The Art of Grammar

D0920099

The Art of Grammar

A Practical Guide

ALEXANDRA Y. AIKHENVALD

Language and Culture Research Centre,
James Cook University

OXFORD
UNIVERSITY PRESS

OXFORD
UNIVERSITY PRESS

Great Clarendon Street, Oxford, OX2 6DP,
United Kingdom

Oxford University Press is a department of the University of Oxford.
It furthers the University's objective of excellence in research, scholarship,
and education by publishing worldwide. Oxford is a registered trade mark of
Oxford University Press in the UK and in certain other countries

© Alexandra Y. Aikhenvald 2015

The moral rights of the author have been asserted

First Edition published in 2015
Impression: 1

All rights reserved. No part of this publication may be reproduced, stored in
a retrieval system, or transmitted, in any form or by any means, without the
prior permission in writing of Oxford University Press, or as expressly permitted
by law, by licence, or under terms agreed with the appropriate reprographics
rights organization. Enquiries concerning reproduction outside the scope of the
above should be sent to the Rights Department, Oxford University Press, at the
address above

You must not circulate this work in any other form
and you must impose this same condition on any acquirer

Published in the United States of America by Oxford University Press
198 Madison Avenue, New York, NY 10016, United States of America

British Library Cataloguing in Publication Data

Data available

Library of Congress Control Number: 2014935566

ISBN 978–0–19–968321–5 (hbk.)
ISBN 978–0–19–968322–2 (pbk.)

Printed and bound by
CPI Group (UK) Ltd, Croydon CR0 4YY

Links to third party websites are provided by Oxford in good faith and
for information only. Oxford disclaims any responsibility for the materials
contained in any third party website referenced in this work.

For Bob,
indefatigable grammar-writer,
grammar-reader,
and the inspiration behind this work

Contents

Preamble: what this book is about

Several thousand distinct languages are currently spoken across the globe, many of them by small tribal communities. Each has its own grammatical system. Comprehensive reference grammars are the basis of our understanding of linguistic diversity, and of cultural diversity as embedded in human languages. Grammars offer a unique window into the structure and cognitive underpinnings of languages, and the ways they reflect the changing world. A reference grammar brings together a coherent treatment of a language as a system, within its cultural context. Ideally, it also touches upon the history of the language.

Comprehensive grammatical analysis of the world's languages is the backbone of linguistics. Grammars are the foundation for any meaningful generalizations about what human languages are like. Linguistic typology—the science of generalizations and predictions about human languages and the underlying cognitive patterns—is based on what we learn from grammars.

Writing a reference grammar is a considerable task. It should outline the distinctive features of the language without being too esoteric. The discussion within the grammar needs to be placed within the established parameters of linguistic typology. And at the same time, a comprehensive grammar will shed light on new, perhaps previously unknown, categories and meanings.

In many ways, a reference grammar serves different masters—experts in the languages of the area, general linguists and linguistic typologists, anthropologists, and other kinds of interested readers. It may also spark the interest of the speakers themselves (who may or may not be co-authors), in uncovering the distinctive genius of their languages. It is up to the grammar writer to satisfy a number of possible readerships.

A reference grammar creates the basis for each of the other, more focused kinds of grammars (e.g. pedagogical or historical grammars), ideally creating a definitive analytic document for a language. It combines scholarly description, documentation, and analysis of language facts. It may even venture an explanation—why the language is the way it is.

Description of linguistic facts goes hand in hand with the analytic perspective one takes on them. The most comprehensive grammars are cast in the typologically informed framework recently given the name of basic linguistic theory (see Dixon 2010a, 2010b, 2012).

Maintaining a subtle balance between being detailed and being comprehensive, between being language specific and yet of interest to a more general audience is an intellectual art. Hence the title of this book, which purports to explain some of the tricks of the art.

My aim in this book is to introduce the principles of grammar writing. The structure of this book in itself follows the ways in which most grammars tend to be organized. One starts with the social and cultural setting of the language, then goes on to its phonetic and phonological make-up, and from there on to the basic building units of a grammar, and then discourse, and lexicon. However, it should not be taken as a prescriptive 'recipe'—it is essential that the grammarian should structure their analysis in the way best for each particular language.

So as to show what a grammar ought to cover, I focus on a discussion of a variety of grammatical topics—and some parameters of their variation—across languages. As a result, the discussion here partly overlaps with topics covered by books on linguistic typology and basic linguistic theory. This is understandable, as we have to cover essentially the same ground—the structure of human languages and their recurrent features.

Note that Dixon's (2010a, 2010b, 2012) three-volume magnum opus on basic linguistic theory differs from this book in three major ways:

- First, the present book addresses a fair number of topics not covered by Dixon in any detail. These include noun classes and classifiers, derivation and compounding, definiteness and specificity, serial verbs and other multi-verb constructions, imperatives and commands, exclamations and versatile sentence types, switch reference, information structure, and issues in linking sentences such as recapitulation and repetition.
- Secondly, the topics Dixon discusses are addressed in more depth and with more examples than will be appropriate here.
- And thirdly, the present book contains hints as to what to include in a grammar, and how to organize it.

My aim is to offer guidelines for writing grammars of spoken languages. These may be judiciously used for sign languages—with the proviso that sign languages are linguistic systems in their own right and not adaptations of the spoken ones.

A further prefatory note is in order. I use the word 'sex' in its traditional meaning, for the difference between women and men, rather than 'gender', which is a grammatical label. This allows me to say 'female sex is marked by feminine gender', which is a clear statement, whereas 'female gender is marked by feminine gender' sounds odd and confusing.

Who this book is for

The word 'linguist' has at least two senses. Some people see a linguist as a polyglot, who knows many languages. There is another sense of 'linguist': an analyst who studies—in a scientific manner—how languages are structured, where they come from, and how they work. This book is primarily for linguists in this second, scholarly, sense.

Its broader audience includes anthropologists, educationalists, and other scholars interested in how languages work and why they are so diverse. It presupposes knowledge of basic concepts of linguistics, such as phoneme and morpheme. The readers are expected to have undertaken a couple of undergraduate courses in linguistics. Many technical terms are explained in the Glossary.

Plea

This book is not the last word on the art of creating, composing, and writing a grammar. I welcome reactions, counterexamples, new facts, new ideas, to further develop, refine, and perhaps redefine the hypotheses and generalizations put forward here. Please send them to me at the LCRC, CASE, James Cook University, Cairns, North Queensland, 4870, Australia, or, in a quicker manner, to Alexandra.Aikhenvald@jcu.edu.au.

Acknowledgements

This book is a product of about thirty years of writing and reading grammars, supervising students, and commenting on grammars written by Post-doctoral Fellows and colleagues, and also conducting annual workshops on grammar-writing for PhD students and Research Fellows, jointly with R. M. W. Dixon. A set of handouts prepared for these workshops were the foundation for this book.

My own experience in writing grammars is at the heart of the book. I have written grammars of three Arawak languages (Warekena of Xié, Baré, and Tariana), one language from Papua New Guinea (Manambu), and two grammars of Hebrew. My typological work, and work on language contact patterns (especially in Amazonia), has helped me enrich my own grammars, and get a feel for what may make a grammar more enticing and more comprehensive. Over the years, I received feedback from many people, of different continents and backgrounds, and am indebted to them all.

My gratitude goes to native speakers of Amazonian languages who taught me their languages. First, my Tariana family: José, Jovino, Olívia, Rafael, Leo, Maria, Diká, Emílio, Juvenal, the late Gracialiano, Ismael, and Cândido Brito, together with other members of the Brito family (speakers of Tariana of Santa Rosa), Marino, Domingo, Ismael, Jorge, and Batista Muniz, and other members of the Muniz family (Tariana of Periquitos). And also Arthur, Amilton, and Floriano Baltazar, and the late Humberto Baltazar and Pedro Ângelo Tomas (Warekena); Ilda Cardoso da Silva, Afonso, Albino, and João Fontes, Celestino da Silva, Cecília and Laureano da Silva, and the late Marcília Rodrigues (Baniwa); the late Tiago Cardoso (Desano, Piratapuya), the late Candelário da Silva (Baré), and Marilda-Mamori and Carlito Paumarí, and Alfredo Fontes (Tucano). I am also grateful to my adopted family in the Sepik area of Papua New Guinea who revealed to me the beauty of their native Manambu (especially Pauline Agnes Yuaneng Luma Laki, James Sesu Laki, David Takendu, and Jacklyn Yuamali Benji Ala).

I am grateful to all my former students and friends from various parts of the world— Simoni Valadares, Marcos Baltar, Cristiane Cunha de Oliveira, Claudete Lucyk, Rute Maria Coelho, Silvana and Valteir Martins, Michael Dunn, Kristina Sands, Rina Marnita, Yunseok Lee, Kazuko Obata, Antoine Guillaume, Carola Emkow, Simon Overall, Mark Post, Chia-jung Pan, Sihong Zhang, Dineke Schokkin, Hannah Sarvasy, Mikko Salminen, Juliane Böttger, Grant Aiton, Kasia Wojtylak, Nick Piper, Valérie Guérin, Elena Mihas, and many more. I have learnt a great deal from them.

My work on Amazonian languages would have been impossible without the assistance, support, and friendship of Lenita and Elias Coelho, and Silvana and Valteir Martins. I continue being inspired by Lenita, Elias, Silvana, and Valteir, and also by the pioneering work of other Brazilian linguists in the Makú-speaking area—Cácio and Elisângela Silva and Marcelo and Claudinha Carvalho.

The members and visitors of our Language and Culture Research Centre within James Cook University—Lourens de Vries, Carol Genetti, Knut Olawsky, Ken Sumbuk, Catherine Travis, Gwen Hyslop, Azeb Amha, Nerida Jarkey, Anvita Abbi—have provided an exciting intellectual ambiance. Mike Wood and Rosita Henry have helped create a wonderful collegial atmosphere, and gave me insight into cultural features which may be included in a grammar. I am indebted to our Post-doctoral Fellows for maintaining high standards of intellectual endeavour—Tianqiao (Mike) Lu, Elena Mihas, Angeliki Alvanoudi, Simon Overall, Valérie Guérin, and Diana Forker.

Invaluable comments on just about every page came from R. M. W. Dixon, without whose incisive criticism, and constant encouragement and support, this book would not have appeared. Hannah Sarvasy, Mikko Salminen, Angeliki Alvanoudi, Kasia Wojtylak, and Nick Piper read through the draft of the book, making sharp comments and correcting errors. Valérie Guérin read through a number of chapters, pinpointing contradictions and inconsistencies. It is hard to find words to express my gratitude to you all!

Brigitta Flick carefully read through various drafts of this book and corrected it with her usual skill, perspicacity, dedication, and good humour. Without efficient and cheerful support from Amanda Parsonage who took many an administrative burden from me, I would never have managed to complete this book.

This volume owes a good deal to John Davey and Julia Steer, the Linguistics Editors of Oxford University Press. Their indomitable support makes an author, and their book, feel wanted.

The stimulating and cheerful atmosphere, encouragement, and warm support of senior management, colleagues, and friends at James Cook University have helped make it all possible.

Conventions

The AFFILIATION and LOCATION of each language is given in brackets at its first mention. The affiliation includes the subgroup if known and generally established, and then the family—for instance, Nanti is introduced as Nanti (Campa, Arawak). I only include a subgroup if it has been firmly established, as is the case with the Campa subgroup of Arawak languages in South America. I cannot expect the reader to remember the affiliation of each and every language. So, this same information is repeated now and again. The index of languages also contains this information.

Examples are numbered separately for each chapter. For instance, examples in Chapter 1 will be numbered 1.1, 1.2, and so on. All language examples are supplied with an interlinear morpheme gloss, and then translated into English. The symbol '+' is used to indicate fused morphemes, e.g. a Tariana form *nhupa* is glossed as '1sg+grab', its underlying form being *nu-* 'first person singular prefix' plus *-hipa* 'to grab'. Portmanteau morphemes are glossed with '.', for instance, Tariana *-mahka* (RECENT.PAST. NONVISUAL). All grammatical morphemes are glossed in small caps while lexical morphemes are in lower case. Pronominal prefixes are shown as 1sg, 3pl, in lower case.

Cross-references are of two kinds:

- Those preceded by § refer to chapter and section number: for instance, §11.1 refers to section 1 of Chapter 11;
- Those beginning with a number refer to examples in the grammar: for instance, 11.1 refers to example 1 in Chapter 11.

References to quoted and cited material are *not* generally given in the chapters themselves. They are included, together with additional notes, in a section 'Notes and sources' at the end of each chapter.

List of tables, figures, and boxes

Tables

Figures

Boxes

Abbreviations

1, 2, 3 – first, second, third person
A – transitive subject
ABS – absolutive
ACC – accusative
ADJOINED.CL – adjoined clause
ADV – adverb
ALL – allative
AOR – aorist
ART – article
ART.DEF – definite article
ART.INDEF – indefinite article
AUG – augmentative
AUX – auxiliary
CA – common argument
CAUS – causative
CC – copula complement
CL – classifier
CL:ANIM – classifier for animates
CL.INAN – classifier for inanimate objects
CoCL – complement clause
CoCL:A – complement clause in A function
CoCL:O – complement clause in O function
CoCL:S – complement clause in S function
COMP – comparative
COMPL – complementizer
COMPL.CL – complement clause
COMPL.DS – complement clause with different subject
COP – copula
COP.INTER – interrogative copula
CORR – correlative marker
CS – copula subject

DAT – dative
DECL – declarative
DEF – definite
DEF.ACC – accusative definite
DEF.ART – definite article
DEF.NOM – definite nominalizer
DEM – demonstrative
DEM.DIST – distal demonstrative
DEP.CL – dependent clause
DEP.CL(DS) – dependent clause different subject
DIR – directional
DS – different subject
du – dual
DUR – durative
E – extended argument
ERG – ergative
EVID – evidential
f – feminine
fem – feminine
FEM – feminine
FINAL.CL – final clause
FOC – focus
FOC.A/S – focused A/S
FUT – future
GEN – genitive
H – high tone
IMPERF – imperfective
IMPERS – impersonal
IMPERV – imperfective
IMPV – imperative
INAN – inanimate

INDEF – indefinite

INDIC – indicative

INF – infinitive

INSTR – instrumental

IPA – International Phonetic Alphabet

L – low tone

LK – linker

LOC – locative

m – masculine

MAIN.CL – main clause

masc – masculine

MASC – masculine

NCL – noun class

NEG – negation

nf – nonfeminine

NOM.MARKER – nominal marker

NOMZ – nominalizer

non.fem – nonfeminine

nsg – nonsingular

NP – noun phrase

NUM.CL – numeral classifier

O – direct object of transitive verb

obj – object

OBJ – object

OBL – oblique

PASS – passive

PERF – perfect

PERT – pertensive

pl – plural

PL – plural

POSS – possessive

POSS/ATTRIB – possessive/attributive

PRED – predicate

PRES – present

PRESENT.DEF – present tense of definite conjugation in Hungarian

PRESENT.INDEF – present tense of indefinite conjugation in Hungarian

PROHIB – prohibitive

REACT.TOP – reactivated topic

REAL – realis

RECIP – reciprocal

REC.P – recent past

REC.PAST – recent past

REC.P.VIS – recent past visual

RED – reduplication

REFL – reflexive

REL – relative clause

REL – relativizer

REM – remote

REM.P.REP – remote past reported

REM.P.VIS – remote past visual

S – intransitive subject

Sa – subject of an active intransitive verb

SAP – speech act participant

SEQ – sequencing

sg – singular

SG – singular

sg.nf – singular nonfeminine

SIM – simultaneous

So – stative of a stative intransitive verb

SS – same subject

subj – subject

SUBJ – subject

TH – theme

TOP – topic

tr – transitive

TRANS – transitivizer

VCC – Verbless Clause Complement

VCS – Verbless Clause Subject

VOC – vocative

1

Introduction: to write a grammar

Linguistics is the science of language, similar to how mathematics is the science of numbers. A reference grammar is a scientific enterprise. It brings together a coherent treatment of each language as a system where everything fits together, within the cultural, and historical, context of the language. The aim of this book is to offer a guide for creating a reference grammar based on empirical facts and combining description, interpretation, and analysis.

Linguistics can be considered a branch of natural science. The great linguist N. S. Trubetzkoy came to the conclusion in 1909 (at the age of 18):

that linguistics was the only branch of 'human lore' with a scientific approach and that all the other branches of this lore (ethnography, history of religion, history of culture, and so forth) would leave their prescientific, 'alchemic' stage only when they followed the example of linguistics. (Liberman 1991: 304)

1.1 The language and its 'genius'

Several thousand different languages are currently spoken across the world. The exact figure is hard to pinpoint. Estimates vary depending on how one counts—whether or not one includes more or less mutually intelligible varieties. Generous counts offer a figure of 6,000, and more restrictive ones suggest about 4,000 or fewer. Only a few of these are spoken by more than a million people. And indeed, English, Mandarin Chinese, Spanish, varieties of Arabic, Portuguese, and French are threatening to take over the world. In 1992, Michael Krauss estimated that at least half of languages spoken then would become extinct during the twenty-first century.

Less than a third of those languages which are still spoken have been extensively described and understood. Analysing and documenting languages on the path towards extinction is a race against time.

Every language is a repository of beliefs, heritage, history, and traditional laws. The loss of a language is bound up with the loss of indigenous knowledge about the environment, its biological diversity and traditional means of sustainable use. Language loss deals a blow to an ethnic group's identity and self-esteem. Speakers of Tariana, an endangered language from north-western Brazil, often complain to me that they have to speak a 'borrowed' language now that their own is being lost. They feel impoverished.

For scientific linguists, loss of a language means loss of a unique system, perhaps a missing link, which might have turned out to be crucial for our understanding of the workings of the human mind, peoples' histories and the ways we interact.

A comprehensive reference grammar—accompanied by a detailed dictionary and a collection of natural stories in the language, as well as audio and perhaps video recordings—will ensure that the language is not irretrievably lost. Ideally, a reference grammar should reflect language use, and its history, and also the ways in which it relates to other languages within its area, and within the world. It will form the basis for further knowledge of the language's history, and for generalizations and predictions about language in general.

A grammar will capture the unique genius of the language—the way meanings are expressed, and how categories are realized. This is how we can understand how languages differ, and why, and what cognitive and other mechanisms they may reflect.

1.2 What linguistic diversity is about

In recent times, a great deal of attention has been directed to biological diversity—what gives rise to it, where it is distributed, its implications, and prognostications for the future. Linguistic diversity is an equally important topic. Why is there a high concentration of different languages in certain areas, but a relative paucity in others? Is linguistic diversity something to be valued, or deplored, and what can we learn from it? How is it being affected by rampant globalization, and what does the future hold?

When we talk about 'diversity' we refer to at least three possible things.

1. DIVERSITY IN NUMBERS. As we survey the world, the number of languages spoken in a certain-sized area differs a great deal. Papua New Guinea (PNG, 463 km²) and Paraguay (407 km²) are of comparable size but there are over 850 distinct languages spoken in PNG and (before the European invasion) Paraguay had only about 20. This difference can partly be explained by geography. PNG has many swamps and high mountains which impede communication, these being absent from Paraguay.

2. DIVERSITY IN ORIGINS. Most languages—with the exception of a few isolates, or linguistic orphans—are known to belong to a genetic family. Multiplicity of families creates diversity in language origins. This is higher in some areas, and lower in others. The island of New Guinea is home to over 60 unrelated families. About 370 Bantu languages are spoken over a considerable-sized area in East and Central Africa. These languages belong to one family, and, despite their distinctness, they share many similarities in their grammars.

Establishing linguistic families is based on fairly strict principles of comparative linguistics—perhaps the most scientific branch of the discipline. And surface similarities between languages should not be taken as indicators of their relationship. More on this later.

Most language communities—with the exception of the few confined to an isolated island or a remote mountain region—are in contact with other communities. The communities interact—through trade, intermarriage, shared festivals and rituals, and also military conflicts. Their languages also interact. They may come to sound similar. Some vocabulary may be borrowed. Some structural features of languages may converge: for instance, neighbouring languages may develop similar systems of noun classes. And yet, the languages remain distinct.

3. Diversity in structures. In some parts of the world, the languages spoken within a given area demonstrate remarkable diversity of structure. In other regions, there is a considerable degree of uniformity for the goodly number of structural and lexical features. Benjamin Lee Whorf (1956) coined the term 'Standard Average European' as a way of drawing attention to the fact that more than a dozen languages spoken in Europe show many similarities in their grammatical properties, lexical extensions, and idioms. These languages have no more than two or three genders, most are straightforwardly nominative-accusatives; many have similar systems of auxiliary verbs. In contrast, languages in a region of the Amazon basin of about the same size as Europe, exhibit a mind-boggling diversity of grammatical structures, lexical subtleties, and culturally-determined aphorisms. The number of gender-like noun classification systems varies from one language to the next. Hardly any language is straightforwardly nominative-accusative. And many categories—such as nominal tense, evidentiality, frustrative modality—are alien to a European centred scholar.

Structural diversity cannot be fully understood without comprehensive grammatical study of each language. This is what a reference grammar is primarily useful for.

No language exists in a vacuum—it is used by people within their own distinct social structure. Linguistic diversity goes hand in hand with social diversity. Diversity in the physical environment and many extra-linguistic features may serve to explain diversity of other sorts. A comprehensive reference grammar will provide a coherent foundation for understanding the language's special character as a system where 'everything fits together'. This is a basis on which the understanding of 'how' and 'why' will then be built.

1.3 The limits of grammar

No two languages are entirely the same, nor are they entirely different. It is as if there were a universal inventory of possible grammatical and lexical categories and meanings, and each language makes a different set of choices from this inventory. Any meaning can be expressed in any language. But it does not have to be.

As Franz Boas (a founding father of modern linguistics) put it, languages differ not in what one **can** say but in what kind of information **must** be stated: '**grammar** . . . determines those aspects of each experience that *must* be expressed' (Boas 1938: 132). French has an obligatory two-term gender system, German has three, while Armenian and Hungarian make no gender distinctions at all in their grammar. In French and in German every noun requires agreement in gender on adjectives and articles. In Armenian and Hungarian the same form will be used with any noun.

However, in every language one can distinguish male from female, as a natural gender—or sex—category. This can be achieved through special words for males and females. The number of distinctions in a lexicon can be unlimited. A grammar forces us to make limited choices. It may focus on gender as it is expressed through an obligatory mechanism. Words for men, women, and other males and females will then be relegated to the lexicon.

That is, every language has a number of obligatory grammatical categories from which a choice must be made in order to construct an acceptable sentence. To translate into French *The child fell down* one must know the gender of the child, since this has to be specified. To translate this sentence into Tariana (from Amazonia) one must specify the source of information on which the statement is based—whether you saw it, or heard it, or inferred it, or were told about it by someone else (this is a grammatical system of evidentiality).

Many languages have a closed set of grammaticalized expressions of location in time: these can involve present, past, and future; or nonpast, recent past, and remote past, etc. Amele, a Gum language from Papua New Guinea, distinguishes four verbal forms which can be defined as: (i) today's past, (ii) yesterday's past, (iii) remote past (what happened before yesterday), and (iv) habitual past—something that often occurred in past time.

Each sentence in Amele has to be specified for one of these parameters. Their application is not rigid: what occurred in the hours of darkness the previous night can be referred to either by today's past tense or yesterday's past tense depending on whether the speaker considers them related to other events on the previous day or on the day of the utterance. English and many other languages have special words for 'today', 'yesterday', 'the day before yesterday', and so on which one may use or not depending on the speaker's whim. So does Amele. A closed grammatical system will coexist with sets of *lexical items* which refer to location in time and a potentially unlimited number of 'composite lexical expressions' for measuring time intervals.

In other words, a closed grammatical system offers limited options. This is in contrast to the lexicon, where the choices are potentially open. So, for grammatical tense, 'even the maximal system would have at most tens of categories, rather than the several orders of magnitude made possible in the lexicon' (Comrie 1985: 9).

A grammar of a language is not a random set of facts. It is rather like a mechanism which organizes the language, or a motor that sets it in motion. At a very early stage of learning a language, a child acquires the principles of grammar and applies them. This is the basis of a speaker's generative ability of creating an infinite number of texts and sentences, based on the rules of grammar. How these principles, and their grammatical meanings, differ from one language to the next is what we aim at discovering.

What is expressed through a grammatical distinction in one language may have to be phrased lexically in another. This is something we have just seen with yesterday's past in Amele. A grammatical form can be shown to develop from a lexical item. This is known as 'grammaticalization'. In Ewe, a major language of Ghana, the word *nO* means 'mother'. The same form can be used as a suffix to names of animals as a feminine marker, for example *nyi-nɔ* (cattle-feminine) 'cow'. Facts like this one are useful to include in a grammar: they show the ways in which the lexicon and grammatical forms interact.

Lexicon and grammar are intertwined. Different classes of lexicon may have different grammatical properties. Grammatically defined subclasses of nouns often include body parts, kinship terms, and place names. Grammatically defined subclasses of verbs may include verbs of perception and cognition, verbs of stance and posture, and verbs of giving. Colour adjectives may behave differently from adjectives referring to size. (We turn to these in Chapters 5 and 8.) Meanings within the lexicon may, at least partly, shape the meanings reflected in grammar. Inasmuch as this is the case, information about lexical categories are relevant as a background for a full grammar.

In summary: the lexicon and grammar of a language are two complementary parts, each in its own right. The lexicon of each language reflects the world in which it is spoken in numerous minute distinctions, realized as many individual items. It is open to new words and notions. The grammar—much more restricted and much more mechanistic—is a closed system. In some ways, it may be seen to reflect some real-life distinctions and depend on them. A reference grammar may address at least some of these.

TO REMEMBER: Every language has a grammar, and no grammar is primitive. However, some grammatical descriptions are. A few missionaries of the colonial era claimed that non-European languages (Chinese, South American—you name it) have 'no grammar'. What they meant was that the grammatical mechanisms of these languages were beyond them to discover: they do indeed differ from what a European might expect. What they also meant is that those languages had no 'prescriptive' grammar. And this is something we turn to in the next section.

Ideally, a reference grammar will be accompanied by a comprehensive lexicon, and a collection of stories of different genres—showing how people actually talk. If appropriate, there may be also a collection of electronically accessible audio and video resources. What is the place of a reference grammar within grammars and language materials of other sorts?

1.4 Serving many masters: a glimpse into the multiplicity of grammars

1.4.1 The essence of a reference grammar

A reference grammar is a comprehensive result of language analysis. A grammarian's first task is to study the complete system of a language at some point in time—that is, focus on its synchrony. As Antoine Meillet (1926: 16) put it, 'une langue constitue un système complexe de moyens d'expression, système où tout se tient' ('a language makes up a complex system of means of expression, a system in which everything holds together'). Scientific linguists who produce comprehensive grammars of languages naturally follow this tenet. Those who look at isolated bits of language, for some particular issue, go against this fundamental principle of systematic analysis.

The study of language can be approached in at least two ways (more details are given by Dixon 2010a). One involves the postulation of a 'formal theory' or a framework which puts forward certain deductive hypotheses about language structure and examines selected language data for confirmation of these ideas. There are, typically, many competing 'formal theories', each making claims about different aspects of language (these have some similarities to competing theories of economics, or of literature). Many 'formal theories' are associated with Chomsky and various generations of his students. These may make some contribution to understanding some aspects of language organization, especially through the prism of European languages—and mostly English—but they never offer a full picture.

A reference grammar (also called 'analytical' grammar and 'descriptive' grammar) will outline the distinctive features of the language—and transmit its 'linguistic genius'—with just the right amount of detail, including reference to the language's history if possible. Ideally, the discussion within a grammar is expected to be placed within the established parameters of linguistic typology—reflecting how languages work, and expanding our understanding of the categories and principles of their organization. At the same time, a comprehensive grammar will disclose new, previously unknown, categories and meanings.

Description of linguistic facts goes hand in hand with the analytic perspective one takes on them. The lasting comprehensive grammars are cast in a typologically informed framework based on cross-linguistic inductive analysis of numerous languages. This framework has been recently given the name of basic linguistic theory (see Dixon 2010a, 2010b, 2012). In this framework, every analytic decision has to be proved, but is not constrained by the requirements of an ad hoc formal model. It is oriented towards expanding our view of structural diversity. This is the perspective taken here.

A reference grammar should last beyond the life-span of its author. This is the main reason why it should not be cast in any of the time-line formalisms which come and go with startling frequency. Two grammars of Bolivian Indian languages—the two isolates Itonama and Movima—were cast in mathematical-type tagmemic framework-of-the-day. They are a puzzle to a modern reader. One gets an idea of the order in which morphemes go, but not a hint on their semantics or any of the intricacies of these languages—which one learns about from later work, cast within a much less restrictive framework. Migliazza's (1972) grammar of Yanomami, a South American language, is cast in the Chomskyan 'generative' framework of the day. His concern was to fit the language into a transformationalist framework, rather than to see what distinctions were expressed in the language itself. As a consequence, there is no mention of classifiers or evidentials (grammaticalized expression of information source). One has to study other, much less restricted, grammars of Yanomami to learn about these—Borgman (1990), Gomez (1990), and Ramirez (1994).

Being able to read and understand a typologically oriented grammar implies being acquainted with basic notions of linguistics, and principles of analysis. A reference grammar is aimed at a scholarly audience, and is based on linguistic analytical methodology which need to be mastered.

1.4.2 *Grammars of further kinds*

Reference grammars are the foundations for other grammars, whose objectives and audiences are more specific.

A purely HISTORICAL grammar focuses on a diachronic approach and the history of a language within the context of its proven linguistic relatives. It is not sensible to run before one can walk. What Leonard Bloomfield (1933: 18) called 'the natural relation between descriptive and historical studies' reflects a common-sense assumption—'the need of descriptive data as a prerequisite for comparative work'. A historical study can 'only be as accurate and only as complete as these data permit it to be' (Bloomfield 1933: 19). In other words, a historical grammar is derivative of a comprehensive statement of facts and their coherent analysis. A reference grammar should ideally be informed by existing historical and comparative studies: these may shed light on otherwise seemingly random and only partly predictable variation.

A PRESCRIPTIVE grammar offers discussion of norms developed through the language's history, often in an artificial way as a result of language reforms. This type of grammar is especially appropriate for a language which has a literary norm, such as many Indo-European and Semitic languages. A prescriptive grammar may contain evaluation of different variants, in terms of how they reflect the class, educational background, and social standing of the speakers.

A PEDAGOGICAL—or a teaching—grammar aims at teaching the language to a wider audience of native speakers, or second language learners, or—not infrequently—those members of a community who had lost the command of a language and wish to learn it back. A pedagogical grammar needs to be organized so as to best suit their aims. It cannot be considered 'primitive', or inferior to any other grammar. This is a different type of enterprise. Importantly, a linguist taking part in this will need to have some training and experience in how to teach languages.

A pedagogical grammar is organized in such a way as to facilitate learning, and may be accompanied by a series of exercises. It may also be suited to a particular language situation (that is, depending on whether the language is actively spoken in a community or not), and to a type of language programme to which it may be tailored. In Mithun's (2007) words, speakers dedicated to preserving their languages 'are acutely interested in the words of the language but also its history, and its special structures'.

A collection of texts, or a dictionary, may be accompanied by a GRAMMAR SKETCH. In contrast to a reference grammar, a grammar sketch—or a sketch grammar—offers the basic grammatical facts of a language, without going into justification and analytical decisions. A sketch grammar may just say: the language has three genders. A reference grammar has to justify why. A sketch grammar is a subsidiary adjunct, while a reference grammar is a complete document in its own right. A sketch grammar can be accompanied by a glossary of morphemes. This serves as an aid to the dictionary, whose purpose is to cater for native speakers, and learners, of the language.

The reference grammar may serve as the basis for a historical grammar. As the definitive analytic document for a language, the reference grammar can be adapted to other purposes—such as teaching, or reclaiming, a language. Using a reference grammar to learn or teach a language, or to issue 'normative' statements, will not be putting it to good use.

Further by-products of a reference grammar may include literacy materials, readers, dictionaries, vocabularies, videos, multimedia resources, and statements of a linguistic norm. Linguists may help, or be instrumental, in translating religious and other materials. Many grammars have been produced by members of the Summer Institute of Linguistics. Further outcome of their activity is translating the Bible—which sometimes gives the people the feeling for a status of their language in the eyes of others. I took part in translating a set of Sunday prayers into Tariana—on the request of the speakers. These additional activities are extraneous to grammar writing.

1.4.3 The place of a linguist

A grammarian—the linguist—does not have to speak the language natively, nor to be born a native speaker of the language. A symbiotic relationship is usually established between the linguist and the community of speakers for whose language the reference grammar is being created. We turn to the ensuing 'priceless partnership' in the Excursus on linguistic fieldwork. The linguist is sometimes bound to take on a social role—in Nora England's (1992) words,

every time we write an article about a language we do several things: we make an analysis of some body of linguistic data, we discuss that analysis in the light of current pertinent theory, we select examples of speech to illustrate our points, and we bring that language into at least momentary prominence. . . . Language prominence resulting from linguistic research has many non-linguistic consequences. (England 1992: 31)

By-products of a reference grammar which we mentioned in §1.4.2 are among the non-purely-linguistic obligations for the linguist.

The linguist is primarily a scholar, and their obligations are scholarly honesty and systematicity. Nora England (1992: 34–5) sums it up: 'publishing descriptions and analyses of the language we work on [which are] of the highest possible quality, and making those publications available to speakers of the language'.

But as we get involved in the social fabric of the language, we cannot help assuming social obligations—involving, in Nora England's words,

1. Recognizing the political and social context for our research and, where necessary, taking the part of the language we study and its speakers;
2. Recognizing the rights of speakers of politically subordinate languages over those languages, and paying attention to public presentation of facts about their languages;
3. Contributing to the training of linguists who are speakers of subordinate languages, at every level from the empirical to the theoretical. (England 1992: 34)

An analytic reference grammar is the responsibility of the linguist. It has their authorship and is ultimately their intellectual property. The cultural heritage belongs to the people linguists work with.

1.5 Documenting a language: an open-ended task

Language documentation in its proper sense involves 'documenting a language as it is used by speakers in various settings from everyday conversation to formal oratory' (Mithun 2007). A reference grammar is its most vital component, together with a comprehensive dictionary, a collection of texts of various genres, and also—if viable—practical orthographies, teaching materials, and multimedia.

Ideally, a reference grammar may include not just the spoken part, and extend to the role of 'body language' as a further modality. Some speech-cum-gesture combinations are a case in point. Saying *yay* (or *yea*) *high* in American English is accompanied by a gesture showing how high an object, or a person, is. Tariana has a set of 'gestural' deictics: a form goes together with a gesture indicating the object's size and shape. Indicating the position of the sun, and direction, is part and parcel of story-telling in Amazonian cultures. A comprehensive multimodal analysis of any language is a task for the future.

To REMEMBER: different audiences value different types of output. Most speakers value dictionaries above grammars. But this is not to say that reference grammars are appreciated by no one but linguistic scholars. On the contrary. Jovino Brito, the President of the Association of the Tariana and a highly competent speaker of the language, said to me, contentedly, after having received a copy of the Tariana grammar and other materials: 'Good, my older sister. Now we have a real language, with a grammar book, a dictionary, a manual, and a book of stories'.

As Mithun (2007) put it, proper language documentation involves

documenting the language as it is used for speakers in various settings from everyday conversation to formal oratory. . . . Particularly in the case of endangered languages, what is documented now will be utilised for purposes well beyond those we can imagine at the present time. (Mithun 2007: 44, 55)

For languages which are still spoken, a linguist is instrumental in providing an 'open-ended' documentation—the more we document now, the fewer unanswered questions will come up in the future.

Modern technology, especially audio-recording equipment, allows us to 'record spontaneous, unscripted speech in real time' (Mithun 2007: 55). Thanks to technological advances, our data and our analyses are more precise. We can now offer an analysis of intonation patterns. Video recordings help register embodied language—gestures and hand and face movements, including lip-pointing, which may well form an integral part of the grammatical structure.

One should not, however, mistake the means for the purpose. Technology should be seen as an accessory, and not an end in itself. If overused, and overtrusted, technological marvels may become a mixed blessing. In a humid tropical environment—such as north-west Amazonia and the Sepik area of New Guinea, with no electricity supply—a computer may become an encumbrance. And the same for video-recorders. We should also recall that speakers of previously undocumented languages, in remote locations, may feel intimidated by flashy gadgets. The constant presence of a video recorder or a computer may do nothing but alienate the fieldworker from the community where they are trying to establish themselves. Even a tape-recorder can be an unwelcome intruder.

There is no doubt that putting conversations, texts, and other information on the world-wide web, and producing videos and web-based archives, is close to the heart of many of our computer-loving linguistic colleagues. But materials without proper grammatical and lexical analysis are of little use to either linguistic posterity or to speakers themselves. For one thing, we can only hope that computerized databases will survive for more than a few years; books have and will survive for centuries. Putting web-based data together may be easier and quicker than painstakingly writing a grammar and producing a competent dictionary. But web-based archives need constant updating, and book pages do not. And if a language is spoken in a remote community, say, in Amazonia, Africa, or New Guinea, with no constant electricity supply, what use is a website? As a colleague from Europe remarked to me, the current focus on computer-based 'documentation' is akin to racism, or 'neo-colonialism', deepening the gulf between the 'haves' and the 'have-nots'. Leo Yabwi, headmaster of a local school in the Manambu-speaking village of Avatip in the Sepik area of New Guinea, concurred: 'We need books. What use are computers to our kids? They need to learn their heritage, and not computer games'.

He had a point here: we must not forget that the more the speakers of a language are exposed to new technologies, the more danger there is that it might get ousted by dominant, 'global', communication devices. Rephrasing Dixon (2007a: 144), 'self-admiration in the looking glass' of computer technology can wait; 'linguistic description must be undertaken now'. Documenting a language in all its cultural manifestations does not involve making a fetish out of appliances.

1.6 The boundaries of a language and the individual voice

What is a language, and what is a dialect? Varieties of speech which are similar to each other and mutually intelligible are called dialects of a single language. A language then can be viewed as an ensemble of dialects. Dialects can be differentiated geographically, for example urban, rural, or regional, or socially, for example standard and vernacular. And when dialects come to differ from each other to such an extent that they stop being mutually intelligible, they will have attained the status of different languages. Brazilian and European Portuguese have a somewhat different pronunciation, grammar, and vocabulary. However, speakers can easily understand each other—we can thus speak about European and Brazilian dialects of Portuguese. Dutch and English are different languages: speakers of Dutch cannot understand English without learning it. The issue can be complicated by the fact that mutual intelligibility may be a matter of degree, and may vary with individual people. Scots English may be unintelligible to speakers of some varieties of American English (to an extent that the Scottish-made film 'Rob Roy' was subtitled in the USA!). Some speakers of Portuguese cannot understand Spanish. Others can—given a certain amount of time, goodwill, and effort.

Mutually unintelligible languages can be referred to as 'dialects' for historical and political reasons. Italian dialects ('dialetti') are not mutually intelligible—a speaker from Rome will not immediately understand one from Sardinia without additional learning. Many of the Chinese 'dialects' are in fact very different linguistic systems. In Arabic linguistics, the term 'dialect' refers to many modern varieties, most of which are not mutually intelligible. This follows an ages-old tradition. The interested reader could learn more about this in Owens' (2006) *Linguistic History of Arabic*.

Norwegian and Swedish provide an opposite example. The standard languages are mutually intelligible. But they are not referred to as 'dialects', as they ought to be on linguistic grounds. These are national languages of two different countries, with different literary traditions. That is, cultural identity and sociolinguistic considerations determine the use of the term 'language' rather than 'dialect'. Even mutual intelligibility may depend not only on linguistic factors, but also on attitudinal and sociolinguistic ones.

As Max Weinreich (1945) put it, 'a language is a dialect with an army and a navy'. Serbian and Croatian are dialects of what used to be called the Serbo-Croatian language. But once Serbia and Croatia became separate states, there was a policy to make words in these two languages as different as possible to try to show that they are totally distinct languages. Orthodox Serbians use Cyrillic script, and predominantly Roman Catholic Croatians use Latin letters: these differences obviously help press the point about them being distinct.

A combination of national and cultural identity, and political and sociolinguistic considerations, often makes it difficult to decide where one language stops and another one begins. In Hock's (1991: 381) words, 'there is no clear line of demarcation between "different dialect" and "different language" ': 'it is gradient, not discrete'. One often finds a range of varieties—dialects in the linguistic sense—spread across a territory. Varieties next to each other will be mutually intelligible. Those at the extremes, far from each other, will not be. This is what we refer to as a 'dialect continuum'.

A grammar, ideally, focuses on just one geographical—or dialectal—variety of a language. However, other dialects may shed light on apparent exceptions or irregularities. A more archaic dialect may provide an explanation for something otherwise bizarre.

How representative do we expect the grammar to be, and whom does it represent? Ideally, a grammar ought to reflect a linguistic community—that is, 'the regular patterns that characterize the natural exchanges in the speech community' (Poplack 1993: 263).

But the notion of community goes only so far. A careful fieldworker may be able to identify groups of speakers along which variation is observed. Among the Urarina, younger people use a somewhat different grammar.

Variation can serve as a 'boundary marker': there may be different forms and rules depending on social class, education, and gender. In a ground-breaking study of physical features of 'women's' speech among the Tohono O'odham (a Uto-Aztecan group from Mexico), Hill and Zepeda (1999) show how women (not men) use a pulmonic ingressive airstream in order to construct a special atmosphere of conversational intimacy, taking advantage of size differences between male and female vocal tracts: such sound production is easier to achieve with the smaller female larynx and pharynx. Physical attributes—including high-pitched voice—typical of women come to be associated with 'female talk'. Just how much of such variation is included depends on the grammar writer and the data, and the size and diversification of the community itself.

If we are dealing with a language used by just a handful of last speakers, the degree of individual variation may be high. This is especially the case in languages which are falling out of use—like Embo Gaelic, Saaroa, or Tariana. Then, in Johnstone's (2000: 411) words, speakers may 'have different grammars'. Describing the special grammar of each individual—however few of them there are—is a strenuous task. This is one of the many problems one faces when working on an obsolescent—or a moribund—language.

1.7 Constructing a grammar

1.7.1 The building blocks

Linguistics is a scientific enterprise where every statement requires substantiation and proof. Creating a grammar involves building up an empirical set of data, and then proceeding towards their organization and explanation by making inductive general-izations, and uncovering the principles behind them. The steps in building a reference grammar are:

I. **Collection of data and their description.** This is done in terms of an overarch-ing typological theory of language structure (each description providing feedback to refine the theory); this is describing 'how' languages are the way they are.

A grammar can be based on numerous sources. If the language is still in use, the major set of data should come from original fieldwork.

In the introduction to his famous anthropological account of the Akwẽ-Shavante, David Maybury-Lewis (1968) comments:

Most anthropological reports nowadays specify how long the author spent in the field, but they do not always indicate how much of that time was actually spent in daily contact with the people studied and how much elsewhere—for example in a near-by city. Nor do they always men-tion other pertinent details of such contacts. We are not always told how the field-worker was received by the people [they] studied and how [they] went about collecting [their] information. It is often difficult to discover whether [they] shared living quarters with the people, or occupied a separate dwelling in the same community, or one at some distance from the community, or whether [they] commuted from another community altogether. . . . I suggest that it is time we abandoned the mystique which surrounds field-work and made it conventional to describe in some detail the circumstances of data collecting, so that they may be as subject to scrutiny as the data themselves. (Maybury-Lewis 1968: xix–xx)

Similar comments are relevant for linguistic accounts of work on little-known lan-guages: as much detail as possible concerning fieldwork, and the narratives, conversa-tions and other materials used for the grammars, should be included.

Older documentation and earlier sources—including texts (recorded or simply writ-ten down)—may also be used, with as much caution and appreciation as necessary. It is de rigueur to always distinguish one's own results and other sources. There are examples of people who muddle up sources—and the results are poor. Written sources in the lan-guage can also be used—but with care. Haspelmath's (1993) grammar of Lezgian heavily relies on translations into Lezgian from Russian, the dominant language (partly due to the limited amount of fieldwork the author chose to undertake). Such materials often reflect the original language and show calques. This is why caution is due. The same applies to web-based examples from Google and such. If the language is no longer in use, one has little choice. But care, caution, and precision are recommended.

II. **Explanation.** This involves addressing 'why' things are as they are. Why does Swa-hili have eight genders, German three, French two, and Hungarian none at all? Why does Hua, spoken in the highlands of Papua New Guinea, have several demonstratives, indicating both 'close' and 'distant', as well as 'level', 'up', and 'down', while English has just *this* and *that*? This may offer a pathway for generalizations about the language type, and the ways in which categories are expressed.

But remember: As Leonard Bloomfield (1933: 20) put it,

The only useful generalizations about language are inductive generalizations. Features which we think ought to be universal may be absent from the very next language that becomes accessible. . . . The fact that some features are, at any rate, widespread, is worthy of notice and calls for an explanation; when we have adequate data about many languages, we shall have to return to the problem of general grammar and to explain these similarities and divergences, but this study, when it comes, will not be speculative but inductive. (Bloomfield 1933: 20)

III. **Prediction**. Synchronic prediction involves saying 'if a language has X, it is highly likely also to have Y'. For example, if verbs have pronominal affixes marking subject and object, then the class of adjectives is likely to be grammatically more similar to verbs than to nouns. Diachronic prediction foresees the way a language is likely to change over time. For example, in English irregular verbs are continually being regularized, as in *strove* being replaced by *strived*. This can be expected to continue, with—in the fullness of time—*sang* giving way to *singed*, and so on.

To fully understand a language, a linguist has to be more than just a scholar of languages. Kate Burridge (2007) makes this point very clear, with regard to the archaic Pennsylvania German spoken by an isolated group of Mennonites in Canada:

But it wasn't long before I realised how inadequate my grammatical descriptions would be if I ignored the social and cultural information. Even my forays into Middle Dutch syntax had taught me that much. In the case of the conservative Mennonites, every aspect of their life style is saturated with symbols that express a commitment to qualities like frugality, equality and humility and, in particular, the subordination of the individual to God's will. These symbols of subordination are evident in the shape of the lexicon, but are also deeply embedded in the grammatical structuring of the language. (Burridge 2007: 39)

1.7.2 *To be precise*

Description of linguistic facts goes hand in hand with the analytic perspective one takes on them. The typologically informed framework recently given the name of basic linguistic theory has been, for centuries, the tacitly accepted framework for those grammars that have outlasted the fads.

A number of principles underlie successful grammar writing:

- A. Clarity of presentation.
- B. User-friendliness.
- C. Explicitness.
- D. Presenting alternative solutions where possible, and assessing each.
- E. The quest for explanation: why?

This is where a synchronic grammar may turn to a diachronic perspective.

1.7.3 Labels, categories, and meanings

What term to use? Basic labels for categories and forms usually reflect functions and a cross-linguistic definition. The term 'serial verb' refers to a sequence of verbs which form one predicate and bear no marking of subordination or coordination of any sort. It is therefore not advisable to extend this term to cover auxiliary verb constructions as in English. However, some linguistic traditions go against general linguistic categories.

A classifier is a morpheme which is chosen, in a particular morphosyntactic context, to categorize the noun in terms of its intrinsic properties. But in Athapaskan linguistics, classifier means 'voice' marker. And 'gender' is used in lieu of 'classifier'. A grammar writer must strike a balance between terminologies of different sorts. Some choose to have a glossary of terms at the end. Or they invent a new, ad hoc term, reflecting a novel or hard to capture notion.

Caution needs to be exercised. As Colin Masica (1991: 774), a major scholar in Indo-Aryan linguistics, puts it,

at one period in the history of structural linguistics . . . traditional grammatical terminology was avoided in favour of *ad hoc terms* arising supposedly only from the exigencies of the language being described, often taken from the form in question itself: "the *te*-form". Whatever the merits of this position in, for example, language teaching, it makes cross-linguistic comparison of different forms with similar functions difficult. For that general labels are needed, and traditional terminology is probably the best source for them, although it needs refinement and standardization. (Masica 1991: 774)

A grain of salt should be added here. There are not enough terms, and new ones keep being introduced. A careful grammarian may initially describe a new phenomenon, for which a label may come years later. Christaller (1875: 144) was the first linguist to have identified the existence of a sequence of verbs which form one predicate in Akan. Without referring to the term 'serial verbs', he identified the phenomenon of verb serialization central to the grammar of many West African, and other, languages. The term 'serial verb' didn't come into general circulation until the late 1950s to early 1960s.

In his magisterial grammar of Takelma, Sapir (1922) did not use the term 'mirativity' (introduced into general linguistic currency by DeLancey 1997). But what he describes as 'surprise overtones' of an inferential evidential (1922: 158, 200) are what is now known as mirative extensions of an evidential (in itself, an obligatory marker of information source).

Whichever term you use, be consistent, clear and explain your choice well—this is the rule of thumb in assigning a proper label for a category.

1.7.4 How to structure a grammar: some hints

And now, to a frequently asked question: how does one go about organizing a grammar? Sadly, some linguists, and especially arm-chair typologists, tend to scour a grammar just for a particular topic (we return to this in Chapter 15). This is why it is important to have a clearly stated organization, and also an index. Others read a grammar from the beginning to end, following the story line as it unfolds—like one reads a novel, or a biography. A reference grammar should be written in such a way that it can be read through like this, with the structure of the language unfolding as the text flows.

A grammar starts with an introduction containing basic facts about the language and its social setting, the family it belongs to, and the cultural background. This is followed by a statement of phonology and phonetics. Then comes morphology, then syntax, then sometimes also discourse properties and some notes on lexical semantics. Other types of organization are also possible. Syntax may be placed before morphology; it is however important that the relevant facts about inflectional morphology be summarized first. Otherwise the discussion of syntax may become unintelligible. A detailed discussion of phonological processes may appear later in the grammar; however, the phonemes of the language have to be introduced at the beginning, as building blocks for the understanding of what follows.

A linguist may choose to put the most exciting part of the language more upfront. Dixon's (1972) classic grammar of Dyirbal begins with a short discussion of word classes and basic inflections in the language, and then turns to the most complicated (and most interesting) part—the syntax. Most of the morphology, phonology and semantics are discussed later. The grammarian decides how to organize the presentation—it just needs to be comprehensive.

The basic rule of thumb is as follows: if the analysis of a category A refers to some facts concerning category B, then the chapter, or section, dealing with B needs to be placed before the section dealing with A.

An important point in grammar writing is choosing appropriate examples to illustrate each phenomenon. To make the language, and the culture, come alive through its grammar, examples need to be based on participant-observation, and accompanied by the context in which they occurred. If they come from traditional narratives, placing them in the context of the narrative makes the grammar an interesting read.

Examples are essential—they support what you are saying, and are the foundation for your argument. In order for the examples to be clear and user-friendly, they need to be glossed. Here is an example of conventional glossing, with lower case for lexemes and pronominal number (sg, du, pl) and SMALL CAPS for grammatical elements.

(1.1)   yaw   s-i-ht   ti   o-d
        3sg.masc:NOM   3sgA-3sgO-look.for   ART:ACC   universal-ACC
        'He looks for a universal'

There can be an additional line if necessary, for phonetic representation. Aguaruna (Jivaroan) is a language with many phonological processes including vowel reduction which obscure morphemic analysis. In his grammar of Aguaruna, Simon Overall (2008) has an additional line for the examples to reflect vowel elision in the surface, pronetic realization. It is up to the grammarian to go for this if necessary, but note that this (a) makes it more strenuous for a reader to process; and (b) makes the grammar longer.

Glossing principles should serve the reader. This can be done in two ways. The linguist may want to always use the same gloss, and not reflect the subtle differences between the meanings of a polysemous term. Or they may choose to reflect in their gloss the actual meaning realized in that particular instance. Either choice is fine—this needs to be stated in an introductory section dealing with glossing and other conventions. The form *nui-takina* in Fijian may mean 'hope for' or 'rely on'. In Dixon's (1988) grammar, each occurrence of this verb is glossed with the meaning it has in that instance of use.

Translation may be another issue. Literal translation may be different from the end result. It may not sound as good as its literary equivalent in the language in which the grammar is written—be it English, French, Spanish, Portuguese, or German. If absolutely necessary, do include a literal translation, and then an explanatory one. In Lango, a Nilotic language, there is a serial verb construction which literally translates as 'I am fat I exceed the king'. It means 'I am fatter than the king'. A literal translation makes the meaning components clearer.

At the very beginning of the grammar, it is useful to have a list of conventions—how the examples are presented, and how they are translated and glossed. There may be special symbols for special purposes. In his grammar of Dyirbal, Dixon (1972) uses / to indicate the end of an intonation unit. If two morphemes are fused together, this may be indicated with +, a dot, or a semicolon. The clearer the conventions, the easier the grammar will be to follow.

For the grammar to remain readable and user-friendly, it is important not to make any of the chapters too long. So, the issue of transitivity classes can be outlined in the chapter dealing with word classes, and then taken up in more detail in a chapter on verbal structure. The same for closed classes. If a language has a highly complex system of demonstratives, their general features can be listed in a word classes chapter, and then addressed separately.

Another issue is how to choose examples from the language. Examples in a grammar serve two purposes: first, they illustrate a point, and secondly, they open the readers' eyes to the riches of the culture and expression. A grammar should make the language come to life through interesting examples—but the author always has to make sure that the examples are not too convoluted, or too complicated to obscure the point they illustrate. (To make parsing examples easier, it is advisable to put square brackets around clausal constituents and indicate their functions by subscripts. The same can be done for noun phrases, especially if they are complex in structure).

A grammar will be incomplete without a selection of texts, about thirty printed pages. Ideally, one should include texts of different genres, from different speakers (men, women, different age groups), or extracts from longer texts. Extracts from conversations are also useful. Within the grammar, the author could use examples from the texts at the end of the grammar, referring to them by numbers, for example Text 1, line 5. This creates a link between the grammar itself and the illustrative texts at the end, and also saves space. A short vocabulary at the end of a grammar is very useful. And, like any academic publication, comprehensive indexes of authors, subjects, and languages will be a help to the readership.

1.8 How this book is organized

This introductory chapter introduces the concept of a reference grammar, and its importance (with a brief overview of further possible types of grammars). A reference grammar is a piece of scientific analysis. The way in which a grammar writer discloses what the language is like, and the way in which they present their discoveries, and analyse them, are not the same.

The Excursus 'Linguistic fieldwork' outlines some basic principles of linguistic fieldwork, focusing on immersion fieldwork and participant-observation as major techniques (with minimal, and judicial, elicitation).

How to start a grammar, so as to capture the audience straight away? Chapter 2, 'A language and its setting', focuses on the language and its setting, including its relatives and neighbours and a typological profile.

Chapters on the language's setting, its phonetics and phonology, and word classes usually come at the beginning of the grammar—in a way, they set the scene for the whole book and provide a backdrop for the rest. But throughout the actual analysis, they may have to be fine-tuned. In a way, the chapters that come first may have to be finalized last.

Before turning to the substance of a grammar, I briefly outline some useful concepts and the building blocks of any grammatical description in Chapter 3, 'Basics'.

Chapter 4, 'Sounds and their functions', addresses the analysis of phonetic and phonological patterns. Chapter 5 focuses on 'Word classes', a discussion which is de rigueur in every grammar. It offers a division into classes of grammatical words based on morphological, syntactic, and also semantic (and sometimes phonological) criteria, and establishes the basis for the rest of the grammar.

Chapter 6, 'Nouns', turns to categories associated with nouns—these include gender, classifiers of various types, number, possession, case, and definiteness, and many more. In many languages, the verb is the only obligatory element in the clause. Verbs tend to have more inflectional complexity than nouns. Chapter 7, 'Verbs', deals with typical categories of verbs, their transitivity classes, and types of complex predicates.

Many languages have a separate word class of adjectives, and also of adverbs— the topic of Chapter 8. Closed classes are discussed in Chapter 9. The ways in which participants are marked are discussed in Chapter 10, 'Who does what to whom: grammatical relations'. The next chapter, 11, focuses on types of clauses and of sentences. This also includes negation as a clausal category. Chapter 12 addresses clause linking and complex clauses.

A language comes alive through the ways in which it is used on a day-to-day basis, and in various genres of narratives and lore. Chapter 13, 'Language in context', deals with various ways of organizing one's discourse—how to make a particular participant salient, how to track participants, and how to judiciously employ repetition and overlaps to keep your listeners interested. It touches upon some issues in semantics and lexicon which may be included in a grammar.

One of the most tantalizing issues in linguistic analysis is the question of explanation—why is a language the way it is? This is what Chapter 14 is about. The final Chapter 15, 'How to create a grammar and how to read one', offers some hints as to how to structure a grammar, how much information on the history of the language to include, how to present the analysis and examples. It also contains ideas on how a grammar could be read to make the most of it. Each chapter focuses on issues that have to be addressed for each topic. Special points are summarized at the end of some chapters. Chapter 15 draws it all together.

At the end, we offer a Glossary of terms, so that the reader may make sure that we always understand each other.

The sequence of the chapters of this book does not offer a cook-book recipe for how to organize a grammar. The exact strategy, and order, of presentation depends on the language itself. One way of tying the grammar chapters together is to offer an initial synopsis of some particularly striking features of the language in a chapter at the beginning—after an introductory chapter or the chapter on phonetics and phonology. Understanding the grammatical relations in Manambu, a Papuan language from New Guinea, is key to grasping the structure of the language. This is why in my grammar (Aikhenvald 2008) grammatical relations are explained even before we talk about word classes as a gateway to the whole language.

Traditionally, a grammar of a language is understood as consisting of morphology and syntax. Some linguists treat phonology as its third part; others regard it as standing apart from grammar. (A relatively new coinage, 'morphosyntax', is sometimes used as an alternative term for grammar, conceived of as syntax plus morphology.) A comprehensive reference grammar goes beyond these limits: it takes account of each aspect of the language, including discourse pragmatics and sociolinguistic parameters.

Notes and sources

§1.1–2: Further figures and information on numbers of speakers for different languages are in Lewis (2009). See chapters in Ameka, Dench and Evans (2006) and van Driem (2007) for the discussion of grammars and holistic approach to them.

§1.3: Roberts (1987: 228–9) on Amele.

§1.4.1: On Itonama, see Judy and Judy (1965), on Movima see Camp and Licardi (1965).

§1.4.2: Exemplary reference grammars include Watters (2002), Dixon (2004a), Kruspe (2004), Olawsky (2006) and Guillaume (2008). Lehmann (2004) offers useful suggestions on the structure and the contents of a historical grammar; an example is Pedersen and Lewis (1937). Examples of pedagogical grammars are Lewis (1953) for Turkish, Hewitt (1996) for Georgian, and Kerr (1995) for Cuiba, a Guahibo language from Colombia. Price (2008) has a strong element of prescriptive grammar. An exemplary sketch grammar is in Silva and Silva's (2012) monograph on Yuhup, a Makú language of north-west Amazonia in Brazil. Reference grammars may incorporate some language learning exercises—an example is Ashton (1947) on Swahili.

§1.5: In recent years, there has arisen a trend to limit the term 'language documentation' to producing computer databases, websites, and electronic archiving which involve little, or no, language analysis. This approach is restrictive and contributes little to the understanding of the internal structure of languages and the development of analytic argumentation. It is also inherently discriminatory: language communities with little internet and electricity will be deprived of access to electronic databases. See also Aikhenvald (2013d) on conflicting priorities for speakers, linguists, and grant-giving agencies.

§1.6: See Dorian (2010) on variation in endangered languages, and the notion of speech community.

§1.7.2: See Dixon (2010a, 2010b, 2012) on basic linguistic theory.

§1.7.3: See Aikhenvald (2006d: 58–9) on the term 'serial verb construction'.

§1.7.4: Noonan (1992: 211–12) on Lango.

Appendix: Excursus—Linguistic fieldwork

Why linguistic fieldwork?

Firsthand knowledge of diverse languages with their different structures is essential for our understanding of how human languages work. Linguistic fieldwork—which involves venturing into a community where the language is spoken, collecting information, and providing a comprehensive analysis and written documentation of the language—is crucial for this. And it is also urgent: in just a few generations many small 'exotic' languages will have passed into oblivion, ousted by encroaching national and other majority languages, which carry more prestige and economic advantages.

Linguistics as a discipline and as a science relies on analytic results based on firsthand information acquired through fieldwork—its backbone. Typologists must rely on careful grammatical descriptions unconstrained by any time-line formalism, in order to bring together language facts and their typological assessments. Linguistic fieldwork is also the best way of 'hands-on' learning the discipline—as Dixon (2007a) puts it, 'get out and do it'. Recording, learning, and analysing a new language as it is spoken in its own environment is a most intellectually exciting and invigorating enterprise. Despite the physical difficulties, frustrations, and sometimes even dangers that living in an unknown environment may bring, you live through a whirlpool of discoveries, and sudden flashes of understanding.

Linguistic fieldwork is a journey of discovery. If you are working with an obsolescent language, it is also a journey of recovery—recovering the knowledge and piecing together the parts of a puzzle which may never be fully solved.

A few years ago doing fieldwork was unfashionable. Self-proclaimed theoreticians—including 'arm-chair' typologists relying on secondary sources—felt intrinsically superior to those who would go out and obtain their own data by fieldwork. Yet, now it appears that the tide has changed. In the early 1990s, a half-baked 'arm-chair' typologist could easily say to a fieldworker: 'you bring us the data, and we will analyse them for you'. Now, more than a decade on, this same person is likely to say, somewhat apologetically: 'you know, I am now planning to do fieldwork myself'. 'Squatting in one's theoretical cocoons and reinterpreting data to fit universal hypotheses and generate PhDs'—to use Dixon's (1977: xvii) words—is falling out of fashion. More value is now placed on fieldwork, and there is more and more interest in how it is done, in its results, and in those who do it.

Immersion fieldwork

Linguistic fieldwork ideally involves observing the language as it is used, becoming a member of a community, and often being adopted into the kinship system. One records texts, translates them and makes sure every bit is fully understood, and at the same time learns to speak the language and observes how it is used by native speakers—ideally—of all age, and social, groups. This is what we call 'IMMERSION FIELDWORK'.

As many previously undocumented languages move towards extinction, they may cease to be used by a community. They may not be spoken at all on a regular basis—just remembered by a few old people. Participant-observation—and with it 'immersion' fieldwork—then becomes almost impossible. We are forced to do what we can with the 'rememberers' through 'interview' fieldwork. This is what happens in many linguistic situations in Australia and throughout the Americas. Such studies, however useful, are bound to produce limited grammars, if compared to the output of fully fledged multi-faceted immersion fieldwork. Fieldworkers who have never had the opportunity of undertaking true immersion fieldwork ought to recognize their limitations, and refrain from teaching others 'how to' and making general pronouncements about the subject.

Many of the manuals of fieldwork, and encyclopaedia articles on this subject, have been written by people who have, at best, some experience of interview fieldwork. They have not lived in a community for a period of months, immersing themselves in daily life and in daily language use. Yet they have the impertinence to instruct students on how to do what they have not undertaken themselves.

'Interview fieldwork' is justified if there is nothing else to be done. It is a very poor option if a speech community is available—but some researchers opt to concentrate on an easy option, that is interview fieldwork with a few speakers conveniently placed in a city or in a township. A grammar of a language spoken by a few million people which is based on work with one consultant in an urban environment could be interesting, but is unlikely to be comprehensive and fully reliable. Opting to study Burmese, Greek, or Serbian—each spoken in their home countries—within the comfort zone of Greater Melbourne, London, or Los Angeles may be good for understanding the subtle influence of the Anglophone environment on a smaller language. But it is bound to give a skewed and partial picture of the language's structure.

Of course, in some cases, the area where the language is spoken is 'off-limits' to the researcher, due to a civil war or other political problems. It is hardly feasible for researchers nowadays to venture into the Caucasus, or conflict-plagued areas of the New Guinea Highlands. One may then have to postpone planned fieldwork until such time as the political situation improves. Meanwhile, there are several thousand other languages on which one can undertake immersion fieldwork.

In some traditions, 'interview' fieldwork involves a whole group of people going to a location for a short time, hastily interviewing the same set of consultants on the principle 'one researcher one problem'. There is no time to establish any true rapport between a linguist and a consultant. The relationship is that of 'paid help' rather than of intellectual partnership. The resulting grammars—of which a few have been published—consist of several chapters each by different people, like a patchwork quilt with colours that do not match. What linguist A considers serial verbs in Chapter X for which A is responsible, linguist B, in their Chapter Y, may happily describe as complement clauses. And so forth.

Another type of malpractice in 'interview' fieldwork involves working on just one aspect, without taking account of the language as a whole. 'If you need to enlarge your database on relative clauses, just go and ask about them in your two-weeks' vacation', was a piece of 'advice' once distributed on the world-wide web by an 'arm-chair' typologist. The results of such interview fieldwork are bound to be flawed.

Field method courses may provide a reasonable background training for someone preparing for real fieldwork. Field methods courses, conducted by such experts as Mary Haas and Harry Hoijer, gave Bhadriraju Krishnamurti (2007) 'adequate confidence and training in phonetics and the methodology for studying a foreign language', so as to enable him 'to undertake fieldwork on unexplored Dravidian languages in Central India'. But field method courses should never be seen as a substitute even for interview fieldwork. A highly lamentable malpractice consists in making this mistake, and publishing a collection of papers from a field methods course, without bothering to explore the language further.

A priceless partnership

What about our relationships with language teachers, or consultants? On the one hand, our consultants are friends, and even adopted family. On the other hand, we are linguists, and can hardly conceal our role as researchers. As Kate Burridge (2007) put it, 'as speakers become friends not just sources of information, it is increasingly difficult to remain the impartial observer'. How close does one get to the people whose language is being described? Being integrated into the Tariana community of Santa Rosa in northwest Amazonia, and into the Manambu community at Avatip in New Guinea, has never been easy for me. The 'adopted' family ties impose moral and financial obligations, and may even hamper further research: I was criticized by my Tariana family for wanting to work with a group speaking a somewhat different variety, who, in their opinion, 'do not speak right'. Yet, just like we live with our 'real families', no matter how difficult they may be, we take our fieldwork environment as it comes, and make the best of it.

Close personal ties enhance a 'priceless intellectual partnership' (in Dixon's 2007a words) with one, or more, consultants. As Burridge says about her consultant friend (2007): 'She knows what I am about to ask, before I have even figured it out myself.' Such consultants are as good as co-authors of our grammars, and are definitely co-analysts.

Learning the language and recording and analysing texts and conversations, are a desideratum for a good fieldworker. Limited elicitation (through the language itself) of paradigms is important for highly fusional languages—such as Dravidian. But if we wish to achieve the goal of language documentation for future generations (of both linguists and communities), we need to learn special vocabulary—for example, of a song language, or a language used when people are in mourning. These can be only discovered through 'spontaneous, unscripted speech'—such patterns may be lost in elicited sentences, and in translations from another language.

As Mithun (2007) puts it, 'the elicitation of sentences translated from a contact language can facilitate direct comparison of languages'—but such comparison will not reveal anything much about the fundamental features of a minority language likely to be 'lost' in translation. We will not learn much beyond what we already know. We may then run the danger of imposing the categories we think should be there onto a language which may truly not have them.

I am often asked what 'prompts' can be taken to the field to discover spatial orientation patterns or positional verbs. In general, it is not advisable to take any special foreign objects and prompts—with the exception of a colour chart and perhaps a body part chart. A set of colour pencils or pens can be used instead of it, and they can then be given to children or to a local school, and thus be useful. Every language has terms for body parts. Instead of pointing them out on oneself, one might bring along a body part chart—a picture of a human body.

A successful fieldworker is a bit of an actor and performer. To get to verbs, one can perform actions one can think of—crouching, jumping, handling things. This is an entertaining and efficient way to get a natural and spontaneous answer which will reflect the use of the language and its meanings. It is useful to take books with pictures—something to talk about, especially pictures of one's own country (if the fieldworker is a foreigner). Pictures of one's family are very useful: this is a way of breaking the ice, and starting an interaction without being intrusive. It is also a good way of learning the kinship system. Simple objects are often a help. A good fieldworker will have a piece of string, needle and thread, matches, and will be able to use any household objects to ask about how one talks about putting them down (thus getting to positional verbs), handling them, and determining what parts they have.

Steps to follow

Here are some hints about how to organize one's work in preparation for fieldwork, and during it.

1 *Preparing to go into the field*

Before you go to the field, you may have to spend time obtaining the necessary ethics and visa permissions, and also an invitation from the community. This time does not have to be wasted. You can try and learn as much as you can about the features of the area you are planning to go to. If possible, do a study of materials available on the language and its relatives. You will then have some idea what to expect in the field.

Having some idea of what kind of stories, or story genres, you may be able to obtain will help you in the initial stages. Many Amazonian peoples have stories about a flying competition between a smaller bird and a bigger bird, and about a deer and a turtle. Hunters like to tell stories about their prowess. The more you know to start with, the easier it will be to learn more—you will be less overwhelmed.

Before departing, make sure you have all the necessary gear (and that it works)—notebooks (to write in), pens, pencils, recorders, medicine, presents, and perhaps a satellite phone just in case. It is good to have a few small notebooks which you carry around with you to write down spontaneous utterances. It is also useful to have a special notebook as a diary, where you will write down your observations at the end of each day.

2 *In the field*

Once in the field, this is what is good to keep in mind.

What we aim to COLLECT includes: stories of varied genres, preferably from more than one speaker (different ages, men and women). These would include folk tales, animal stories, traditional stories, autobiographies, procedural texts about how to make things, and stories of other sorts. To be able to record, transcribe, and fully understand songs, spells, incantations, or any ritual genres is wonderful. But this is a secondary priority and may not be achieved until a later stage when you understand the language better and speakers trust you with culturally important texts. It is also wonderful to record, transcribe, and understand spontaneous dialogues and discussions (including those at meetings and in Church). However, these are notoriously difficult to transcribe, and to get translated. Collection of these may be better left to a later stage.

Our PARTICIPANT-OBSERVATION will allow us to get a feel for how the language is used on a daily basis. Certain phenomena—for example, direct speech reports, or some very abrupt commands—will be sparingly used in stories. But you will hear them, learn how to use them and write them down as you communicate with the people, and hear the language around you. Not everything has to be recorded. A good grammar can be produced based on three to four hours of good recordings, transcribed and fully understood.

It is also important to collect lexical items. This is where—in the beginning at least—you may have to use elicitation in the lingua franca or the national language. It is important to get a list of body parts, kinship terms, and names of flora and fauna. Identifying flora and fauna may be a strenuous task, best achieved in collaboration with experts. Kinship terms are best learnt through establishing people's genealogies, and discussing their own kin (and perhaps the fieldworker's) and how they speak about and address their relatives. For each bird or mammal, a fieldworker is advised to get some facts about its habits—what it eats, where it lives, how big it is. In this way, working with the lexicon can provide you with examples of grammar.

What we aim to ACHIEVE is, first and foremost, a comprehensive grammar which will ultimately reflect different genres, including spontaneous speech. We also will compile a dictionary, or at least a word list, and produce a collection of texts.

What communities value most is dictionaries, story books, and also primers. These are important by-products which reflect something one can 'give back' to one's teachers.

When one is first confronted with a new fieldwork language, one needs to learn some words—body parts are a good start. For plants and animals, it is good to have books with pictures as a means of orientation (but these can be misleading since they may not reflect the actual size and shape of the object).

A WAY TO START work can be recording a short text and then transcribing it with a speaker. (This may not be the same person as the one who has told you the story). Carefully go through the recording with a speaker, and try and get it translated and understood. You will stumble upon grammatical constructions for which you will require clarification. Try and do this through the language itself. Speakers will appreciate your tenacity, and will help you.

In all your relationships with people, try and use the contact language as little as possible. You will learn the new language by listening, repeating, and getting corrected.

It is advisable to ORGANIZE YOUR DAY in the field following a routine. In the morning, you can start with activities which demand more concentration and intellectual effort—recording, transcribing, and grammatical analysis and grammatical questions. When you—and your consultants—are somewhat tired, a good way to change is to start asking lexical questions. This may involve some amount of 'show-and-tell' on your part. For instance, if you try and establish what positional verbs are you may walk around the house lifting and putting down things of different shapes and sizes, and creating general amusement. Lexical elicitation of the type 'let's now talk about kinds of birds we have here' is better left to the end of the day.

Make sure that for each text, and each written down bit of information for participant-observation you record the name of the person and the date. We may be dealing with a language with high variation from one speaker to another. This is typically the case for many obsolescent languages. Variation may also reflect a familylect—a way of speaking characteristic of a family, or of a clan. Noting the details of each speaker may turn out to be crucial for the grammar.

REMEMBER: Successful fieldwork is a sine qua non for producing a high-quality, theoretically-informed grammar. The following principles ensure attaining this goal.

Box 1.1 Essential principles for successful fieldwork in linguistics

1 Grammatical analysis should primarily be based on study of texts and conversations, *not* on elicitation through a lingua franca.

2 If the language is still actively spoken, fieldwork should be conducted in a community where it is spoken by all (or most) members as a first language, and where the linguist will be welcomed.

   It is not satisfactory to work with a limited number of speakers in a town, or anywhere away from a major language community.

   (A single linguist—or linguist and spouse—can fit into a small community, and be accepted by them. For more than a hundred years, all successful linguistic fieldwork has been on this basis. It has occasionally been suggested that a 'team' of linguists should be involved, each working on a topic. This is neither sensible nor practicable; it has never produced quality results, and would never be likely to do so.)

3 A fieldworker must make an effort to achieve substantial competence in the language of study in order to interact with members of the speech community. This is 'immersion fieldwork' (as opposed to 'interview fieldwork').

   Participant observation will provide invaluable materials, supplementing the textual corpus. This involves: (a) noting what speakers say during everyday activities; and (b) noting how speakers correct the fieldworker's attempts at speaking the language.

Cont.

Box 1.1 *continued*

4 It is good to record texts from a range of speakers, in terms of status within the community, age, and if possible sex (but this is sometimes not possible). And from a range of genres. These may include a selection from: traditional legends, accounts of recent historical events, announcements, procedural instructions on how to garden or hunt or cook or construct artefacts, and so on.

   Sometimes the people who record texts will also assist in their transcription and analysis. At other times different consultants are needed for these two tasks. Typically, some of the best texts may be told by elder members of the language community, with younger, and perhaps more literate, relatives playing the major role in helping with transcription and analysis.

   There will generally be a smallish number of consultants who will become well attuned to the fieldworker's methods and aims. But care must be taken not to work *just* with one or two fine consultants. A reasonably wide range of speakers should be involved.

5 Texts to be included in the corpus must be transcribed, translated, checked, and analysed in the field, in consultation with speakers. If, at a late stage, the fieldworker feels able to make a draft transcription on their own, this must be checked with consultants. It is bad practice to attempt to transcribe and translate texts away from the field.

6 Grammatical elicitation should come in at an intermediate stage of the work, and must always involve asking about sentences in the language (not in a lingua franca). Once grammatical hypotheses have been proposed, on the basis of textual and other materials, sentences can be constructed to test them, and put to consultants. These may commence with variations on sentence patterns in the corpus (for example, if a certain construction type has been observed with 'see', one can then test to see whether it is also used with 'hear') and gradually generalize from these.

   When a putative sentence is put to a speaker it is generally appropriate to place it in a context. For instance, the linguist may ask: 'if someone said X [a sentence in the corpus], could you reply with Y [a sentence generated by the fieldworker]?'

   It is not sufficient to accept a 'yes' from the consultant. They must be asked to themselves say the proffered sentence. Not infrequently, speakers respond 'yes' but then when asked to say the sentence themselves, cast it in a slightly different way from that offered. (They may be accepting a certain aspect of the sentence—say subject-predicate gender agreement—but the sentence may err in some other respect—say, constituent order.)

   It is often sensible to check tricky grammatical points with more than one good consultant. But this can be overdone; there is seldom need to check anything with more than two or three speakers.

Cont.

Box 1.1 continued

7 If there is no existing dictionary of the language, an extensive vocabulary should be gradually built up during the fieldwork. Elicitation is useful for some semantic domains (flora, fauna, artefacts, body parts, etc.). All lexemes which come up in texts or are noted during participant observation should be included. It is useful to have vocabulary files arranged in two ways—by semantic field, and also alphabetically.

If there is an existing (full or partial) dictionary this can be a useful basis, but must be checked, corrected, and expanded, as necessary.

8 Equipment should be kept to a minimum. Too much flashy machinery may alienate the linguist from members of the community and make it more difficult to achieve success in immersion fieldwork. And the more machinery one takes into the field (and the more complicated it is) the more there is to go wrong.

A good-quality robust recorder is essential. In case this might fail, there should be a back-up recorder of the same type.

The experience of practised fieldworkers is that to introduce a video camera into a fieldwork situation too soon may gravely disturb the chance of establishing a close relationship between linguist and speech community. Overuse of flashy gadgets may severely jeopardize the likelihood of success for a standard linguistic description (grammar, texts, and dictionary).

Similar remarks apply for computers. In addition, many fieldwork situations have no electricity, or else an occasional and unreliable supply. If a linguist takes into the field a reliance on computers, it is highly likely that they will, from time to time, become frustrated with their productivity being impaired. Energy which has to be spent on computational matters is far better directed towards learning and analysing the language.

9 Each fieldwork situation is subtly different and culturally specific. It is generally not sensible to attempt to employ questionnaires which were not constructed with this language community in view. Video clips from another society (and materials like 'Pear' and 'Frog' stories) are often confusing and are unlikely to produce reliable data in the way that immersion fieldwork will. Such extraneous 'aids' and 'prompts' are best avoided.

10 Fieldwork should never be seen as a business deal (or a contract of employment) between linguist and consultants. Rather, sound fieldwork is based on friendship, cooperation, interest, and trust. Consultants should of course be compensated. Ways of doing this vary widely, depending on the fieldwork situation; sometimes it is appropriate for money to be involved, sometimes just goods.

It is always appropriate to offer other kinds of help. For instance, providing advice on how to deal with government agencies, writing to officials on the community's behalf, writing other kinds of letters as requested.

Cont.

Box 1.1 continued

A language community often values the linguist's input to teaching programmes. It may be appropriate, on a second field trip, to take elementary vocabulary books and primers. But, within the time-limits of a PhD course or a Post-Doctoral Fellowship, the amount of time devoted to such concerns must not be allowed to grow out of proportion.

11 It is not sensible to publish anything on a grammatical or phonological topic until the linguist has gained a good overall picture of every aspect of the structure of the language. If one publishes part-way through a study, there is a fair likelihood that later work may show that the initial analysis requires radical revision (in a nutshell, that it is wrong). This piece of advice has to be balanced against the present-day pressure to publish (something, anything, anywhere) in order to advance to the next rung of the academic ladder.

Notes and sources

More on immersion fieldwork and its advantages is in Dixon (2007a, 2010a); see also Aikhenvald (2007a), and Mithun (2007). A view on language documentation through electronic means (often unstable and unreliable in the long run) is presented in Chelliah and de Reuse (2010).

2

A language and its setting

The first chapter of a reference grammar is a gateway to the whole book. This is where the reader will learn the basic facts — where the language is spoken, how many people speak it, and what its cultural background is like.

The primary audience for a reference grammar are linguists. A linguistic profile of the language will highlight its most distinctive and noteworthy features. Further points to be addressed in the introductory chapter include genetic affiliation and the names of the language, the speakers' social organization and relationships with neighbours, previous studies of the language and the people, and the materials for the reference grammar.

2.1 To launch a grammar: the language and its profile

A general profile of the language highlights features that give the grammar its distinctive character. Every category in a language warrants a typological perspective. This helps us predict what is plausible, and what is not, what to expect in a new language, and what is unusual. The introductory chapter will, ideally, offer a typological outline of the language with its general features, and a selection of features which the linguist considers most noteworthy.

Let's look at some general typological parameters. First, languages can be classified depending on whether words neatly divide into parts with one meaning each. In ISOLATING languages, like Vietnamese, every form has one meaning. In an AGGLU- TINATING language, like Turkish, a word may consist of several morphemes but the boundaries between them are clear-cut. There is typically a one-to-one correspondence between a morpheme and its meaning, and a morpheme has an invariant shape which makes it easy to identify. And in a FUSIONAL language, like Latin, one little form can combine many meanings: for instance, *i*, the shortest form in Latin, has a complex meaning of 'you singular go! (imperative)'. A language can be agglutinating with some fusion. Hungarian, a predominantly agglutinating language, allows for some change of form on morpheme boundaries, known as vowel harmony, for example Hungarian *ember-ek-ben* (man-PLURAL-INNER.LOCATIVE) 'in men', but *ásztal-ok-ban* (table- PLURAL-INNER.LOCATIVE) 'in tables'.

Languages can also be classified depending on number of meaningful parts—that is, morphemes—within a word. ANALYTIC languages tend to have a one-to-one correspondence between word and morpheme; they have few if any bound morphemes. Vietnamese and Mandarin Chinese are good examples of analytic languages. In SYNTHETIC languages a word consists of several morphemes, and there are numerous bound morphemes. Hungarian and Latin are synthetic languages. Some languages are only mildly synthetic. In English, and in many languages of the Jê family from South America, the number of morphemes per word is often not more than two. Languages such as Eskimo (including Greenlandic, Yup'ik and Cup'ik) are at the opposite extreme. The bound morphemes often express semantic content reserved for lexemes in languages of other types. In Nahuatl, from Mexico, one word *ni-naka-kwa* (1sg-meat-eat) has a complex meaning of 'I eat meat'. These 'megarich' structures are sometimes called polysynthetic.

The degree of synthesis and the treatment of morphological boundaries are independent typological parameters. For a description of a previously undocumented language, it is not enough to say that it is 'analytic', or that it is 'isolating'. It is true that isolating languages tend to be analytic, but the reverse would be wrong: English, which has a lot of fusional morphology, makes extensive use of analytic constructions.

Languages can be classified based on further parameters. One such parameter concerns the order of the meaningful elements. Languages vary as to the order of syntactic constituents within a clause. In English, the verb has to follow the subject, as in *I saw a dog*. But in Fijian, the verb generally has to come first. So, English is verb-medial, and Fijian is verb-initial, while Manambu, from New Guinea, is verb-final. Order of individual words within a constituent—especially a noun phrase—is another parameter. For instance, English and Latin have prepositions, Hungarian has postpositions, and Estonian has both.

It is worth mentioning whether the language has prefixes, suffixes, or both (and maybe also discontinuous confixes and transfixes). It is useful to include a summary of open and closed word classes (with a reference to a chapter which will discuss them).

Distinct phonological features can be included—tones, vowel length, number and special features of consonants and vowels. And also special processes—reduplication, vowel harmony and assimilation, and defining features of the phonological word. A detailed profile would also include possession classes of nouns, whether there are genders and classifiers, and what the most prominent grammatical subclasses of nouns are (these may include kinship terms and body parts, or part–whole relations). Further specific nominal, and verbal, categories may include number, tense, aspect, modality, information source (or evidentiality), person, and more.

The major questions to be addressed in delineating the typological profile of a language are:

- How are grammatical relations expressed—that is, if the language is nominative-accusative, or absolutive-ergative; or perhaps it combines features of both types?

- What are the transitivity classes of verbs, and predicate structure?
- What are its clause types?
- What are the orders of constituents within a clause and of words within a phrase?

Besides these few basics, there is hardly any 'recipe' for this initial profile. There are no musts. Some categories in some languages stand out as strikingly unusual. East Tucanoan languages from Colombia and Brazil have obligatory marking of information source—or evidentials: in every clause one needs to specify how one knows things. Many of these languages also have half a dozen special forms for commands—whether the activity is to be performed straight away, or later, or in a different location, or on someone else's order. Many languages of Papua New Guinea have long chains of verbs each of which tells us whether its subject is the same or not as that of the main verb, known as switch reference. In Panoan languages of Peru, Brazil, and Bolivia, the choice of switch reference marker depends on whether the verb is transitive or not. Many South American and Australian languages have different tense distinctions on verbs and on nouns. In Kham, and its many Tibeto-Burman relatives, case markers express grammatical relations on nouns; when used on verbs, case markers link clauses. Many Oceanic languages of the Austronesian family have a way of classifying nouns in possessive constructions, depending on how these can be handled—eaten, drunk, worn, sold, etc. A short and snappy profile will bring to light some of such features.

2.2 The language and its speakers

This part includes names under which the language and the people who speak it are known. There may be several names—the name under which the language is known in the literature, the name(s) which the speakers use (known as autodenominations), and the names by which they are referred to by other groups, if different (known as exonyms). The language known as Wanano (or Guanano) is called, by the speakers, Kotria or Kotiria (literally, people of the water). Its Tariana-speaking neighbours refer to the Wanano as Panumape (literally, 'one mouth' in Tariana). The name of the people who speak the language can be different from the language itself. The Tolai of New Britain speak a language they call Kuanua.

People may refer to themselves simply as 'us', or 'people', or 'real people'. An Arawak language from Peru, known as Piro, is called Yine by some native speakers. The word *Yine* means 'human race, people', and can also refer to any 'non-white'. When speaking Piro, the Piro also refer to themselves as *Wumolene* 'our kinspeople'.

Most languages are known in the literature, and to the speakers, under many different names. It is useful to list these, to be as comprehensive as possible. A reference grammar is the only place where all this information will be consolidated and discussed.

A grammarian confronted with a multitude of names may have a hard time choosing one. A name which has gained currency in the literature may be felt to be offensive to the community of speakers. Papago used to be an accepted name for a Uto-Aztecan language spoken in south-eastern Arizona and north-west Mexico. This name is derived from *ba:bawiko'a*, meaning 'eating tepary beans'—a pejorative name used by enemy tribes of the same linguistic group. The Spanish had misheard this as Papago. The people themselves have recently rejected this name, and renamed themselves as Tohono O'odham meaning 'Desert People'.

But if you wish to change the main name, do so with care. One thing a grammarian should try to avoid is to create further havoc in language names. Establishing the exact meaning of an additional name may require detective work. The Piro language is also known as Simirinche or Simiranch. In a few languages of the neighbouring Campa-speaking groups, also from the Arawak family, the root *shimirin*- refers to 'enemies', or to people who live downstream. This makes us suspect that *Simirinche* is an exonym, that is, a name by which the Piro are known to others.

It is also important to include known dialects, and their precise location. Mention how much dialectal diversity there is (or was). And how this is manifested (phonological and/or morphological and/or syntactic and/or lexical differences). Ideally, a map should be included. This section should also contain demographic information—that is, approximate numbers of speakers in each location, inasmuch as is possible. If there is a discrepancy between the number of members of ethnic group and those who speak the language, this should also be included here.

Then comes a crucial point: is the language spoken by all the members of the community, and is it being learnt by children? Is it spoken in all circumstances, or does it co-exist with another, more dominant one employed in schools and official gatherings? Are there school programmes in the language? Is the language used on the radio, or television? Is there any literary variety? Some of these points will overlap with the ones mentioned in §2.4.

2.3 The language, its relatives, and its neighbours

To place a language within its broader context, we need to outline its genetic and areal connections—teasing apart its various similarities to other languages.

2.3.1 *Chance similarities and shared structural features*

When you start learning a new language, you may wonder why a word in one language is similar to a word in a language you already know. This situation can result from pure chance. In Latin, 'two' is *duo/dua*. We know this from such English words as *dual*, or *dualism*. In Malay, the language of Malaysia, *dua* also means 'two'. Goemai (a Chadic language from Nigeria) and Manambu, a Ndu language of Papua New Guinea, both happen to use *a:s* for 'dog'. And numerous languages of the world have a negator *ma* or *ma:*. These are coincidences, curious facts which tell us nothing about the history of these languages, or of those who speak them.

Linguistic categories can be similar because they are universal. Every language has some way of asking a question or of framing a command. In every language, there is a way of negating a statement. Such similarities due to universal properties of language are of interest for general linguistics.

Languages spoken in different parts of the world and bearing no relation to each other can share grammatical features. Shilluk, a Nilotic language from Kenya, distinguishes three information sources: what one saw, what one inferred, and what one was told. This is similar to what one finds in Shipibo-Konibo, a Panoan language from Peru, and in Quechua, spoken by millions of people in Peru and Bolivia. Quechua, Turkish, and Hungarian are agglutinating in terms of how morphemes are arranged inside a word. These structural similarities are interesting for a typologist. But they tell us nothing about the history of languages or their speakers. Let us turn to those similarities that do.

2.3.2 *Common origins and genetic connections*

Number words in English and in German are very similar to each other because these languages are related: they come from a single common ancestor. This is no chance coincidence. They are Germanic languages and belong to the Germanic subgroup of Indo-European. Their similarities are due to **genetic inheritance**: an example is in Table 2.1.

That is to say, a shared feature may be based on common linguistic origin. The languages can then be shown to have descended from the same ancestor (this is achieved by using the rigorous procedures of historical and comparative linguistics). They will then retain features of the shared 'proto-language'.

TABLE 2.1. No chance coincidence: 'one' through 'four' in English and German

English	German
one	*ein(s)*
two	*zwei*
three	*drei*
four	*vier*

If two languages descend from the same ancestor, and thus belong to one family, they are likely to have similar categories, and meanings expressed by similar forms. For a similarity to be recognized as a mark of genetic affiliation it must involve shared forms. In other words, the forms and their meanings must be either identical or else relatable, through established rules for phonological change and semantic change in the languages (within the limits of what types of phonological change and of semantic shift are possible, and plausible).

Genetic affiliation of the language may shed light on a wider context of the history and prehistory of the speakers of a language. Edward Sapir (1936) compared Navajo, an Athapaskan language from the American Southwest, with its proven genetic relatives in the north, where the majority of Athapaskan languages are spoken. He arrived at a few important conclusions, to do with the culture and possible origins of the Navajo people. First, the gourd was not originally an element of Southern Athapaskan culture. Secondly, spoons were made of horn (since the word meaning 'spoon' in Navajo means 'horn' in other languages of the family, and especially those in the north). Thirdly, corn, a staple food nowadays, was at one time felt to be an alien food: the Navajo word for 'corn', *nà.dą́,* if compared with other Athapaskan languages spoken in the north, can be analysed as 'enemy food'. Fourthly, linguistic evidence suggests that the Navajo—who now live in arid areas—used to have knowledge of canoes. All these features show that the Navajo are different from their current neighbours in the Southwest of the USA. The four conclusions—and especially the fourth one—point towards a non-Southwestern origin of the Navajo, and more specifically towards their possible migration from the north to where they are now.

Languages of the world are divided into proven families—such as Indo-European, Uralic, Algonquian, Athapaskan, Arawak, Jê, Panoan, Carib, Tupí, to name just a few. Based on occasional shared formal similarities and shared typological features, speculative groupings have been suggested such as Indo-Pacific, Ge-Pano-Carib, Macro-Equatorial, Amerind, Pama-Nyungan, Nostratic, Trans-New Guinea etc.). Putative long-distance groupings—unless proved—remain, in Matthews' (2007: 268) words, 'the kind of hypothesis one believes to the extent that one believes in that kind of hypothesis'.

To REMEMBER: A genetic family is a fact. A grammar is not a set of beliefs—unproven fantasies are out of place in it. A typological similarity—in terms of a category, a construction, a morphological technique—is not a mark of genetic relationship. Shared and regularly corresponding forms are.

2.3.3 Geographical proximity and language contact

Forms and meanings across languages can be similar for yet another reason. Languages—and dialects—do not exist in a vacuum. Speakers of different languages come into contact with each other: they may trade, intermarry, meet for ceremonies, and so on. Languages are then in contact, with many speakers of one having some knowledge of the other. Speakers naturally borrow linguistic features back and forth—habits of pronunciation, significant sounds (phonemes), grammatical categories, vocabulary items, and even some grammatical forms. Thus, contact is another source of similarity between languages, whose speakers adjust their speech habits to make sure they understand their neighbours. No feature is absolutely borrowing-proof. When speakers of different languages interact, they borrow forms and meanings. How much they borrow depends on cultural and social factors, including the degree of knowledge of each other's languages, speakers' sense of purism, and also on the structure of the languages in contact. Complex morphological patterns in a language can make the incorporation of a foreign word difficult, and thus serve as a natural obstacle to foreign intruders.

Languages which are not in contact with each other may have borrowed the same form, or the same pattern, from some common source, or from different sources. For instance, the Arabic word *nabī* 'prophet' was independently borrowed into Persian, Swahili, and Malay.

Every language has been, to some extent, influenced by another. There are no 'pure' languages in this respect. In English, we find many words which are not our 'own'. The word *very* comes from French *vrai* 'real', and familiar *cherries* come from French *cerise*. The impact of language contact is easy to see in some languages. In others, it is not so easy. Hungarian has very few words taken from other languages: speakers prefer to coin their own words rather than borrow foreign ones. The English word 'cosmonaut', literally 'world navigator', comes from Greek. Hungarian *űr-hajós* ('world navigator') means the same: but all the forms are native. Most languages of Europe use the word *president* for the head of a company or a republic. Not so in Hungarian: the word for president is *elnök*. Literally, this means 'first one'.

Borrowings and structural similarities due to contact may extend over all or most of the languages in a geographical region, no matter whether they are related or not. We then get large-scale linguistic diffusion, defining the region as a linguistic area (or Sprachbund). Then, languages may remain different in many of their forms, but their structures will converge towards a similar prototype.

Languages within an area will share a fair number of distinctive diagnostic traits. And they will distinguish them from their relatives. For instance, Romanian is a Romance language: its forms are very similar to its relatives French, Italian, and Spanish. But articles in Romanian follow the noun—rather than preceding it as in other Romance languages. This is a feature Romanian has borrowed from its neighbours, South Slavic languages spoken in the same area. Such languages can be called 'aberrant': they differ from their relatives, and for a good reason.

2.3.4 *The language in its genetic and areal context: what to include*

Every language—except for a handful of so-called isolates, or linguistic orphans—belongs to an established genetic family. For some languages, we can be precise as to which subgroup within a family they belong to. So, Romanian is a member of the Eastern Romance subgroup of the Romance group of Indo-European. Maori belongs to the Polynesian subgroup of the Oceanic group of the Austronesian family. No putative or unproven grouping should be included in a scholarly work.

No language is spoken in a vacuum. To show which languages may be relevant for understanding the impact of language contact, one needs to place the language in the areal context. Romanian is a Romance language spoken in the Balkans area, surrounded by South Slavic languages: this explains some of the features which make it different from other Romance languages.

The pieces of information to be included are: an established genetic family and (if possible) a subgroup, and the areal context of the language. If any of these are putative, say so.

Teasing apart similarities due to genetic inheritance and those due to borrowing of varied kinds is one of the hardest problems in linguistics. As Dench (2001) puts it,

we should leave open the possibility that all questions may turn out to be undecidable. It may not be possible to show conclusively for any particular innovation that it results from genetic inheritance rather than that it is motivated by contact with another language. If enough such cases occur, then the suspicion we might attach to any putative inherited innovation will mount and we should become increasingly sceptical of any suggested genetic classifications. (Dench 2001: 113–14)

Long-term divergent development can obscure the erstwhile genetic relations. In Sapir's (1921) words,

may it not be, then, that many instances of morphological similarity between divergent languages of a restricted area are merely the last vestiges of a community of type and phonetic substance that the destructive work of diverging drifts has now made unrecognizable? (Sapir 1921: 204)

We may never be able to answer this sort of question. In this case, a grouping becomes 'putative'. A scholar need not be afraid to say 'I do not know' if the evidence is not comprehensive or a conclusion cannot be substantiated.

The genetic and areal links of a language are not just curious facts: if carefully understood, they offer a crucial glimpse into the prehistory and development of each language, ultimately helping us understand the 'why' of each language (more on this in Chapter 14).

2.4 The language in its social setting

The social setting of each language is a complex issue. The first question to ask is, how many languages do the speakers of the language know—that is, how multilingual are they? If speakers know more than one language, what are the relationships between these? Is one dominant over the other? Are they distributed in different spheres of use—for instance, is one restricted to religious ceremonies or contacts with neighbours, and the other one used in daily life? How much multilingualism (and multi-dialectism) was there in traditional times? Did speakers from other communities understand the language? Did speakers of this language understand other languages?

If speakers of a language do not speak any other language nowadays, but used to, it will then be up to the linguist to disclose this—based on stories or historical records. The language itself may hold a clue. Urarina (or Shimaku) is an isolate from the remote basin of the Chambira River in the north-western Amazonian region of Peru. Urarina has no known relatives. The Urarina people are only in sporadic contact with the local Spanish-speaking population. There are no stories, or memories about being in contact with any other group. But the language has number words (three to nine) which are similar to Quechua, the major trade language of the area. How come? A careful historical study shows that a few hundred years back the Urarina were a powerful group in charge of trade along the whole Chambira river area. They were then trading with speakers of Quechua. Since then, the Urarina have been decimated by illnesses and encroaching Peruvian invaders, and retreated into swampy regions of difficult access. It is their language—and historical archives—that tell us their story.

GENERATIONAL DIFFERENCE is a further important point. Younger people—especially if they are shifting to a different language—may speak differently from their elders. For instance, older speakers of Urarina have cross-referencing patterns no longer used by younger people. Younger speakers of Tariana tend to replicate verb-final constituent order common in the dominant Tucano language. If such differences are too extensive or too significant, they may be accorded a special section or chapter later in the grammar. The grammar of Anong, a Tibeto-Burman language influenced by Tai languages, contains a chapter dealing with how Anong has been affected by Tai, in its vocabulary and its grammar.

There may be other sociolinguistic differences, and speech varieties. Communities, in numerous languages in North America and Siberia, as well as a few in Amazonia, have conventionalized registers known as 'women's speech' and 'men's speech'. Other special sublanguages may include song language, special mythological genres, taboos and drum languages, and whistle languages.

In some societies, non-spoken language varieties may be used under special circumstances. For instance, a ritual sign language continues to be used among the Yolngu of northern Australia in circumstances when spoken language cannot be used: as when people are in mourning. This same sign language is also used for communication between, and with, deaf people.

This section is also where one can summarize the existing literary tradition—stories, songs, poems, and whether there were (or still are) song styles and poetry styles distinctive in their subject matter, accompaniment, and metrical patterns. Any of these genres may have had special phonological, lexical, or grammatical features. If a substantial amount of information is available, just a summary may be placed here (with details in a further chapter).

2.5 How the people used to live: non-linguistic background and social organization

This is the place to provide a brief summary of the habitat, lifestyle, political organization, kinship system (if it proves possible to work this out), ceremonies and beliefs, naming practices, and non-verbal communication. If relevant, and if sufficient information is available, these can also be discussed in appropriate places throughout the grammar—especially if these parameters correlate with linguistic features. For instance, one would not expect an extensive lexicon to do with waterways and travel by water if people live in a desert area. And one will not be surprised to find a system of demonstratives referring to uphill and downhill if the people who speak that language live in a hilly environment. Location on the banks of a large river, or on a small rivulet, or on the seashore may determine the orientation system.

This section offers a view of the traditional environment and lifestyle—in view of pervasive globalization, many peoples have embraced modernity, where cultural differences come to be submerged. A summary of the anthropological literature, if it exists, may also be placed here.

The non-linguistic parameters are expected to include the following points.

(I) PHYSICAL ENVIRONMENT, such as rainforest/open woodland/desert/arctic; flat/ hilly; on island(s) or by the seaside or on a river (large or small).

The next point is the climatic zone—tropical, subtropical, temperate, and so forth, hot/cold, and whether there is a definite distinction of seasons—for instance, wet season and dry season. The area may be inaccessible (flooded or snowbound) for part of the year. All this may influence peoples' seasonal movements and lifestyle, which may or may not be reflected in their languages.

(II) LIFESTYLE, including means of subsistence, that is whether speakers of the language are hunters/gatherers, or practise slash-and-burn agriculture (also known as swidden agriculture), or rotating crop agriculture, or whether they are urban dwellers; whether animals are domesticated for food; whether a major part of their diet is meat, fish, or vegetables; whether there are taboos on eating certain foods (at all times, or during certain seasons), or for people in certain states (pregnant women, or men during initiation).

(III) MATERIAL CULTURE, including whether permanent houses are built (for use during all or part of year); whether there are pottery and ceramics (for cooking, and/or water storage); whether there is metalwork; and what sorts of weapons are or were used (e.g. bow and arrow, spear, blowgun, boomerang, guns) and what sorts of implements were known (axes, hooks). Mention whether clothing was used traditionally—if so, whether woven or hanging grass, etc. The traditional ways of sleeping may have been on the ground, on beds or raised ledges, in a hammock, etc. The traditional methods of cooking food—boiling, steaming, roasting in coals or in a ground oven; whether meat/fish was ever eaten raw—can be mentioned here.

(IV) TRANSPORT, including use of rafts or canoes on rivers (canoes can be bark or dug-out), craft with sails (on sea); animals used for transportation (dogs, donkeys, ox carts, camels, etc.).

(V) STYLE OF LIVING, including a whole village living in one longhouse, with special parts dedicated to nuclear families; or one house per nuclear family; or all the men in one house, each woman and children in their own house; or an extended family in one house.

One then turns to further aspects of social relations:

(VI) DIVISION OF LABOUR. In most societies, men do the hunting of large animals and women look after children and do the daily cooking. But the division of other tasks varies. If there is information available, say who is mainly responsible for: getting small animals (e.g. lizards); fishing (men and women may both fish, but using different methods); gathering shellfish etc.; cooking on ceremonial occasions; building houses; making gardens; weeding gardens; gathering food from gardens; gathering wild food from outside gardens; weaving baskets; making pottery; trading goods with neighbours.

(VII) RELATIONS WITH NEIGHBOURS may be basically friendly (trading goods and wives) or essentially hostile; or friendly with some, hostile with others. What kind of trading was used, and what objects were exchanged? Were there regular inter-group meetings for ceremonies/dances/games (at which marriages may be arranged, disputes settled, pacts made, etc.).

(VIII) POLITICAL SYSTEM AND SOCIAL HIERARCHY. There may be a small tribe or tribes with no designated chief. Or there may be a chief living the same sort of life as everyone else, getting their own food, but just having organizational responsibilities. In many north-western Amazonian societies, there used to be a hereditary division into groups—within each tribe—perhaps consisting of shamans, warriors, dance-masters, and 'soldiers' (who would perform duties for others). Or a chief/king may live in a different style from others, being provided with food, goods, wives, etc. There can be a fully fledged hierarchy (king, nobles of varying degrees), on a hereditary basis, which rules either as an oligarchy, or as a democratic government, chosen by election. This is also where mention can be made of any special speech styles (politeness levels) associated with the relative level of speaker and addressee in the social hierarchy. Different speech styles associated with different groups in a community (with no overtones of politeness—e.g. different moieties) can also be mentioned. Some of this information overlaps with what was mentioned in §2.4, and can be discussed together with socio-linguistic features of the language.

(IX) ARMY AND WARFARE. This reflects whether there is a permanent army and whether there is regular warfare, with a group of armed men attacking a neighbouring nation/tribe for goods/women/land (or in revenge), and whether there is a class of slaves (hereditary and/or taken in war). This can be especially important from the point of view of contact change in the language. The Matses, a war-like Panoan group in Peru and adjacent regions of Brazil, used to practise polygamy. If they did not have enough eligible women, they would attack a neighbouring tribe, kill the men, and kidnap women and children. Women would learn Matses, but continue speaking their own languages—some of these languages were related to Matses, and some not. A major impact on Matses comes from these women's languages. The same applies to conquered tribes, amalgamated and assimilated to the tribe of the conqueror—as is the case with the influx of Norman French loans into English since 1066. Warfare and assimilation of groups is a factor in creating typologically unusual languages; this point feeds into what we mentioned under §2.3.3.

(X) KINSHIP AND MARRIAGE. Here one may address kinship terminologies—we will see, in §5.4, that kinship terms are very often a separate subclass of nouns. To offer a comprehensive description of the kinship system, one needs to know whether there is a classificatory kinship system, with everyone related to everyone else, or merely a limited 'nuclear family' kin system. Is the descent patrilineal or matrilineal? Is residence patrilocal or matrilocal? Does the wife have to move to the husband's residence (virilocal) or will the husband move to live with the wife's family (uxorilocal)? Any polygyny, or polyandry? Are there any moieties/sections? What are the rules for who can marry whom? In some cultures, one has to marry one's classificatory cross-cousin (marrying a parallel cousin is as bad as incest). In a few societies, one marries someone who comes from a different language group.

There may be a further distinction of kin into (a) those to be avoided (with whom a special speech style may have to be used); (b) those with whom one can be very intimate, for example make dirty jokes with; (c) a middle class, treated neither very formally nor very informally. If there is arranged marriage, it is important to know who arranges it, and whether it is, or used to be, arranged many years in advance or at the time. If marriage is not arranged, it is useful to state whether free choice is involved.

(XI) RELIGION. At present, most people across the world may belong to one or more large religions (Hinduism, Buddhism, Christianity, Moslem, etc.). One needs to know how long they have had this affiliation, and if possible which sect or subdivision of, say, Christianity they profess. (Seventh Day Adventists impose special dietary restrictions, and so on).

Do speakers of the language have a traditional religion? If so, provide a brief description, including type of gods (whether or not ancestors). What are the responsibilities of people to gods? What do they expect from gods in return for sacrifices and gifts? Are there any traditional praying, and religious ceremonies (note that many societies have a major world religion and a local religion side by side).

Is there any class of priests/shamans, and consequently, any special language or style used in religious ceremonies? Any belief in an afterlife or in where spirits came from at birth and where they will go at death? Any belief in animals being changed into humans (or vice versa)? Any sacred animals (totemic or otherwise)? How should one behave towards them? Ideas about the causes of death may also belong here—whether most deaths (except of the very young and very old) are believed to be caused by sorcery (or poison) from another group, and should be avenged (by armed attack to kill someone of the guilty group, or just by counter-sorcery).

It is useful to mention if there are any origin myths, about the people coming into their present territory from a certain geographical direction or from a different sort of terrain (e.g. used to live in plains country, now in hilly country)? This information may be crucial for understanding the peoples' origins—and even some possible features of the language which might otherwise be hard to understand.

Information about consumption of human bodies (or cannibalism) can also be discussed here. It is important to point out if the bodies consumed

(a) were of their own group or of other groups;
(b) after they had died naturally, or been killed for a misdemeanour; or had been killed simply to be eaten;
(c) were eaten as a matter of honour, to make sure that the valour of the deceased passed on to the descendants who eat the corpse, as among the Yanomami and numerous peoples of the Vaupés.

Finally, it is instructive to list the benefits believed to accrue to someone who eats human flesh (or drinks human blood).

Consumption of a human body may have been associated with a ceremony—the next point.

(XII) INITIATION, CEREMONIES, ETC. Are there special ceremonies for (a) male, and/or (b) female initiation? At what stage(s) of life are men/women initiated? What does initiation consist of? Is there any special language/style used by initiated men/women or at initiation ceremonies?

Are there any other important ceremonies, for example installing a new chief or king, funeral, wedding, new harvest, or bestowing a name? Are any special languages or special speech styles used at them?

(XIII) NAMING. Every culture has its own rules for naming. This is the place in the grammar where these rules can be summarized. Names often form a special grammatical subclass of nouns. There may be secret names (given at birth but only used later, at a certain stage in life, e.g. initiation, or perhaps always kept secret). Some names are associated with taboos, and may be regarded as 'protections'.

Many societies have a name taboo. When someone dies their name(s) may not be pronounced by members of their local group for a period of time. And sometimes any lexical item that is phonologically similar to the tabooed name is also tabooed (some-times it may return to use after an interval of time, other times this leads to permanent lexical replacement). In some societies across the Sepik area of New Guinea, names are a token of special wealth and have protective powers. Personal names are often a special subclass of nouns (see §5.4); so the information given here may be highly rele-vant for the grammar itself.

(XIV) WRITING SYSTEM. If there was an indigenous writing system, briefly describe it and how long has it been in use; and about what proportion of the population were (and are) literate. A number of different writing systems may have been suggested (perhaps by rival missionary organizations). These can be discussed and compared either in this section, or at the end of a chapter dealing with phonology and phonetics (see §4.6).

(XV) NON-VERBAL COMMUNICATION. This may include the following:

First, how verbal expression, and conversely, silence, is valued by the people in the society. In some cultures (e.g. Anglo-Saxon), explicit verbal expression is generally favoured, while in other cultures (e.g. Japanese and Western Apache, perhaps one of the most extreme cases) it is not. The norms of verbalization and silence in the given culture can be addressed here.

Secondly, the norms of non-verbal communication may vary, along the following lines. What kinds of greetings, gestures, and facial expressions are observed in the course of conversation? How much distance is placed between the interlocutors? Do people touch each other in public? How distinct is the contour/pitch/loudness diffe-rence between male and female speakers, in public and private speech, or with regard to different topics?

For each of these, it will be useful to have a summary of the rules in relation to the sex/age/social status/intimacy of the interlocutors, social situations (formal/infor-mal, private/public), etc. The linguistic side of these means of communication can be addressed in a later chapter (see §13.3).

Thirdly, to what extent are explicit emotional expressions such as laughing and crying, and manifestation of involuntary bodily functions—such as belching and farting—allowed, praised or restricted?

And, finally, what kind of explanations are given in that culture/society with regard to the points listed above? Such explanations can be of a historical or a religious nature.

In this section, the grammarian can also briefly discuss gestures, including those involved in pointing (which may cover lip-pointing, eye-pointing, and finger-pointing).

2.6 Previous studies of the language

Unless the amount of previous scholarship is too large, it is important to provide an exhaustive list of publications and manuscripts on the language, with a summary and brief evaluation of each with respect to its scope and degree of reliability. It is truly important to be honest about previous work. This is one way of explaining why further work is required. For instance, the fact that Slater's (2002) lengthy grammar of Mangghuer was based on work with only one speaker justifies a further, more elaborate grammatical study of this complex language. In terms of argumentation and clarity of analysis, Owens' (1985) grammar of Harar Oromo is among the best descriptions of any Cushitic language. But as it was based on work with just one speaker, a further, more comprehensive, grammar is warranted.

If there is just too much to cover, the linguist may choose the most important works— books, or papers published in high-status journals. The rest can be summarized.

It is always good to include information about the first outside contact ever made with the speakers of the language, and when the language, or the people who speak it, were mentioned in print for the first time. All of this may involve work in archives and older sources.

2.7 Materials and speakers: basis for the grammar

This is where one gives details about how the materials for the grammar were gathered—where, when, how long was spent in the field, the number of consultants, their sociolinguistic background, discussion of texts, types of texts, size of lexicon, and methodology. This always involves recording, transcribing, translating, and analysing texts (sometimes with elicitation to refine hypotheses, or limited elicitation, with back-up from texts) and, importantly, participant-observation. This section is important: the reader will be better able to appraise the grammar if they have an idea what its potential limitations are.

If the grammar is based on fieldwork, it is important to describe the conditions, and maybe even provide pictures. In Maybury-Lewis' (1968) words,

Of course it is the quality of the interaction that counts, not the quantity. A good field-worker may obtain better data in six months than an indifferent one in two years. But this is all the more reason for insisting that the quality of this experience should be described as minutely as possible, so that readers of the ensuing report may be in a proper position to evaluate its content. (Maybury-Lewis 1968: xix–xx)

It is important to state whether the data were gathered from a speaker who has now settled in some town or city, or whether the linguist actually undertook fieldwork and went to a community where the language was spoken on a daily basis. One needs to be precise about how many consultants were involved, and in what capacity (as story tellers, as helpers in translations and transcriptions, and so on). It is useful to say what age groups they belonged to, how many of them were women, and how many men, what their educational background was, and so on. Whether the data on which the grammar is based were gathered by elicitation or by analysis of texts together with participant observation is equally crucial. The approximate number of hours of recording and length of texts on which the grammar is based are also important details.

The introductory chapter makes the book an ethnographic document and brings the culture to life. It may also contain an overview of the texts at the end of the grammar, and the principles behind their choice.

A final word of warning. Any grammar needs to have a chapter dealing with the whereabouts of the language, its relatives, and its neighbours. This chapter will also include as many cultural and societal features of the people as is reasonable, and possible. A chapter of this kind creates a general background for the rest of the grammar. This is also the part that will be refined, and perhaps even rewritten, over and over again as more information on the language will be disclosed through other chapters. A grammar writer may have to fine-tune the typological profile as new features of interest emerge. What is drafted first may have to be finalized last.

What the reader learns from this chapter will help them follow the language examples. This chapter will also offer some help towards explaining why the language is the way it is (see Chapter 14).

Notes and sources

§2.1: On typological classification of languages, see Sapir (1921); a brief summary in Aikhenvald (2007b) and Dixon (2010a). Greenberg (1963) is a classic piece on the order of meaningful elements (not to be confused with word order). Further information on evidentiality systems is in Aikhenvald (2004a), and on Amazonian languages in Aikhenvald (2012a), and references there.

§2.3: See Hock (1991), Anttila (1989) on methodology of historical linguistics, Weinreich (1953) and Winford (2003), inter alia, on contact-induced change and linguistic areas; and a summary on similarities between languages and contact-induced change in Aikhenvald (2006a).

§2.4: See Dean (2009) and Olawsky (2006) on Urarina; see Sun and Liu (2009) on Anong.

§2.5: See Fleck and Voss (2006) on Matses; Basso (1970) on Western Apache.

3

Basics

We now review some basic concepts of language analysis. The glossary, at the end of the book, includes notions specific to individual parts of grammar.

3.1 Sound systems

The PHONEME is the basic concept of phonology. Phonemes distinguish words and morphemes with different meanings. If we replace the final /t/ in English *pat* with /d/ we obtain a different word, *pad*. Each phoneme has a set of phonetic realizations, or allophones. They are VARIANTS, or ALLOPHONES, of a phoneme. The choice of a variant may depend on the position of the phoneme, speed of speech, and speech style. At the beginning of a word, English /p/ can be pronounced as [pʰ] with slight aspiration, as in [pʰæt]. If it follows another consonant, there won't be any aspiration: an example is [spæt], past tense of *spit*. If this form is pronounced as [spʰæt], it is still recognizable as '(he) spat', but sounds strange. Following usual conventions, phonemes are written between slashes, and allophones between square brackets.

Two sounds may be allophones of a phoneme in one language, and different phonemes in another. Tariana word *phia* is the pronoun 'you'. If I pronounce the initial consonant as *p* and say *pia*, this will mean 'you go!' Such contrasting pairs—known as MINIMAL PAIRS—demonstrate which distinctions are important, and which are less so.

Native speakers of any language intuitively recognize phonemes as different entities, and allophones as mere variants. This is often reflected in the way speakers spontaneously write their languages. In Manambu, labio-dental [β] is an allophone of [p] between vowels. A loanword [sup] 'soap' with an instrumental suffix *-ar* meaning 'with' will be pronounced as [suβar]. My young teacher spontaneously wrote it as *supar*, 'with soap'. Ideally, an alphabet—within an orthography created by a linguist, or an insightful native speaker—will have one letter per phoneme.

Phonemes can be classified in terms of distinctive features—phonetic properties which set one apart from the other. 'Voicing' is a distinctive feature in English since this is what differentiates pairs like *bin* and *pin*. In Tariana, aspiration is distinctive.

Phonemes in a language include vowels and consonants. Semi-vowels (*y* and *w*) may sound like vowels, but may share properties with consonants. The system of phonemes defines the SEGMENTAL phonology.

Phonemes combine into SYLLABLES, a further basic universal unit of analysis. Each syllable has a nucleus. A nucleus can consist of a short vowel (as in English *pat* /pæt/), a long vowel (as in English *peep* /piːp/), a diphthong (as in English *bait* /beit/) or a triphthong (as in *flour* /flaʋə(r)/), or a syllabic consonant (as in English, *bottle* /bɔtl/). What precedes it is called ONSET, and what follows it is a CODA. A diphthong or a triphthong is a complex vowel nucleus and always constitutes one syllable.

Occurrences of consonants in coda and onset positions are captured under PHO-NOTACTIC RESTRICTIONS. Distinguishing VOWEL SEQUENCES and DIPHTHONGS may not be straightforward.

A word on notation. V is a symbol for a vowel. It is thus logical to use the notation VV for a vowel sequence, NOT for a long vowel or for a diphthong—otherwise the reader may get the impression that two vowel nuclei are involved in a diphthong or a long vowel. A long vowel is best represented as V:. (The same applies for long consonants: a unitary segment will be represented as C:; while a sequence of two segments is CC).

SUPRASEGMENTAL features extend over several minimal elements in succession. STRESS applies to the syllable as a unit, and more specifically, to its nucleus. Here are some basic principles:

- The syllable is a stress-bearing unit.
- If a syllable is stressed, stress applies to the whole syllable, not to a part of it.
- One syllable cannot contain more than one vowel (this can be a diphthong or a triphthong).
- If there is a sequence of two vowels such as either may be stressed independently of the other, they belong to separate syllables. More on this is in Chapter 4.

A syllable can be open (ending in a vowel) or closed (ending in a consonant). The notation is CV (consonant vowel) or CVC (consonant vowel consonant). Syllables can also be classified in terms of weight, as HEAVY and LIGHT. A light syllable will contain a short vowel. A heavy syllable may contain a long vowel, a complex vowel nucleus (a diphthong or a triphthong), or have a coda. For some languages, it is useful to introduce the notion of mora. Then, a light syllable will count as one mora and a heavy one as two morae. Mora is a unit which may be useful for understanding the placement of stress, and choice of variants of morphemes (or their allomorphs).

A STRESSED syllable may be heard as more prominent than other syllables. This prominence may correlate with loudness, vowel quality, pitch, length, or a combination of these. Relative pitch height may depend on the intonation contour of the utterance, and illocutionary force, or emphasis. This is, in a nutshell, a stress system (which can also be called intensity stress). Or the stressed syllable can always display a higher level of pitch. This is known as a pitch accent system (Donohue 1997: 348–9 contains a concise explanation). Stress, and pitch accent, may or may not be contrastive.

Syllables or their sequences can be distinguished by levels of pitch, or by changes in pitch—for example, low, high, and mid-level. Then, the language has distinctive

TONES. Register tones have a specific level of pitch. Contour tones are characterized by a movement in pitch—falling (high-low), rising (low-high), and so on.

A tone can be assigned to each syllable. Or it can be a feature of a larger unit—a PHONOLOGICAL WORD. Word in this sense is a basic unit of pronunciation. Criteria for delimiting a phonological word always include suprasegmental features (stress or tone). Other suprasegmental features, or prosodies, which operate on the word as their domain may include vowel and consonant harmony, retroflexion, and nasalization. There can be special segmental features which appear at the beginnings, or at the ends of words—such as final devoicing (as in German or Russian) or initial aspiration of voiceless labial consonants, as in English *pit* [pʰit].

Pitch movements form an intonational contour. Intonation distinguishes different types of clauses—often rising or falling for questions and commands, level for statements, rising for exclamations and so on.

3.2 The unit 'word'

A phonological word can be pronounced on its own. Its limits are determined by phonological features. A grammatical 'word' is a unit which has conventionalized coherence and meaning, and may consist of one or more grammatical elements (morphemes). Its components occur together rather than scattered through a clause, and tend to have a fixed order. Properties of grammatical words are specific to each language.

Some grammatical words cannot stand on their own. They have to 'lean' on another element—their 'host'—to form a proper phonological word. These are CLITICS. The term 'clitic' comes from the Greek root *klin-* 'lean'. Clitics which precede their hosts are called proclitics. Those which follow the hosts are enclitics. There can be—albeit rarely—mesoclitics (or endoclitics) which occur inside the host (see Chapter 4).

One grammatical word may consist of more than one phonological word. Or one phonological word may consist of more than one grammatical word. We return to these in Chapter 4.

The term 'word' can be used with further meanings, for special purposes. A unit of syntactic analysis may be referred to as a syntactic word. An entry in a dictionary may be called a lexical word. What is written between spaces can be called an orthographic word. Nevertheless, for a grammatical analysis, the phonological and grammatical word are the most basic notions.

3.3 The building blocks of a grammatical word

The basis of a grammatical word is a root, to which morphological processes may apply. A grammatical word is composed of MORPHEMES—grammatical units with distinct meaning and status. For instance, *dis-taste-ful-ness* contains four morphemes: the root *taste*, one prefix *dis-*, and two suffixes *-ful* and *-ness*.

Morphemes can be classified as FREE and BOUND. Affixes are bound morphemes; they can be classified according to their positions with respect to roots into prefixes, suffixes, and confixes or circumflexes. Affixes cannot occur on their own (which is why they are called 'bound'). Some roots may occur on their own. These are 'free' morphemes. Two or more roots can be joined to form one grammatical word, creating compounds. Combinations of roots and affixes may be called 'stems'.

A morpheme can have different realizations, known as ALLOMORPHS. For example, the plural marker in English has three allomorphs -z as in /dɔg-z/, *dogs*; s, as in /kæt-s/, *cats*; and -əz as in /hɔ:s-əz/, *horses*. Phonological changes which are restricted to specific morphological environments (e.g. boundaries between affixes, or affixes and roots) are called 'morphophonological'.

Special morphological processes can be applied to a stem, or a root, to produce new grammatical meanings. These include (a) affixation (adding some material to the root), (b) reduplication, (c) shift of stress or tone change, (d) internal vowel or consonant change, and (e) subtraction (removing some material from the root, for example the formation of the plural in Tariana: compare singular *ātʃaɾi* 'man', plural *ātʃa* 'men'). Suppletion involves full replacement of one form with another, to express a grammatical meaning, for example *went* as the past tense of English *go*.

Clitics are also bound morphemes since they may not occur on their own. Their differences and similarities with affixes are outlined in Table 4.6. It is convenient to distinguish between affix boundary (-) and clitic boundary (=).

Morphological processes in a language can be presented in several ways. In fusional languages, the focus of a grammarian is often on how words as a whole contrast within paradigms, rather than on their internal structure. This is reflected in the 'WORD-AND-PARADIGM' approach: words are compared to each other as wholes within a paradigm rather than focusing on their internal structure and morpheme-per-morpheme divisions. So, for instance, the Latin first person present form *amō* 'I love' is characterized as a whole in its opposition to second person form *amās* and third person form *amat*. It will be characterized as singular by its opposition to the plural form *amāmus*. And as indicative, it will be contrasted with the imperative form *ama!* 'Love!'.

Table 3.1 illustrates a sample paradigm of the verb 'to love' in the indicative mood:

TABLE 3.1. A sample paradigm in Latin: the verb *amāre* 'to love': indicative mood

	Singular number	Plural number
1st person	*amō*	*amāmus*
2nd person	*amās*	*amātis*
3rd person	*amat*	*amant*

This approach is prevalent in the descriptions of many classical languages including Latin, Greek, and Sanskrit (especially for teaching purposes), and of some other fusional languages, such as the Kiranti languages from the Tibeto-Burman family.

The 'ITEM-AND-ARRANGEMENT' approach takes morphemes as basic building blocks realized by one or more alternating morphs. Larger units ('words') consist of arrangements of morphemes. So, the English form *un-grate-ful-ness* will be analysed as a sequence of four morphemes: the negative *un-*, the root *-grate-*, and suffix *-ful* followed by another suffix *-ness*. This approach may work well for agglutinating languages.

If forming a grammatical word involves the root undergoing successive processes of affixation, internal vowel change, etc., the 'ITEM-AND-PROCESS' approach will be most appropriate. If we take the English form *unbroken*, it can be seen as derived from the root *break* by internal change followed by suffixation of *-en* and prefixation of *un-*.

Each of these two approaches has its merit, for languages of different morphological types, and may be applied as appropriate. A grammar which consists mostly of paradigms will bore the reader. But a sample of paradigms may be useful to show how the system works.

3.4 Inflection and derivation

In many languages, morphological processes and affixes can be classified as inflectional and derivational. In a nutshell: derivational processes result in the creation of new words with new meanings; they are optional. In contrast, inflectional processes include obligatory grammatical specifications characteristic of a particular word class. Typical inflectional categories are those which involve agreement within a phrase or on the clausal level, that is nominal categories such as gender (or noun class), number agreement and case, and verbal categories such as aspect and tense. Typical derivational categories are diminutives and augmentatives, nominalizations of verbs, and verbalizations of nouns. Table 3.2 summarizes typical properties of inflection and derivation.

Inflectional categories are typically regular and predictable, in both form and in meaning. Derivational categories, on the contrary, can be idiosyncratic. Derivations often have to be listed in a lexicon, and the derivational history of each word may have to be described separately.

The English prefix *en-* is an example of a morpheme which exhibits most derivational properties. It can change grammatical class if used to derive verbs from nouns. Its meaning is not quite predictable. With adjectives it means 'provide with a quality of', as in *en-rich* or *en-able*. When used with nouns it usually means 'enter into' or 'put into', as in *en-train*, *en-cage*, or *en-chain*. Its meaning may be partly unpredictable, as in *en-tangle* or *en-gulf*. It is also used to derive prefixed verbs; in this case it does not change grammatical class, for example *en-wrap* (see further examples in Marchand 1969: 162–4).

TABLE 3.2. Typical properties of inflection and derivation

	Inflection	Derivation
1.	usually obligatory	optional
2.	final process (if affix, on rim of word)	pre-final process (if affix, between root and inflection)
3.	forms a complete word	derives a stem which takes inflections
4.	defining characteristic of a word class (e.g. nouns inflect for case)	usually specific to a word class
5.	does not change word class	either derives a stem of a different word class, or adds some semantic specification to a root without changing class
6.	may indicate grammatical relation- ship between words, function within a clause, and/or participate in agreement	never indicates grammatical relationship between words or participates in agreement
7.	usually does not show gaps in the paradigm	often shows gaps in the paradigm
8.	generally semantically regular	often semantically irregular
9.	tend to form smallish systems	may form large systems
10.	tend to have high frequency	likely to have lower frequency
11.	tend to be monosyllabic; can consist of a single consonant (or be even shorter)	may be monosyllabic or longer

A category or a process may be inflectional in one language and derivational in another. Gender markers in some languages straddle the boundary between inflection and derivation: they may mark agreement within a noun phrase, and can also derive new words. Number may be derivational if it is not obligatory, and does not involve agreement within a noun phrase.

Distinguishing inflectional and derivation processes can be a useful analytical tool. But this distinction is not universal. In many South American languages, tense, aspect, and many other verbal categories are optional. The distinction between inflection and derivation is useful inasmuch as it is applicable to a particular language, and has explanatory power.

3.5 Delineating word classes

Grammatical words divide into WORD CLASSES, defined, in the first place, by their grammatical properties. The equivalent term used in traditional grammar is 'parts of speech'. OPEN classes are those whose members cannot be listed exhaustively, and which are potentially expandable through borrowings, and through derivation from other classes. Typical open classes are Noun and Verb (see Dixon 2010a: 102–5, 2010b: 37–61 for a definitive statement, and references). Some linguists refer to open classes as 'lexical classes'. Such terminology confuses grammatical classes and lexicon, and is best avoided. CLOSED classes are those whose members can be listed fully, and no new members added. Typical closed classes are content question words, quantifiers, and, in most languages outside Southeast Asia, personal pronouns.

Each class has a set of its own grammatical categories—that is, a closed set of distinctions that have to be expressed. These grammatical categories are realized through grammatical systems. Some of these, such as polarity (or negation) and person, are universal. Others, such as tense, aspect, mood, evidentiality, and gender are not.

The essential criteria for establishing word classes are:

(i) morphological structure and grammatical categories—obligatory or optional—that apply for each word class, and

(ii) syntactic functions of a member of this class.

Additional criteria may include possible phonological differences between classes. Word classes may also differ in terms of their semantic core, and even discourse functions. Nouns can be said to designate objects (including humans and other animates, places, things, etc.); verbs designate activities, processes, and states; adjectives denote qualities, attributes, and states, while adverbs denote manner, time, location, and further attributes of actions or properties.

Such semantic features are intuitively obvious. But in practice they are difficult to apply as steadfast criteria. 'States' can be denoted by verbs, such as 'be poor', and by adjectives, such as 'poor'. Verbs denote activities, but so do deverbal nouns. This is why semantics is concomitant, rather than criterial, in distinguishing word classes.

3.6 Categories and strategies

For each grammatical category of each word class we distinguish:

(a) the meanings of its terms (e.g. masculine versus feminine term for gender; singular versus non-singular for number);

(b) its realization—through a clitic, an affix, another morphological process, or a separate grammatical word;

(c) further features of its expression—for instance, whether the category has to be marked on each word within the phrase (as is the case in some languages with gender agreement), or just once.

Each feature and category has a role within morphology, and within syntax. It can be called 'morphosyntactic' if it has to be included in a morphological paradigm and also marks syntactic function. Case affixes are a case in point. They can be mentioned as characteristic of nouns, in the chapter on word classes, and then further discussed in a chapter on grammatical relations.

Not all meanings, and not all functions, have a dedicated means of expression in a language. One language may require obligatory marking of information source (known as evidentiality). Another may co-opt other means—conditional modality or reported speech—to express similar meanings as required. Many languages have a dedicated imperative paradigm used for commands. Some do not: they use a subjunctive or another verb form instead. If a language does not have a dedicated construction of a certain type, for example complement clause, or imperative, it may render the relevant meanings by using an established construction in a secondary sense. This is then a 'strategy': we can have evidentiality strategies, imperative strategies, complementation strategies, and so on. Discussing strategies alongside categories makes grammars informative for typologists: languages are then easier to compare in terms of which meanings are expressed, and how. Over time, a strategy may acquire the status of a category.

3.7 Phrases and clauses

A PHRASE is a syntactic unit smaller than a CLAUSE, and which functions as a whole within it. A NOUN PHRASE (NP) can consist of just a noun, or have a noun as its HEAD accompanied by one or more modifiers. The HEAD of the noun phrase determines the form of the modifiers (e.g. gender and number marking on adjectives in Latin or French). Modifiers within a Noun Phrase may include one or more adjectives, numbers (ordinal and/or cardinal) and/or quantifiers, articles, demonstratives, interrogatives, and other nouns. A possessive Noun Phrase (NP) is an NP embedded within another NP, for example *[the old emperor]'s*$_{Possessor}$ *[new clothes]*$_{head}$. A Noun Phrase has a structure and an order for the components—or grammatical words within it—which need to be stated.

Other grammatical categories can be expressed through the verb ('head' of predicate) and associated elements which constitute a VERB PHRASE (VP). In synthetic languages the verb tends to have a rich morphological structure, and all or most categories will be coded by affixation or other morphological processes within it. In analytic languages, a VP typically consists of a verb and words modifying it. A VP has a structure, and a fixed order of words.

A CLAUSE—a further basic unit—is a description of an activity, state, or property. A simple SENTENCE consists of a single clause. Complex sentences involve several clauses linked together or embedded within one another. A clause has a syntactic function, and a pragmatic function.

3.8 Clauses and speech acts

The pragmatic functions of each clause reflect the type of speech act (also termed 'mood'). Three major clause types are: statements, commands, and questions. Exclamative clauses are a minor type. Each of the clause types has appropriate marking. A statement bears an indicator of the declarative (or indicative) mood, while a command contains a marker of the imperative mood, and a question that of the interrogative mood, or interrogative words. Pragmatic functions of distinct clause types may show further complexities: a command could be expressed by a statement, or by what looks like a question. More on this in Chapter 11.

3.9 Clause types and clause structures

Each clause has an internal structure: it consists of the PREDICATE (which typically, but not exclusively, is a verb) and a number of arguments. CORE ARGUMENTS must either be stated within a clause, or be understood and recoverable from the context. PERIPHERAL ARGUMENTS (also called obliques, or adjuncts) are optional.

Note that the term 'predicate' is sometimes used in the different sense of LOGICAL predicate. This covers everything in the sentence or a clause except the subject. This is generally not used in writing typologically informed grammars.

The notion of GRAMMATICAL predicate is used by the majority of linguists. This refers to the pivotal element in a clause typically inflected or modified by tense–aspect–modality (TAM) elements. This is the sense of predicate in terms of which the grammatical structure of clause is described. The verb is the typical head of a predicate.

There are the following main clause types, depending on the number and roles of participants involved, and the predicate type (more on clause types is in Chapter 11).

A. TRANSITIVE CLAUSES:

   (i) contain a transitive predicate;
   (ii) require two core arguments A (transitive subject) and O (transitive object);
   (iii) in many languages, only a verb can be the head of a transitive clause.

B. INTRANSITIVE CLAUSES:

   (i) contain an intransitive predicate;
   (ii) require one core argument S (intransitive subject).

In some languages, only a verb can be the head of an intransitive predicate. In others, a member of other word classes—nouns, adjectives, pronouns, and so on—can head an intransitive clause. Non-verbal predicate heads may have fewer choices of verbal categories (including TAM) available to them.

C. Copula clauses:

 (i) have a copula verb or element which takes some or all of the TAM possibilities open to predicates in transitive and intransitive clauses, as their predicate;

 (ii) require two arguments: copula subject (CS) and copula complement (CC) (note that CC is an argument of the copula verb and not part of the predicate);

 (iii) contain a copula predicate which has a relational meaning, that is, establishes a relation of equation, identity, etc. between CS and CC, as in *My son is a dentist* and *The teacher is stupid* (more on this in Chapter 11).

In some languages there is a copula clause type with CS and no CC, as in Latin *Deus est* (God is) 'God exists'.

D. Verbless clauses:

 (i) are similar to copula clauses but lack a copula verb or element. No constituent takes TAM (they can be said to have a null predicate);

 (ii) require two arguments: verbless clause subject (VCS) and verbless clause complement (VCC).

A VCS has similar properties and possibilities to CS, and VCC will be similar to CC. But just how similar? This is the question to address. Some languages, including English, simply lack this type.

Intransitive and transitive clauses may fall into further subtypes. An intransitive clause may contain an obligatory argument (E) with different properties from the O of the transitive verb. This is known as EXTENDED INTRANSITIVE. Similarly, a transitive clause can have a further core argument, for example location for English verb *put,* or recipient for verbs of 'giving'. This is an EXTENDED TRANSITIVE, or DITRANSITIVE, VERB.

We thus have the following clause types, which can be mapped onto verbal transitivity classes, or verb types:

		obligatory arguments
(a)	plain intransitive	S
(b)	extended intransitive	S + E (e.g. dative or locative)
(c)	plain transitive	A + O
(d)	extended transitive	A + O + E (e.g. dative or locative)

It may be the case that every language has types (a), (c), and perhaps also (d). Type (d) (extended transitive, or ditransitive) is always a special type of transitive—one argument can be identified as A and one as O. Some languages have two arguments which appear, on the surface, to be marked as O—then syntactic tests may have to be applied to distinguish them.

Typical type (d) verbs are ditransitive 'give', 'show', 'tell', and also 'lend', 'borrow', 'bestow a name'. It is always the Donor/Shower/Talker who is the A. Languages differ as to which argument is the 'primary' O (that is, an O with full object properties): (1) first, the gift/thing shown/news can be the O; (2) secondly, the recipient/person to whom shown/addressee can be the O; and (3) thirdly, there may be two construction types, one with possibility (1) and one with (2).

Type (b) is rarer. It has two 'participants', like a plain transitive, but the two constructions can be distinguished in terms of the syntactic functions they include.

In Tongan for instance we get (translating literally into English):

type (c) John (A) hit Mary (O)
type (b) John (S) saw/likes Mary (locative)

In (b) 'John' behaves like an S, while in (c) 'John' behaves like an A for coordination and case marking. (Coordination rules apply differently for A and S in this language.)

A, S, O, and E are the basic CORE GRAMMATICAL RELATIONS. They define the ARGU-MENT STRUCTURE of a clause. Recapitulating the labels:

Subject of a transitive verb—**A** is an abbreviation for this.
Object (or: second core argument) of a transitive verb—**O** is an abbreviation for this.
Subject of an intransitive verb—**S** is an abbreviation for this.
A further argument of an extended intransitive verb (second core argument of this verb) and a further argument of an extended transitive, or ditransitive, verb (third core argument of this verb—**E** is an abbreviation for this.

The labels A, S, O, and E are syntactic and not semantic. They are nicknames, and do not stand for any abbreviated term. That is, A does NOT imply Agent; and O does NOT imply Patient. They may correspond to a variety of different semantic roles: A can be the agent of hitting, and O someone who gets hit; A can be the one who sees something (not a semantic Agent at all), and O something seen (not a Patient) and so on.

Predicates of the (a)–(d) clause types, and their arguments (A, S, O, CS, CC, VCS, and VCC) constitute functional slots within each clause. Members of distinct word classes may differ in the slots they may occur in (without undergoing derivational 'word class changing' operations). For instance, in some languages, only verbs can occupy the predicate slot.

The expression of core arguments—or the argument structure—is the basis of who does what to whom. Languages with nominative-accusative grammar group together A and S, in terms of their marking and syntactic behaviour. Languages with absolutive-ergative grammar group together S and O. A number of languages combine nominative-accusative and absolutive-ergative properties. And there are certain universal structures which operate in terms of either S/A (e.g. imperatives) or S/O (e.g. noun incorporation).

The basic grammatical relations may be marked with cases, or with verbal cross-referencing (or by other means, such as constituent order). In some languages, ellipsis is more frequent than in others, and the identity of arguments under ellipsis has to be inferred from the context. Mechanisms of inference, however, do not override the existence of core arguments.

'Subject' and 'object' are grammatical labels; they can be applied only if properly defined in terms of grammatical properties in a given language. One can, and ought to, provide morphological and syntactic criteria for these. It makes no sense to talk of 'logical subject' or 'logical object' (unless one is doing logic, and not writing a grammar). The same case marking may be used for one of the basic core grammatical relations (that is, for a core argument) and for a peripheral argument. For instance, accusative case may also be used to mark direction. This overlapping marking does not invalidate the existence of the basic grammatical relations. On the contrary: the fact that the same marking corresponds to two different grammatical functions may indicate that in fact we are dealing with homonymous case forms. More on this in Chapter 10.

3.10 Order of words and order of constituents

Each argument and the predicate are not just 'words'. They are constituents within a clause. It is sensible to distinguish the order of individual words within phrases—'word order'—from the order of constituents within a clause. The order of clausal constituents may be fixed, as in English, where it reflects grammatical relations—who did what to whom. Or it can be relatively free, as in Russian and Latin, and reflect the pragmatic attitude of the speaker. Ditto for the order of words within each constituent. The order of words within a constituent reflects its structure. The order of clausal constituents may define a clause type. In many languages, V-S/O order is a feature of imperative clauses. In each statement of clausal order, it is essential to give information about the relative position of A, S, O, and V (and E, if applicable).

3.11 Sentence and discourse

Clauses combine together to form sentences (the topic of Chapter 12). A sentence consists of at least one MAIN clause, and may include DEPENDENT clauses. We distinguish:

- RELATIVE CLAUSES (RC), which modify the head of the NP filling an argument slot in the main clause or a further subordinate clause, e.g. *The man [who won the prize]*_{REL.CL} *emigrated.* A relative clause may have a fixed place in the NP structure and should be discussed jointly with it.

- COMPLEMENT CLAUSES (CoCL), which fills an argument slot in another clause, for instance, an object (O) in I_A *hear [that Brazil won the football match]*$_{CoCL:O}$, or intransitive subject (S), as in *[That Brazil won the football match]*$_{CoCL:S}$ *is not surprising.*
- DEPENDENT CLAUSES expressing TEMPORAL RELATIONS, CONSEQUENCE, CONDITION, ADDITION, and CONTRAST, for instance, *[When I get home]*$_{TEMPORAL.}$ $_{DEPENDENT.CLAUSE,}$ *I will do my homework.*

Various techniques may be employed in clause linking, including conjunctions, special verbal forms, and clause chaining (see Chapter 11). It is advisable to put clauses within square brackets in language examples, indicating their functions (as, for instance, relative clause, or complement clauses).

Sequences of sentences may form an utterance, as a unit of DISCOURSE. A coherent succession of utterances can be referred to as discourse, or as a subdivision of discourse such as a paragraph, or 'stretch' of discourse. What links parts of such a unit together may be a shared TOPIC—something the discourse (or a sentence) is about. A part of a sentence, or of a stretch of discourse, that is given prominence and is contrastive with respect to other participants, or parts of a sentence, is a FOCUS. Discourse organization may depend on genres, speakers' intentions, and conventions. See Chapter 13.

The ways of speaking may depend on speakers' sociolinguistic backgrounds. Subtle differences between what appear to be 'free variants' in phonology, morphology, syntax, and discourse, may in fact be determined by speakers' gender, age, level of education, and perhaps other, not purely linguistic, parameters.

Notes and sources

Sections 3.1 and 3.2 formulate the basics for Chapter 4. Sections 3.3–3.5 form the background of Chapter 5. Notions in Section 3.6 are relevant for most chapters. Sections 3.6–3.10 are especially relevant for Chapters 11–12; and Section 3.11 is important for Chapter 13. Additional references are at the end of each of these chapters.

§3.1: For further details on basic notions of phonetics and phonology see Abercrombie (1967), Ladefoged (1975), and Ladefoged and Maddieson (1996). Dixon (2010a, 2010b) contains a comprehensive discussion of fundamental notions.

§3.2: See Dixon and Aikhenvald (2000).

§3.3: See Hockett (1954) on various approaches; further critique in Dixon (2010a: 146–8).

§3.4: See Payne (1990), Anderson (1992: 77ff), Aikhenvald (2007b) for distinguishing between inflection and derivation, Dixon (2010a: 142–3) for some further caveats.

§3.5: See Dixon (2010a: 102–5, 2012: 37–61), Aikhenvald (2011a).

4

Sounds and their functions

Every grammar should have a chapter on the phonological, and phonetic, make-up of the language. This chapter generally comes fairly close to the beginning. Based on what the reader learns from this chapter, they will be able to get a feeling for how the language sounds. Established phonemes will provide the basis for writing down the examples, and the foundation for an orthography. As the linguist discovers morphological alternations, and phonological properties of words, morphemes, and clauses, these will have to be included, or at least cross-referenced, in the phonology chapter.

Examples and forms within the phonology chapter have to be presented in phonological transcription, ideally using the International Phonetic Alphabet (IPA). (Phonetic transcription reflecting the allophones can be included inasmuch as it is relevant.) Then any scholar will be able to understand the meaning of each symbol in articulatory terms. Examples in the rest of the book can be presented in a practical orthography, but only if the orthography is true to the language, and thus acceptable to a linguist. More on this in §4.6.

The order of sections in this chapter follows the way in which most grammarians present phonological systems. A phonological description will normally start with a statement of consonants and vowels, and the range of phonetic realizations for each phoneme in different environments. But this is in no way prescriptive. Some grammarians may choose to start with syllable structure before they present the segmental system. But if you veer from the standard ordering, you should explain why.

It is appropriate to give minimal, or quasi-minimal, pairs for contrasts between phonemes, especially if the contrasts are not so usual cross-linguistically, or potentially problematic for the language. If a language has several rhotics, glottalized consonants, long vowels, or distinctive stress or tone, minimal pairs will provide a convincing illustration. It is unnecessary to overwhelm the reader with a meticulous list of minimal pairs for every possible combination.

Spectrograms are an important aid to a description which is primarily based on perception, articulation, and observation of the speaker's articulatory movements. However, the analytic decision—of what is a phoneme, and what is an allophone, and how best to present them—is best made by the grammarian: this cannot be delegated to mechanical analysis.

4.1 Segmental phonology

Each language has a system of consonants, and a system of vowels. It is important to establish the systematic oppositions of consonants and of vowels within the language, and then list possible allophones which occur either interchangeably (free variation), or in different, mutually exclusive positions (complementary distribution). English has a phonological voicing distinction in consonants. The aspirated variant of the voiceless bilabial /p/ appears at the beginning of words. It is thus an allophone condition by its position.

It is not sufficient to say that the language has a 't'. This conventional orthographic symbol may be misleading. It does not tell us any specific details about 't': whether it is apico-dental, or apico-alveolar, and so on—that is, how its main realization is pronounced. Similarly, it is not enough to say that a language has an /i/—this symbol needs to be interpreted in terms of the actual features. Statements like '*i* in the language is the same as *i* in English *pit*' should be used very sparingly in a reference grammar—if at all. Some authors of pedagogical grammars, and even anthropologists who quote examples in a language, use this device. But it is essentially sloppy: the responsibility of understanding the nature of a phoneme is simply passed on down the line.

Why do we need such detail? First, because our first commandment is 'be precise'. Secondly, because once we embark on a next stage—comparing the language with its relatives and reconstructing a proto-language—minute details of articulation may give us insights into historical changes.

4.1.1 Consonants

Let's start with a sample matrix of consonants, in Table 4.1. In tables of consonants, columns usually reflect places of articulation. Rows list manner of articulation. Each should be labelled, following the conventional terminology.

Some linguists present a similar matrix without labels. The result is misleading because it is vague—for instance, for a *t* we will have to guess if it is apico-dental, apico-postalveolar, or apico-alveolar. Others give a list of phonemes in their orthographic representation—another unsatisfactory option.

A. 'PLACES OF ARTICULATION'. Place of articulation is defined by cooperation of a movable or active articulator, for example lower lip, towards a fixed or passive articulator, for example upper teeth: the result may be expressed by using a hyphen, for example a labio-dental consonant, such as /f/. In order to describe each consonant with precision, one needs to state not just the fixed passive articulator, but also the moving part—the active articulator. Table 4.2 offers a list of passive articulators and their labels (adapted from Dixon 2010a: 268–9).

Table 4.3 presents a list of active articulators, passive articulators they combine with and the conventional labels.

TABLE 4.1. **A sample consonant matrix**

Active articulator	apico-			lamino-	dorso-	labio-		
Passive articulator	dental	alveolar	post-alveolar	palatal	velar	labial	dental	glottal
unaspirated voiceless stop	t				k	p		ʔ
aspirated voiceless stop	tʰ					pʰ		
voiced stop	d			ɟ		b		
voiced affricate				dʒ				
voiceless fricative		s	ʃ				f	h
voiced fricative		z	ʒ					
nasal	n			ɲ	ŋ	m		
lateral		l		ʎ				
rhotic		r	ɹ					
semi-vowel				j	w			

TABLE 4.2. **Passive articulators and their labels**

Articulator	Label
upper lip	labial
upper teeth	dental
gum ridge	alveolar
front (hard) part of palate	palatal
back (soft) part of palate, or velum	velar
uvula	uvular

TABLE 4.3. Active articulators, passive articulators they combine with, and their labels

Active articulators	Combining with passive articulators	Labels
lower lip (labio-)	with upper lip	bilabial (that is, labio-labial)
	with upper teeth	labio-dental
tip of tongue (apico-)	with upper teeth	apico-dental
	with gum ridge	apico-alveolar
	with hard palate	apico-palatal
tip of tongue turned back so that the underside touches the back of the gum ridge	gum ridge	apico-postalveolar (also called 'retroflex', describing the bend in the tongue)
blade of tongue (lamino-)	with upper teeth (or with both sets of teeth)	lamino-dental
	with gum ridge	lamino-alveolar
	with hard palate	lamino-palatal
back of tongue (dorso-)	with hard palate	dorso-palatal
	with velum	dorso-velar
	with uvula	dorso-uvular
root of the tongue (or epiglottis just below it)	back wall of the pharynx	pharyngeal
vocal folds (or vocal cords)	glottis	glottal

To create a glottal sound, the 'vocal cords' or 'vocal folds' may be brought tightly together and then released, producing a glottal stop. Or the cords may be held just apart, the noise of air as it is squeezed between them producing a glottal fricative.

Some articulators are 'multifunctional'. The uvula is the passive articulator for dorso-uvular stops and fricatives. But in a uvular trill, the uvula is in motion and is then considered the active articulator.

To clearly understand exactly how a consonant is pronounced one may need to watch how the speaker does it, and discuss this with them. This is something one cannot do sitting in one's office listening to a recording—a further reason to get an accurate transcription while you are in the field.

B. MANNER OF ARTICULATION AND NATURAL SUBCLASSES OF CONSONANTS. The major manners of articulation can be grouped into natural classes using the labels in Table 4.4. The labels 'obstruent' and 'sonorant' allow one to group phonemes into natural classes. The discussion in the grammar may need to refer to these classes.

Laterals and rhotics form a natural class. They share similarities in their articulation. Young children who cannot produce a rhotic will often substitute a lateral for it. Liquids may occupy privileged places in the syllable structure. In a number of Jê languages of South America, a complex onset must contain a rhotic or a lateral.

The term 'rhotic' covers a family of sounds each of which bears resemblance to at least one of the rest. All the varieties of rhotic are written, in the IPA tradition (derived from the Greco-Roman writing) as variants of the letter 'r'. The unity of the class is a matter of some controversy.

The most prototypical rhotic is an apico-alveolar trill made with the tip or blade of the tongue (IPA symbol *r*). The sides of the tongue are raised and the tip, located close to the gum ridge, vibrates as air is pushed past it. A tap (*ɾ*) is a trill with just one such vibration. A flap is similar to a tap, except that it involves a sliding motion; this is found in some dialects of Spanish. In production of a uvular trill (ʀ) the uvula vibrates against the back of the tongue. A rhotic can also be realized as a dental or alveolar approximant (ɹ) or a uvular approximant (ʁ). Across the dialects of English, the most common rhotic is a continuant with air flowing through a trough in the tongue.

The lateral flap sounds a bit like an *r* and a bit like an *l*, and combines properties of both lateral and rhotic. It is articulated like a flap, by drawing the tongue tip back and making a brief ballistic contact in passing (usually) in the post-alveolar region behind the gum ridge, but 'one side of the tongue remains low so that air can flow continuously through a lateral escape channel' (Ladefoged and Maddieson 1996: 243). In Korean, *l* and *ɾ* are in complementary distribution: *l* appears in syllable codas, and *ɾ* in the onset position.

The motion associated with a 'trill' does not have to involve a rhotic. A bilabial trill (a rare sound) involves lips as passive and active articulators.

Semi-vowels (also called 'glides') occur in the coda or the onset of a syllable (but not as its nucleus, as a vowel would). The laminal semi-vowel *j* or *y* is similar to high unrounded front vowel /i/. The bilabial semi-vowel *w* involves the back of the tongue raised towards the velum and the lips brought together, thus relating to both dorso-velar and bilabial columns in the matrix in Table 4.1. This proximity in articulation is reflected in the matrix by placing the two columns closely together. A cover term for bilabial and dorso-velar sounds made at the periphery of the mouth is PERIPHERAL.

TABLE 4.4 Natural classes of consonants by manner of articulation

Manner	Description of manner	Subclass	Natural class	Description of natural class
stop	complete closure of active articulator against passive one	} obstruent	obstruent	obstruction to the air flow at larynx or above it
fricative	a small gap between articulators creates audible friction			
affricate	a stop released into a fricative			
nasal	the velum is lowered and the air exits through the nose	liquid } sonorant	sonorant	the air flows without any obstruction, directed in a specific way
lateral	the centre of the tongue is raised so that air flows past one or both sides			
rhotic	the sides of the tongue are raised so that air flows through an opening in the middle			
semi-vowel	similar articulation to a high vowel (see §4.1.2) but belongs to consonant system			

In a few languages, a bilabial semi-vowel contrasts with a dorso-velar one. A continuant rhotic is associated by some linguists with semi-vowels (and the term 'glide', or 'approximant', is applied to this grouping).

Stops may vary in terms of the air stream mechanism involved. Those produced with the pulmonic air stream have air pushed by the lungs through the vocal tract by the respiratory mechanism. Some stops, and a few fricatives, are formed with an egressive glottalic air stream, producing EJECTIVE STOPS—a prominent feature of Northeast Caucasian, Salish, and some Chadic languages. There, the upward movement of the glottis acts like a piston to push air out. IMPLOSIVE STOPS are produced by 'downward movements of the larynx which lower the pressure of the air in the vocal tract'; they are a feature of many West African languages and also Sindhi, an Indo-Aryan language.

In a few languages, stops can be FORTIS (or strong, pronounced with greater articulatory strength) or LENIS. A regular part of the consonant system of many languages in southern Africa are types of stop known as 'CLICKS': the ingressive air stream is initiated by trapping air between the back of the tongue in contact with the velum and a second closure further forward in the mouth. Clicks can be voiced, voiceless, nasal, velar, uvular, affricated, and aspirated.

Further parameters involve VOICING and ASPIRATION. For sounds produced on a pulmonic air stream, the glottis can be open and the sound produced as voiceless. Or the glottis can vibrate, and the sound is then voiced. Voiced and voiceless realizations can be contrasting for some or all of the obstruents, and only occasionally for sonorants. There can be whispered voice (glottis narrowed), creaky voice (laryngealization, with vocal cords vibrating slowly), and breathy voice (or murmur). These are contrastive in some languages of Africa and of Southeast Asia.

Friction at the glottis, as a lip or mouth closure is released, provides aspiration at the end of the stop or an obstruent (voiced or voiceless). If glottal friction precedes closure, we get pre-aspirated stops.

Stops can also contrast in length. Phonologically, one should be able to distinguish between geminates or long stops and a sequence of two identical stops—this is what occurs in English on some morpheme boundaries, for example *hip pocket*. It is up to the grammarian to make a coherent argument in favour of or against geminates, or sequences of identical consonants.

Affricates have a complex articulation—as Ladefoged and Maddieson put it (1996: 90), they 'are an intermediate category between simple stops and a sequence of a stop and a fricative'. Historically, they may come from such a sequence.

Sounds with a 'complex' articulation may pose similar problems. Many languages of New Guinea have sequences of nasals and homorganic stops known as prenasalized stops and written as *mb*, *nd*, and *ŋg*. There can also be prenasalized affricates and fricatives. There can additionally be prestopped nasals, as in some African languages and in some Makú languages of northern Brazil, e.g. ^{d}n, ^{b}m. Various further combinations of mechanisms may involve glottalized, palatalized, and labialized obstruents and also sonorants. In each case, a coherent argument in favour of each being a unitary segment will have to be made.

A unitary segment must be shown to contrast with other proven unitary ones. No epenthetic vowel can intervene between the two parts of the articulation. Box 4.1 contains some suggestions of how to go about distinguishing a complex segment from a unitary one. Similar principles will apply to long vowels—see §4.1.2.

Box 4.1 One segment or more?

Principal ways of distinguishing a sequence of segments from one unitary segment include:

 (i) unitary segments (including geminates) cannot be interrupted by epenthetic vowels or any other interruptions, such as glottal stop insertion; complex segments can be;

 (ii) when dictated or pronounced v-e-e-ry slowly, complex segments may be clearly realized as several units;

 (iii) a putative subcomponent of a unitary segment cannot undergo any phonological process by itself; a component of a complex one can;

 (iv) native speakers tend to perceive unitary segments as one unit, not as two; and often write them accordingly.

4.1.2 Vowels

The three main parameters involved in production, and analytic representation of vowels are:

 (i) Referring to the horizontal position of the part of the tongue raised to produce a vowel: 'FRONT' (towards the hard palate) versus 'BACK' (towards the velum); there can also be a 'central' position in-between.

 (ii) Referring to the height of the tongue as it is raised towards the roof of the mouth, contrasting HIGH versus LOW (or CLOSE versus OPEN).

 (iii) Referring to whether the lips are ROUNDED or UNROUNDED.

These parameters are related. Front vowels are typically unrounded and back vowels are usually rounded (occasionally, this is not the case). Higher vowels are usually more rounded than lower vowels.

The eight primary Cardinal Vowels (so named by Daniel Jones) are shown in Table 4.5. These are used as fixed reference points for describing vowels in any language. They delimit the space within which each vowel is articulated. Note that rows reflect height of vowels (parameter (ii)) and columns reflect the position of the tongue and roundedness.

Additional vowels are sometimes called 'secondary' cardinal vowels. Some languages have a rounded high front vowel [y], or an unrounded back vowel [ɯ]. A high central unrounded [ɨ] is a pervasive feature of Amazonian languages. The schwa vowel /ə/ is central and unrounded. In some languages one or more vowels are pronounced as /ə/ (a schwa) in certain positions—for instance, in an unstressed syllable, or at the end of a word. Then the underlying identity of the vowel can be determined by placing the vowel under stress—for instance, adding an affix and changing the stress placement. Alternatively, a schwa may be a distinctive phoneme.

TABLE 4.5. Primary cardinal vowels

Front Unrounded		Back Rounded
i	close = high	u
e	close-mid = high-mid	o
ɛ	open-mid = low-mid	ɔ
a	open = low	ɑ

NASALIZED vowels are produced when the velum is lowered so that air escapes through the nose as well as the mouth. These are typical in Amazonian languages, and also some Romance languages, such as French and Portuguese. There are never more nasal vowels than oral vowels. A general tendency is for lower vowels—rather than higher vowels—to have nasal counterparts. If a language has nasal high vowels, it is likely to have nasal low vowels, too. A vowel can be nasalized contextually—for example, if preceded or followed by a nasal consonant. Nasalization of vowels often accompanies consonants produced through pharynx and glottis.

In many West African languages and in Karajá, a South American language, vowels differ in the position of the tongue root: it is more, or less, retracted. This is the essence of the ATR (advanced tongue root) distinction. This can also be important in vowel harmony. Vowels can be PHARYNGEALIZED, TENSE, or LAX.

Numerous languages—including English—distinguish long and short vowels. In just a few languages three vowel lengths are contrastive. These include Mixe, a Central American language, Yavapai and Wichita, from North America, and possibly Estonian, a Balto-Finnic language. A phonetically long vowel may result from a sequence of identical short vowels. It is important to remember that vowel length can be reinforced by stress. In French and in Gulf Arabic, long vowels are always stressed. In Czech, Finnish, and Classical Latin, vowel length is contrastive in unstressed syllables. Cairene Egyptian Arabic does not allow long vowels in antepenultimate position.

It is convenient to map vowel realizations in the language onto the Cardinal Vowel matrix, positioning the main allophone of the vowel within the phonetic space it occupies. This is a way of indicating the phonetic place of its main variant with respect to other vowels in the system. In a small system of three or four vowels, there may be substantial allophonic variation. Each phoneme may then occupy a substantial phonetic space: /i/ may subsume [i], [e], and also [ɛ]. In a larger system, the space will be reduced. Just as with consonants, it is not enough to just say that the language has an [o], or a [u].

We can recall, from §4.1.1, that semi-vowels are akin to high vowels in their articulation, but function within the consonant system. Other sonorants (nasals and liquids) can also function as syllabic nuclei, akin to vowels. English has syllabic /l/ and /n/ word-finally, as in *bottle* /botl̩/ and *sadden* /sædn̩/. Syllabic liquids can be heard, and transcribed as liquid-vowel sequences into other languages. For instance, the famous collection of Vedic hymns, called *R̥gveda* in Sanskrit, is known, in many European languages, as Rig-Veda. *Vltava*, the longest river within the Czech Republic, is *Wełtawa* in Polish.

Vowels and syllabic consonants constitute nuclei of the next segmental unit—the syllable. This is what we turn to now.

4.1.3 Syllable structure

In many languages, a syllable can consist of just a sequence of a consonant and a vowel (CV) or just a vowel (V). Or there can be complex onsets consisting of two or three consonants: C_1C_2V, or even $C_1C_2C_3V$. There can also be a simple coda, as in VC, or a complex one, for example $VC_1C_2C_3$. The syllable structure is usually presented as a formula, reflecting all the possibilities. For instance, Modern Standard Arabic has syllables of CV, C_1VC_2, and $C_1VC_2C_3$ structure. The general formula for the syllable can then be presented as $C_1V(C_2)(C_3)$. Tucano, a Tucanoan language from Brazil, and Sanuma, a Yanomami language from Brazil and Venezuela, have just two syllable patterns, V and CV. The general pattern is (C)V.

Some languages of the world have complex onsets. The syllable structure in Southern Nambiquara languages from Brazil is $C_1(C_2)(C_3)(C_4)VC_5$, (with CV being the most common syllable type). An example of a complicated syllable onset with four consonants is *kwhʔaʔ³kaʔ³li³-su²* 'a kind of deer' (raised numbers indicate tones).

Vowels can be ellipsed in fast speech, creating phonetic syllables (different from underlying phonological ones). In Sanuma, this results in phonetic (C)VC syllables, for example slow speech [aloamɨ kɨkɨ], fast speech [aloam kɨk] 'jararaca snake'. We may then postulate different syllable possibilities depending on speech register or speed. Unusual forms may have syllable structures not found anywhere else. In Sanuma, consonant clusters *pl* and *kl* are only found in onomatopoeia (see §4.1.5).

Each syllable has one nucleus. It can be simple—consisting of just one vowel, short or long. A long vowel may have to be distinguished from a sequence of identical vowels. Box 4.1 contains some ideas of how these can be distinguished. In Sanuma, if two identical vowels occur together, a glottal stop may appear between them. Therefore, such sequences are analysed as two vowels, VV.

Which vowels can occur in sequences (if any)? This may belong to the domain of phonotactics (§4.1.4). However, distinguishing between complex vowel nuclei, and vowel sequences often impinges upon the structure of the syllable.

Phonological diphthongs are complex vowel nuclei (see §3.1). Phonetically, a diphthong consists of a vowel of continually changing quality, as in [ia] and [ai]. One of the two vowel qualities is usually more prominent than the other. The less prominent one can be a preceding glide, or an on-glide, such as [jɛ] in Italian *viene*. Alternatively, the less prominent quality is a following glide, or an off-glide, as in English *way*. A diphthong will bear just one stress, since one vowel nucleus has one stress. In Tariana, a sequence of two vowels, *a* and *i*, contrast with the diphthong *ay*. The contrast can be demonstrated by a minimal pair *kaí* 'to hurt' (where the second vowel bears stress) and *káy* 'like this, thus' where the semi-vowel cannot be stressed.

When we encounter a phonetic sequence such as /ua/, we could, in principle, have three options of analysing them as (a) a diphthong, (b) a sequence of a consonant (semi-vowel)-vowel, or (c) a sequence of vowels involving *i* or *u* reduced to a semi-vowel, that is [wa].

Option (c) will be preferred if stress may go on either of the vowels, or if two articulations can be pronounced as distinct vowels in slow register. The choice between (a) and (b) may depend on the overall structure of the phonological system. By postulating a set of diphthongs (solution (a)), a linguist expands the vowel system. Opting for solution (b) may necessitate a re-statement of the syllable structure: if V-y or V-w are considered VC syllables, this may expand the range of syllable types (perhaps only for semi-vowels as codas). If a language does not allow complex onsets, postulating that a sequence *wa* or *ya* is a CV syllable may result in changing the syllable structure to CSemi-vowelV. In these cases, the linguist should follow the principle of maximum economy and coherence of description.

Other language-internal phenomena may help. Sequences *ⁱa*, and *ᵘa* in Warekena, an endangered Arawak language spoken in north-western Brazil, can be interpreted in any of the three ways (a), (b), or (c). The following piece of evidence rules out (a). Warekena has special pausal forms (see §4.5) marked by putting an extra syllable, *-hṽ*, after the word. The vowel in this 'pausal' syllable is a copy of the last vowel of the word, for example *ibu* 'head', *ibu-hũ* 'head (pause follows)'. If the 'pausal' syllable is added to a word ending in *ⁱa* or *ᵘa*, only the vowel 'a' will be repeated, for example *piya* 'you', *piya-hã* 'you (pause follows)', *waɾawa* 'our supply', *waɾawa-hã* 'our supply (pause follows)'. Options (b) and (c) are equally plausible. Not to complicate the vowel system, I opted for solution (b) in Aikhenvald (1998).

The choice of variants of morphemes—or allomorphs—may help make a decision. A word in Dyirbal has the shape CV(C)(C)CV(C), and the language has no vowel sequences. A word like [yalgai] 'road, track' has to be phonologically analysed as /yalgay/ ending in a semi-vowel, that is, a consonant rather than a vowel sequence. This can be supported by examining the choice of variants of case markers. The locative case has the form *-ŋga* after a disyllabic stem ending in a vowel. After a consonant, its form is *-Ha* (where H is a stop homorganic with the preceding consonant, that is, *ba* after *m*, *da* after *n* and *j* after *ñ*). 'Road' takes the form *-ja*; thus, 'on a road' is *yalgay-ja* (and not **yalgay-ŋga*), thus proving that the final element of 'road' is a consonant (solution (b)).

Any language which has syllables of VC structure (that is, closed syllables) will have syllables of (C)V structure (or open syllables), but not the other way around. There are usually more options for consonants in the onset position than in coda position. Usually, any consonant can occupy the syllable-initial position in CV syllables. But there can be constraints on which consonants occur in CC sequences (clusters) and in codas. The matter of which consonants, and vowels, occur in which positions within a syllable belongs to the domain of phonotactics.

4.1.4 Phonotactics

Phonotactic restrictions are normally formulated in terms of occurrences of consonants and vowels in various positions within a syllable or a phonological word. In Mandarin Chinese and in English, the dorso-velar *ŋ* only occurs in syllable- (and word-)final positions. In other languages, such as Dyirbal and other Australian languages, there is no such restriction. There may be restrictions on what consonants can occur in the coda position. In Baniwa, an Arawak language from north-western Brazil, only nasals can occur in the coda position. The syllable structure is $(C_j)V(:)(n)$.

Only some consonants may occur in clusters. In many Jê languages, clusters in the onset position are limited to labial and velar stops and nasals followed by a liquid, for example Kaingáng *pra* 'to bite', *krɛ* 'burrow', *ŋrɛn* 'to dance'. In Gulf Arabic, two consonants which differ from each other in nothing but voicing, or only manner of articulation, cannot form a cluster: there are no clusters **sz*, **ts*, or **bm*.

Principles of and restrictions on vowel sequences can be formulated in terms of a sonority hierarchy: low vowels > mid vowels > high vowels. In Warekena vowel sequences, a lower vowel is typically followed by a higher vowel (not the other way round). Thus there are vowel sequences *ia*, *ie*, *ua*, and *ue*, but not **au* or **ei*.

Phonotactic restrictions on glottal stops may have to do with a unit larger than the syllable. In some languages—such as Bamileke, a Bantu language, or Desano, from the East Tucanoan family—a glottal stop is a phoneme, like any other. In other languages, its distribution is limited. Glottal stop in Hausa, the major language of Nigeria, from the Chadic branch of Afroasiatic, occurs in loanwords from Arabic, word-initially before a vowel, and after short vowels before a pause. An affirmative 'grunt', 'yes', in many languages contains a glottal stop or a velar fricative, often accompanied by a nasalized vowel. This may be a unique form in a language with no other instances of glottal stop.

In a grammar, a special section on phonotactics may follow that on syllable structure. In many languages, phonotactic restrictions interrelate with possibilities for consonants or vowels within a phonological word. Different kinds of consonant clusters and vowel sequences can occur word-initially, word-medially, and word-finally. Then, it may be a better choice to include them after the discussion of the phonological word, or even within it (see §4.3) or add a cross-reference in each section.

Languages may also have different phonotactic restrictions for different types of morphemes, and different word classes. For example, fricative *s* and affricate *ts* occur in roots, but not in affixes in Hebrew and other Semitic languages. Or nouns may differ from verbs in their phonological make-up. In Igbo most nouns have an initial vowel (noun class prefix) whereas all verbs begin with a consonant. We return to this in §5.3.

4.1.5 Unusual sounds in unusual forms

In any language, there are forms that sound unusual. When a new word is taken from one language into another, the resulting loan word may be pronounced as it was in the source language. If a sound which appears in a loan word is absent from the non-borrowed forms in the language we are describing, we are dealing with loan phonology—that is, the phonological make-up of essentially foreign elements. In Cairene Egyptian Colloquial Arabic, post-alveolar voiced fricative [ʒ] appears only in loans from European languages; in English it is found predominantly in loans from French, as in *pleasure, leisure*. The dorso-uvular stop /q/ in Gulf Arabic is found in just a few 'classicisms' associated with written Arabic, such as /qurʔaːn/ 'Koran'. Such phonemes can be seen as forming a special subsystem in a language, one which coexists with that of native forms.

Foreign words may be 'recast in a form already acceptable to the borrowing language' (Henderson 1951: 131). For instance, loans from Sanskrit and European languages into Thai may conform to Thai phonology: they do not have any unusual sounds, or patterns. Or they 'may retain some alien features, and so introduce new phonological patterns'. Mazateco, from the Oto-Manguean family in Mexico, has the sequence *nt* only in loans from Spanish, such as *siento* 'one hundred'. In native words, *d* and *t* are not distinguished.

In a synchronic description, phonemes which occur just in loans can be included in the general phoneme chart in brackets, or with an asterisk (which will be explained in a comment). Alternatively, a special 'loan' phoneme chart can be provided.

Ideally, most grammars need a section dealing with linguistic assimilation of loans and their special phonological properties. We can recall from Chapter 2 that languages vary in how 'receptive' they are to foreign forms. In some languages these tend to be avoided, as is the case in many languages within the Vaupés River Basin linguistic area in Brazil and Colombia.

Peculiar sounds, and peculiar patterns, are often found in onomatopoeia, interjections, and exclamations. In Thai, only onomatopoeia may have CV:C structure, as in *kuːk* (call of a bird). They can also occur in repeated form, as in *kaːp kaːp* 'quack quack'. Ideophones in Cilubà, a Bantu language from the Democratic Republic of Congo, differ from words of any other kinds by having a sequence of a consonant and a semivowel, as in *kwàà* 'noise of something disappearing into bushes', and by having a nasal in a final position, for example *nzen* 'duration'.

Interjections may contain sounds not found anywhere else. In Fries and Pike's (1949: 45) words, 'the glottal stop seems to be an essential part of English /mʔm/ or /ʔmʔm/, or /haʔə/ (each with dropping pitch) "no". The English form indicating disapproval or commiseration contains an alveolar click (*tsk tsk*).

Child language and baby talk may have their own phonological features. In Manambu, a rare sound—the bilabial trill B —appears in one word in baby talk: *Bu* 'water'. A salient property of Manambu baby talk is CV-CV reduplication, for example *didi* 'poo', for *di* 'feces', and *yæ-yæːy* for *yæy* 'paternal grandmother'.

Languages used in special circumstances may have a special phonological makeup. Traditionally, many Australian Aboriginal groups had a special speech style used between initiated men and taught to youths during initiation. The Lardil people in northern Australia had a special initiation language, Damin. The 'lay' Lardil language had four vowels, and Damin had three. It had eleven of the seventeen consonants of the lay Lardil. But in addition, it had thirteen very unusual phonemes—such as nasal clicks, a bilabial trill, and an ejective velar stop. Damin was the only language in the world outside Southern Africa to have phonemic click sounds.

Special sounds, or patterns, found in unusual forms may or may not warrant a special section. They may be included in the statement of phonemes (accompanied with an asterisk, or within brackets), and then explained.

4.2 Beyond segments: stress and tone

Suprasegmental or prosodic systems which extend over a sequence of segments include stress, tone, glottalization, labialization, rhoticization, and vowel (and sometimes consonant) harmony. They may have scope over part of a syllable, a complete syllable, or a phonological word.

If a language has STRESS (see §3.1), the stress-bearing syllable will be perceived as having more energy than an unstressed one. Loudness, vowel quality, higher pitch, and length may contribute to this perception. In some languages, stress is contrastive. In English, there are pairs like noun *import* /ˈimpɔt/ with stress on the first syllable and verb *import* /imˈpɔt/ with stress on the second syllable. In Russian, getting the stress right will help you distinguish /ˈpisatj/ 'to pee' from /piˈsatj/ 'to write'. In contrast, stress always falls on the last syllable in French and in many Jê languages of South America. Then, it does not have a contrastive function. It does have a delimitative function, helping us perceive where one word ends and another begins.

Rules for stress placement may be less straightforward. Syllable 'weight' (and the notion of 'mora': see §3.1) can play a role. In Modern Standard Arabic, syllables which contain a long vowel and a coda, or a short vowel and a complex coda, are 'heavy'; the heavy syllable always bears stress, for example *rijáːl* 'men', *billáwr* 'crystal'. If a word of three syllables or less contains only light syllables, stress falls on the penultimate syllable, for example *málik* 'king', *madrása* 'school'. And if a word with more than four light syllables contains a long vowel, this long vowel is stressed, for example *munáːsaba* 'occasion'. Otherwise the antepenultimate syllable is stressed, for example *katábtuhu* 'I wrote it'.

An additional secondary stress may occur in longish words. In Abkhaz, polysyllabic compounds may have an additional secondary stress which is less strong than the primary stress. The placement, and the nature, of the secondary stress need to be specified.

Tone languages employ differences in pitch to differentiate words and meanings. The following two words in Yuhup, from the Makú family in Amazonia, differ in tone only: *nĩh* is a marker of negation, 'not', and is pronounced with high pitch, and *nĩh*, with low pitch, marks possession, like English *of*. These are REGISTER tones each with a specific level of pitch. There can also be CONTOUR tones characterized by a movement in pitch—falling (high–low), rising (low–high), and so on. The following pairs in Yuhup are only distinguished by pitch movement. The form *nĩh* 'not exist' with low-high (rising) and the form *nĩh* 'from' with high-low (falling) differ only in tone.

Tone can be a feature of each syllable, or of the whole word. It is important to mark tones, and stress (if contrastive and not predictable) throughout the grammar. Not specifying the tone is like missing out a feature that distinguishes words—like writing *ban* for all of *pan*, *ban*, and *man*. Only sloppy grammarians do that.

Tone assignment can correlate with word class. In Lango (Western Nilotic, Uganda) nouns, adjectives, and prepositions all have fixed tones. The choice of tone for verb roots is determined by aspect–mood marking—see §5.3.

Tone, stress, and further prosodic features (discussed in the next section) are crucial for defining the phonological word.

4.3 Phonological word

A phonological word is defined on entirely phonological principles—primarily based on prosodic features. These include STRESS (or ACCENT) and/or TONE assignment. Further prosodies include NASALIZATION, ASPIRATION, RETROFLEXION, and GLOTTALIZATION. In many East Tucanoan languages, every morpheme can be either intrinsically oral, intrinsically nasal, or 'chameleon'. An intrinsically nasal morpheme engenders the spread of nasalization within a phonological word.

This can be best illustrated in how personal names borrowed from Portuguese or Spanish are rendered in East Tucanoan languages. A name which contained a nasal vowel in the original language (Portuguese) is pronounced as nasal throughout: *João* 'John' is pronounced as *ñũ*). A name without a nasal vowel is realized as oral throughout (even if the 'original' did have a nasal consonant) 'Maria' is pronounced as *Baɾia*.

VOWEL HARMONY consists in adjusting vowels within a word. We can recall, from §2.1, that in Hungarian vowels within a word have to be either all back, or all front: this spreads from beginning to end (progressive harmony). Compare: *az-ak-ban* (that-PLURAL-INNER.LOCATIVE) 'in those', but *ez-ek-ben* (this-PLURAL-INNER.LOCATIVE) 'in these (ones)'. There are different types of vowel harmonies depending on which feature is 'harmonized', or adjusted.

A phonological word can be also be defined in terms of phonotactic restrictions. These may include number of syllables, and syllable weight. In many languages, including Guaraní Mbyá, and Walmatjari, an Australian language, a phonological word has to contain at least two syllables. In Tariana, and many other North Arawak languages, a monosyllabic word has to contain a long vowel or a diphthong. Some consonants can be restricted to word-initial, word-medial, or word-final position. In this way, they indicate the beginning, the middle or the end of a phonological word. As mentioned above, in English, dorso-velar -*ŋ* is not found word-initially. Gulf Arabic has no word-final three-consonant clusters.

A phonological word may be the playground for a range of phonological processes. These may include vowel fusions, vowel reduction, and tone sandhi. Consonant mutation in Celtic languages applies within the phonological word.

4.4 Grammatical word versus phonological word

Phonological processes within a phonological word may interrelate with its grammatical structure, and with grammatical word (see §3.2). Vowel fusion and vowel harmony may apply over the boundaries of affixes with roots, as is the case in Hungarian. Most North Arawak languages are largely agglutinating. Processes of vowel fusion apply on the boundary between prefixes and roots.

Affixes may have their own prosodic properties. Some derivational suffixes in English have to be stressed, while others do not. Compare *expectátion* with *expéctancy*. Both nouns are derived from the verb *expéct*, stressed on the final syllable. The suffix -*ancy* does not require stress shift; the suffix -*ation* does. This is the kind of information that needs to be included about every affix—if relevant for the language.

If two morphemes with different tones combine in one word, their tones may change following special rules. Mundurukú, a Tupí language from Brazil, has two tones, high (shown by acute accent) and low (not marked). Each morpheme has its own tone. If a suffix with high tone attaches to a root with Low–High pattern the result is Low–Low–High: *wəñə́* (L–H) 'Brazil nut' becomes *wenə̄ -ʔá* (nut-CL:ROUND.OBJECT) 'Brazil nut pod'. This is an example of tone assimilation in tone sandhi. Other processes may involve tone copying, polarization, and floating tones. A grammatical category may be marked just by tone alternation. In Yuhup, perfective and imperfective aspect forms differ just in their tone: rising for the former, falling for the latter.

A grammatical word, and a phonological word, may be composed of morphemes with different prosodic properties. As mentioned in §3.2, clitics are morphemes which lack phonological independence and behave as if they were bound. They differ from affixes in that they may form a separate grammatical word. Personal pronouns in Romance languages are clitics: in French, *je te le donne* 'I give it (to) you' is pronounced as one phonological word. And yet, there are four grammatical words. This is an example of mismatch between phonology and grammar.

Clitics and affixes may carry the stress in a phonological word. They may also vary in their segmental properties and phonotactics. For instance, in Tariana, no affix contains the nasal vowel õ; clitics and roots do. (This has to do with the fact that numerous clitics in the language recently grammaticalized from roots.)

Clitics only superficially resemble affixes. But there are crucial differences. These are summarized in Table 4.6.

TABLE 4.6 Contrasting clitics and affixes

Features	Affix	Clitic
1. Selectivity of host: what it attaches to	a root or a stem, the whole functioning as one grammatical word	a host defined phonologically, e.g. the first word in the clause
2. Is it an independent phonological word?	no	no
3. Is it an independent grammatical word?	no	generally
4. Special phonological rules apply on boundaries	often	seldom
5. Restrictions on occurrence	always restricted, sometimes to forms of just one word class and linked to it	fewer restrictions, often none at all
6. Position in grammatical word	closer to roots	typically, outside affix+root or root+affix sequence; may have movable position and attach to various hosts
7. Relative order	precede or follow the root and/or other affixes	precede or follow affixes; there may be special constraints on order between clitics in clitic strings
8. Scope	grammatical word or a phrase	phonological word, phrase, clause, or sentence
9. Lexicalization and creation of idiosyncratic combinations	frequent	less frequent

A major difference between affixes and clitics is that when an affix is added to a root (or a stem) it will form one grammatical word with it. An affix is always limited in its application and scope: one finds verbal affixes, nominal affixes, and so on. In contrast, a clitic can generally be added to a variety of hosts: it is thus less selective. And it can form a separate grammatical word. A clitic—for instance, a topic marker—may have the whole clause within its scope.

In most languages, affixes have a fixed position in a grammatical word. Clitics may attach to a fixed host, or appear at the edge of a phrase. Or they may occur in the second position in a clause (called Wackernagel's position, after the scholar who first discovered this principle applying to Indo-European languages).

Phonological processes will frequently apply on the affix–root or affix–affix boundary. (They can be then called 'morphophonological' since their application involves access to information on the morphological status of morphemes and not just their phonological make-up.) Examples of clitic–affix or clitic–clitic boundary processes are not so easy to find. In Romance and Germanic languages, fusions are attested on clitic+clitic boundaries, for example German *im* 'in him' (from *in* 'in' + *dem* 'dative form of definite masculine and neuter article), or Portuguese *na* 'in her' (from *em* 'in' + *a* 'feminine singular definite article'). Clitics tend to be added to a well-formed grammatical word—that is, after all derivational and inflectional affixes have been applied. As a consequence, we find clitics on the rims of words: a proclitic will precede all the prefixes, and an enclitic will follow the suffixes.

There are few examples, in the world's languages, of clitics interrupting the root. This is known as endoclisis (or mesoclisis). In Udi, a Nakh-Dagestanian language, the third person singular marker =*ne* is a clitic: it can attach to any focused word. 'Bread' is focused in the sentence in (4.1):

(4.1) xinär-en   lavaš=**ne**   uk-sa
       girl-ERGATIVE bread:ABSOLUTIVE=3sg.CLITIC eat-PRESENT
       'The girl eats **bread**'

This marker can also be inserted into a monomorphemic word, between a vowel and a consonant of the root. This is what happens in the following example, where the action, eating, is focused:

(4.2) xinär-en   lavaš   u=ne=k-sa
       girl-ERGATIVE bread:ABSOLUTIVE eat=3sg.CLITIC=eat-PRESENT
       'The girl **eats** bread'

Clitics can be called prosodically deficient. Word classes which are on the 'watch list' for potential cliticization include many closed classes—pronouns, interrogatives, conjunctions, adpositions, discourse markers, and auxiliaries. Only a few members of open classes may be capable of becoming clitics.

In synthetic languages, different affixes occupy different places in a word. They may vary in their properties—some change stress, others do not. Similarly, there can be more than one type of clitic. Some clitics in English can have an alternative realization as fully fledged phonological words, for example *'s* versus *is*, *n't* versus *not*. Others do not offer such an alternative, for example possessive *'s*.

In many languages, a grammatical word and a phonological word coincide most of the time. However, mismatches between phonological and grammatical words may arise. Typical suspects include:

(a) REDUPLICATION. This typically creates one grammatical word—bearing one marker of grammatical categories. This is the case in Arrernte, an Australian language, with full reduplication. Reduplicated grammatical words consist of two phonological words. First, each reduplicand bears stress. Secondly, the initial /a/ before a retroflex consonant (e.g. *rl*) can be palatalized; this is a word-initial feature showing that one grammatical word contains two phonological words, for example *arlátyeye* 'pencil yam (plant)', *arlátyeye-arlátyeye* 'area with lots of pencil yam plants'.

(b) COMPOUNDING. This also creates one grammatical word. However, the compounded forms may retain their independent stresses, as in Arrernte, where both bear stress: *antékerre-ikngérre* 'southeast'.

(c) INCORPORATION. Incorporating a noun into a verb creates one grammatical word (more on this in §7.4). But both components may keep their own stress, as in Fijian *unu-tii* 'drink tea'.

A pause—an audible break in delivery—tends to coincide with a word boundary. In many languages, including Jarawara, Cup'ik, Dagbani, and Georgian, pauses can only occur between phonological words and not within them. Pauses may delimit units larger than the phonological word. This takes us to our next section.

4.5 Beyond the 'word'

Two or more phonological words can form a phonological phrase—defined in terms of stress placement and strength. In Modern Standard Arabic, a phonological phrase contains one phonological word with major stress. The stress on other words is heard as weaker and secondary. In Warekena, the stress on the first component of a phonological phrase is perceived as less prominent, as compared to the stress on the second component, and is shifted one syllable to the right. The word for 'bone' in isolation is *ʃimápi*, and for 'monkey' is *puátʃi*. Together they form a possessive noun phrase realized as one phonological phrase, *ʃimapí puátʃi* (bone [of] monkey) 'a bone of a monkey', where the stress on the first component is shifted to the end, and has less intensity than the stress on the second component.

Properties of phonological phrases require further cross-linguistic examination. Their suprasegmental features may be important for determining constituency boundaries and additional phonological processes which operate beyond a word.

Back to pauses. Pauses may be marked by changes in the segmental and suprasegmental make-up of the prepausal word, also known as 'pausal forms'. These are especially familiar for students of Semitic languages (particularly Arabic and Biblical Hebrew). Pausal forms mark the end of a word especially in citation, a phrase, or a whole clause or sentence.

Their formation in Classical Arabic involves truncations of the short vowels *a* or *u* and the change of *an* > *ā*. Pausal forms in Biblical Hebrew have a set of vowel alternations, among them vowel lengthening and vowel lowering spread over the last phonological word before the pause, and also stress shift. In the text of the Old Testament, they are signalled by special 'pausal' accent marks. Pausal forms in the Arawak languages Bare and Warekena involve vowel nasalization and *h*-insertion. Correlation between pause and nasalization is a feature of a number of South American languages and Alamblak, a Sepik Hill language from New Guinea. A glottal stop can mark a pause, as in Tokyo Japanese and Hausa.

The use of pausal forms goes beyond word boundaries. In a few West African languages, including Dagbani, Fula, and Gokana, a glottal stop precedes a pause at the end of an utterance. Pauses mark ends of sentences in Modern Standard Arabic. Some tonal languages are known to have a special 'boundary' tone, distinct from other tones, that occurs only at the end of phrases, clauses, and sentences.

Distinguishing different intonation patterns may hold a clue to clause types. A statement, or a question, may differ from a command only by its intonation. In Tamambo, an Oceanic language from Vanuatu, a clause within a series of clauses ends with an upward pitch contour, and the last clause in the sentence has a downward contour. Imperative clauses in Tamambo have a falling contour, similarly to declaratives. Unlike declaratives, the imperatives 'tend to start at a higher pitch and fall more sharply' (Jauncey 2011: 44). Interrogative clauses are characterized by a sharp rise in pitch, and then a sharp fall. Modern linguistics is still trying to grapple with the many uses of intonation—including pragmatic and emotional overtones. The more your grammar can describe, the better.

Finally, a word on speech registers. In rapid, informal speech there may be more vowel reduction than in slower, more careful pronunciation (for instance, that used in a classroom, or directed at a foreigner). In Jordanian city dialects (such as that of Amman), the following variants of consonant occur, depending on the speaker's level of formality and education:

(4.3) 'informal/uneducated' 'semi formal'   formal educated
       (apico-dental stop)   (apico-dental fricative) interdental fricative
       matal   *masal*   *maθal*   'example'
       dihin   *zihin*   *ðihin*   'mind'

Each register may have to be described and analysed, as to its sociolinguistic context, and its correlation with the speed of speech.

4.6 How to decide on an orthography

One outcome of fieldwork is the development of a practical orthography for a previous unwritten language, or the fine-tuning of an existing one. The most straightforward way to go about this is to use letters of the Roman alphabet for sounds that are similar (however, perhaps not identical) to those conventionally represented by them. The voiced bilabial fricative /β/ can be represented with *v* which is, in many languages including English and French, normally used for the voiced labio-dental fricative. The high central vowel *ɨ* can be written as *y*, *ü*, or even *u* (if *o* is used to cover one phoneme with [o] and [u] as allophones). The fewer diacritics are used, the easier the language will be to write down.

Some languages have more phonological distinctions than the Roman alphabet can offer. All of these need to be reflected in the orthography. If the existing practical orthography does not recognize them, it needs to be amended or abandoned. Fleck, in his grammar of Matses, a Panoan language, tells a cautionary tale. The orthography proposed by earlier missionaries employed the same symbol for retroflex and palatal fricatives, and affricates. He used this writing system throughout his MA and PhD, but then realized its deficiency—and had to retranscribe each example containing these (Fleck forthcoming). The moral is: all contrastive distinctions in the language—involving consonants, vowels, stress, or tone—must be shown in writing.

A section on practical orthography can be included in the introductory chapter (where sources on the language are discussed). Or it may be more appropriate to add it to the phonology chapter, as a logical follow-up to the analysis of what the language sounds like.

Notes and sources

General readings on phonetics and phonology include Abercrombie (1967), Ladefoged (1975), Ladefoged and Maddieson (1996), and Dixon (2010a: 264–88).

§4.1.1: See Ladefoged and Maddieson (1996: 244–5), Dixon (2010a: 270–1), and especially Lindau (1985) for further details on rhotics. See Ladefoged and Maddieson (1996: 243) on the articulation of flaps; Ladefoged and Maddieson (1996: 78) for a description of ejective stops; Ladefoged and Maddieson (1996: 278) contains a summary table of possible articulations for click, and their symbols. An example of possible analyses of palatalized consonants as unitary segments or as sequences of a consonant and a palatal glide in Cavineña, a Tacana language from Bolivia, is in Guillaume (2008: 32–4) (see also Guillaume 2004).

§4.1.2: The connection between nasality and glottality was captured by James Matisoff (1973) under the term 'rhinoglottophilia'; see Parker (1996), and Ladefoged and Maddieson (1996: 106–16) for a further explanation. For a further discussion of these, and other distinctions, in vowels, see Ladefoged and Maddieson (1996: 306–20). See Holes (1990: 274) on Gulf Arabic, and Holes (1995: 50) on Cairene Egyptian Arabic.

§4.1.3: See Holes (1995: 49) on syllables in Modern Arabic, Ramirez (1997) on Tucano, Borgman (1990: 222–3) on Sanuma, Lowe (1999) on Southern Nambiquara; see Padgett (2007) on phonetic properties of diphthongs. See Dixon (2010a: 198–9) for language-internal evidence in favour of treatment of phonetic [ai] as VC in Dyirbal and as VV in Fijian; Aikhenvald (1998) on Warekena.

§4.1.4: See Rodrigues (1999: 180) on Jê languages, Holes (1990: 267) on Gulf Arabic, Burquest and Payne (1993) on the sonority hierarchy; Newman (2000: 228, 401) on Hausa; Parker (1996) on 'yes'; Ikoro (1996) for a summary on Igbo.

§4.1.5: See Gary Olmsted and Gamal-Edin (1982: 121) on Cairene Egyptian Colloquial Arabic; Holes (1990: 265) on Gulf Arabic; Henderson (1951: 131, 141) on Thai; Fries and Pike (1949) on Mazateco, Kabuta (2001: 141–2) on Cilubà; Hale (1973: 442–6) and Dixon (2002: 92) on Damin.

§4.2: A summary on stress is in Dixon (2010a: 281); see Hewitt (1979: 263) on Abkhaz; Silva and Silva (2012: 82) on Yuhup; and Noonan (1992) on Lango.

§4.3: For further data on nasalization in East Tucanoan languages, see Jones and Jones (1991: 14) and Barnes (1999); see Rice (1990: 9–10) for a discussion of phonological rules and their domains.

§4.4: See Picanço (2005: 311) on Mundurukú; Hyman (1975: 224–5) on tones; Silva and Silva (2012) on Yuhup. Unusual positioning of clitics may be accounted for as a kind of 'historical accident' (see Halpern 1998: 112, on this in European Portuguese). See Harris (2000) and Schultze (2004) on Udi. Dixon (2007b) offers an analysis of English clitics. See Henderson (2002: 112–13) on Arrernte, Dixon (1988, p.c.) on Fijian. Aikhenvald (2002a) provides further parameters for classification of clitics and a survey of relevant references; also see Dixon and Aikhenvald (2002) and Dixon (2010b: 24–7), especially on the relationships between a grammatical and a phonological word. See Holes (1995: 51) and Aikhenvald (2002a) on pauses.

§4.5: See Gray (1971), Steuernagel (1961) on pausal forms in Semitic languages, Aikhenvald (1996) on pausal forms in Arawak; Rodrigues (1983) on South American languages, Bruce (1985: 96) on Alamblak; Vance (1987: 13) on Tokyo Japanese; and Newman and van Heuven (1981: 13) on Hausa; Hyman (1988) on glottal stop at the end of utterances; Holes (1995: 52–3) on pauses in Modern Arabic; Hyman (1990) on boundary tones in Luganda and Kinande, two Bantu languages. See Jauncey (2011: 43–4) on Tamambo, and Holes (1995: 59) on Jordanian city dialects of Arabic. Fries and Pike (1949: 44–5) offer a discussion of speech registers.

5

Word classes

5.1 A statement of word classes

Every language has open and closed word classes (see §3.5). Open classes typically include nouns and verbs. Adjectives and adverbs are open classes in some languages, and closed in others. Definitional properties of open classes are generally discussed at the start of the word class chapter. A discussion of each open class will subsume a discussion of semantic subclasses determined by their specific grammatical properties.

Open word classes can accept new members either through loans, or via word-class-changing derivations. There can never be an exhaustive listing of all members of an open class. Onomatopoeia and interjections may be considered open to new members, but hardly ever by derivation.

In contrast, membership of each closed class is limited; they can be listed exhaustively. Closed classes may include demonstratives, personal pronouns, prepositions, postpositions, and possibly also adjectives, time words, locationals, copulas and other, more language-specific items. The chapter on word classes can contain a brief characterization of each of the closed class type, with more detailed discussion later on (see Chapter 9).

We start with the morphological and syntactic features instrumental in distinguishing word classes.

5.2 Essential features of word classes

The essential criteria for distinguishing between word classes include (i) morphological structure and categories, covering obligatory inflections and optional derivations for each word class, and (ii) syntactic functions of the representatives of the class reflecting the relationships between word classes and functional slots in a clause (see §3.9). Concomitant features may involve phonological criteria, additional morphological processes, and semantic properties.

5.2.1 Morphological categories

Typical morphological categories of nouns include case (marking grammatical function of a noun phrase in a clause), inherent number, inherent gender, classifiers, possession marking, and sometimes also degree (diminutive, augmentative) (more on these in Chapter 6). Typical categories associated with verbs are person, number, and gender of core arguments, tense, aspect, modality, evidentiality, mood, and valency-changing derivations (see Chapter 7). Typical categories of adjectives are agreement gender, and agreement number, both determined by the noun within a noun phrase, and comparison (see Chapter 8). This means that gender marking of an adjective is determined by the noun it modifies (and is not inherent to the adjective). There may also be nominal tense on nouns (usually independent of tense on verbs), verbal classifiers on verbs (independent from classifiers with nouns), and special adjectival affixes (e.g. dimunitives, or affixes which change word class).

The marking of categories on different word classes can overlap. Throughout the Arawak language family, the same set of prefixes marks possessor on nouns and the subject of the clause on verbs (that is, the A of transitive verbs and the S of active intransitive verbs). In many familiar Indo-European languages, inherent gender on nouns can be expressed in the same way as the agreement gender on adjectives, for example Portuguese *menino* (boy:inherent.masc.sg) *bonito* (handsome:agreement. masc.sg) 'handsome boy'. In Estonian adjectives have fewer case distinctions than nouns. All of these features may be useful to draw additional distinctions between word classes.

Polyfunctional morphemes can be used with more than one word class. In Classical Sanskrit, the suffix *-tara* was used to form 'the comparative degree of adjectives and rarely . . . of substantives', 'added (in older language) to adverbs . . . and (in later language) to verbs' (Monier-Williams 1899: 438). The comparative on adjectives marks comparison of qualities, and the comparative on verbs marks comparison of the extent of actions or states (that is, how actions and states are similar or different).

Degree markers—diminutive and augmentative—in Tariana occur on verbs, on nouns and on adjectives. The diminutive with nouns implies a small size or young age of a referent. With verbs, it marks the small extent of an action, that is, doing something 'a little bit', and with adjectives it expresses the small degree of a property. The augmentative on nominals expresses the large size of a referent; on adjectives it indicates the degree of a quality (e.g. 'very big'); and on verbs it marks an intensive action or state (and also has an additional overtone of 'really').

The comparative in Sanskrit is primarily an adjectival category, extended to verbs and adverbs. In contrast, 'degree' in Tariana is a category equally characteristic of nouns, of adjectives and of verbs. Such versatile categories are ancillary for determining word classes.

5.2.2 *Syntactic functions: word classes and functional slots*

Syntactic criteria reflect the relationships between word class and functional slot. Recapitulating from §3.9, the criterial functions are:

WITHIN A CLAUSE:

(a) obligatory predicate or head of predicate;
(b) obligatory core arguments A, S, O, and E (extended argument, for instance, of a ditransitive verb), and also Copula Subject (CS);
(c) Copula Complement (CC);
(d) Peripherals or Obliques.

WITHIN A PHRASE:

(i) head of a noun phrase (including possessor and possessee within a noun phrase);
(ii) modifier within a noun phrase;
(iii) modifier of a verb.

In some languages, for example Latin and Dyirbal, the head of a transitive or an intransitive clause has to be a verb, and arguments and obliques can only be nouns, while adjectives are copula complements and modifiers in noun phrases. In Nootka and other languages from the Wakashan, and also Salish, families, predicates, and core arguments can be nouns or verbs. A similar problem appears to exist in Tagalog. But in each of these, the morphological differences between nominals, adjectivals, verbals, and adverbials are sufficient to distinguish between the word classes. For instance, in Tagalog only verbs can be inflected for aspect.

In Tariana, verbs, nouns, adjectives, and adverbs can head an intransitive predicate. Only verbs can head a transitive predicate. Nouns and adjectives, but not verbs or adverbs, can be heads of NPs. Only adjectives are typical modifiers in NPs, and normally just adverbs modify verbs. A summary of correlations between word classes and functional slots is in Table 5.1.

The asterisks in Table 5.1 indicate that a morphological derivation has to be applied for the word classes to occupy these slots. An adjective or a noun has to take a derivational suffix (in this, as in many other languages, the same as the causative) to be able to head a transitive clause. To head an NP, or to serve as a modifier, a verb must take a classifier in its derivational function. The very existence of word-class-changing derivations, and the necessity of applying them under given syntactic circumstances, demonstrates the reality of word classes. This is despite some syntactic overlap between them.

The four word classes in Tariana differ in their morphological categories. Nouns have inherent genders, and determine the choice of classifiers of various types. Nouns also possess number, case, possession, nominal tense, diminutive, and augmentative. Verbs have bound pronouns expressing grammatical relations, tense, aspect, modality, evidentiality, and valency-changing categories. Adjectives have to agree in noun class and in number with nouns (in addition to the category of 'degree' and approximation specific just to them).

TABLE 5.1. Word classes and functional slots in Tariana

	Verb	Adjective	Noun	Manner adverb	Time word
Head of intransitive predicate	yes (all)	yes	yes	yes	yes
Head of transitive predicate	yes (some)	no*	no*	no	no
Head of NP	no*	yes	yes	no	no
Modifier in NP	no*	yes	no*	no	no
Modifier of verb	no	no (very few exceptions)	no	yes	yes (some)

In Fijian, verbs, adjectives, and nouns can head an intransitive predicate, but only verbs can head a transitive one. All three can head an NP (though this is a primary function only for nouns), but only adjectives can be consistently used as modifiers in noun phrases. So much for those who have claimed that Fijian does not distinguish word classes.

Members of different word classes can take different subsets of morphology depending on their function. For instance, in Turkish, nouns and adjectives as predicate heads take agreement suffixes, but cannot take the nominal plural marker. The option of having a noun or an adjective as predicate head should not be confused with zero-derivation from a non-verb to a verb. For instance, in Tariana any noun can head a predicate. But this does not make it into a verb. A noun as predicate head allows only a subset of verbal categories—for instance, it cannot occur with the imperative mood. It still has all other grammatical properties of a noun.

Box 5.1 offers a checklist of functional slots for each word class. This can also be applicable for their grammatically defined subclasses.

5.2.3 Derivation between word classes

Languages vary in their possibilities for extending open classes through derivation. In Yidiñ, an Australian language, just about any non-verbal stem can be verbalized. In Djabugay, a neighbouring language, verbalization is said to apply just to adjectives. Babungo, a Bantu language, Supyire, from the Gur family, and Tauya, from the Papuan area, have no ways of deriving verbs from any other word class. In contrast, Kobon, another Papuan language, has no derived nouns; but verbs can be derived from adjectives, and adjectives can be derived from nouns and verbs. In English and Ilocano,

---

Box 5.1 Word classes and functional slots: a checklist

Can each of VERB; NOUN; ADJECTIVE; MANNER ADVERB; TIME WORD; LOCATIONAL WORD; and OTHERS be used in one or more of the following functional slots?:

A. WITHIN A CLAUSE:

- argument (A, S, O, E) or oblique—PROTOTYPICAL CHOICE: nouns
- copula complement—PROTOTYPICAL CHOICE: adjectives and nouns
- head of intransitive predicate—PROTOTYPICAL CHOICE: verbs
- head of transitive predicate—PROTOTYPICAL CHOICE: verbs

B. WITHIN A NOUN PHRASE:

- head of NP—prototypical choice: nouns
- possessee in NP—PROTOTYPICAL CHOICE: nouns
- possessor in NP—PROTOTYPICAL CHOICE: nouns
- modifier in NP—PROTOTYPICAL CHOICE: adjectives

C. WITHIN A VERB PHRASE:
- modifier of a verb—PROTOTYPICAL CHOICE: manner adverb; time word; locational word

If the word class cannot be used in a functional slot without applying a derivational process, this needs to be said.

---

an Austronesian language from the Philippines, nouns, adjectives, and verbs can be derived from each other. Maale, an Omotic language from Southwest Ethiopia, has only one word-class-changing derivation: from adjectives to nouns.

Nouns derived from verbs may have fewer nominal (morphological and syntactic) features than simple, underived, nouns. This may justify considering them a special subclass—see §5.4.

5.2.4 *One form, several functions*

What if the same form can be used as a 'verb' and as a 'noun', in terms of its syntactic and morphological properties? English offers numerous examples. Pairs like *spy* (verb)—*spy* (a person who spies), *sleep* (verb)—*sleep* (action noun), *knife* (noun)—*knife* (verb: use a knife to attack someone), and *mother* (noun)—*mother* (verb: behave as a mother does) can be understood as doing 'double-duty'. Another way of describing them is as zero-derivations or as 'conversions'.

Can we say which function is primary? Yes, in most cases we can. Many polyfunctional roots in English can be identified by speakers either as primarily verbal, and secondarily nominal, or the other way round. *Stand, call, drink*, and *spill* are primarily verbs, and the nominal usages of *stand* (as in a stadium), *call* (as in *phone call*), *drink* (as in *have a drink*) and *spill* (as in *have a spill)* are clearly secondary. In contrast, *mother, father,* and *knife* are primarily nouns. And note that typically only generic nouns tend to develop a verb-like usage. For instance, a primary noun *stone* can be used as a verb, as in *to stone (someone),* but more specific nouns, such as *pebble, rock, gravel* are not used this way. Only the general noun *flower* has a verbal usage (as in *the tree is flowering*), but specific names for flowers do not—that is, one does not hear **to lily,* **to tulip,* or *to daisy).

The meaning correspondences between the 'double-duty' forms may be rather idiosyncratic, even for nouns from the same semantic field. *To mother* means 'behave as a mother to', and *to father* means 'to be progenitor of'. Other kinship terms can be—often jokingly, or in an ad hoc fashion—employed in the sense 'to use THE TERM as term of address' ('don't you aunty me!' = 'don't you call me an aunty'), or 'treat as THE TERM', for example *to baby somebody* means 'treat as a baby'.

Nouns used as verbs may have further idiosyncrasies. In British English, the verb *to table* means 'bring (a matter) forward for discussion or consideration at a meeting'. In American English it means the opposite: 'postpone consideration (of a matter)'.

Polyfunctionality of forms, and of roots, is pervasive in numerous Austronesian languages (especially Philippine and Oceanic languages), and in Wakashan and Salish languages from the Pacific Northwest. In two Austronesian languages, North-east Ambae and Taba, a number of roots can act as verbs and as nouns depending on morphological markers and syntactic environment. In each of these cases, a special argument needs to be made as to whether the root is really polyfunctional, or whether some can be considered primarily nominal, and others primarily verbal. Some scholars consider such roots 'pre-categorial'—that is, neither nominal nor verbal. Their exact status as nouns or as verbs would then depend on the morphology they may take in a specific context, and the syntactic slot they occur in.

Having polyfunctional roots does not rule out having word-class-changing derivations. North-east Ambae has a number of nominalizing devices, and employs reduplication to derive intransitive verbs from some nouns, and verbal modifiers (= adverbs) from verbs. Taba has a nominalizing derivation. That is, verbs and nouns are distinct grammatical classes notwithstanding some overlap between them. The freedom for members of word classes to occupy different functional slots in a clause may correlate with the amount, and productivity, of word-class-changing derivations. This is a matter for typologists to investigate.

5.3 Concomitant features of word classes

Concomitant features of a word class are important, but not criterial, to its definition. Each word class has its core meaning—nouns tend to designate objects, and verbs refer to activities, processes, and states. Adjectives denote qualities and attributes.

Adverbs refer to manner, time, location, and so on. However, such semantic criteria cannot be definitional because they are not steadfast. Deverbal nouns—such as *running*—denote activities, and yet they are not verbs. 'Hungry' is a state—and yet the concept is expressed by an adjective in English, but with a verb in Latin. Attempts to define word classes on purely semantic grounds are bound to be unsatisfactory if taken to a cross-linguistic perspective.

It is nevertheless essential to comment on the semantic content of each word class. One may wish to specify, for instance, if the verb class in language X includes stative verbs which correspond to adjectives in other languages (that is, express concepts which refer to qualities and attributes). A correlation of this may be that X has only a small closed adjective class. Or, in another language, the noun class may only include nouns with concrete reference—in some languages there are no abstract nouns (e.g. 'sincerity', 'beauty', 'truth', 'height').

In some languages different word classes have different segmental phonological possibilities; in others different word classes have different root structure. In most Arawak languages, polysyllabic roots are always nominal. In Lango, a Western Nilotic language from Uganda, nouns have lexical tones; their roots can be longer than one syllable. Verb roots are one syllable long, and their tone is determined by aspect–mood marking. In Hua (East Central Highlands family, Eastern New Guinea Highlands stock) verb stems always end in a vowel; nouns have no such constraints (but some subclasses of nouns—proper nouns and most kin terms—end in a glottal stop).

Word classes may differ from each other in their morphological processes and their semantic effects. In Saaroa, an Austronesian language from Taiwan, infixation is a property of verbs. In many Oceanic languages, reduplication can apply to nouns, verbs, and adjectives, with different semantic effect and grammatical consequence. In Tamambo, CVCV reduplication of many nouns has the meaning of 'plurality', for example *hinau* 'thing', *hina-hinau* 'things'. Reduplication of intransitive verbs may produce a progressive meaning, for example *sahe* 'go up', *sahe-sahe* 'be going up'. Reduplication of forms referring to states (corresponding to adjectives in other languages) indicates intensity, for example *duhu* '(be) good', *duhu-duhu* 'be wonderful'. And reduplication of transitive verbs makes them intransitive, for example *lavo* 'plant something', *lavo-lavo* 'plant' (intransitive)'.

Major word classes are not homogenous. More often than not, they are composed of subclasses defined in terms of semantic features and specific grammatical properties.

5.4 Grammatically defined subclasses of nouns

Nouns can be divided into subclasses defined by a combination of semantic and grammatical properties. Some will have fewer case or number distinctions than others. Some may have restrictions on their syntactic functions. Subclasses of open classes are semantic groupings with special grammatical features. That is, every language will have locational nouns and kinship terms. But it is not the case that in every language these will have grammatical peculiarities setting them apart from nouns of other groups. Incorporability of nouns is another potential parameter for their classification—in Amazonia, it is body parts and inalienably possessed nouns in general that can be incorporated.

We now turn to a selection of typical subclasses of nouns, defined in terms of semantic and grammatical features.

A. Free (unpossessed) and obligatorily possessed nouns. In many languages, some nouns have to always occur with a possessor stated. These are obligatorily possessed, and typically include body part terms, part–whole relations, and sometimes kinship terms. An alternative term for this is 'inalienably possessed'. Other nouns may or may not occur with a possessor: they are known as alienably or optionally possessed. Still other nouns may never be possessed at all; for instance, in some South American languages one cannot possibly say 'my moon' or 'my cockroach' (see §6.3).

B. Human nouns. In languages with optional number marking and number agreement, these are more likely to have an overt morpheme indicating their number, and to trigger number agreement. Nouns with human referents may bear an overt marker for gender, and have a special classifier, a vocative form, and more case forms than other nouns. Nouns with human referents may be used as modifiers to other nouns, specifying their gender, as in Tucano.

C. Animate versus Inanimate nouns. Like human nouns, animate nouns are often likely to bear an overt exponent of number and gender, and to trigger number and gender agreement. Nouns with animate referents may have separate subsystems of cases (for instance, some Slavic languages have a special animate sub-declension).

D. Kinship terms. These may stand apart from the rest in their possessive marking and occurrence in possessive constructions, as in Ritharngu, an Australian language, Koyokon (Athapaskan) and Jarawara (Arawá). In Mandarin Chinese, the possessive marker *de* can be omitted only in constructions with kinship nouns. Nouns referring to kinship may have irregular number forms (as in East Tucanoan languages) and gender markers. Such nouns are often unique in that they distinguish between address terms and referential terms, nursery forms, and forms of endearment (e.g. English *Mom, Mommy*) which other nouns lack. In terms of their grammatical behaviour—including their use in possessive constructions—kinship terms may further divide into consanguineal (blood relationships) and affinal (relationships by marriage).

Kinship terms and kinship relations are especially important in small societies with classificatory kinship systems—where everyone is related to everyone else. The systems will have to be established via painstaking genealogies, and participant observation. Some of the features of the system should be mentioned in the introductory chapter.

E. BODY PARTS. These may have unusual possessive forms, or always be possessed. To be used without a possessive construction, they may have to take a special affix marking them as 'unpossessed', as in Koyokon and Arawak languages. Body parts may also be used to express spatial relations and undergo grammaticalization, for example 'face' > 'front'.

F. COUNTABLE versus UNCOUNTABLE NOUNS. Mass nouns, or uncountable nouns, may differ from other nouns in terms of whether they can take number markers, what kind of classifiers they occur with, and how they trigger number agreement with modifiers (if at all). Some languages have special quantifiers with countable and uncountable nouns, for example English *much* versus *many*.

G. INHERENTLY LOCATIONAL NOUNS are likely to have fewer locative cases than nouns of other groups (or they may appear unmarked for location, as in American English *We go places*). In Saaroa, most nouns can be reduplicated, with the meaning of plural. Locational nouns include nouns referring to direction and orientation, and place names can neither be reduplicated nor marked for plural.

H. INHERENTLY TEMPORAL NOUNS may have fewer case distinctions than other nouns. They may not be able to appear in some syntactic functions, for example A, or head a possessive NP. These features may be shared by inherently locational nouns.

I. PERSONAL NAMES or PROPER NAMES may differ from nouns of other groups in that they may not be modifiable by adjectives or demonstratives, may have vocative forms, and are inherently definite. In numerous languages, the formation of associative plural, for example *The Smiths* 'Smith and those associated with him', is restricted to just personal names (see §6.2). Proper names can constitute a closed set. This is sometimes a feature of small-scale societies, especially if proper names are believed to possess special magic power and are to be used only under special (ritual) circumstances. They may have special gender markers, as in Manambu. In many European languages, proper names do not take articles at all. In Fijian, proper names have special noun phrase markers. In Chamorro, the Austronesian language of Guam, proper names of humans take the noun marker *si* (*si Pedro*), proper names of non-humans including locations take the marker *iya* (*iya Guam*) while other nouns take *i* (*i lahi* 'man'). In Ilocano, personal names take the singular noun marker *ti*, plural *dagiti* if they are core arguments, and *titi* and *kadagiti* if they are in oblique functions. Common nouns in core functions take singular *ni*, plural *da*; if they are in oblique functions, they occur with singular *kenni* and plural *kada*.

J. NOUNS DERIVED FROM VERBS, including ACTION NOMINALIZATIONS and NOMINAL-IZATIONS OF OTHER SORTS may constitute a separate subdivision with fewer nominal properties than other subclasses. In Tariana deverbal action nominalizations cannot be pluralized, and do not occur in A or S functions. So-called infinitives in Finnish and Estonian take a reduced number of cases.

Nominals derived from verbs may retain some verb-like features. For instance, in Latin, participles—traditionally considered adjectives derived from verbs—distinguish present, past, and future. Alternatively, their categories may be different from those of declarative verbs: in Turkish, the action nominals have relative tense and not absolute tense. Having such strikingly different sets of categories may warrant considering derived nominal-like forms a special word class.

There may be other, language-specific, subclasses. Manambu has a special subclass of address terms which have only a few nominal properties: they cannot be pluralized or used in possessive constructions. For each of such 'deficient' subclasses, there is the alternative option to consider them as word classes in their own right.

5.5 Grammatically defined subclasses of verbs

In most languages, verbs are an open class. Some grammatically defined subclasses of verbs can be listed exhaustively (and thus can be considered closed). Identifying these may reveal grammaticalization paths. For instance, motion and posture verbs may grammaticalize into auxiliaries and then into exponents of tense and aspect. In a few languages in New Guinea (including Kalam and Sko languages) verbs form a largish but closed class. These languages show an array of verb combinations in the form of serial verbs, each of which constitutes a single predicate.

The major division of verbs is based on their argument structure and the expression of grammatical relations. A copula verb—as the head of the predicate of a copula clause—may be a special subclass of verbs, or a separate closed class.

Typical grammatical categories of verbs include person, number, gender, tense, aspect, modality, mood, evidentiality, and valency-changing derivations (causative, passive, reflexive, etc.) (see Chapter 7). Grammatical subclasses of verbs vary in terms of these categories.

5.5.1 Transitivity classes

The major division of verbs is into transitivity classes. TRANSITIVE VERBS have two obligatory arguments, and INTRANSITIVE VERBS just one. This division may be considered universal (§3.9).

In some languages every verb is either strictly transitive, or strictly intransitive. In others, some verbs can function either transitively or intransitively. These verbs are ambitransitive.

For AMBITRANSITIVE VERBS it is important to specify the identity of arguments between the transitive and intransitive use of each verb. The O of the transitive version can be the same as the S of the intransitive one. This is the case for English *break*: I_A *broke the glass$_O$* versus *The glass$_S$ broke*. This type of ambitransitivity is transparently referred to as S = O ambitransitive. Alternatively, the A of the transitive version can be the same as the S of the intransitive one. Consider English *eat*: I_A *have eaten dinner$_O$* versus I_S *have already eaten.*

Some verbs can be both S = O and S = A ambitransitive. The verb *-awa-* in Jarawara can be used transitively with the meaning 'see, look at, look for', for example *We$_A$ 'awa' moon$_O$* 'We see the moon'. It can be used as an S = O ambitransitive, with the meaning 'be visible', for example *The moon$_S$ 'awa'* 'The moon is visible'. Or it can be used as an S = A ambitransitive, meaning 'look'. In this case, the S has to include the noun 'eye': *(He) eye 'awa'* 'He looks'.

For each ambitransitive verb, one needs to state what kind of ambitransitive it is. Languages vary in how much fluid transitivity is allowed. When one language, or one dialect, comes in contact with another, patterns of transitivity may change. The recent intransitive (S = A) use of *enjoy* in British and Australian English—as in the encouragement to enjoy food, *enjoy!*—is due to North American influence.

Further transitivity classes include DITRANSITIVE, or EXTENDED TRANSITIVE, verbs. These have A, O, and E as core arguments, and typically include verbs of giving, lending, and borrowing, and also 'bestowing a name' (see §3.9). EXTENDED INTRANSITIVE VERBS include S and E as core arguments.

Ambitransitive verbs may be similar to elliptic structures with omitted arguments. Teasing them apart may not be an easy task. Distinguishing between core arguments and obliques may be a further problem. A core argument must either be stated or understood from the context. An oblique is like an optional add-on—perhaps needed for saying what one wants to say, but not required by the verb.

Some transitive verbs may be used intransitively with an inherently reflexive meaning, for example English *shave* or *wash*. *I shaved* means *I shaved myself*. Verbs can also have an inherently reciprocal sense when used intransitively, for example *kiss, meet*: *We met* implies *We met each other*. Inherently reflexive and inherently reciprocal verbs may constitute separate subclasses. Inherently reciprocal verbs in English do not have to occur with the reciprocal 'each other'. In Yidiñ and Guugu Yimidhirr verbs with inherently reciprocal meanings always take a reciprocal marker.

Transitivity classes can be addressed in the word class chapter, and then taken up in more detail in a special chapter dealing with verbal structure, or with grammatical relations. More on this in Chapter 10. Grammatical features of other subclasses of verbs will, in all likelihood, include special transitivity properties.

5.5.2 *Further grammatical subclasses of verbs*

Further semantic-cum-grammatical subclasses of verbs may be established based on the selection of grammatical categories (e.g. formation of imperatives, causativization, and passivization), expression of grammatical relations, and other syntactic properties available in the language—for example occurrence in serial verb constructions and types of complement clauses they may take. Recurrent subclasses include:

A. ACTIVE versus STATIVE VERBS. In all languages, verbs can be divided, on a semantic basis, into active and stative. Active verbs denote a process or a volitional activity, and comprise motion and posture verbs such as *go*, *run*, or *stand up*. Stative verbs refer to states, such as *be poor*, and non-volitional activities, such as *fall*, *cough*, or *stumble*. In some languages, these have special grammatical properties, on the basis of which active and stative verbs will be considered grammatical, and not just semantic, groupings. In Onondaga, an Iroquoian language, imperatives cannot be formed on stative verbs: this sets them apart from other verbs.

We recall from §3.9 that in most languages, S—the sole argument of an intransitive clause—is marked in the same way as A in a nominative-accusative system; or in the same way as O, in an absolutive-ergative system. In what are known as 'split-S' languages, active intransitive verbs mark their S argument in the same way as an A. Stative verbs mark their S argument as O. This is called a split-S system. (We return to such systems in §10.5.2.) In these languages, the division of verbs into active—or S_a—and stative—or S_o—is grammatically justified, and essential.

B. Verbs of perception such as 'hear', 'smell', 'see', etc. exist in every language. In some languages they may form a special grammatical subclass. The choice of a complementizer or a type of complement clause with a perception verb may serve to express meanings related to how one knows a particular fact. In English, different complement clauses distinguish an auditory and a hearsay meaning of the verb *hear*: saying *I heard John cross the street* implies that I did hear John stamping his feet, while *I heard that John crossed the street* implies a verbal report of the result. A *that-* clause with perception verbs can refer only to indirect knowledge. Similar structures have been described for Boumaa Fijian. Perception verbs differ from other verbs in their complementation strategies in Korowai and in Manambu, from the Papuan area. Perception verbs in Luwo, a Nilotic language, allow the omission of a perfective marker, which is impossible with action verbs.

Verbs of perception can share grammatical and semantic properties with verbs of cognition, and of emotional states. In a number of North-east Caucasian and in South Caucasian languages, the subject of such verbs is marked with dative case rather than with nominative or ergative case (see §10.6).

Verbs of perception and also of cognition may be limited in terms of whether they can take derivational affixes. In Tariana, the verb 'see' cannot be passivized or causativized, and can occur in only a few idiomatic symmetrical serial verbs. In Manambu neither 'see, look' nor 'hear, listen' can occur in a full range of verbal compounds, or be causativized.

C. The verb 'give' may be the only ditransitive verb in the language. In a number of Papuan, Dravidian, and Caucasian languages, it has different forms depending on the person or recipient. Enga, the largest Papuan language of PNG, distinguishes *maingi* 'give to third person' and *dingi* 'give to first/second person'.

D. Verbs of motion may always occur in serial verb constructions (Chapter 7), or require directional markers. In Barasano, an East Tucanoan language, direction markers occur only in the imperatives of motion verbs. In Chalcatongo Mixtec, motion verbs have more aspectual distinctions than verbs of other groups. Verbs of motion may have irregular forms—in Figuig, a Berber language, they have suppletive imperatives with unusual gender marking. DIRECTIONAL VERBS may be a subclass of verbs or a subdivision within motion verbs. In many Papuan languages (including Abelam, Alamblak, and Manambu) they require a special directional morpheme. Their reference changes with the speaker's position and orientation (similar to 'shifters': §5.8). Their use may be determined by geographical factors of the terrain and general patterns of orientation (see also Chapter 14).

E. POSITIONAL VERBS as a separate subclass of verbs may display correlations with the type of object positioned (coming close to classificatory verbs: §6.1.5). They may overlap with EXISTENTIAL VERBS and COPULAS. They may have special number forms, as in Omaha-Ponca, and suppletive imperative forms.

F. VERBS OF SPEECH may constitute a separate subclass, in terms of valency-changing derivations applicable to them, the meanings of directionals, and types of complement clauses and strategies they occur with. They may obligatorily occur with direct speech reports whose status may be different from that of complements of other types. Verbs of speech are obligatorily serialized in Tariana.

G. WEATHER VERBS and VERBS REFERRING TO NATURAL PHENOMENA may be special. In a sense, they have no semantic roles at all. In English the impersonal *it* has to be added, to satisfy the syntactic requirement that each clause contains something in the subject slot, so in English we obtain *It is thundering*, and *It is raining*. In Northern Subanen meteorological verbs can optionally have the noun 'world' as their subject (S); they differ from other verbs in the meanings of applicative and other suffixes. In many languages—including Udihe, from the Tungusic family—imperatives cannot be formed at all on such verbs. They typically constitute a closed subclass.

H. DERIVED VERBS may stand apart from the rest. In Irakw (South Cushitic), verbs derived from adjectives are either inchoative, for example 'black'—'become black', or causative 'blacken'—'make black'. Their syntactic possibilities are determined by the transitivity class they are assigned to. Denominal verbs in the Lolovoli dialect of North-east Ambae are derived only from words for clothing, and mean 'to dress in this type of clothing'.

There may be further, language-specific subclasses. Complement-clause-taking verbs which typically include verbs of perception, cognition, and speech may be considered a special class (see §12.2.2). In a number of highly synthetic languages of North America, and some northern Australian languages, kinship relationships are expressed through verbs. For instance, in Nahuatl, a Uto-Aztecan language from Mexico, 'mother' is a transitive verb ('I am your mother' is, literally, 'I mother you'). Kinship verbs form a closed subclass of verbs, defined by an exhaustive set of kinship relations within a kinship terminology, and by grammatical properties—including grammatical relations, imperative formation, and applicability of valency-changing derivations such as causatives, or reflexives, and reciprocals.

A large proportion of non-inflecting verbs in Cavineña, a Tacana language from Bolivia, are borrowings from Spanish. Similarly to adjectives (see §5.6), non-native elements may stand apart from the rest of their word class.

5.5.3 Secondary concept verbs

So far we have addressed the verbs which refer to activities and states. These can form a clause on their own with appropriate noun phrases filling argument and oblique slots, and can be called 'primary concept verbs'. In contrast, verbs expressing 'SECONDARY CONCEPTS' provide 'semantic modification of some other verbs, with which they are in a syntactic or a morphological construction' (Dixon 2005: 96–101). Such verbs may express modal meanings such as 'want', 'need', 'must', phrasal meanings—to do with beginning and ending the activity of the other verb, duration ('continue'), trying, daring, and so on. The subject of the secondary concept verb may be the same as that of the verb it modifies: this is the case with 'try', or 'begin', for example *The farmer tried to kill the chicken*. Or the secondary concept verb may introduce an additional participant, as is the case with 'want' and verbs of causation 'make', 'force', and others, for example *The farmer wants the labourer to kill the chicken*.

Secondary concept verbs may constitute a closed subclass of verbs. They may be morphologically deficient: for instance, in English modal verbs do not form imperatives (one cannot say *Must kill the chicken!*). In other languages, they may not undergo the same valency-changing derivations as primary concept verbs. Secondary concept verbs are generally lacking from languages with extensive verb serialization, where such concepts are expressed through serial verb constructions.

Auxiliary verbs are somewhat similar to secondary concept verbs. An auxiliary is usually defined as a closed subclass of verbs which (a) form part of one complex predicate in combination with a verb from a large open class; (b) take the person, number, gender, aspect, tense, mood, and/or modality specifications; and (c) may impart a modal, or an aspectual meaning to the whole construction. An English complex tense form *have been doing* contains two auxiliaries, *have* and *be*, which impart aspectual semantics to the predicate. In Balto-Finnic languages, an auxiliary verb *e-* marks negation in declarative clauses. Unlike secondary concept verbs, auxiliaries tend to have purely grammatical meanings, and few verbal properties. Depending on how many true verbal properties they have, auxiliaries may have to be discussed jointly with other verbal categories in the chapter on verb structure, rather than as a special type of verb.

5.5.4 Copula verbs and copulas

Copula clauses are often a separate clause type (see §3.9) which stands apart from other clauses in terms of its grammatical relations and semantics. Copula verbs establish a relationship between the copula subject and the copula complement, including (a) identity: *The man is a student*; (b) attribution: *The man is stupid*; and also (c) benefaction: *This book is for me*; (d) location: *The tree is in the garden*; and (e) possession: *The garden is ours*. However, semantic criteria can never be definitional for copula verbs (nor for any other word class).

The copula subject can be marked in the same way as the S of an intransitive verb. In some languages it is not: for instance, in Mojave, a Yuman language, the copula subject takes the accusative case while S takes the nominative case. The copula complement typically takes no marking. In Kamaiurá, a Tupí-Guaraní language from Brazil, a copula complement marked with attributive case *-ram* refers to a temporary state of the copula subject, or to their occupation. Estonian has an 'essive' case with a similar meaning, for example *mina olen õpetaja* (I am teacher) 'I am a teacher', *olen siin õpetaja-na* (I am here teacher-ESSIVE) 'I am here as a teacher, in a teacher's role'. In many languages, the copula complement is not cross-referenced with bound pronouns. Copulas may stand apart from other verbs in their morphological possibilities: they may not be passivized, or causativized, or form imperatives. They may have special suppletive negative forms.

A copula verb may take just one argument, the copula subject, as in Latin *Deus est* 'God exists', or Tucano *sĩ'í nĩî-mi* (this exist-PRESENT.VISUAL) 'This one exists'. In many West African languages, an existential copula clause or a locative clause may have possessive meanings: for instance, in Likpe, a Kwa language from Ghana, *a-táàbí kpé o-saní ɔ́-mɔ́* (CLASS.MARKER.PLURAL-money be.in CLASS.MARKER-man AGREEMENT-DEFINITE) 'the man has money' literally translates as 'money is in the man'. Alternatively, a language may have possessive verbs, such as 'have' or 'belong'. These may also form a separate class in terms of their grammatical features—for instance, 'have' in English cannot be passivized.

A copula may have hardly any verbal properties at all. The copular marker *d* in North Berber languages including Kabyle and Figuig is a case in point. It is then best treated as a separate closed class.

5.6 Grammatically defined subclasses of adjectives

Many languages of the world have a special word class of adjectives—words which provide a specification for the head noun in a noun phrase, and/or make a statement that something has a certain property. Functional slots typical for adjectives are: (a) modifier to a head noun in an NP, and (b) either (i) head of intransitive predicate, or (ii) copula complement. In many Indo-European and Semitic languages, adjectives are recognized as a large open class. But an adjective class can be closed to new members, and vary in size. Yimas, from the Lower Sepik family in Papua New Guinea, has just three adjectives: *kpa* 'big', *yua* 'good', and *ma* 'other'. Further semantic types subsumed under adjectives are expressed through nouns and verbs. In most languages, there tend to be fewer monomorphemic (or underived) adjectives than nouns or verbs. In Warekena all adjectives are derived.

Typical grammatical categories of adjectives may include gender, noun class, number, and also case. These same categories are typical of nouns, but they have a different nature. A noun has inherent gender or noun class. Number in a noun reflects the number of its referent, and its case—the noun's function in a clause. If realized on adjectives, each of these may reflect agreement with the head noun: that is, gender, number, and case are inherited from the head noun, and not inherent. Thus, the feminine gender and singular number of *menina* 'girl' in Portuguese is inherent to the referent 'girl'. When we use the feminine singular form of the adjective *bonita* 'beautiful: feminine singular' in a noun phrase *menina bonita* 'a beautiful girl', the adjective's gender and number are in a way secondary—they reflect the properties of the main noun. Adjectives may have categories just of their own, including comparative forms (see Chapter 8). They may be able to modify verbs directly, as in American English, where the adjective *quick* can be used as a verbal modifier, as in *go quick!*

Across languages, adjectives vary in their functional possibilities and morphological categories. They may share properties with verbs and with nouns, or have features of their own. In many Oceanic languages adjectives can be considered similar to stative verbs. In many Romance languages, they may well be treated as a subclass of nouns. How can the differentiation be made, and why is it important? We return to this in Chapter 8 (where the reader will find a snap-shot of semantic types typically associated with adjectives).

Grammatical subclasses of adjectives may correlate with their semantic types. Manambu has two subclasses of adjectives. One consists of three adjectives which mark gender and number agreement; two of them cover DIMENSION and agree with the head noun when used as modifiers, and with the subject when used as copula complements; one referring to VALUE only agrees with the head noun when used as modifier. The other subclass has about sixteen members (but can be considered open because it accepts loan forms). All adjectives can modify a noun and occur as copula complements. Only agreeing adjectives can be used as modifiers to verbs, and in comparative constructions.

Tariana has a closed class of thirty adjectives. DIMENSION adjectives form a separate subclass (they have irregular plural forms). COLOUR adjectives have a special derivational suffix. Other semantic types are split across subclasses defined by the possibilities of use as verbal modifiers, in compounds, and so on.

Grammatical subclasses may partly overlap with semantic types. Japanese has two adjective classes. So-called 'inflected adjectives' form a closed class of about 700 members (all the monomorphemic ones are native). So-called 'uninflected' adjectives constitute a large open class (which contains native forms, and also loans). All adjectives modify verbs, and can be modified by an intensifier. Only inflected adjectives can modify a noun directly (while uninflected adjectives require a postposition *na* or *no*).

Uninflected adjectives—noun-like in many features—can be used as copula complements, and inflected adjectives—which share features with verbs, and have restricted
phonological possibilities—cannot. Inflected adjectives subsume AGE, COLOUR, and
SPEED; while DIMENSION, PHYSICAL PROPERTY, and VALUE are found in each class. In
Swahili, one closed subclass of about fifty native adjectives take agreement markers
corresponding to the noun they modify. The other subclass involves a number of borrowed adjectives which do not take agreement markers. That is, borrowings behave
differently from the rest.

If there can be more than one adjective in an NP, preferred ordering of these may
follow the established semantic types. In English, a value adjective typically precedes
a DIMENSION adjective, which precedes an adjective referring to PHYSICAL PROPERTY;
a SPEED, AGE, and COLOUR adjective will follow, as in *a good big fast new white car*.
Ordering can be an additional parameter for subclassification of adjectives.

5.7 The elusive class of 'adverbs'

Open classes may also include adverbs whose typical function is to modify a verb. The
term 'adverb' is used in a number of different ways (often as a kind of residue class).
The concept of 'adverb' is perhaps the most problematic of all word classes. Adverbs
may be open by derivation; for instance, in English adverbs can be derived with the
suffix *-ly* from adjectives. In terms of their semantics, adverbs overlap with adjective
types. They typically cover MANNER, SIMILARITY, QUALIFICATION and QUANTIFICA-
TION, EPISTEMIC MEANINGS (to do with possibility and probability), and LOCATION
IN SPACE and IN TIME. Specific grammatical categories of adverbs may include derivational markers, and comparative forms (similar to adjectives of corresponding semantic types) (see §8.5).

Each of these semantic subgroups may—alternatively—constitute a separate closed
class. Similarity may be expressed with special affixes. In serializing languages, manner
may be expressed through verbs within a serial verb construction. The existence of a
word class of 'adverbs' in these languages is problematic.

5.8 Closed word classes and their properties

The exact nature and types of closed word classes are specific for each language. In
some languages, adjectives as a grammatical class are closed (and concepts associated
with adjectives in other languages are expressed through other word classes). Time
words ('today', 'yesterday', etc.), locationals, quantifiers, number words, and copulas
are potential candidates for closed classes. Number words (also called numerals, or
counting words) can constitute a small class of their own, or be grouped with quantifiers ('many', 'few', '(a) little'). In most Amazonian communities, the practice of
counting, or enumerating, used to be traditionally very limited. As a consequence,

underived number words in most Amazonian languages are restricted just to one, two, and three. In European languages, and a number of Papuan languages, one can count indefinitely. But since the pool of forms and derivations is restricted, numbers are best considered a type of closed class.

The term 'shifters' was introduced by Jakobson (1957) to cover pronouns whose reference changes depending on the speaker, and also demonstratives whose use is determined by the speaker's location. These tend to be prime candidates for closed classes. In every language, demonstratives (or deictics) and interrogative words can be exhaustively listed. They also tend to have special properties not found among other word classes. The animacy distinctions in the interrogatives 'who' and 'what' are independent of any other animacy-based divisions found in the grammar. Different animacy forms for 'who' and 'what' can be reconstructed for proto-Uralic. Yet no Uralic language has genders, or noun classes, where animacy would play a role.

Those familiar with grammars of languages of Europe, the Americas, Africa, and the Pacific might take it for granted that personal pronouns would form a closed class, restricted and easily listable. However, this may not be the case in languages of Southeast Asia—including Thai and Lao. Pronouns and terms of address are particularly tailored to allow people to express differences in social standing, respect, and deference. As a result, there is a wide range of alternative pronominal forms, many of which are co-opted from kinship terms, names and certain nouns (such as 'your humble servant').

For each of the closed classes we need to discuss its grammatical categories, and the functional slots its members may be able to occupy. Demonstratives may have the same gender distinctions as adjectives: this is the case in French. In Baniwa, an Arawak language, demonstratives have two agreement genders, but adjectives take a wider variety of noun class markers. In Manambu, demonstratives agree in number and gender with the head noun (just like the agreeing adjectives). But they stand apart from all other word classes, thanks to their own system of directional markers.

Closed grammatical systems used to express grammatical categories may include articles and noun phrase markers (Chapter 6), adpositions (a cover term for prepositions and postpositions), modals, discourse markers of topic, focus, attention-getting and discourse prominence, and markers of coordination and subordination, or connectives.

We saw in §4.1.5 that interjections, and onomatopoeic, or sound-symbolic, expressions, may stand apart from other word classes in their phonological make-up. Interjections are grammatical words which express an emotion or a sentiment of the speaker, for example English *ugh! shhh! yuk!* or Portuguese *eca!* (expression of disgust). Interjections typically do not enter into syntactic relations with other words (however, they may serve as a basis for derivations, as in English *yukky* 'disgusting', or function as copula complements). The syntactic and derivational possibilities for interjections (usually, a closed class) vary.

Ideophones may be a large class of onomatopoeic, or sound-symbolic, forms, especially typical for African, Southeast Asian, South American, and Papuan languages. In Doke's (1935: 118) definition, an ideophone is 'a vivid representation of an idea in sound', an onomatopoeic word 'which describes a predicate, qualificative or adverb in respect to manner, colour, sound, smell, action, state or intensity'. Ideophones are subsumed under the category 'expressives'. They form a potentially open word class which may be defined by special and unusual phonological features (sometimes replicating the sound they refer to), inherent reduplication, or even tri- and quadriplication, and repetition, and limited syntactic possibilities (usually as independent clauses, and modifiers of verbs).

The list of word classes addressed here is not exhaustive. Many Australian languages—including Yawuru, Wardaman, and Njul-Njul—have complex predicates. Each consists of an uninflected coverb and a simple verb which bears inflection. The simple verb *-ga-* in Yawuru means 'carry'. In combination with coverbs, the meanings are made more specific and are not quite predictable, for example *ŋanjbi -ga-* 'carry, holding under the arm or by the side of the body', *ŋanjdja -ga-* 'carry in the mouth (as a dog does)', *wirrb -ga-* 'oppose (carry a grudge against someone)'. The number of simple verbs is often limited to a few dozen, and the class of coverbs is open.

5.9 Summing up

Every comprehensive reference grammar must have a chapter on word classes. This chapter sets the scene for the whole grammar, and offers the most basic distinctions which will then be elaborated upon in the following chapters. This chapter presents the division of grammatical words based on morphological, syntactic, semantic, and sometimes also phonological criteria. It is important to distinguish between open classes and closed classes. For each open class, a grammarian needs to strive to delineate grammatically and semantically defined subclasses, going into as much detail as appropriate for the analysis and their level of expertise.

The description of each word class within the word class chapter may be presented as a summary, with a more detailed discussion to follow in a separate chapter (if there is enough justification to do so). For example, in my grammars of Tariana and of Manambu I summarized the major grammatical categories, and grammatically-motivated subclasses of both verbs and nouns in the word class chapter. Then, each category was discussed in a separate chapter in more detail. The exact choice—how much to include where—depends on the demands of the language.

A draft of the word class chapter is usually prepared at an early stage of grammatical analysis, and then refined and even rewritten as the analysis proceeds. Similarly to the Introduction, it may have to be finalized after all the other chapters have been written.

Notes and sources

§5.2.1: Further readings on the typology of word classes and how to differentiate them include Schachter (1985), Dixon (2010a, 2010b), Vogel and Comrie (2000), Aikhenvald (2007b), and also Evans and Osada (2005). Polyfunctional possessive morphemes are further addressed in Aikhenvald (2013a: 41–4). See Aikhenvald (2003: 195, 366–7) on Tariana.

§5.2.2: See also Schachter (1985: 12) on Wakashan and Salish languages; van Eijk and Hess (1986) on Salish; Jacobsen (1979) on Makah, a Wakashan language; Schachter and Otanes (1972: 59–85) for Tagalog; Aikhenvald (2003) for Tariana; Dixon (1988: 238) and Milner (1956) for Fijian; Underhill (1976: 40) on Turkish.

§5.2.3: See Dixon (1977: 364ff) on Yidiñ; Patz (1991: 291) on Djabugay; Schaub (1985) on Babungo; Carlson (1994) on Supyire; MacDonald (1990) on Tauya; Davies (1981) on Kobon; Amha (2001: 74–5) on Maale; and Rubino (1997) on Ilocano.

§5.2.4: 'Conversion' is defined as 'changing a word's syntactic category without any concomitant change of form' by Bauer and Huddleston (2002: 1640–3). See Bauer and Huddleston (2002: 1640–3); Brinton (2000: 91–3) and Dixon (2005: 57–8, 2014) on 'double-duty' forms in English, and also Clark and Clark (1979). See Hyslop (2001: 91–2) on the Lolovoli dialect of North-east Ambae; and Bowden (2001: 113–14, 395–6) on Taba.

§5.3: See Noonan (1992) on Lango; Haiman (1980) on Hua; Pan (2012) on Saaroa (or Lha'alhua); Jauncey (2011: 133–9) on Tamambo. If there are correlations between type of morphological process and word class, this may justify having a separate chapter on morphological processes after the word classes have been defined, as was done by Pan (2012). It may be suggested that the semantic effects of reduplication are the consequences of the semantic features of a lexeme (see, for example, Beck 2002). Thus, words which refer to properties will be marked for intensity, and words referring to objects will be pluralized, using reduplication. This holds for Tamambo, but not for Dyirbal and many other languages where reduplication marks plurality on nouns and adjectives, e.g. *jambun* 'grub', *jambunjambun* 'many grubs', *bulgan* 'big', *bulganbulgan* 'many big (things)'; see Dixon (2010b: 87).

§5.4: A: Further information and references on possession classes and body parts are in Aikhenvald (2013a) and Dixon (2010b: Chapter 16).

  B: The principle concerning correlations between humanness, animacy, and number marking was first formulated by Smith-Stark (1974).

  C: See Corbett (1991), Aikhenvald (2000: 48) on animate subdeclensions of nouns in Slavic languages.

  D: Dixon (2002: 400) on Ritharngu, Thompson (1996: 655, 659–60) on Koyokon, Dixon (2004a) on Jarawara, Luo (2013) on Mandarin Chinese, Barnes (1999) on East Tucanoan.

  F: See Aikhenvald (2000) and references there for mass and count nouns.

G: Pan (2012: 167) on Saaroa.

I: Moravcsik (2003) on the associative plural. See Rubino (1997: 30–1) on Ilocano; Topping (1973: 98–100) on Chamorro.

J: On nominalizations in Turkish, see Lewis (1967: 254), Comrie and Thompson (1985: 362) and Aikhenvald (2011a) on nominalizations and derivation in general.

§5.5: See a summary in Pawley (1987, 1993), and also Ingram (2006) on verbs as closed classes in some Papuan languages.

§5.5.1: 'Labile' is an alternative term for ambitransitive verbs describing this kind of 'fluid' transitivity. Some scholars employ the terms 'unergative' and 'unaccusative', which cover fluid transitivity and also the division of verbs into active and stative. Apart from being used to cover different parameters for the division of verbs, these terms are additionally confusing because they bring in a further independent parameter of ergative and accusative which reflects the classification of languages by the marking of grammatical relations (§3.9) (see Dixon 2010b: 155–7 for a snapshot of different uses of these two unfortunate terms). Terminological clarity is an important prerequisite to adequate analysis and exposition (see also §1.7.3): confusing terms which mix unrelated parameters are best avoided. Olawsky's (2006) analysis of Urarina, an isolate from Peru, illustrates the difficulties in distinguishing ellipsis from ambitransitivity.

See Dixon (2005: 64–6; 2012: 138–86) on inherently reciprocal and reflexive verbs in English and elsewhere; see Dixon (1977) on Yidiñ and Haviland (1979: 65, 98) on Guugu Yimidhirr.

§5.5.2: A. See Chafe (1970: 20–1) on Onondaga; Guillaume (2008: 151–4) on Cavineña.

B. A concise analysis of complement clauses with verbs of perception in English in the context of complementation in general is by Dixon (2005: 270–1). On Boumaa Fijian, see Dixon (1988: 267–79); on Korowai, see de Vries (2013); on Manambu, see Aikhenvald (2013b); on Luwo, see Storch (2013). Other special features of perception verbs as a special class are in Brenzinger and Fehn (2013) for Khoisan languages. Onishi (2001) offers discussion of the special marking of perception verbs in Caucasian languages, and further references.

C. See Lang (1973: 17, 62) on Enga, and general discussion and further examples in Comrie (2003).

D. Jones and Jones (1991: 76–8), on Barasano; Macaulay (1996: 134–5) on Chalcatongo Mixtec; Kossmann (1997: 125–6) on Figuig.

E. Aikhenvald (2000) on classificatory posture verbs; Rankin (2004) on classificatory verbs in Omaha-Ponca; Aikhenvald (2010) on suppletive imperative forms.

F. See Aikhenvald (2011b) on speech verbs and a snap-shot of their properties.

G. Daguman (2004) on Northern Subanen, Nikolaeva and Tolskaya (2001) on Udihe.

H. Mous (1993: 186–8) on Irakw; Hyslop (2001: 356) on North-east Ambae.

On kinship verbs in North American languages, see Halpern (1942), Mithun (1996); in Australian languages, Evans (2000); in Nahuatl, Amith and Smith-Stark (1994: 355).

§5.5.3: For further discussion of secondary concept verbs see Dixon (2005: 96–101). On auxiliaries, see Heine (1993), Kuteva (2001).

§5.5.4: Munro (1976: 269–70) on Mojave; Seki (2000: 110–11) on Kamaiurá; Ameka (2013: 237) on Ewe, Likpe and other West African languages; Laoust (1928: 110), Chaker (1983: 169), Kossmann (1997: 297–8) on Berber languages.

§5.6: Further readings include Dixon (1982, 2004b, 2010a, 2010b), and also (Givón 1970). See Foley (1991: 93) on Yimas; Sohn (1994: 239) on Korean; Aikhenvald (2008) on Manambu and (2004a: 120–1) on Tariana. On the order of adjectives in English, see Dixon (1972: 24–6).

§5.7: See Dixon (2005, 2014) on adverb derivation in English.

§5.8: On counting in Amazonian languages, see Aikhenvald (2012a: Chapter 13); see Aikhenvald (2000: 440) and references there on animacy in interrogatives. Goddard (2005: 19–25) provides an illustration of open classes of pronouns and address forms in a selection of Southeast Asian languages. Ameka (1992) offers a general perspective on interjections. Useful sources on ideophones and expressives include papers in Kilian-Hatz (1999) and Voeltz and Kilian-Hatz (2001). See Dixon (2002: 184–201) and references there on coverbs in Australian languages.

The term 'particle' is used by some linguists with an overwhelmingly large array of meanings, sometimes covering all uninflected word classes, and also clitics. To avoid confusion and misunderstandings, it is advisable to use it sparingly.

6

Nouns

In every language, nouns form a large open class. Syntactically, a noun is the head of an NP which functions as an argument of a verb. Some, or all, nouns can also be used as modifiers. As we saw in §5.4, nouns may fall into distinct subclasses depending on their special morphological and syntactic features. Meaningwise, nouns tend to refer to entities or objects. Nouns derived from verbs and from adjectives may also refer to actions and to states.

Grammatical categories associated with nouns can reflect the referential properties of a noun (or a noun phrase). Such categories include GENDERS (also known as noun classes) and CLASSIFIERS of various types, NUMBER, POSSESSABILITY, and DEFINITENESS or SPECIFICITY. The category of CASE is functional: it relates to the noun phrase's role within a clause. The values of a category can be categorical, presupposing a determined choice. For instance, in a two-term gender system, a noun is assigned to either feminine or masculine gender. Alternatively, the values can be gradient, and determined relatively to one another. For instance, in a many-term number system, a noun can be marked for paucal (small number) or for plural depending on the speaker's choice, rather than the exact number of objects or people.

Nominal derivational categories include diminutives, augmentatives, and pejoratives. New nouns can be derived through compounding. At the end of this chapter, we turn to the structure of a noun phrase.

6.1 Reference classification: genders and classifiers

The continuum of reference categorization devices covers a range of means, from the lexical numeral classifiers of Southeast Asia to the grammaticalized gender agreement classes of Indo-European languages. They share meanings, and one can develop from the other. They provide a unique insight into how people categorize the world through their language in terms of humanness, animacy, sex, shape, form, social status, and function.

Reference classification devices are morphemes which denote some salient characteristics of the entity to which the noun refers. They are restricted to noun phrases, or verb phrases which require their presence. Their choice is primarily dictated by the semantic characteristics of the head of a noun phrase. They offer a strong criterion for determining what the head is.

6.1.1 Genders

The term 'gender' is perhaps one of the oldest in the linguistic tradition. Indo-European languages such as Greek, German, and Russian have three genders—'masculine', 'feminine', and 'neuter'. Latin had a similar system, but during historical change neuter nouns were redistributed between the other two genders, giving the modern system of masculine and feminine in French and Italian.

When Europeans came to study African languages, they discovered larger gender-like agreement systems with eight or more possibilities in languages like Swahili. These often did not even have a straightforward masculine/feminine distinction. The term 'noun class' came to be used for systems of this type. The terms 'noun class' and 'gender' are often used interchangeably. Genders are found in more than half of the languages of the world.

Genders are realized, as agreement markers, for example on modifiers, and also outside the noun phrase (on the verb, agreeing with its subject and object participants). The number of genders varies—from two, as in French or Portuguese, to eight or ten as in Bantu languages, or even to several dozen, as in some South American languages. The Portuguese word *menin-o* 'boy' is recognizable as belonging to the masculine gender by its ending (masculine singular), and also by the agreement markers it triggers on the article, and the accompanying adjective, for example, in *o menin-o bonit-o* (ARTICLE:MASC.SG child-MASC.SG beautiful-MASC.SG) 'the beautiful boy'. Its feminine counterpart *menin-a* is recognizably feminine by its ending *-a*; it also triggers feminine agreement: *a menin-a bonit-a* (ARTICLE:FEM.SG child-FEM.SG beautiful-FEM.SG) 'the beautiful girl'.

This is an example of OVERT gender marking: you can tell, by the form of the noun, what its gender is. In other languages, the form of the noun tells you nothing about its gender. In German, *Mond* 'moon' is masculine and *Gabel* 'fork' is feminine. We only know this because *Mond* requires the masculine form of the article, *der Mond* (and of modifiers). And *Gabel* occurs with the feminine form of the article, *die Gabel*. This is known as COVERT gender marking.

In Swahili, a Bantu language, gender (or noun class) is shown by a prefix on the noun, on the adjective and any other modifier, and on the verb. The gender-marking prefixes correlate with number. The singular prefix *ki-* of a class which contains names of inanimate objects has the form *vi-* in the plural:

(6.1) ki-kapu   ki-kubwa   ki-moja
       NCL.INAN.SG-basket   NCL.INAN.SG-large   NCL.INAN.SG-one
       ki-li-anguka
       NCL.INAN.SG-PAST-fall
       'One large basket fell'

(6.2) vi-kapu   vi-kubwa   vi-tatu
       NCL.INAN.PL-basket   NCL.INAN.PL-large   NCL.INAN.PL-three
       vi-li-anguka
       NCL.INAN.PL-PAST-fall
       'Three large baskets fell'

Genders are intrinsic for nouns: every noun belongs to one. The gender of a noun determines the gender form of an adjective or another modifier. This is the essence of the noun being 'head' of a noun phrase. More on this in Chapter 8.

Genders can, to a greater or lesser extent, be semantically transparent. Natural gender and grammatical—or linguistic—gender do not have to coincide. In German, the words *Mädchen* 'girl' and *Weib* 'woman' belong to the neuter gender. The choice of a gender can be based on semantic, morphological, and also phonological criteria. In Hausa, nouns denoting people or large animals which are biologically male have masculine gender. Those that are biologically female have feminine gender. The choice of genders for other nouns is not straightforward. Most geographical locations are feminine, and months are masculine. Native Hausa words which end in -*ā* are feminine: this is an example of how the phonological form of a noun indicates its gender. In German, some derivational suffixes are associated with one particular gender. For instance, -*ung* 'action nominalization' is feminine, and nouns with one of the two diminutive markers -*chen* and -*lein* are neuter. That is, gender assignment is conditioned by the morphological form of a noun. The word for girl, *Mädchen*, contains the diminutive suffix -*chen* and thus belongs to the neuter gender.

The defining properties of genders are as follows:

FIRST, the number of classes is always limited and countable.

SECONDLY, each noun in the language belongs to one (or occasionally more than one) class.

THIRDLY, there is always some semantic basis to the grouping of nouns into classes. Languages vary in how transparent the meanings are. Typical meanings include animacy, humanness, and sex, and sometimes also shape and size.

FOURTHLY, some constituent outside a noun itself must agree in gender with the noun. Agreement can be with other words in the noun phrase (adjectives, numbers, demonstratives, articles, etc.) and/or with the predicate of the clause, or an adverb. Genders are typically realized through affixation, or other morphological processes.

The meanings of genders may involve:

- sex: feminine vs masculine: we find this in many European, Afroasiatic, and Nilotic languages;
- human vs non-human, as in some Dravidian languages of India;

- rational (humans, gods, demons) vs non-rational as in Tamil and other Dravidian languages;
- animate vs inanimate, as in Siouan, from North America.

The term 'neuter' is often used to refer to irrational, inanimate gender, or a residue gender with no clear semantic basis. Genders can also reflect shape and size. In languages of the Sepik region of New Guinea, short, squat, and round objects are feminine. Tall, long, and wide ones are masculine.

In some languages most nouns are assigned to just one gender. In others, different genders can be chosen to highlight a particular property of a referent. Manambu, a Ndu language from the Sepik area, has two genders. The masculine gender includes male referents, and feminine gender includes females. But the gender choice is not cast in stone: if an object is exceptionally long, or large, it is assigned masculine gender; if it is small and round, it is feminine.

Rules for the semantic assignment of genders can be more complex. The Australian language Dyirbal has four genders. Three are associated with one or more basic concepts: Class I—male humans, non-human animates; Class II—female humans, water, fire, fighting; Class III—non-flesh food. Class IV is a residue class, covering everything else. There are also two rules for transferring gender membership. By the first rule, an object can be assigned to a gender by its mythological association rather than by its actual semantics. Birds are classed as feminine by mythological association since women's souls are believed to enter birds after death. The second transfer rule is: if a subset of a certain group of objects has a particularly important property, for example being harmful, it can be assigned to a different class from the other nouns in that group. Most trees without edible parts belong to Class IV, but stinging trees are placed in Class II.

Establishing links and connections between seemingly disparate meanings of genders is one of the most rewarding exercises for a fieldworker. One can spend hours discussing why one noun is feminine and another is masculine.

6.1.2 *Noun classifiers*

Noun classifiers are independent of any other element in a noun phrase or in a clause. They are often independent words with generic semantics (but can also be affixes to nouns). In Yidiñ, an Australian language, one would not generally say: 'the girl dug up the yam'. It is more felicitous to include generics and say 'the person girl dug up the vegetable yam', as in (6.3). Classifier constructions are in square brackets.

(6.3) [mayi   jimirr]   [bama-al   yaburu-ŋgu] jula-al
       CL:VEGETABLE:ABS yam:ABS CL:PERSON-ERG girl-ERG   dig-PAST
       'The person girl dug up the vegetable yam'

Not every noun in a language has to take a noun classifier. A noun classifier does not involve any agreement. Each noun may occur with more than one classifier. This is where noun classifiers differ from genders.

In Minangkabau, a Western Austronesian language from Sumatera in Indonesia, different noun classifiers may be used with the same noun to express different meanings. *Limau* can refer to a lemon tree or a lemon fruit. One says *batang limau* (CL:TREE lemon) specifically for 'lemon-tree', and *buah limau* (CL:FRUIT lemon) for 'lemon-fruit'.

A noun classifier is always chosen by the noun's meaning (and not its form). The meanings expressed may reflect the referent's social status, function and nature, and also physical properties, for example shape. In some Australian languages noun classifiers developed into noun class agreement markers: the interested reader will find more on this in Dixon (2002: 496–506).

Constructions superficially similar to noun classifiers are found in Indo-European languages. In English one can use a proper name together with a descriptive noun phrase, as in *that evil man Adolf Hitler*, but this kind of apposition is only used to achieve rhetorical effect. Lexico-syntactic mechanisms of this kind may well be a historical source of noun classifiers. Noun classifiers are not the same as parts of compounds known as class nouns, such as *berry* in English *strawberry* or *blackberry*. Class nouns—in contrast to classifiers—are not very productive, and are restricted to a closed subclass of nouns. The meaning of a compound containing a class noun may not even be transparent: a *blackberry* is indeed a kind of berry which is black in colour, but a *strawberry* is not made of straw.

6.1.3 Numeral classifiers

Numeral classifiers are used with a lexical number word, and sometimes also a quantifier. They categorize the referent of a noun in terms of its animacy, shape, and other inherent properties. Uzbek, a Turkic language, has fourteen numeral classifiers. A classifier for humans is in (6.4).

(6.4) bir   nafar   âdam
       one   CL:HUMAN   person
       'one person'

Inanimate objects are classified by their form. In (6.5), 'cabbage' is head-shaped, and so it has to occur with the classifier *bas*:

(6.5) bir   bâs   karâm
       one   CL:HEAD.SHAPED   cabbage
       'one (head of) cabbage'

Numeral classifiers are relatively frequent in the isolating languages of Southeast Asia; in the agglutinating North Amazonian languages of South America, in Japanese,

Korean, and Turkic; and in the fusional Dravidian and Indic languages. There is no obvious link between morphological type and the presence of numeral classifiers.

Numeral classifiers may be independent words, or affixes to number words and quantifiers. Their choice is always determined by the meaning of the noun. In a language with a large set of numeral classifiers, the way they are used often varies from speaker to speaker, depending on their social status and competence. In this they are much more similar to the use of lexical items than to a limited set of genders. Not every noun in the language has to be associated with a numeral classifier. Some nouns take no classifier at all. Others take more than one classifier, depending on which property of the noun is in focus. Numeral classifiers may be obligatory on small numbers only.

Numeral classifiers are typically chosen based on animacy, physical properties (such as dimensionality, shape, consistency, nature), functional properties (e.g. object with a handle) and arrangement (e.g. bunch). There can also be specific classifiers for culturally important items, for example canoe or house. Numeral classifiers can be sortal. These just characterize a referent, as in (6.4–6.5). Mensural classifiers provide information about how the referent is measured, or what kind of arrangement it occurs in. In Tzeltal, a Mayan language, the noun *lagrio* 'brick' takes one sortal classifier *pech* 'rectangular, non-flexible object'. It can occur with several mensural classifiers: *latz* 'stack of bricks', *chol* 'aligned bricks', and *bus* 'pile of bricks'.

Almost every language, whether it has numeral classifiers or not, has quantifiers, the choice of which may depend on the meaning of the noun. In English, we include *head* in *five head of cattle, stack* in *three stacks of books, flock* in *two flocks of birds*, and so on. Saying **five cattle* is ungrammatical. Why are the measure terms *head, stack*, and *flock* not numeral classifiers? The main reason is that they do not fill an obligatory slot in the numeral–noun construction. In fact, they occur in a type of construction which is also employed for other purposes. The quantifier construction in English *five head of cattle* is a subtype of an all-purpose possessive-like construction.

For each language, a special argument must be made for how measure terms can be distinguished from classifiers. The meanings of 'quantity' and 'arrangement' may be present in a noun classification system. This does not make all classifiers into quantifiers.

6.1.4 Classifiers in possessive constructions

Classifiers within a possessive noun phrase can categorize the possessive relation itself, that is, the way a noun can be possessed, or manipulated. This is done through RELATIONAL CLASSIFIERS. In (6.6), from Tamambo, an Oceanic language from Vanuatu, one classifier is used to categorize a yam as a plant that I own:

(6.6)   bula-ku   dam
      CLASSIFIER:LIVE.OBJECTS.ONE.OWNS-1sg   yam
      'my yam I own (growing)'

In (6.7), another classifier is used to refer to a yam I am expected to eat:

(6.7) ma-ku   dam
       CLASSIFIER:EDIBLE-1sg   yam
       'my yam to eat'

Alternatively, a special set of morphemes, POSSESSIVE CLASSIFIERS, categorize the possessed noun in terms of its physical properties (shape, form, consistency, function) or animacy. An example is from Panare, a South American language from the Carib family:

(6.8) y-uku-n   wanë
       1sg-CL:LIQUID-GENITIVE   honey
       'my honey (mixed with water for drinking)'

The ways in which classifiers are used in possessive constructions tends to be linked to possession classes: in many languages, only alienably possessed items require a classifier. Classifiers are always chosen on semantic principles; there is usually variability in their use. Their meanings are typically to do with shape, function, and social status (of humans). Not every noun has to occur with a possessive classifier. This reminds us of noun classifiers and numeral classifiers.

6.1.5 *Verbal classifiers*

VERBAL CLASSIFIERS (also called VERB-INCORPORATED CLASSIFIERS) appear on the verb, categorizing a noun, which is typically in S (intransitive subject) or O (direct object) function, in terms of its animacy, shape, size, structure, and position. In (6.9), from Waris, a Papuan language from the Border family, the classifier -*put*- 'round object' is used with the verb 'get' to characterize its O argument, coconut, as a round object.

(6.9) sa   ka-m   put-ra-ho-o
       coconut   1sg-to   VERBAL.CL:ROUND-get-BENEFACTIVE-IMPERATIVE
       'Give me a coconut (lit. coconut to-me round.one-give)'

SUPPLETIVE (OR PARTLY ANALYSABLE) CLASSIFICATORY VERBS are a subtype of verbal classifiers. Classificatory verbs can categorize the S/O argument in terms of its inherent properties (e.g. animacy, shape, form, and consistency). In Mescalero Apache and other Athapaskan languages of North America, there is no one way of saying 'give me tobacco'. Different shapes and arrangements of an object (such as tobacco) are reflected in the forms of the classificatory verb in bold in (6.10):

(6.10) *Nát'uhí* **shán'aa** 'Give me (a plug of) tobacco'
        Nát'uhí **shánkaa** 'Give me (a can, box, pack) of tobacco'
        Nát'uhí **shánłtįį** 'Give me (a bag) of tobacco'
        Nát'uhí **shánłtįį** 'Give me (a stick) of tobacco'

Classificatory existential verbs can categorize the S/O argument in terms of its orientation or stance in space, and also its inherent properties. In Enga, a Papuan language from the New Guinea Highlands, a verb meaning 'stand' is used to talk about the existence of referents judged to be tall, large, strong, powerful, standing, or supporting, for example men, houses, trees; and 'sit' is used with referents judged to be small, squat, horizontal, and weak, for example women, possums, and ponds. Existential classificatory verbs are a feature of many Papuan and Tibeto-Burman languages.

6.1.6 What reference classification devices are good for

Reference classification devices—gender, noun classifiers, numeral classifiers, classifiers in possessive constructions, and verbal classifiers—share their meanings of shape, form, consistency, and sometimes gender, and may develop from one another. Each type has its own preferred semantic parameters. Numeral classifiers typically categorize nouns by shape. Verbal classifiers may also involve orientation. Animacy and humanness are normally the semantic core of genders. Classifier types interact with other categories. Possessive and relational classifiers show dependencies with possession classes (§6.3). In some—but far from all—languages with numeral classifiers, the expression of number on nouns is optional. Only genders can be marked through agreement, and have to be assigned to every noun in a language. No other noun classification devices do this.

Genders are often semantically opaque. A gender choice interrelates with choices in the number system. In many languages, including Russian and German, gender is distinguished in the singular, but not in the plural.

TABLE 6.1. **How numeral classifiers in Burmese highlight different meanings of one noun**

NOUN	NUMBER	CLASSIFIER	TRANSLATION
miyiʔ	*tə*	*yaʔ*	river one place (e.g. destination for a picnic)
miyiʔ	*tə*	*tan*	river one line (e.g. on a map)
miyiʔ	*tə*	*hmwa*	river one section (e.g. a fishing area)
miyiʔ	*tə*	*'sin*	river one 'arc' (e.g. a path to the sea)
miyiʔ	*tə*	*θwɛ*	river one connection (e.g. connecting two villages)
miyiʔ	*tə*	*'pa*	river one sacred object (e.g. in mythology)
miyiʔ	*tə*	*'khu*	river one conceptual unit (e.g. in a general discussion of rivers)
miyiʔ	*tə*	*miyiʔ*	river one river (the unmarked case)

In some languages, classifiers and also genders distinguish what can be encoded with different lexemes. We saw in (6.6) and (6.7) how, in Tamambo, the ways a yam as a commodity and as food are distinguished by classifiers. In Burmese a river can be viewed as a place, as a line (on a map), as a section, as a connection between two places, or as a sacred object. These meanings are distinguished through the use of different numeral classifiers, as shown in Table 6.1.

A language can combine several means of reference classification. Many Dravidian languages have genders and numeral classifiers. In many languages of South America, New Guinea and Southeast Asia, the same set of morphemes can appear in several classifier contexts.

In (6.11), from Tariana, the classifier *-dapana* 'house, human habitation' is used as an agreement marker on a demonstrative 'this', an adjective 'big', a number word 'one', a possessive pronoun 'their', a verb 'do, make', and on the noun 'medicine' (forming the term for 'hospital'):

(6.11) ha-dapana   pa-dapana   na-tape-dapana
        this-CL:HOUSE   one-CL:HOUSE   3pl-medicine-CL:HOUSE
        na-ya-dapana   hanu-dapana heku na-ni-ni-dapana-ka
        3pl-POSS-CL:HOUSE   big-CL:HOUSE wood 3pl-make-PASS-CL:HOUSE-REC.P.VIS
        'This one big hospital of theirs has been made of wood'

Tariana is an example of a multiple classifier language. That the same set of markers can fulfil the role of all the reference classification devices discussed here is another argument in favour of their unity.

6.2 Number

Number distinguishes reference to one individual from reference to more than one.

6.2.1 *The meanings of number*

The most common types of number distinctions with examples are shown in Table 6.2. These are:

I. SINGULAR/PLURAL. This is by far the most common system. It is found in English and many other Indo-European languages, Hungarian, Hausa, Swahili, Quechua, and many more. The terms are SINGULAR (referring to 'one') versus PLURAL, or NON-SINGULAR (referring to 'many').

II. SINGULAR/DUAL/PLURAL. This type of system is fairly common. It is found in many Semitic and some Indo-European languages, and also many Oceanic, Australian, and South American languages. The terms are SINGULAR (referring to 'one') versus DUAL (referring to two) versus PLURAL (referring to 'more than two').

TABLE 6.2. Number systems: a snapshot

NUMBER OF INDIVIDUALS REFERRED TO	1	2	THREE OR A FEW	MANY	VERY MANY
I. English	singular *boy*	plural/non-singular *boys*			
II. Sanskrit	singular *pitā́* 'father'	dual *pitárau* 'two fathers'	plural *pitáraḥ* 'more than two fathers'		
III. Manam	singular *áine ŋára* (woman that:3sg) 'that woman'	dual *áine ŋara-díaru* (woman that-dual) 'those two women'	paucal *áine ŋara-díato* (woman that-paucal) 'those few women'	plural *áine ŋára-di* (woman that-pl) 'those women'	
IV. Ngan'gityemerri	singular *ngayi* 'I (singular)'	dual *ngarrgu* 'we two'	trial *ngarrgunime* 'we three'	plural *ngagurr* 'we (many)'	
V. Fula	singular *ngesa* 'field'	plural *gese* 'fields'		greater plural *geseeli* 'very many fields'	

III. SINGULAR/DUAL/PAUCAL/PLURAL. This type of system is less common than I and II. It is found in a few Oceanic languages, including Manam, Sursurunga, and Fijian. The terms are: SINGULAR (referring to 'one') versus DUAL (referring to 'two') versus PAUCAL (referring to 'three', or 'a few'') versus PLURAL (referring to 'more than a few').

IV. SINGULAR/DUAL/TRIAL/PLURAL. The type of system with the trial number (that is, with a special term referring to 'three') is rare. It is found in some Oceanic languages and in a number of Australian languages such as Wunambal and Ngan'gityemerri. The terms are: SINGULAR (referring to 'one') versus DUAL (referring to 'two') versus TRIAL (referring to 'three') versus PLURAL (referring to 'more than three').

V. SINGULAR/PLURAL/GREATER PLURAL. This type of system is infrequent, and is found in Fula and a number of other languages in Africa. The terms are: SINGULAR (referring to 'one') versus PLURAL (referring to 'many') versus GREATER PLURAL (referring to 'very many').

Some languages, for example Syrian Arabic, distinguish singular/dual/plural/greater plural. Warekena has singular, plural, greater plural, and an even greater

TABLE 6.3. Number in Warekena

NUMBER OF INDIVIDUALS	1	Many, about 2–6	Very many, about 40–50	Very many indeed, uncountable
	singular *abida* 'pig'	plural *abida-pe* 'pigs'	greater plural *abida-nawi* 'very many pigs'	even greater plural *abida-pe-nawi* 'very many pigs indeed'

plural: see Table 6.3. When my teacher of Warekena was explaining the system to me, he commented that if pigs are 'very many indeed', one cannot even count them.

Languages can have more plurals, with a variety of meanings. Hamer, an Omotic language from Ethiopia, distinguishes 'particular plural', e.g. *k'úlla* 'the goats', and 'global plural', e.g. *k'últono* 'all goats'. The collective plural refers to a group. In Syrian Arabic nouns denoting insects, vegetables, and fruits have a collective form, for example *dəbbān* 'flies'. If one has to specify 'one fly', a singular form *dəbbāne* is used. Distributive plural refers to individuals all over the place, as in Quileute (a Chimakuan language from North America) *tukôˑyo'* 'snow' versus *tutkôˑyo'* 'snow here and there'.

The associative plural has the meaning 'X and associates'. This is most often marked on proper names, kinship terms, and nouns with human reference. In English 'the Smiths' may not be a simple plural of various individuals called 'Smiths'. 'The Smiths' may refer to 'Smith and his (or her) gang': these may include John Smith, his family members, and some friends. As associative marker can be followed by a dual or a plural. In Central Alaskan Yup'ik, *Cuna-nku-k* (Cuna-ASSOCIATIVE-DUAL) means 'Cuna and his associate (for example, one friend)', and refers to two people. *Cuna-nku-t* (Cuna-ASSOCIATIVE-DUAL) means 'Cuna and his associates (friends, family, etc.)' and refers to more than two people. The associative plural, and the associative dual (that is, the associative or non-singular) constitute a useful criterion for personal names, or kin terms as a separate subclass of nouns—something we discussed in §5.4.

Number can have an absolute numerical value: in systems I, II, and IV the distinction between terms is exact. Or it can have a gradient, or relative reference. The exact distinction between 'a few' and 'many' in a type III system depends on the speaker's choice and perspective. (So does the choice between plural ('many') and greater plural ('very many') in a type V system.) In Boumaa Fijian, 'there is no fixed number of people below which it is appropriate to use a paucal pronoun and above which a plural should be employed. . . . The only constraint is that plural must refer to *more* participants than paucal'. In one announcement about village work, the village crier used the paucal to address one-third of the adult village population (twenty or so people), and plural when addressing all the villagers (about sixty adults).

The label 'plural' may be somewhat misleading. It may refer to 'many' individuals, as in English; or 'strictly more than two' as in Sanskrit, or 'more than three', as in Manam, or 'more than three', as in Ngan'gityemerri, all depending on each individual system. It is up to the grammar writer to specify what they mean, and to be precise.

6.2.2 *How number is expressed*

Number can be marked on nouns. In English, and in Sanskrit, we can tell by the form of the noun if it refers to one person or more than one. That is, number is marked overtly. In Manam, an Oceanic language from the Solomon Islands, we can tell how many people or things the noun refers to only by the form of a modifier, 'that', as in Table 6.2. The noun *áine* 'woman' has the same form no matter how many women we are talking about. This is an example of covert number marking. In some languages number is expressed on pronouns, but not on nouns—an example from Ngan'gityemerri, an Australian language, is in Table 6.2. Examples (6.1) and (6.2), from Swahili, show how number is marked on nouns (as inherent category), adjectives, and verbs. It can also appear on demonstratives, interrogatives, and other modifiers. Number on verbs codes how many arguments take part in the action. ('Verbal number' is sometimes used to refer to frequency or intensity, as a type of adverbial modification of a verb, e.g. 'he did it lots of times'.) Number, like gender, is often an agreement category. The marking of number within the noun phrase is dictated by the head noun.

Most languages of the world show a number contrast in free pronouns. Non-singular first person pronouns ('we') can be of two types: inclusive, that is with addressee included, and exclusive, that is, not including the addressee (see also §9.1.1). For instance, Motuna, a Papuan language from Papua New Guinea, has the following system:

(6.12)   PERSONAL PRONOUNS IN MOTUNA

1sg   *ni*   { 1pl inclusive *nee* (referring to speaker and addressee)

1pl exclusive *noni* (referring to speaker plus someone other than addressee)

2sg   *ro*   2pl   *ree*

The expression of number may correlate with the meaning of a noun. In Boumaa Fijian, a number specification must be made if the referents are human, and is optional otherwise. So, a third person singular pronoun can be used to refer to one, two, or a lot of things. In Koasati, the nominal plural is marked only on nouns that refer to human beings. This reflects a universal tendency discovered by Smith-Stark (1974): that overt number marking, and even number agreement, is more likely with humans and higher animates than with inanimates.

Number can be an obligatory inflectional category, as in English or Arabic. In many languages, number is optionally marked. The unmarked form can be called 'general': it is not specified for number. For instance, the noun *midin* 'possum, possums' in Dyirbal is neutral with respect to the number of individual possums, and can refer to one or more animals. If the dual number marking is attached, *midin-jarran* will refer to two possums, and the plural *midin-midin* (marked with full reduplication) refers to three or more possums. General, or transnumeral, forms are found in many Nilotic and Cushitic languages, in languages of South America, and in many isolating languages of Southeast Asia. Optional number can be considered derivational in nature.

In synthetic languages such as Latin or Sanskrit, obligatory specification of number is fused with case and with gender. The choice of gender may depend on choices made in the number system: in many languages, including Russian, gender is distinguished in the singular but not in the plural.

6.2.3 Number in its further guises

The number of a noun can also be expressed through quantifiers, for example 'many', 'much', 'few'. Many languages have a lexical class of number words with exact numerical reference. These tend to form a separate closed class—see §9.5.

Non-singular number forms can have polite overtones. In many European and some non-European languages, such as Fijian and Tamambo, plural forms of verbs, and non-singular pronouns, indicate respect (also see §9.1.2). Politeness, and other categories to do with interpersonal relations, can also be expressed through other grammatical systems: the imperative is one of these. Back to this in Chapter 11.

6.3 Possession classes of nouns

Every language has a way of expressing possession. This can be done through a noun phrase: *John's house*, *my car*, or *the leg of the table*. Possession can also be expressed in a clause, as in *John has a car* or *A car belongs to John*. We turn to possessive clauses in Chapter 11.

6.3.1 What can be possessed

In many languages, nouns divide into categories depending on whether or not they have to be used with a possessor. Some nouns—including body parts, plant parts, and kinship terms—always require a possessor. These are called 'inalienably', or obligatorily possessed. The nouns 'father' and 'arm' in Mussau-Emira, an Oceanic language from Papua New Guinea, cannot be used on their own. One always has to include the possessor, stating whose arm, or whose father it is: *nima-m* 'your arm' and *tama-ghi* 'my father'. One cannot just say **nima* 'arm' or **tama* 'father': it would be ungrammatical.

Nouns that can be used on their own are 'alienably', or optionally possessed. The word *ateva* 'chicken' in Mussau-Emira does not require a possessor. In a number of languages, some nouns are never used with a possessor. In Dakota, a Siouan language, land, water, animals (e.g. dogs) cannot occur with a possessor because 'under aboriginal conditions they could not be exclusive property of anyone' (Boas and Deloria 1941: 128).

Kinship nouns can stand apart from other nouns in terms of how they are used in possessive constructions. In Mandarin Chinese, the marker *de* 'genitive' has to be used in possessive constructions involving body parts and possessees of other sorts. Its omission will produce an ungrammatical construction:

(6.13)   wǒ de   shǒu   not * wǒ shǒu
          1sg GEN   hand
          'my hand'

(6.14)   wǒ de   fángzi   not *wǒ fángzi
          1sg GEN   house
          'my house'

Not so for kinship terms: if a kinship term is possessed, *de* can be omitted:

(6.15)   wǒ de   dìdi   or wǒ dìdi
          1sg GEN   younger.brother   1sg younger.brother
          'my younger brother'

The division of nouns into alienably and inalienably possessed is especially salient in indigenous languages spoken by small communities. It is crucial in many languages of North and South America, Oceania, and Australia.

6.3.2 *How to express possession*

Possession can be expressed by a special form, for example *de* in Mandarin Chinese, or *'s* and *of* in English. In a few languages, possessor and possessee are simply juxtaposed to each other. This is the case in Tucano: *yi'i pako*, literally, 'I mother', means 'my mother'. Or there can be a marker on the possessor. This is known as 'genitive case'. A typical example is Latin:

(6.16)   passer   meae   puellae
          bird   my:feminine.sg.genitive   girl:genitive.singular
          'my girl's bird'

There can also be a pertensive marker on the possessed noun, or the possessee. An example is from Nêlêmwa, an Oceanic language spoken in New Caledonia:

(6.17)   khoo-t   aayo
        food-PERT   chief
        'chief's food'

The choice of marking may correlate with what is being possessed. In Yidiñ, a genitive marker is added to the possessor if the possessee does not have to be possessed—that is, is alienably possessed. A dog does not have to be possessed:

(6.18)   waguja-ni   guda:ga
        man-GEN   dog
        'man's dog'

A man's foot does not exist without a man—it is inalienably, or obligatorily possessed. Then, the possessor and the possessee are simply juxtaposed, as in (6.19):

(6.19)   wagu:ja   jina
        man   foot
        'man's foot'

A man's foot is closely associated with the man as part of him. A dog is an independent entity, independent from its owner. Such conceptual proximity is reflected in the expression of possession: a closer, 'inalienable' relationship requires less marking. Such a correlation between meaning and expression is reflected in the principle of 'iconic motivation' outlined by Haiman (1983); we return to this in Chapter 14.

The division of nouns into possession classes depending on how they are used in possessive constructions may be crucial for determining grammatical subclasses of nouns (see §5.4). Classifiers in possessive constructions tend to be used with alienably possessed nouns only, as mentioned in §6.1.4.

6.3.3 *The meanings of possessive constructions*

What grammar writers describe as possessive constructions may cover a wide range of meanings. In many languages, including English, a possessive noun phrase can express part–whole relationships (*John's head*), kinship (*John's father*), property, and association in general. So, *John's house* may refer to the house John owns, or the house he lives in (but does not own), or the house he is somehow associated with—for example, designed, or built, or drew a picture of, or talked about. Expressions of quantity in English are superficially possessive-like, for example *a kilo of sugar*. A similar construction refers to material, for example *a house of stone*, or even a characteristic of a person, e.g. *a bear of a man* or *a man of honour*. But note: we cannot rephrase these expressions with the possessive verb have. Neither can we ask '*Whose kilo is it?*'. Rephrasing a superficially possessive or associative constructions with a predication, or a question, may offer a useful test for distinguishing it from possession proper.

A language can have a polysemous possessive construction encompassing many meanings, not all of them to do with possession. Or there may be a special construction just to express what one has. Within these constructions, some languages distinguish past and non-past possession: what I used to have before, and what I have now. In Macushi, a North Carib language from Brazil, *u-ye* (1sg-tooth) means 'my tooth that I have now', and *u-ye-rî'pi* (1sg-tooth-FORMER.POSSESSION) means 'my former tooth (that I no longer have)'.

6.4 Case

Case indicates the function of a participant in a clause. Case systems often mark core grammatical relations. We can recall, from §3.9, that these are the transitive subject nicknamed A, the intransitive subject, S, and the object, O, and also the Extended argument of a transitive verb, E. In (6.20a), from Turkish, the suffix *-ı* indicates that 'apples' is an O, and is labelled 'accusative' case. The suffix *-a* indicates that 'man' is the recipient and E the argument of the verb 'give', and is labelled 'dative' case. The 'giver', Mehmet, bears no overt marking. This argument is an A, and is marked with a zero—as is typical for a nominative case in a nominative-accusative system like the Turkish one.

(6.20a)   Mehmet   adam-a   alma-lar-ı   ver-di
          Mehmet.NOM   man-DAT   apple-PL-ACC   give-PAST.3sg
          'Mehmet gave the apples to the man'

This same marking is used for an intransitive subject, the S, in (6.20b):

(6.20b)   Otobüs   gel-di
          bus.NOM   arrive-PAST.3sg
          'The bus has arrived'

In (6.21), from Dyirbal, the A is a 'woman', marked with the suffix *-ŋgu*. This special marking of A is known as the ergative case. 'Man' is in the O function, and it is marked with zero—this is known as absolutive case:

(6.21)   yara   yibi-ŋgu   balga-n
         man:ABS   woman-ERGATIVE   hit-PAST
         'The woman hit the man'

Core cases mark who did what to whom—the topic of Chapter 10. Typical core cases are nominative, accusative, ergative, absolutive, and also dative.

Peripheral participants can also be marked with cases. The most common peripheral (or oblique) cases are local cases, including locative 'in', ablative 'from', allative 'towards', perlative 'course of action, through', and prolative 'along'. Instrumental case refers to the instrument with which an activity is accomplished, for example Tariana *hipada* 'stone', *hipada-ne* '(hit someone) with a stone'. Comitative case covers someone or something in whose company the action was taken, for example Manambu *du* 'man', *du-a-wa* (man-linker-COMITATIVE) '(do something) together with a man'.

Case meanings can be more elaborate. Many Tupí-Guaraní languages of Brazil have two locative cases: 'punctual locative' indicating location at a specific point, and 'diffuse locative', indicating a location within a bigger area. Uralic, Caucasian, and some South American languages have spectacularly large case systems. Table 6.4 shows a selection of oblique cases in Estonian.

The genitive stands apart from the rest. It is mainly used to indicate how nouns relate to each other in a noun phrase. In (6.22), from Latin, genitive marks the possessor within a noun phrase. In some languages, objects (O) of some verbs can be marked with the same case form, also called genitive, instead of accusative. In Latin, objects are normally marked with the accusative case:

(6.22)   Carpe   diem
         seize   day:ACC.SG
         'Seize the day' (meaning: enjoy the day)

TABLE 6.4. **A selection of oblique cases in Estonian:** *kivi* 'stone'

CASE	FORM	MEANING
Inessive: location inside	*kivi-s*	'in the stone'
Illative: direction inside	*kivi-sse*	'into the stone' (e.g. a hole in a stone)
Elative: out of inside	*kivi-st*	'out of the stone, from the stone'
Adessive: on the surface	*kivi-l*	'on the stone'
Allative: towards (the surface, or the whole object)	*kivi-le*	'onto the stone, to the stone'
Ablative	*kivi-lt*	'off the stone'
Terminative	*kivi-ni*	'up to the stone'
Instrumental-comitative	*kivi-ga*	'with the stone'
Abessive-privative	*kivi-ta*	'without the stone'
Translative	*kivi-ks*	'into the state of being a stone'
Essive	*kivi-na*	'as the stone, in the state of being a stone'

In Latin, verbs of remembering and forgetting require that their object take the genitive case:

(6.23)   Diēi   meminerit   cōnsul
         day:GEN.SG   remember.FUTURE.PERFECT:3sg   consul.NOM.SG
         'The consul will remember the day'

Core, and oblique, cases may share form and function with other cases. This is known as 'case syncretism'. In Russian, plural animate nouns have the same form for genitive and accusative case. In many ergative languages, ergative and instrumental case have the same form. In (6.24), from Dyirbal, the noun *yugu* 'stick' takes the instrumental ending -*ŋgu*, identical in form to the ergative case marker which occurs on the noun 'woman', in A function, also in (6.24):

(6.24)   yara   yibu-ŋgu   yugu-ŋgu   balga-n
         man:ABS   woman-ERGATIVE   stick-INSTRUMENTAL   hit-PAST
         'The woman hit the man with a stick'

Why can ergative and instrumental not be considered the same case? Evidence from Dyirbal supports their analysis as two independent cases. Dyirbal has an antipassive derivation (see §7.3.1) which makes a transitive clause into an intransitive one. Then, the A argument goes into S function, the O takes the dative case, and the instrument has the same marking as before. The verb takes a derivational suffix -*ŋa-*:

(6.25)   yibi   yugu-ŋgu   yara-gu   balgal-ŋa-ñu
         woman:ABS   stick-INSTRUMENTAL   man-DATIVE   hit-ANTIPASSIVE-PAST
         'The woman hit the man with a stick'

That is, the ergative and the instrumental share their form, but behave differently depending on the syntactic environment.

In some languages, like Latin or Finnish, every word within a noun phrase receives a case marker. Case can then be considered an agreement category, similar to gender and number. In other languages, case markers may go onto the last word of a noun phrase, as in Hungarian. Most case markers in Estonian appear on every word in a noun phrase. Some—including the instrumental -*ga*—go onto the last word of a noun phrase. This reflects the historical fact that this case marker only recently developed from a postposition meaning 'with'.

Nouns and other word classes, including pronouns, may have different case distinctions. This may serve to differentiate them: see Chapter 9.

6.5 Definiteness and specificity

DEFINITENESS implies reference to a uniquely identifiable individual or set of referents. A grammatical system 'DEFINITE' versus 'INDEFINITE' is found in a minority of
the world's languages, particularly in Romance and Germanic, and also in Hungarian
and Arabic. It is essentially a discourse category, relating to the predicate argument
fully specified by the referential information included in the NP. For instance, *the man
who lives next door* refers to the one man who does so. *The King of Spain* is unique. A
definite marker can also refer anaphorically to a participant already introduced in the
discourse. For example: *A snake came into our house. My brother screamed but then my
father killed the snake*—that is, the one that had come into our house.

The most straightforward way of marking definiteness is by articles; these often
combine information about definite/indefinite status with gender/noun class and
number. In some languages, for example English, they correlate with the division of
nouns into countable and uncountable. Note that the definite article in English is used
for both singular and plural. The indefinite article *a(n)* cannot be used with plural
nouns; it may sometimes be replaced with *some* if a noun is plural. In English, the definite article *the* can be used in a generic sense, as in *I dislike the bagpipes*. So can the
indefinite *a(n)* and the plural form; but the implications are different:

(6.26a)   The fox is a cunning animal—comparing the prototypical fox to other animals
(6.26b)   A fox is a cunning animal—any unspecified member of the set of foxes
(6.26c)   Foxes are cunning animals—the whole class

The definite member of a definiteness system has often developed from a deictic, or
a third person pronoun (as in Nama, a Khoisan language). Conversely, the indefinite
article often develops from the number word 'one'.

There can be inherently definite nouns (e.g. possessed nouns; proper names, personal and other pronouns) and inherently indefinite nouns (e.g. generic nouns like
'thing', or 'people').

Overt noun class marking on a noun can signal its definiteness. In Gola, a West
Atlantic language, class-marking prefixes and suffixes act similarly to definite articles. An indefinite noun is unmarked for noun class, for example *gbalia* 'a dwarf
antelope', and a definite noun is marked with a noun class, by means of a prefix and a
suffix, for example *o-gbalia-a* 'the dwarf antelope'. In the Australian languages Nung-
gubuyu and Warray the presence of a noun class prefix on a noun is correlated with
definiteness or givenness, and its absence indicates focus and foregrounding. Noun
classifiers function similarly to markers of definiteness. A noun is usually introduced
with the indefinite marker (homophonous with the number word 'one'), or without
a classifier. Noun classifiers may be used when it is mentioned for the second time.
Numerous Uralic languages have different cross-referencing paradigms for indicative

verbs depending on definiteness and topical continuity of the O. Definite and specific nouns hardly ever undergo incorporation, while nouns with non-specific and generic reference do.

Objects or individuals may be specific or generic. In Longgu, an Oceanic language, a noun with a specific referent is marked by a singular clitic =*i* or the plural clitic =*gi*. Nouns with generic reference are not marked. In Tariana and Tucano specific objects in non-subject role take an overt case marker.

In many Oceanic languages noun markers are sometimes misleadingly called 'articles'. In Boumaa Fijian, *a* is used with a common noun, and *o* with personal names, place names and pronouns, for example *a 'oro* (NOUN.MARKER:COMMON.NOUN village) 'a/the village', *o Waitabu* (NOUN.MARKER:PROPER.NOUN Waitabu) 'Waitabu (name of a village)'. These markers bear no relation to definiteness or specificity. They help mark the boundaries of a noun phrase.

6.6 Making new nouns: derivation and compounding

A new noun can be derived from a member of another word class. Such 'word class changing derivations' include forming nouns from verbs, or deverbal nominalizations. Nominalizations can describe an activity or result of the verb, for example English *development* from *to develop* or Estonian *kirjuta-mine* 'writing' from *kirjuta-ma* 'to write'. Or they can represent a core or a peripheral argument of the verb. English *payment* is an object nominalization of *to pay*, and *employ-er* is an agent nominalization of *employ*. In English, nouns can also be formed from adjectives, for example *nicety* from *nice*. This is deadjectivization.

A noun can be derived from another noun. Typical 'non-word class-changing derivations' include diminutives and augmentatives. Diminutives refer to small objects or people (often with overtones of endearment), for example Portuguese *menina* 'girl', *menininha* 'small girl, girlie'. Augmentatives are in a sense the opposite of diminutives: they refer to bigger objects, for example Portuguese *casa* 'house', *casarão* 'big house'. An augmentative may have pejorative overtones: in Spanish, an augmentative *perrazo* may mean 'a big dog' or 'a mean, nasty dog' (formed from *perro* 'dog'). There may be special evaluative markers. Tariana has a pejorative suffix -*yana*, and augmentative -*pasi* with no overtones of value. One can say *tsinu-pasi-yana* (dog-AUGMENTATIVE-PEJORATIVE) 'a big mean dog'. English has a wide variety of nominal derivational affixes, a number of them with a negative meaning, for example *non-* as in *non-entity* or *non-smoker*, *mal-* as in *mal-practice*, and *counter-* as in *counter-example*.

Compounding involves forming a new grammatical word by combination of at least two nouns, for example English *fox-hunting*, *station-master*, or German *Brief-kasten-schlüssel* 'letter box key'. Compounds form one phonological word in English. They are stressed on the first of two elements, *bláckbird* 'a type of bird known as *turdus merula*' as opposed to *bláck bírd* 'any bird which is black'. In contrast, in Boumaa Fijian, parts of compounds are independent phonological words, for example *cagi.laba* 'cyclone', lit. 'murdering wind', from *cagi* 'wind' and *laba* 'murder'.

Compounds fall into a number of subtypes.

I. ENDOCENTRIC compounds denote items referred to by one of their components. For instance, Estonian *vana-linn* 'old town, downtown' is a kind of town, and English *boathouse* is a kind of house.

The semantic relationship between the components of endocentric compounds can be of a genitive or part–whole type, for example English *soap-dish* 'dish for soap' or Estonian *sõja-vägi* (war:GENITIVE-force) 'military force, army' (lit. force of war). Or one may modify the other, for example English *black-bird*, Sanskrit *mahā-rāja(-)* (big-king) 'great king'.

II. EXOCENTRIC compounds denote something which is different from either of their components. Portuguese *quebra-cabeça*, literally 'break head', refers to a puzzle, or a cross-word, and not to a kind of breaking, or a kind of head. Similar examples are English *egghead* 'a type of intellectual' or *bottleneck* 'a narrow place at which the flow of production is constricted; an impasse': none of these can be reduced to any one of its components.

The Sanskrit term 'bahuvrīhi' (lit. 'the one who has a lot of rice') is used to describe exocentric compounds which refer to a person, or an object with a quality described by a compound; thus *Snow-white* is someone who is white as snow, and English *bird-brain* 'stupid person' is someone who (metaphorically) has a brain no bigger than that of a bird.

III. COORDINATE compounds (known by the Sanskrit term 'dvandva', lit. 'two and two') consist of two juxtaposed nouns which refer to a unitary concept, for example English *bitter-sweet, actor-manager.*

IV. SYNTHETIC compounds consist of a verbal root with its argument, typically direct object (O), for example Portuguese *lava-louça* 'dish-washer', English *dish-washer*, or intransitive subject (S), for example English *snow-fall.*

V. ALLITERATIVE compounds are a special, and understudied, type, for example English *mish-mash, chit-chat, argie-bargie* or Manambu *sawle-pawle* 'great quantity'.

Compounding is especially prevalent in isolating languages, such as Vietnamese (which have few if any bound morphemes).

Nouns may have further categories. In many synthetic languages from South America and Australia, a noun can have a special marking for tense and information source. This is independent from tense or information source on the verb, or in a clause. In (6.27), from Tariana, 'wife' is marked for nominal future (since we are talking about a future wife). The verb is marked for past:

(6.27)   di-sado-pena   aĩse   du-yã-pidana
         3sg.nf-wide-NOMINAL.FUTURE   there   3sg.fem-live-REM.PAST.REPORTED
         'His future wife was reported to live there'

In Chapter 7, we return to the expression of tense, aspect, and information source in general.

6.7 Unravelling a noun phrase

A noun phrase (NP) can be a core, or a peripheral argument in a clause. An NP can consist of just a noun, or contain modifiers to the nouns as its head. The head of an NP is a grammatical word which may stand for the whole NP, or dictates its properties to the non-head components. We saw in §6.1.1 how the gender of a noun may determine the form of adjectives and other modifiers in an NP. Gender and number agreement are powerful means of determining what is the head.

The first thing to determine is what kinds of heads noun phrases can have. Besides nouns, heads may include pronouns, and adjectives. Nouns themselves may be complex in their structure. Derivational markers usually come closer to the noun's stem or root than inflectional ones (see Table 3.2). Case suffixes usually come last after number and gender. And some categories, such as number, may have to be marked more than once. In example (6.28), from Tariana, the noun 'my hand' contains two noun classifiers followed by a plural marker, an augmentative suffix also followed by a plural marker, and then a locative case marker:

(6.28)   di-kapi-da-ma-pe-pasi-pe-se
         3sg.nf-hand-CL:ROUND-CL:SIDE-PL-AUG-PL-LOC
         'in the sides of the round part of his huge hands'

The structure of a noun in a synthetic language like Tariana needs to be addressed before the NP structure. Classification of NPs is the next issue. This can be done based on type of head, type of modifier, and type of relationship between two or more nouns in an NP.

An NP consists of a head accompanied by modifiers. These can precede the head (pre-head modifiers) or follow it (post-head modifiers). Modifiers typically include one or more adjectives, demonstratives, quantifiers, or number words, and also relative clauses. Nouns can modify other nouns but the choice of nouns which can act as modifiers tends to be limited. In many languages, only human nouns can be modifiers within an NP, as in Portuguese *filho homem* (son man) 'son, male child' and *filha mulher* (daughter woman) 'daughter, female child'. A possessive NP involves one noun being the owner, or whole, and the other being owned, or part, as in *John's shoes* or *John's nose*.

> 1 Noun marker or 'article'
> 2 Number word or quantifier
>
> **HEAD**
>
> 3 Adjectival modifier
> 4 Demonstrative modifier

FIGURE 6.1 Structure of an NP in Longgu.

In many Oceanic languages, an NP is recognizable by a noun marker. In Boumaa Fijian a common noun is signalled by the marker *a* and a proper noun by *o*, sometimes misleadingly called 'articles'. Articles in Germanic and Romance languages also mark an NP; additionally, they reflect definiteness and specificity of the head noun (see §9.3).

Oceanic-style noun phrase markers and European articles occur on the periphery of an NP, and may be followed or preceded by other modifiers. Demonstratives also tend to occur towards the NP's edges. The structure of an NP can be represented schematically, in terms of the ideal order of its components. Figure 6.1 offers an example of a typical NP structure in Longgu. The Noun phrase with a common noun as head can contain up to two pre-head modifiers, and two post-head modifiers:

The order of words within an NP can be fixed, as in Longgu. Or it can be free, as in Dyirbal or Latin. Components of an NP may have to occur together. In some languages, we encounter split NPs where a modifier and the head do not appear next to each other. *Inaru matʃia-ma* (woman beautiful-NOUN.CLASS:FEMININE) in Tariana is an NP meaning 'beautiful woman'. In (6.29), the head and the modifying adjective are separated by the verb.

(6.29)   inaru   nu-keta-ka   matʃa-ma
         woman   1sg-meet/find-RECENT.PAST.VISUAL   beautiful-NOUN.CLASS:FEMININE
         'I found a beautiful woman'

'Woman' and 'beautiful' form one NP because 'woman' triggers noun class agreement on the adjective. Properties of an NP help us determine its unity as a constituent (see Chapter 3). Splitting an NP in Tariana is a way of focusing on the modifier: in this instance, the fact that the woman was 'beautiful' was new and important to the speaker. Discourse parameters which determine the order of words within an NP, and the conditions under which it may become discontinuous, can be discussed in the chapter on nouns, or in a later chapter dealing with discourse structure.

6.8 Summing up

Grammatical categories of nouns can be discussed in one chapter, or split across a number of chapters, as the grammarian judges appropriate. Let's recapitulate a number of points which have to be covered, for each of the categories discussed here.

With regard to the REFERENCE CLASSIFICATION OF NOUNS, it is important to state if the language has genders (sometimes called 'noun classes') or classifiers (numeral, noun, possessive, verbal, or other types). With regard to genders, one needs to say how many genders there are, and how they are realized. It is important to say where agreement is shown, and whether marking is covert or overt. Extensive comment on the meanings of genders, and their assignment is de rigeur. We need to know if gender assignment is variable, or whether every noun has one fixed gender. The expression of gender may depend on other categories, for example number, of the noun, and this needs to be stated as appropriate.

If the language has noun classifiers, it is important to say how many there are, what meanings they express, and under what conditions they can be omitted (if at all). The same questions need to be addressed for numeral classifiers. It is also important to state whether they are used with all number words, or just with some, and with quantifiers, and whether the language distinguishes between sortal and mensural classifiers.

If the language has classifiers in possessive constructions, important points include: potential differences between relational and possessive classifiers, and the meanings expressed with classifiers. Classifiers may correlate with possession classes of nouns, and if so, this should be addressed. If the language has verbal classifiers, it is important to say how many there are, how they are expressed (that is, through affixes, or suppletive verbs), and what their meanings are.

With regard to NUMBER, one needs to state how many terms there are in the number system. It is important to investigate whether number is marked on nouns, adjectives, pronouns, verbs, and other contexts. If language has number agreement, one needs to show if it is obligatory. It is important to address the meanings of each term in the number system, whether the language has associative or distributive plural, and whether the expression of number correlates with other categories, such as gender and case.

With regard to POSSESSION CLASSES OF NOUNS, we need to focus on how possessive relationships are marked (by apposition, or a special marker on possessor or possessee, or in another way), and if there is a distinction between inalienably and alienably possessed nouns. It is important to mention what the head of the possessive construction is, how ownership, kinship and part–whole are expressed, and whether possessive constructions have any other meanings.

With regard to CASE, it is important to state whether cases are used for marking core and peripheral participants, how the cases are marked, where they appear in a noun phrase, and what their meanings are. A further important point is whether all word classes which occur with case markers have the same case distinctions.

With regard to DEFINITENESS and SPECIFICITY, it is important to state whether there is any special marking for each of these, and if so, whether nouns with inherently definite, or inherently generic, meanings occur with these markers.

With regard to MAKING NEW NOUNS, it is important to outline word class changing derivations (e.g. verbs from nouns and nouns from verbs) and their meanings, and then the non-word class-changing derivations, focusing on their meanings. If language has nominal compounding, one needs to state what types of compounds are attested, whether or not compounds form one grammatical and one phonological word.

A statement of the NOUN PHRASE STRUCTURE needs to address the order of components within it, types of 'head' that an NP can have (nouns, pronouns, demonstratives, etc.), types of modifiers and the criteria for determining the head of an NP. It is interesting to know if an NP can be split, and what the motivations could be for changing the order within an NP, or for splitting an NP.

Notes and sources

§6.1.1: On the history of the notion of 'gender', see Aikhenvald (2000, 2004c, 2006b), and Dixon (forthcoming); on shape in gender systems see Aikhenvald (2013b). An earlier discussion of genders in a limited number of languages is in Corbett (1991). See Newman (2000: 200–15) on Hausa; Ashton (1947) on Swahili; Dixon (1972: 308–12, 2014) on Dyirbal. There are a few languages with two gender-like agreement systems, one marking masculine and feminine, and the other one having different semantic distinctions. It is then convenient to use the term 'gender' for the first system, and the term 'noun class' for the second one: see Aikhenvald (2000: 67–76, 2009) on Paumarí and other languages, and Aikhenvald (2012a: 280–5) on Amazonian languages in general.

§6.1.2: See Dixon (1982: 185) on Yidiñ; Marnita (1996) on Minangkabau.

§6.1.3: See Beckwith (1998) on Uzbek; Berlin (1968: 175) on Tzeltal.

§6.1.4: See Jauncey (2011: 207–9) on Tamambo; see Lichtenberk (1983a), Aikhenvald (2000) on relational classifiers, and further references in Aikhenvald (2012a).

§6.1.5: See Brown (1981: 96) on Waris; Rushforth (1991) on Mescalero Apache; Aikhenvald (2000) on other, minor, types of classifiers.

§6.1.6: For an overall justification for the continuum of noun categorization devices, see Aikhenvald (2000, 2006b); dependencies between grammatical systems (including number and gender) are in Aikhenvald and Dixon (2011b); see Becker (1975: 113), on Burmese.

§6.2: See Lichtenberk (1983b: 267) on Manam; see Reid (1990: 118–19) on Ngan'gityemerri; Evans (1994) on Fula (or Pular); Cowell (1964: 297–302, 369) and Corbett (2000: 32) on Syrian Arabic; Aikhenvald (1998) on Warekena; Dixon (1988: 52–3) on Boumaa Fijian; Dixon (1972, 2012: 52) on Dyirbal; Dimmendaal (2000) on Nilotic; Kimball (1991: 403) on Koasati; Mithun (1999: 94) on Central Alaskan Yup'ik. Moravcsik (2003) contains an in-depth analysis of associative plurals and their meanings. See Coates (2003: 33–4), Brown and Levinson (1987: 198–9), and Aikhenvald (2010: 219–223) on plural as exponent of politeness.

§6.3: For further information and references on possession, see Chapter 16 of Dixon (2010b), and Aikhenvald (2012a); Luo (2013) on Mandarin Chinese; Bril (2013: 75) on Nêlêmwa, Dixon (2010b: 284–5) on Dyirbal; Abbott (1991: 86–7) on Macushi. Many Polynesian languages distinguish controlled and uncontrolled possession (a summary is in Aikhenvald 2012a: 18–19).

§6.4: Blake (2001) is a basic source on case and additional problems of how to distinguish a case from an adposition; see Dixon (2010a: 128, 188) on Dyirbal; Viitso (2007: 33) on Estonian.

§6.5: See Dixon (2011) on English, Heine and Kuteva (2002) on the development of articles from deictics, Hill (1992: 220–1) on Longgu, Dixon (1988: 35–6) on Boumaa Fijian. See Aikhenvald (2000: 320–33) for correlations between definiteness, noun classes, and classifiers; Abondolo (1998) discusses definite and indefinite declensions in Uralic languages.

§6.6: On derivation and compounds, see Bloomfield (1933: 180), Marchand (1969: 13–14), Dixon (2014), Aikhenvald (2011a, 2007b) and references in the latter; Grandi (2002), on diminutives and augmentatives and their meanings to do with value; Dixon (1988: 226) on Boumaa Fijian; see Nordlinger and Sadler (2004), Aikhenvald (2012a: 158–63) on nominal tense, aspect and evidentiality.

§6.7: See Hill (1992: 200) on Longgu; Aikhenvald (2003: 479–82) on split NPs in Tariana. Note that the form *matʃa-ma* (beautiful-NOUN.CLASS:FEMININE) in (6.29) cannot be considered as an independent predication because it does not have the tense-evidentiality specifications necessary for a clausal predicate.

7

Verbs

In the majority of the world's languages, verbs form a large open word class. The verb is often the only obligatory element in a clause. Its syntactic function is to head the clausal predicate. Verbs fall into several transitivity classes, depending on the number of arguments they require (see §5.5.1). Other grammatical subclasses of verbs may include verbs of perception, stance and motion, and copula verbs (see §5.5.2). Person, number, and gender of arguments, spatial setting, and a set of categories under the umbrella of non-spatial setting are typically associated with the verb. Non-spatial setting includes tense, aspect, mood, modality, reality status, and evidentiality. Valency-changing derivations and noun incorporation are also characteristic of verbs.

Special verb forms may occur only in non-main clauses: we turn to these in Chapter 12. Categories expressed within the verb—especially non-spatial setting—have the whole clause as their scope. They can be referred to as clausal. Negation (or polarity) also has clausal scope, and is intertwined with types of clauses. In many languages clausal negation is marked on the verb—see Chapter 11.

A verbal predicate may contain two or more verbs. In synthetic languages, categories associated with the verb are coded within one verbal word. In languages with a more analytic profile, some of the categories may be expressed through independent words modifying the head verb of a verb phrase. In the last section, we look at the order of components within the verbal word and the verbal predicate.

7.1 What may go onto a verb

A verb tends to be the most versatile part of the grammar. Grammatical information coded within the verb, or the verb phrase, may include core participants. A most common technique is through bound personal pronouns (also known as cross-referencing markers). These may occur on the verb itself, as affixes, or within a verb phrase. Bound pronouns may refer to 'subject' (A/S). In Latin, they combine information about the number, and the person of the intransitive subject (S), as in (7.1), and the transitive subject (A), as in (7.2). Latin is a fusional language, and the information on the person, the number, and the tense is fused into one suffix:

(7.1)   Cant-o
        sing-1sgPRESENT
        'I sing, I am singing'

(7.2)   Ama-t   vir   puellam
        love-3sgPRESENT   man:NOM.SG   girl:ACC.SG
        'A man loves a girl'

Bound pronouns in Manambu refer to the A and S of the verb. There is an additional set that refers to the O. Gender of the A, S, and O is expressed separately, also with a suffix:

(7.3)   ya-l-wun
        come-feminine(S)-1sgS
        'I (woman) come, am coming'

(7.4)   və-l-wun-a-də-mən
        see-feminine(A)-1sgA-LK-masculine(O)-2sg.mascO
        'I (woman) see you (man)'

These are examples of a nominative-accusative system (see §3.9). In absolutive-ergative systems, bound pronouns may refer just to A (transitive subject). In Paumarí, an Arawá language from Brazil, pronominal prefix *bi-* refers to the third person A, the transitive subject. There is no special bound pronoun for objects.

(7.5)   kaba'i amakari(-a)$_A$ bi-noki-'i-hi   ida   ojoro
        then   monkey(m)-ERG   3sg.tr-see-ASP-THf this.fem.sg turtle
        'Then the monkey saw this turtle'

In Basque, the S is cross-referenced on an intransitive verb, as in (7.6):

(7.6)   n-ator
        1sg-come
        'I come, I am coming'

A transitive verb contains bound pronouns referring to A and to O:

(7.7)   d-akar-t
        3sgO-bring-1sgA
        'I bring it'

If a clause contains an E (for instance, a recipient), this can also be cross-referenced. This is done through a combination of prefixes and suffixes:

(7.8)   d-akar-ki-zu-t
3sgO-bring-LINKER-2sgA-1sgDAT
'You bring it to me'

In Chapter 10 we consider further intricacies of marking grammatical relations, A, S, and O.

We can recall that the verb in Swahili bears the noun class agreement prefix determined by its subject (A or S): we saw this in examples (6.1)–(6.2). In (7.5), from Paumarí, the O, 'turtle', is feminine; and this is reflected in the feminine form of the final thematic marker. Gender/noun class, number, and person can be considered verbal agreement categories.

All the languages cited here also have independent free personal pronouns. These can be added—often if the participant has to be emphasized or focused on. Free, and bound, personal pronouns may have somewhat different forms and different categories. In Tariana, a free personal pronoun consists of a combination of bound personal pronominal prefix with the suffix *-ha*, for example *nu-hpani* (1sg-work) 'I am working', *nu-ha* 'I'. Bound pronouns distinguish genders in third person singular only, and free pronouns also distinguish genders in all persons of the plural. We return to pronouns in Chapter 9.

Information on the participants signalled on the verb can be supplemented by a noun phrase. This is what we saw in (7.2), from Latin. The question of whether the marking on the verb is 'more important' than the noun phrase itself, or the other way round, bears upon surface realization rather than the underlying structure, and is somewhat futile. Interested readers can turn to Dixon (2010a: 39–40), for more discussion.

The number of participants can be shown on the verb. The suffix *-tu-* in Manambu means 'all'. It indicates that all S (as in 7.9) or all O (as in 7.10) took part in the activity:

(7.9)   du-taːkw   ata   vya-tu-d
man-woman   then   kill-ALL:O-3sg.masc
'Then he killed all the people (lit. man-woman)'

(7.10) du-taːkw   ata   gəpə-tu-di
man-woman   then   run-ALL:S-3pl
'Then all the people ran away'

The marking of verbal number may have non-spatial overtones of repetition and intensity of action. In Warekena, reduplication of the final CV syllable of a verb may refer to many S, for example *wa-wayata* (1pl-talk) 'we are talking', *wa-wayata-ta* 'we are talking as a large group', or many O, as in *nu-paka* (1sg-break) 'I broke (e.g. one glass)', *nu-paka-ka* 'I broke many (e.g. glasses)'. Reduplication can also imply intensity of action: *kuneta* means 'frighten', and *kuneta-ta* means 'frighten very much'. It can also refer to doing something many times and all over the place, as in *mita* 'fly', *mita-ta* 'fly to and fro, many times over'. This is the essence of 'pluractional' verbs—see §7.2.3.

The spatial setting of a clause is typically shown with oblique noun phrases and adverbs. In some languages, it is also shown on the verb. Meanings 'here' and 'there' in Filomeno Mata Totonac, from Mexico, are expressed on a verb, for example *či-ʼan* 'arrive here' and *ča-ʼan* 'arrive there'. Mam, a Mayan language from Guatemala, has twelve morphemes within the verb phrase which express direction and motion, for example away from, toward, down, up, returning from here, and passing.

Cavineña, a Tacana language from Bolivia, has eleven suffixes which combine reference to the orientation of motion ('towards' or 'away from' a reference point, the stability of motion target (temporary or permanent) and the location of the event. For instance, the suffix *-na-* means 'come temporarily', the suffix *-eti* means 'come permanently', *-diru-* means 'go permanently'. Further suffixes mark the spatial position of the subject: *iwa* means 'wait', *iwa-jara* means 'wait in a horizontal position', while *iwa-bade* means 'wait in a hanging position'.

Meanings covering direction, position, and motion of action are sometimes covered by the term 'Aktionsart'. More on this in the next section.

7.2 Non-spatial setting and speech acts

In most languages of the world, verbs or verb phrases code a plethora of non-spatial parameters. These include mood (§7.2.1), tense (§7.2.2), aspect and various facets of the structure of activity (§7.2.3), modality (§7.2.4), evidentiality (§7.2.5), and reality status (§7.2.6). Their expression can be fused into one morpheme. Their meanings and realization interrelate with one another. For example, the meanings of a present tense may overlap with progressive aspect, and past tense may have perfective overtones. The meanings and expression of non-spatial setting are sometimes concisely referred to as the TAM (tense–aspect–modality), or TAME (tense–aspect–modality–evidentiality) complex.

7.2.1 Moods, speech acts, and sentence types

In every language one can make a statement, ask a question, or tell someone else what to do. These communicative tasks have special grammatical structures reserved for them. A typical form of a statement is declarative, that of a question is interrogative, and that of a command, advice, good wish, and entreaty is imperative. In some languages, each of these may have a special syntactic construction. In others, there may be a special particle or an affix marking a speech act type.

These three major speech acts are conventionally referred to as 'mood'. We have:

- a *statement*, characterized by *declarative mood* (also called *indicative mood*);
- a *command*, characterized by *imperative mood*;
- a *question*, characterized by *interrogative mood*.

Speech acts correspond to three sentence types. The declarative mood, or sentence type, is the default one, and often bears no special marking. An interrogative mood marker occurs for questions in only a few languages. One example is West Greenlandic: here, every question is marked with a special suffix on verbs. Interrogative sentences in many languages are marked with question words—more on these in Chapter 11.

For many linguists, language learners, and language teachers, 'imperative' implies just a command to a second person. These 'canonical' imperatives are central to the paradigm of imperative forms in every language. However, commanding expressions can be addressed to someone other than 'addressee'. These 'noncanonical imperatives' include commands directed to first person 'me', or 'us' which may also be referred to as 'hortatives', and commands to third person which may also be called 'jussives'.

A canonical imperative form can bear a special affix, or a clitic. In Yidiñ, the imperative verb appears marked with -*n*, as in (7.11):

(7.11) ŋanda wiwi-n   waŋal
        I:DAT   give-IMPV   boomerang:ABS
        '(You) give me (your) boomerang!'

A bare root or stem of the verb can be used as a canonical imperative. One of the shortest words in Latin is a canonical imperative, *i!* 'go!', from the verb *īre* 'to go'. The second person singular imperative regularly coincides with the stem of the verb. So, from *amāre* 'to love' one forms the second person singular imperative *amā!* 'love!', and from *audīre* 'to listen', *audī!* 'listen!'. That is, compared to second person declarative *amas* 'you (sg) love' and *dicis* 'you (sg) say', imperatives appear impoverished—they bear no overt expression of person or tense. The English imperative also bears no markers of person or tense. A personal pronoun is obligatory in a statement in English, but is normally omitted in an imperative, for example *Sit! Go!* But adding a pronoun to an English imperative has stylistic effects. *You sit!* usually implies a stern order with the 'commander' asserting their authority.

The imperative form used for a second person singular addressee tends to be the least formally marked. The forms employed for non-singular (plural, dual, or paucal) addressee can involve a special number marker. Typically, fewer verbal categories are expressed in imperatives than in declaratives. Imperatives may vary in terms of their degrees of politeness. There is usually a special intonation contour; and they may be accompanied by an eye-gaze.

Imperatives have their own spatial and non-spatial setting. Their special categories include distance in space, roughly translatable as 'do here' versus 'do there'. Imperatives tend to be oriented towards the future. A few languages distinguish 'immediate imperative' and 'future imperative', that is, 'do now' and 'do later on'. Tariana has separate forms for distance in space used just in imperatives: (7.12a) and (7.12b) illustrate a 'proximal' and a 'distal' imperative:

(7.12a)   pi-hña-si
          2sg-eat-PROXIMATE.IMPERATIVE
          'Eat here (close to the speaker)!'

(7.12b)   pi-hña-kada
          2sg-eat-DISTAL.IMPERATIVE
          'Eat there (far from the speaker)!'

Distance in time is marked with a different suffix:

(7.12c)   pi-hña-wa
          2sg-eat-FUTURE.IMPERATIVE
          'Eat (later)!'

These meanings are especially frequent in North and South American Indian languages, and a few languages from the New Guinea Highlands. Imperatives often have their own means of negation. Not every language has distinct imperative forms; but in every language one can express a command, an order, or a request. Non-imperative forms are then used, as 'command strategies'. Deploying non-imperative forms in lieu of the imperative itself may serve various pragmatic purposes: the imperative may sound too brusque. Saying *Could you pass the salt* in English is a way of phrasing a polite request, and will not be understood as a question by anyone who knows the language well. Imperatives and their use often reflect relationships within the society where the language is spoken; more on this in Chapter 14.

7.2.2 Tense

Every language has a way of talking about the time of an event, or of a state. There is typically a set of lexical items which refer to location in time, for example 'yesterday', 'today', and so on. 'Tense' refers to a closed set of grammaticalized expressions of location in time. Grammatical tense may involve present, past, and future. So, in Lithuanian we have present (*dirb-u* 'I work, I am working'), past (*dirb-au* 'I worked, I was working') and future (*dirb-siu* 'I will work, I will be working'). Many languages distinguish just two terms. One possibility is past versus non-past (which covers future and present), as in Estonian *armasta-n* (love-1sg) 'I love, I will love' and *armasta-si-n* (love-PAST-1sg) 'I loved'. No language distinguishes present versus non-present in its system of grammatical tense.

Many languages have several tense forms for the past. Tucanoan languages from Brazil distinguish recent past and remote past. Yimas, from New Guinea, has four past tenses:

- the near past, marking events which occurred yesterday,
- the far past, covering past events from the day before yesterday to a year or even a few years ago,
- the remote past, which may refer to events at least five days removed from today, and more distant events, if they are not 'vivid to the narrator', and
- the perfective, which marks events 'which have already occurred and been completed during today, including last night'.

There are, in addition, two future forms—the near future 'covers events expected to happen tomorrow', and the remote future refers to what will happen from the day after tomorrow into the indefinite future.

We can recall from Chapter 1 that Amele, a Gum language from Papua New Guinea, has four verbal tense forms: (i) today's past, (ii) yesterday's past, (iii) remote past (what happened before yesterday), and (iv) habitual past—something that often occurred in past time. Two future forms include the 'absolute' future describing an event to happen in future time, and the 'relative' future for an event which is about to happen.

We can thus see that the exact time span covered by a tense is language specific. And the choice of a tense may well depend on a speaker's perspective, and their attitude to the event they are talking about.

No language has more tense distinctions in the future than in the past. The full tense system is usually expressed in declarative clauses. Imperatives may have their own tense distinctions, typically, immediate versus remote future.

In some languages, tense marking is optional. Tense in Boumaa Fijian is not expressed at all if a statement is generic or timeless. Tense can be absolute and reflect the time of speech. Or it can be relative, and adjusted to the tense in which the rest of a sentence or a narrative is cast. Relative tense is especially visible in non-main clauses whose tense marking may have to be adjusted to that of the main clause. The so-called sequence of tenses in Standard English is a prime example. Suppose John said 'I will come tomorrow'. This can be rendered as indirect speech, by *John said that he would come tomorrow* using a special future-in-the past. Saying **John said that he will come tomorrow* is not grammatical.

A number of languages do not have grammatical tense. Various facets of the internal composition of the action, or aspects, or reality status have to be marked instead. In the Lolovoli dialect of North-east Ambae, the realis forms cover past, present, and definite future; and the irrealis forms refer to any future. Numerous markers specify various facets of the action. For instance, *u* 'telic aspect' indicates that a past event has an endpoint, and *bei* 'just, for the first time' indicates that the event has just occurred in the recent past. Toqabaqita, another Oceanic language, has an array of preverbal particles whose meanings include immediacy (covering immediate past or immediate future), completion, anteriority, and many others—but no tense. Lexical time words can be used to specify when the event happened, if necessary.

'Present' tense is enigmatic and elusive. As Dixon (2012: 13) put it: 'present time is but a moment, yet only an event with duration can properly be described as "present"'. What is traditionally called 'present' in English has habitual, or generic, overtones. *I get up late* refers to what I usually do. And if I need to say what I am doing right now, I will use a so-called progressive form, *I am getting up*. The future does not relate just to time. Any statement about the future may have overtones of possibility, probability, and prediction. In many languages, future can be considered a kind of modality—we turn to these in §7.2.4.

7.2.3 Aspect, and the structure of activity

Verbal aspect reflects the grammatical representation of the internal structure and composition of activity. In its narrow definition, the basic aspectual opposition is between PERFECTIVE and IMPERFECTIVE aspect. Perfective aspect implies that the event is regarded as a whole, without any account of its temporal constituency or composition. Imperfective aspect makes explicit reference to the internal temporal constituency of the event. Aspectual systems are salient in Balto-Slavic languages, and in Greek. Perfective and imperfective aspect are contrasted in 7.13, from Russian:

(7.13)   Kogda ja voshel   v   komnatu,
         when   I come.PERFECTIVE.PAST.masc.sg   into room:ACC.SG
         otec   chital
         father   read.IMPERFECTIVE.PAST.masc.sg
         'When I came into the room, father was reading'

The verb in the first clause presents the situation in its totality with no reference to its temporal organization. The verb in the second clause indicates an action taking place over a certain period of time which both preceded and followed my entering the room.

In a broader perspective, 'aspect' is used to capture a number of further parameters. COMPLETION of activity involves the opposition between perfect and imperfect. Perfect refers to an activity completed before the present time, which still has relevance to it. Imperfect refers to an activity which began before the moment of speech and is still continuing. The perfect aspect suffix -*wa* in Cavineña refers to an action completed in the immediate past; and the imperfect suffix -*ya* marks on-going and habitual actions (in the past, present or near future). Perfect aspect can also be termed completive. Imperfect can be referred to as incomplete, continuative, on-going, or progressive. the continuative aspect in Chamorro indicates that an action is continuing, 'or at least is not completed', for example *sásaga* 'be staying' as opposed to the unmarked aspect *saga* 'stay'.

In terms of its temporal extent, an action can be PUNCTUAL: then, the activity takes place once for a brief moment. Or it can be DURATIVE. Then the activity lasts over a longer time period. TELICITY, or boundedness, is a further facet of representation of activity. An activity is telic when it has a specific endpoint, and atelic when it does not. Perfect aspect has telic overtones; and imperfect, durative, and progressive aspects tend to be atelic. The telic aspect in the Lolovoli dialect of North-east Ambae describes an event in the past which has reached its endpoint.

An activity can be viewed with respect to its FREQUENCY. Amele has a habitual aspect, which describes a situation that used to be characteristic of an extended period of time, for example *nuo-lo-i* (go-HABITUAL-3sg) 'he used to go'. The iterative aspect in Amele describes successive occurrence of several instances of the same activity, and is expressed via reduplication, for example *qu-qu* (REDUPLICATION:ITERATIVE-hit) 'hit many times'.

DEGREE of activity may acquire special marking. Kolyma Yukaghir, a Paleo-Siberian isolate, has the suffix *-s'ī* 'slightly, shortly, a little bit', for example *morie-* 'wear', *morie-s'ī-* 'wear for a short time, just a little bit'. Three preverbal markers in Toqabaqita express low degree, or low intensity of an activity. Degree markers on the verb in West Greenlandic include *-alug* 'rather, a bit', *-ngajag* 'almost', *-(r)piar* 'really/exactly', *-qqar* 'barely', *-qqinnar-* 'exactly', and *-rujug-* 'a little'.

A further parameter in the non-spatial setting indicates the PHASE of activity—whether it is beginning, continuing, or finishing. Kolyma Yukaghir has an inchoative suffix meaning 'begin', for example *leg-* 'eat', *leg-ie-* 'begin to eat'. West Greendlandic has an inchoative suffix *-lir-* 'begin' and a terminative suffix *-junnar-* meaning 'finish'.

One non-spatial marker can cover a number of meanings. The suffix *-ja-* in Dyirbal can indicate 'many S' in an intransitive clause, or 'many O' in a transitive clause. *Banin-ja-ñu* (come-many(s)-PAST) means 'many (people or animals) came', and *gundal-ja-ñu* (put.in-many(o)-PAST) means that the man (A) put many objects (into his bag). The same suffix *-ja-* can indicate that the action was repeated: *ŋandan-ja-ñu* (called-REPEATED-PAST) means '(he) called out many times in many directions'. The term 'pluractional' describes polysemous forms which may refer to a multiplicity of objects, subjects, and repetition and even intensity of activity (as in Warekena, in §7.1).

Telicity, phase, duration, and completion may interrelate with the meanings of the verb itself. In Kolyma Yukaghir, inchoative marking usually applies to verbs which denote processes and atelic situations. Perfective aspect in Slavic languages often has overtones of telicity and completion, depending on the meaning of the verb.

Further non-spatial meanings on the verb may include speed. Dyirbal has a suffix *-nbal ~ -galiy* 'do it quickly'. The marker of 'velocity' in Urarina, *-uri*, means 'do it quickly' and is also used as a marker of politeness in commands. West Greenlandic has special suffixes meaning 'be hard to VERB', 'be easy to VERB', and 'be good at

VERBing'. Bora uses a set of instrumental prefixes to the verb, for example *to-* 'do with the hand', *ti-* 'do with the teeth', *tʰa-* 'do with the foot', *kʰa-* 'do with something pointed', *kʰi-* 'do with some cutting tool', *pʰi-* 'do with something like a saw', and *kpa-* 'do by a series of blows'. A series of verbal clitics in Tariana describe manner of action, for example *-su* 'suddenly', *-khuli* 'by slipping away', *-holo* 'by spilling', and even a speaker's reaction to it, as in *-ñu* 'do by stepping on something and feeling sharp pain'. Elaborate sets of markers for non-spatial setting within the verb are a feature of highly synthetic languages across the world.

7.2.4 Modality, and attitude to knowledge

A further facet of non-spatial setting involves the actuality of the event in terms of its certainty, speakers' attitude towards its possibility, probability, and their obligation or ability to perform it. These meanings are captured under the label of 'modality'. An epistemic modality covers degree of certainty, as does the clitic *=ni* 'maybe' in Cavineña. Potential modality in Finnish (marked with the suffix *-ne-*) indicates probability, for example *Heikki ottanee sen* (Heikki take:POTENTIAL:3sg it:ACC) 'Heikki may (or can) take it'. The suffix *-hat/het-* in Hungarian may express possibility, permission, or ability: a form like *ír-hat* (write-POTENTIAL.3sg) may mean 'he can write', 'it is possible for him to write', 'he is allowed to write', and 'he is able to write'. West Greenlandic has several suffixes expressing obligation, for example *miri-niru-sariaqar-putit* (drink-more-MUST-2sgINDICATIVE) 'You must drink more!'. This is known as deontic modality.

Desiderative modality expresses the meaning of 'wanting', for example Manambu *ya-kər* (come-DESIDERATIVE) 'want to come'. Lakhota has three optative forms: one expresses 'probability of fulfilment of wish', another one expresses 'improbability of fulfilment', and a further one marks a wish which cannot be fulfilled. Intentional modality expresses the speaker's intention and planning, as in West Greenlandic *kati-ssamaar* (get married-INTENTIONAL) 'plan to get married'. The frustrative modality covers actions done 'in vain', that is, failing to achieve the result. Frustrative in Tariana is expressed through the suffix *-tha*. The form *nu-emhani-tha-na* (1sg-walk-FRUSTRATIVE-REMOTE.PAST.VISUAL) means 'I walked in vain'. This is a feature of a number of Amazonian, Australian, and New Guinea languages.

Other meanings relating to the speaker's attitude to information, and their reaction to it, can be included in the verb or the verb phrase. Urarina has a verbal clitic expressing 'warning', and another one expressing reassurance. The clitic *=shama* in Cavineña marks 'pity' a speaker may feel for someone. Quite a few languages have some grammatical marking of surprise, sudden discovery, or revelation. This is known as mirativity. Chechen, a North-east Caucasian language, has a 'mirative' suffix *-q* added to the verb if 'the situation is unexpected and surprising for the speaker'.

7.2.5 *Evidentiality*

In every language one can say HOW one knows what one is talking about. A quarter of the languages of the world have grammaticalized information source. They have 'evidentiality' as a grammatical category. In the same way as 'tense' refers to closed grammatical systems which grammaticalize the expression of time, 'grammatical evidentiality' refers to a closed set of obligatory choices of marking information source. The size of systems varies.

Many languages have just a marker for reported information—that is, what one knows from being told by someone else. In Língua Geral, a Tupí-Guaraní language of north-west Amazonia, adding a particle *paá* to a statement indicates that you got the information from hearsay, or from someone else. Quechua languages distinguish three information sources: direct evidence, conjecture, and report. Tariana has five evidentials marked on the verb. If I saw José play football, I will say 'José is playing-*naka*', using the visual evidential. If I heard the noise of the play (but didn't see it), I will say 'José is playing-*mahka*', using the non-visual. If all I see is that José's football boots are gone and so is the ball, I will say 'José is playing-*nihka*', using the inferential. If it is Sunday and José is not home, the thing to say is 'José is playing-*sika*' since my statement is based on the assumption and general knowledge that José usually plays football on Sundays. And if the information was reported to me by someone else, I will say 'José is playing-*pidaka*', using the reported marker. Omitting an evidential results in an ungrammatical and highly unnatural sentence.

Evidentiality does not bear any straightforward relationship to truth, the validity of a statement or the speaker's responsibility. The 'truth value' of an evidential may be different from that of the verb in its clause. Evidentials can be manipulated to tell a lie: one can give a correct information source and wrong information, as in saying 'He is dead-reported', when you were told that he is alive, or correct information and wrong information source, as in saying 'He is alive-visual', when in fact you were told that he is alive, but did not see this. The ways in which semantic extensions of evidentials overlap with modalities and such meanings as probability or possibility depend on the system, and on the semantics of each individual evidential. In many languages, including Quechua, Shipibo-Konibo, Tariana, and Abkhaz, markers of modality and of irrealis can occur in conjunction with evidentials on one verb or in one clause. This shows that these are all different categories.

The maximal number of evidentials is distinguished in statements. The only evidential possible in commands is reported, to express the command on behalf of someone else: 'eat-reported!' means 'eat following someone's command!'. The text's genre may determine the choice of an evidential. Traditional stories are typically cast in the reported evidential. Evidentials can be manipulated in discourse as a stylistic device. Switching from a reported to a direct (or visual) evidential may imply that the speaker had participated in the event, and is confident of what they are saying. Evidentiality is intertwined with conventionalized attitudes to information and precision in stating its source.

Every language has some lexical way of referring to an information source, for example English *reportedly* or *allegedly*. Such lexical expressions may become grammaticalized as evidential markers. Non-evidential categories may acquire a secondary meaning relating to information source. Conditionals and other non-declarative moods may acquire overtones of uncertain information obtained from some other source, for which the speaker does not take any responsibility. The best known example is the French conditional known as *conditionnel de l'information incertaine*. It is frequent in newspaper reports. For example, the sentence *la flotte britannique* **aurait quitté** *ce matin le port de Portsmouth* 'The British Navy would have left the port of Portsmouth this morning (we are told)' has the overtones of reported information relayed by the author of the statement. This interpretation is imparted to the sentence by the conditional form (in bold).

The choice of a complementizer, or a type of complement clause, may serve to express meanings related to how one knows a particular fact. In English, different complement clauses distinguish an auditory and a hearsay meaning of the verb *hear*: saying *I heard Brazil beating France* implies actually listening to a radio commentary. In contrast, *I heard that Brazil beat France* implies a verbal report of the result—that someone told me about this fact. These evidential-like extensions are known as 'evidentiality strategies'. Historically, they may give rise to grammatical evidentials.

7.2.6 Reality status

In many languages, an event or state can be marked for its 'reality status', as 'realis' or as 'irrealis'. Realis implies that the activity or state expressed by the verb is a fact, or something that has happened or is happening. 'Irrealis' is, in Edward Sapir's words (1930: 168), something 'unreal, i.e. either merely potential or contrary to the fact'. Irrealis may cover statements about future, and epistemic modalities. Both realis and irrealis may acquire a special marker. Alternatively, realis (but not irrealis) may be formally unmarked.

Realis in Terêna, an Arawak language from Brazil, appears in 'definite statements about the past, about things already taking place in the present, and in definite assertions about the future'. Irrealis is reserved for 'statements about events that have not started at the time of speaking'. This includes imperatives and assertions about something that may or could happen. So, *pih-a* (3sg+go-REALIS) means 'he went', *pih-o* (3sg+go-IRREALIS) means 'let him go' as a command to 'him'. Terêna does not have a tense system, just the realis/irrealis contrast. Manam, an Austronesian language from the Solomon Islands, also has a realis/irrealis distinction. Irrealis is used to mark commands, warnings, counterfactual, and hypothetical events.

Reality status may be independent of a tense system. Or it may interrelate with tense. Irrealis in Yimas co-exists with an intricate tense system. It refers to events 'located outside of the continuum of real time: they must be completely timeless, in the legendary past or in the indefinite future'.

The exact meanings of realis and of irrealis are not the same across languages. In Central Pomo and in Amele, commands are cast in irrealis (as may be expected). In Maricopa, a Yuman language, imperatives are marked as realis. Negated clauses in Jamul Tiipay, from the same family, are marked for irrealis. In Mesa Grande Diegueño, another Yuman language, they are cast in realis.

In some languages, including Tamambo and Manam, irrealis forms have habitual overtones. This usage echoes Brinton's (1988: 140–1) discussion of English aspectual categories, and her observation that 'habitual aspect has similarities to epistemic modality because a present habit is presumed to continue into the future; the statement of habit is a kind of prediction'.

7.3 Valency-changing derivations

In many languages, one can change the number of arguments of the verb (or its valency), or rearrange them. These processes are typically marked by an affix on the verb, or by a periphrastic multi-verb construction (see §7.6). They form a 'voice' system.

7.3.1 Reducing valency

A core argument may be removed from a transitive clause, which then becomes intransitive. PASSIVES and ANTIPASSIVES are the two common valency reducing derivations. Passive forms and passive constructions are a familiar feature of European languages. In English, one can say *The dog bit the child*, using an active construction, or 'active' voice. This can be made into a passive construction, *The child was bitten* (*by the dog*). This construction is a complex predicate with an auxiliary. It allows us to focus on the child—which was the O of an active clause, and is now the S of the passive one. It also offers an option of not mentioning the culprit, the dog: this is now an oblique 'extra', 'demoted' from being the A of a transitive active clause. Box 7.1 summarizes the criterial features of a passive.

Box 7.1 How to recognize a passive

A passive has the following features:

    (i) it applies to an underlying transitive clause and forms a derived intransitive;

   (ii) the former O becomes S of the passive;

  (iii) the former A argument goes into a peripheral function, being marked by a noncore case or an adposition; this argument can be omitted, although there may be the option of including it—that is, a passive can be impersonal (or 'agentless'), or an A can be included;

  (iv) there is some explicit formal marking of a passive construction—this can be a verbal affix, or a periphrastic construction.

A passive can be expressed through a verbal affix. A basic transitive clause in Mam is in (7.14):

(7.14)   ma   ch-ok   t-b'iyo-7n   [Cheep]$_A$ [kab'   xjaal]$_O$
         PAST 3pl+O-DIRECTIONAL 3sg+A-hit-DIR José   two   person
         'José hit two people'

A passive is marked by the verbal suffix -*eet*, in (7.15). This clause is intransitive. The erstwhile A argument, José, is no longer obligatory and is an oblique:

(7.15)   ma   chi   b'iy-eet [kab'   xjaal]$_S$ [t-u7n   Cheep]$_{OBL}$
         PAST 3plA hit-PASS two   person 3sg-AGENT José
         'Two people were hit (by José)'

There can be impersonal passives which do not allow the inclusion of the erstwhile A at all.

An antipassive removes the O of a transitive active clause, and makes it intransitive. In other words, the 'A' becomes the 'S', and the O is accorded the status of an oblique. The focus is on the subject, or the activity itself. Box 7.2 summarizes the criterial features of antipassive, illustrated in examples (6.24)–(6.25).

An antipassive derivation is not exactly the 'opposite' of a passive. A transitive clause 'The woman hit the man with the stick' in (6.24), from Dyirbal, can be intransitivized using the antipassive derivation -*ŋa*- in (6.25), as 'The woman hit ((at) the man) with a stick'.

Passives are found in nominative-accusative and in absolutive-ergative languages. A major function of a passive is foregrounding the former O which is now an S of a derived intransitive (passive) clause, and downplaying the former A. A major function

---

Box 7.2 How to recognize an antipassive

An antipassive has the following features:

(i)   it applies to an underlying transitive clause and forms a derived intransitive;
(ii) the former A becomes S of the antipassive;
(iii) the former O argument goes into a peripheral function, being marked by a non-core case; this argument can be omitted, and there may or may **not** be the option of including it;
(iv) there is some explicit formal marking of an antipassive construction—this is usually a verbal affix.

of an antipassive is foregrounding the former A, now an S of a derived intransitive (antipassive) clause, and downplaying the former O. In addition to these discourse-pragmatic functions, they have a role in tracking referents across clauses: we turn to this, and the notion of pivot, in Chapter 12.

Further valency-changing derivations may include reflexives, reciprocals and causatives, and applicatives. Reflexives—meaning 'do something to oneself'—and reciprocals—'do something to each other'—may be expressed through a verbal affix. A reciprocal meaning in Huallaga Quechua is expressed with the suffix *ku-*, which makes a transitive verb into an intransitive one. Consider the following pair of examples:

(7.16) arma-n versus arma-ku-n
        bathe:TRANS-3person bathe:TRANS-REFL-3person
        'He bathes (him, e.g. a child)' 'He bathes himself'

The suffix *-naku-* in Huallaga Quechua has a reciprocal meaning: *qara-naku-n* (feed-RECIP-3) means '(they) fed each other'. In other languages, the same suffix may have a reflexive meaning if the subject is singular, and a reciprocal meaning if it is plural, for example Warekena *pi-yutʃia-na-wa* (2sg-kill-REFL-IMPERFECTIVE) 'you kill yourself', *na-yutʃia-na-wa* (3pl-kill-RECIP-IMPERFECTIVE) 'they kill each other'.

7.3.2 Increasing valency

The most common means for increasing valency are CAUSATIVES and APPLICATIVES. Causatives add an argument, typically, an A, to the intransitive clause. Box 7.3 summarizes features of a causative (see also §7.3).

The suffix *-ta* in Warekena is a typical morphological causative. An intransitive verb *pi-yueta-wa* (2sg-return-NONACCOMPLISHED) means 'you returned, came back'. If the suffix *-ta* is added, the newly formed transitive verb *pi-yueta-ta-wa* means 'you returned (something)'. (Similar examples are 10.1–10.2).

Box 7.3 What is a causative?

(a) Causative applies to an underlying intransitive clause and forms a derived transitive.
(b) The argument in underlying S function ('the causee') goes into O function in the causative.
(c) A new argument ('the causer') is introduced, in A function.
(d) There is some explicit formal marking of the causative construction: there can be morphological causatives, syntactic causatives, and causative serial verb constructions.

When a causative is formed on a transitive verb, a new argument (A) is introduced. What happens to the erstwhile A and O depends on the language: in some languages, the former A becomes the new O, and the former O becomes an oblique. This is what we have in Warekena. The obligatorily transitive verb *kurua* 'drink' is shown in (7.17a).

(7.17a)   nu-tani   kurua   weni
         1sg-child 3sg.nf+drink water
         'My son is drinking water'

The morphological causative derivation, *kuua-ta*, means 'to make drink'. 'My son' is now the O, and 'water' is an oblique marked with a postposition 'with', in 7.17b:

(7.17b)   nu-kurua-ta   nu-tani   weni   ima
         1sg-drink-CAUS 1sg-child water with
         'I made my son drink water'

In Imbabura Quechua, the erstwhile O and the new O (former A) both take the accusative suffix -*ta*.

(7.18)   Juzi-ka   Maria-ta-mi   Juan-ta   riku-chi-rka
         José-topic Maria-ACC-EVID Juan-ACC see-CAUS-PAST
         'José caused Maria to see Juan'

Are they both objects (O), or can they be distinguished? We return to this in §10.9.

Specific meanings of causatives may include control, volition, and affectedness of the causee, and directness, intention, and involvement of the causer. In Carib languages and in Cavineña different causative markers apply to transitive, and to intransitive verbs. Urarina has one causative -*a* with the meaning of 'direct' causation: 'make' somebody do something. Another causative, -*erate*, means 'have somebody do something through someone else'. A number of Amazonian languages have a 'sociative' causative indicating that the 'causer' is involved in the caused action.

Causative meanings can also be expressed through serial verb constructions, complex predicates, or even a sequence of two clauses. As we will see in §7.5, a marker of a morphological causative may derive new verbs from nouns and adjectives.

Applicative derivations are somewhat similar to causatives in that they add an argument. The functions of an applicative are different depending on the transitivity of the verb—see Box 7.4. When applied to an intransitive verb, applicative increases the number of arguments. When applied to a transitive verb, it rearranges them, making a new O more prominent.

Box 7.4 What is an applicative?

For an intransitive verb: an applicative involves *Adding an O argument, S becoming A.*

(a) Applicative applies to an underlying intransitive clause and forms a derived transitive.
(b) The argument in underlying S function goes into A function in the applicative.
(c) A peripheral argument (which could be explicitly stated in the underlying intransitive) is taken into the core, in O function.

For a transitive verb: a peripheral argument becomes an object

(a) Applicative applies to an underlying transitive clause and maintains transitivity, but with an argument in a different semantic role filling O function.
(b) The underlying A argument stays as is.
(c) A peripheral argument (which could be explicitly stated in the underlying transitive) is taken into the core, in O function.
(d) The argument which was in O function is moved out of the core into the periphery of the clause, or alternatively stays as the second O (and may be omissible).

And in each case

(e) There is some explicit formal marking of an applicative construction, generally by an affix or some other morphological process applying to the verb.

Examples (7.19)–(7.20), from Yidiñ, illustrate a comitative applicative: the former oblique 'with wife' becomes a core argument (an O) as a consequence of the applicative derivation.

An applicative involves making an intransitive verb transitive by taking an oblique into the O function. The erstwhile S becomes A, and there is an explicit marking of this on the verb. Example (7.19), from Yidiñ, is an intransitive clause. The oblique, 'with wife', may or may not be included—it is not part of the core.

(7.19)   wagu:ja$_S$ ñina-ŋ   (waga:l-ji)
         man:ABS sit-PRESENT wife-COMITATIVE
         'The man is sitting (with (his) wife)'

In (7.20), the verb takes the suffix -ŋa- and is transitive. 'Wife' is now the object; and the new A, 'man', is marked with the ergative case.

(7.20)   wagu:ja-ŋgu$_A$ wagal$_O$ ñina:-ŋa-l
         man-ERG   wife:ABS sit-APPLICATIVE-PRESENT
         'The man is sitting-with his wife'

Other common applicatives include locative, 'goal', and instrumental, each named after a constituent it applies to.

7.4 Noun incorporation

The term 'noun incorporation' covers morphological structures in which a nominal constituent is added to a verbal root, and the resulting form remains a verb. Incorporation can help derive new verbs. It may affect the valency of the verb, or help organize the flow of discourse by foregrounding an important participant and backgrounding the less important one. Incorporation is a morphological process which brings word formation and syntax close together. It is especially prominent in synthetic languages.

The simplest kind of noun incorporation is a lexical compound. A noun and a verb form a new lexical item. The process typically applies to just a handful of nouns, and of verbs, to refer to a 'name-worthy' unitary activity, such as English *baby-sit* and *fundraise*, or Mandarin Chinese for example *jié-hūn* (tie-marriage) 'marry' and *kāi-dāo* (open-knife) 'operate on'.

Noun incorporation may be highly productive, and may have a consistent syntactic effect. It may also make a transitive verb intransitive. The transitive clause in (7.21) comes from Guaraní, a Tupí-Guaraní language spoken in Paraguay:

(7.21)   A-jogua-ta   petei   mba'e
          1ACTIVE-buy-FUT   one   thing
          'I will buy something'

The object, 'thing', can be made part of the verb. The verb becomes intransitive, and the combination 'thing-buy' refers to a unitary activity, 'shopping' in general:

(7.22)   A-mba'e-jogua-ta   ko-ka'aru
          1ACTIVE-thing-buy-FUT   this-afternoon
          'I'll go shopping (lit. thing-buying) this afternoon'

Noun incorporation may result in re-arranging the verb's arguments. In Paraguayan Guaraní there are two ways of saying 'I washed your face'. If I am talking about your face, I will say (7.23).

(7.23)   (Che) a-johei   nde-rova
          I   1ACTIVE-wash 2:INACTIVE-face
          'I washed your face'

And if my focus is on you, rather than a part of you (that is, your face), I will say (7.24). As a syntactic position was vacated by the incorporated noun, 'face', the erstwhile possessor, you, becomes the direct object.

(7.24) (Che)   ro-hova-hei
        I   1subj/2obj-face-wash
        'I washed your face' (lit. I face-washed you)

This is also known as possessor ascension, or 'raising'.

An incorporated noun is usually indefinite, and refers to a general, non-specific object. Only nouns in S, O, or oblique function can be incorporated; a transitive subject 'A' never is. In many languages, including Paraguayan Guaraní (examples (7.23)–(7.24)), a noun is incorporated in its free form. In other languages, such as Nahuatl, a phonologically reduced form of a noun is incorporated. A whole possessive noun phrase with generic reference can be incorporated in some languages, including Bou-maa Fijian, for example *saqa.-['e-dra-i'a]* (cook-[their-edible.thing-fish]) 'cook their fish'. Noun incorporation does not change word class and has a syntactic and pragmatic effect—this is how it differs from deverbal nominalizations.

7.5 Making new verbs

A new verb can be derived from a member of another word class—nouns, adjectives, adverbs, and closed classes. The meanings of verbs derived from nouns include 'BECOME something', for example Dyirbal *baryan* 'youth', *baryan-bi-* 'become a youth'; 'HAVE something', for example Indonesian *anak* 'child', *ber-anak* 'have children'; 'DEPRIVE of something', for example English *dis-arm, de-caffeinate*; 'BEHAVE/WORK as something', for example English *burglar-ize*. Further, a denominal verb may have a broad range of causative-like meanings, including 'PROVIDE with something', for example Tariana *-ipitana* 'name', *-ipitan-eta* 'bestow a name'; 'PRODUCE something', for example Warekena *inena* 'egg', *inena-ta* 'lay an egg'; 'TRANSFORM, MAKE into something', for example English *victim-ize, crystal-ize*; or 'MAKE something come about', for example English *glor-ify*. Delocutive verbs mean 'say NOUN', as in Indonesian *bapak* 'father', *ber-bapak* 'to use "father" when addressing someone'.

A derivational affix may have a plethora of meanings. Consider the verbalizer *–ify* in English whose meanings include the following:

  (a) A makes O into X: *gas-ify, mummi-fy*
  (b) A puts O in/on X: *class-ify, cod-ify*
  (c) A provides X to/for O: *beauti-fy, dirti-fy*
  (d) A represents X of/for O: *exempl-ify, sign-ify*
  (e) A makes O have (some of) the characteristics of X: *countri-fy, person-ify*.

Verbs derived from adjectives often mean 'become ADJECTIVE', as in Russian *krasnyj* 'red', *krasnetj* 'become red', 'be ADJECTIVE', for example Boumaa Fijian *rewa* 'high', *va'a-rewa-* 'be raised (of a flag)', causative 'make ADJECTIVE', for example English *American-ize, simpl-ify*. Verbs can be derived from other word classes. For instance, in Finnish verbs can be derived from numbers and quantifiers, as in *kahdentaa* 'duplicate' from *kaksi* 'two', or *monistaa* 'multiply' from *moni* 'many'. In many European languages, delocutive verbs can be derived from personal pronouns which distinguish politeness, for example Estonian *sina-ta-ma* vs *teie-ta-ma*, German *du-zen* vs *sie-zen*, French *tu-toyer* vs *vou-voyer*, Latin American Spanish *tu-tear* vs *vos-ear*, which all mean 'say thou' and 'say you (pl) as a mark of respect', respectively. In Dyirbal, the delocutive suffix *-(m)ba-y* derives intransitive verbs from onomatopoeia and interjections, for example *yabu-yabu-ba-y* 'call yabu yabu (a call of terror)'.

The same affix can derive a morphological causative from a verb, and a verb from another word class. The causative suffix *-chi-* in Imbabura Quechua can derive verbs from nouns, for example *shuti* 'name', *shuti-chi-* 'bestow a name', and from adjectives, for example *ali* 'good', *ali-chi-* 'make become good, repair'. In Huallaga Quechua, many noun-to-verb derivations with *-chi-* have a hard-to-predict meaning, for example *noochi* 'night', *noochi-chi-* 'pass the night'.

A verb can be derived from another verb. English boasts a multiplicity of derivational prefixes, for example *over-rate* from *rate*, *under-estimate* from *estimate*, or *sub-let* from *let*. In many cases the meaning of a derived verb does not bear any straightforward relationship to the one it is derived from—obvious examples include *over-take* 'to go past someone' or *under-take* versus *take*.

A causative derivation may produce an unpredictable semantic effect. In combination with some verbs, the causative suffix *-chi* in Huallaga Quechua creates new meanings and can no longer be described as a simple valency-changing derivation. Examples include *taapa-chi-* (cover-CAUSATIVE) 'keep vigil (at a wake)' and *tushu-chi-* (dance-CAUSATIVE) 'bounce (a child) on one's lap'. We can recall, from Table 3.2 in Chapter 3, that semantic idiosyncrasies are typical of derivation (but not of inflection). For each derivation, whether word-class changing or not, it is important to state how productive it is, and how predictable its meaning.

Compounding is another way of forming new verbs. Noun–verb compounds usually refer to unitary, name-worthy activity, as in English *problem-solve*, or *home-deliver*. The meaning of a compound may not be easily inferred from the meanings of the parts. That is, these compounds are semantically 'non-compositional'. For example, a Korean compound *kil-tulta* (road-enter) means 'get used to'. In Hungarian *világ-latszani* (world-see) means 'travel'; and in Paumari *-va'i-hoki* (liver-be alive) means 'remember'. Compounds can consist just of verbs. English has a handful of these. Some describe two simultaneous actions, for example *stir fry*, *crash land*, and *sleep walk*, others refer to actions in sequence, for example *strip search* or *drink drive*. These compounds are restricted—one could list all of them in a dictionary. And the meanings are somewhat idiosyncratic: for example, *strip search* describes a particular kind of search one may have to undergo, say, at immigration. One-word serial verbs are unlike verb–verb compounds in that they are fully productive and tend to be compositional in their meanings. More on this in §7.6.

7.6 Multi-verb constructions

A single predicate may consist of several verbs. The most common kinds of multi-verb predicates are (i) serial verb constructions (§7.6.1), and (ii) constructions with auxiliaries and support verbs (§7.6.2).

7.6.1 Serial verb constructions

A serial verb construction, or a serial verb, is a sequence of verbs which form one predicate. Each verb can be used independently. The construction contains no overt marker of coordination or subordination. A serial verb will have a common tense, aspect, mood, modality, and polarity value. That is, its components cannot be negated separately. For example, within a serial verb, one verb cannot be cast in the past, and another one in future. A serial verb describes what can be conceptualized as a single event. In (7.25), from Kristang, a Portuguese-based Creole language spoken in Malaysia, a serial verb 'finish go' means that going was completed. Components of a serial verb are underlined.

(7.25) kora yo ja   chegá nalí eli ja   <u>kaba</u> <u>bai</u>
        when 1sg PERF arrive there 3sg PERF <u>finish</u> <u>go</u>
        'When I arrived there he had gone'

Serial verbs can be used to express modal meanings, for example desiderative (wanting), as in (7.26), from the Lolovoli dialect of North-east Ambae.

(7.26) ra-mo   <u>tarani</u> <u>vano</u> lo   sitoa
        3nsgS-REAL <u>want</u>   <u>go</u>   LOC shop
        'They want to go to the shop'

Causation may be expressed through serial verbs. Example (7.27), from Taba, an Austronesian language from Indonesia, describes one event: the death of a pig comes 'as a direct and immediate consequence of the pig's being bitten' (Bowden 2001: 297–8).

(7.27) <u>n=babas</u> welik <u>n=mot</u> i
        <u>3sg=bite</u> pig   <u>3sg=die</u> 3sg
        'It bit the pig and it died'

What happens if the same verbs are coordinated and no longer form one predicate? Example (7.27) shows two independent verbs, 'bite' and 'die'. In (7.28) the bite and the death of a pig are not immediately linked: 'there may have been a considerable time elapsed between the biting and the pig's eventual death by bleeding'; that is, the death of the pig was not a direct result of the bite.

(7.28) <u>n=babas</u> welik <u>n=mot</u> do
        3sg=<u>bite</u> pig 3sg=<u>die</u> REAL
        'It bit the pig (so that) it (the pig) died'

Serial verbs usually share their subjects. In causative serial verbs, like the one in Taba (7.27), the object of the first verb is identical to the subject of the second one. This is 'switch-subject' serialization.

Serial verbs can be of the contiguous type: then the components have to be next to each other, as in (7.25) and (7.26). They can be non-contiguous, as in (7.27). In the examples discussed so far, serial verbs consist of several grammatical and phonological words. In some languages, serial verbs form one grammatical and phonological word, as in (7.29), from Alamblak. This is sometimes referred to as 'root serialization'.

In terms of their composition, serial verbs are of two major types. ASYMMETRICAL serial verbs consist of a 'minor' verb from a small closed subclass—typically, a modal verb, verb of beginning or finishing, or a verb of posture or motion—and another, 'major', verb from a large open class. Examples (7.25) and (7.26) illustrate asymmetrical serial verbs. 'Minor' verbs ('finish' in 7.25 and 'want' in 7.26) provide modal and aspectual specification for the whole serial construction.

SYMMETRICAL serial verbs consist of verbs from open classes; the relationship between the verbs can be that of cause–effect, as in (7.27), or of a sequence of sub-actions, as in (7.29), from Alamblak, a Papuan language of New Guinea:

(7.29) mɨyt   ritm   <u>muh-hambray</u>-an-m
        tree   insects <u>climb-search.for</u>-1sg-3pl
        'I climbed the tree searching for insects'

Verbs can only combine to form a serial verb construction if the sequence of subactions makes sense to the speakers. In Alamblak, one cannot combine 'climb and see', as in 'I climbed to see the stars': this is not what a person would normally do.

Minor verbs within serial verb constructions can become bound grammatical morphemes: that is, they grammaticalize. The proto-Oceanic verb *la- 'go' survives in Toqabaqita only as a directional morpheme with a general meaning 'away'. Symmetrical serial verbs tend to develop unpredictable meanings, for example Igbo kà-sá (say-spread.open) 'spread information, rumours', cè-fù (think-be.lost) 'forget', and may have to be listed in a dictionary rather than discussed in the grammar.

Serial verb constructions are a prominent feature of languages of West Africa (such as Akan and Ewe), Creole languages, and many languages of Southeast Asia, Oceania, New Guinea and South America.

7.6.2 Constructions with auxiliary verbs and support verb constructions

An auxiliary is a member of a closed subclass of verbs which

(a) may form part of one complex predicate in combination with a verb from a large open class;
(b) may take person, number, gender, aspect, tense, mood, and modality specifications; and
(c) may impart a modal or an aspectual meaning to the whole construction.

An auxiliary occurs together with a lexical verb. It may take the inflection for some categories covering non-spatial setting (tense, modality, mood, and aspect), rather than the verb taking the inflection.

Auxiliary verbs have a wide range of functions across the world. In many European languages, including English, they are used to express tense and aspect. Continuous forms in English involve the verb *be* as an auxiliary, for example *He is writing a book*. The verb *have* is used as an auxiliary to refer to something which commenced previously to the time of speech, for example *He has written a book*. Future involves modals auxiliaries, *will* and *shall*, as in *He will write a book*. To negate, and to question a clause, one employs the auxiliary *do*, as in *He does not write books*, and *Does he write books?*

Auxiliaries 'be' and 'have' are often used to express passives, especially in familiar Indo-European languages. English uses the verb *be*, as in *A man was robbed*. Tamil, a Dravidian language, employs the verb *paṭu* 'experience, suffer, undergo' followed by a nominalized form of the 'main', or lexical verb. Quechua has two passives: one is formed with the auxiliary *ka-* followed by a nominalized form of the verb. The resulting construction has no implication of change of state. The other one involves the auxiliary *tuku-* 'become', and implies transition from one state to another.

An auxiliary does not have to be used as a full verb in the language. The auxiliary *i-* in Paumarí combines with a nominalized verb to express the passive: this is the only function it has. The auxiliary takes on all aspect and person marking. A special auxiliary *-riy* in Yagua has just a modal 'frustrative' meaning, 'fail to do something'. In a number of languages, negatives are used with a special negative-only auxiliary verb which takes person, number, and also tense marking. This is a feature of Balto-Finnic languages, for example Finnish *tule-n* (come-1sg) 'I come', *e-n tule* (NEG.AUX-1sg come:stem.combining.with negation) 'I don't come'. Auxiliaries may have just some properties of verbs (and thus be defective). The negative auxiliary in Finnish has no nominalized forms, and cannot be passivized. A different auxiliary has to be used to form a negative command, for example *Tulkaa!* (come+2pl.IMPV) 'Come (you many people)!', *Älkää tulko* (NEG.IMPV.AUX+2pl come+IMPV) 'Do not come (you many people)!'.

Auxiliary verbs may have other functions. In Jarawara, many verbs, such as *amo* 'sleep', cannot take inflection directly, and require an auxiliary to express tense, aspect, evidentiality, and other predicate features.

In many languages ideophones, onomatopoeia, borrowings, and other non-verbal forms can only be used as predicates if accompanied by a 'support' verb. Its only function is to enable a non-verbal element to be used as a predicate. Verbs borrowed from Turkish into Kurmanjî, an Iranian language, typically occur only in combination with the Kurmanjî verb 'be' or 'do'. In many languages auxiliaries have this, 'support verb', function. Spanish loans in Cavineña require a support verb, for example *aterisa ju-* 'to land' consists of the borrowed equivalent of Spanish *aterizar* 'to land' and *ju-* 'intransitive auxiliary' and *acepta a-* 'accept' consists of Spanish *aceptar* 'to accept' and *a-* 'transitive auxiliary'.

Auxiliary constructions can express a multitude of meanings. A main verb accompanied by an auxiliary always comes in a dependent, or nominalized, form. Usually, no other constituents can intervene between an auxiliary and the main verb. Auxiliaries vary in (a) whether they are also used as full verbs in the language; (b) how many properties of full verbs they have; (c) what kind of form of the main verb they occur with.

7.6.3 Multi-verb predicates in their further guises

In many Cushitic, Omotic, and also Tibeto-Burman languages, a multi-verb construction consists of a main, inflected verb and another verb marked as dependent to it. The form may vary (and so does terminology: in some traditions, the dependent form is called 'infinitive', in others 'participle', and in others 'gerund', or 'converb'). The components of multi-verb constructions with dependent verb forms act together as a single predicate, and usually share their subjects.

'Converb' constructions in Wolaitta, an Omotic language from Ethiopia, consist of a lexical verb marked with a converb suffix and another verb which may provide aspectual, directional, or degree meaning to the whole construction. So, the verb *y-* 'come' marks the direction of action as being 'towards' the speaker, as in *ʔekk-í y-iisi* (take/bring-CONVERB come-3sg.masc.PERFECTIVE) '(he) brought (the goods)'. This construction contains just one predicate, because no constituent can intervene between the two forms, neither can be negated or questioned separately, the two have to share their subject, and one provides a directional specification to the construction.

A causative, 'making someone do something', can be expressed analytically. A causative in English involves a combination of the verb *make* with the plain form of the other verb, as in *He made them write a letter*. Similarly, in French and Spanish verbs meaning 'make, do'—*faire* in French and *hacer* in Spanish—form one predicate with another verb to form a causative.

In a number of Australian languages, complex verbs consist of one or more uninflected forms (termed 'coverbs') and a simple verb. A simple verb will have a broad generic meaning, and a coverb will make this meaning more specific. The simple verb *-ga-* in Yawuru has a general meaning 'carry'. If a coverb is added, the meaning of a resulting complex verb is more specific, for example *ŋanjbi -ga-* 'carry holding under the arm or by the side of the body', *ŋanjdja -ga-* 'carry in the mouth (as a dog does)'. The meaning of the combination may not be at all transparent: *wirrb -ga-* means 'carry a grudge against someone, oppose' and *mardalj -ga-* means 'make noise, be noisy'. Australian languages vary as to how many simple verbs, and coverbs, there are. In some, only a handful of simple verbs combine with coverbs. Further information is in Dixon (2002: 183–201).

For each multi-verb construction, the grammarian will need to ascertain the status and the form of the components, and establish (a) that the multi-verb construction forms one predicate; and (b) what its properties and meanings are.

7.7 Verbal word and verb phrase

Many of the categories expressed within a verb characterize the clause as a whole. Mood, tense, aspect, and information source are clausal categories. Their marking tends to be associated with the verb. We can recall, from §6.6, that noun phrases can have their own tense, aspect, reality status, and modality marking which may or may not be the same as that of the clause (see example 6.27).

In synthetic languages, the verb tends to have a complex structure. Following the principles in Table 3.2, markers of derivational categories—that is, the ones likely to produce a new verb—will tend to appear closer to the verb's root than categories referring to non-spatial setting. Markers of valency-changing derivations will generally be followed by those indicating the internal structure of the activity and aspect. Exponents of tense, mood, modality, and evidentiality will appear further away from the root. Person, number, and also gender agreement markers are usually expected to occur on the very edge of the verb. These principles are reflected in the order of morphemes in synthetic languages such as Quechua, Tariana, or Jarawara.

The order of verbal affixes may not be fixed. In Quechua, the order of verbal suffixes changes if the meaning changes. For instance, *asi-chi-naku* (laugh-CAUSATIVE-RECIPROCAL) means 'make each other laugh', and *asi-pa:-nakU-chi* (laugh-BENEFACTIVE-RECIPROCAL-CAUSATIVE) means 'make (people) laugh at each other'.

In languages with a more analytic profile, categories associated with the verb are expressed within a verb phrase. The order of possible components of a verb phrase in Tamambo is as follows:

Subject pronoun

Marker of realis

Aspectuals and negative aspectuals

Manner modifiers

Head of the verb phrase

Manner modifiers, directionals

Adverbs and adverbial modifiers are sometimes included in the verb phrase. The structure of the verbal phrase across the world's languages allows for much more variation than the structure of a noun phrase.

7.8 Summing up

A description of the structure of the verb must include a statement of verbal categories, including pronominal cross-referencing, marking of non-spatial setting and of spatial setting (including motion, direction, and location of the action). Discussion of non-spatial setting will cover mood (that is, the distinctions between declarative, interrogative, and imperative), modality (e.g. possibility, probability, and obligation), attitude to knowledge, evidentiality (or grammticalized information source), tense, aspect and the structure of activity, and reality status. An important question concerns the ways in which these categories interact: for instance, not all aspects may be distinguished in all tenses. Additional checklists for each of these can be found in Dixon (2012: 40–1).

In analysing valency-changing derivations, one needs to check how each applies to transitive and to intransitive verbs. If there are several passives, or several causatives, it is important to discuss semantic and pragmatic differences. If the same verbal derivation may have a reflexive and a reciprocal meaning, investigate how the two may be distinguished.

If the language has productive noun incorporation, a major question is: what are its syntactic and discourse functions? And what are its pragmatic effects? Forms with incorporated nouns and compounds may or may not form one phonological word.

If the language has serial verb constructions, their defining properties will include shared values of tense, aspect, modality, information source, negation, and illocutionary force etc. Most languages distinguish asymmetrical and symmetrical serial verbs. These can express different meanings. A major issue in analysing serial verb constructions is sharing arguments (subject, objects, and also obliques), their contiguity and wordhood (that is, whether verbs within a serial verb construction form one grammatical and one phonological word, or not), and the expression of shared values of tense, aspect, negation, and so on.

Serial verb constructions differ from other complex predicates, including support verb constructions and constructions with auxiliary verbs. Each of these needs to be addressed, in terms of types of auxiliaries, grammatical meanings expressed, and properties, of the complex predicate.

Some of the verbal categories may warrant a special chapter each, depending on the language. The analysis of the verb will be incomplete if the grammar lacks a statement of the structure of the verbal word and verb phrase.

Notes and sources

§7.1: See Dixon (2010a: 116–17; 2010b: 210–23), for more on the general characteristics of bound pronouns. Bound pronouns can also be realized as clitics; they may then be placed after the first constituent of a clause, in a typical clause-second clitic position (mentioned in §3.2 and §4.4). For more details on Basque, see Hualde and Ortiz de Urbina (2003: 2005–12) (the gloss 'pre-dative' has been replaced with 'linker' for the sake of simplicity); Saltarelli (1988: 238–45). For Paumarí see Aikhenvald (2009), Chapman and Derbyshire (1991).

See Aikhenvald and Dixon (2011c: 155–6), and Newman (1990: 53–87) on verbal number. See McFarland (2009: 191) on Filomeno Mata Totonac; England (1983: 167–74) on Mam, Guillaume (2008: 212–36, 307–20) on Cavineña.

§7.2.1: See Aikhenvald (2010: 2), on the notion of mood, and also Dixon (2010a: 95–6). See Fortescue (1984: 4–9; 287–98) on West Greenlandic; Dixon (1977: 370), on Yidiñ; see Aikhenvald (2010) for a detailed study of imperatives, and references there. For an in-depth discussion of English imperatives, see Huddleston (2002) and Davies (1986).

§7.2.2: See Dixon (2012: 9–21), Comrie (1985), Timberlake (2007), Chung and Timberlake (1985), on tense. See Foley (1991: 241–4, 247–9), on Yimas. See Roberts (1987: 227–31) on Amele. See Mithun (1999: 152–3) for a discussion of Washo, and other languages with numerous distinctions in past and future. See Hyslop (2001: 236–55) on the Lolovoli dialect of North-east Ambae, and Lichtenberk (2008: 165–227), on Toqabaqita.

§7.2.3: See Comrie (1976a), and Dixon (2012: 30–40) on aspect and related categories. See Guillaume (2008: 170–8) on Cavineña; Foley (1991: 249–51) on Yimas; Topping (1973: 258–9) on Chamorro; Roberts (1987: 247, 252) on Amele, Maslova (2003: 201–2, 209) on Kolyma Yukaghir; Dixon (1972: 248) on Dyirbal; Olawsky (2006: 471–3, 546) on Urarina; Fortescue (1984: 282–3) on West Greendlandic; Thiesen and Weber (2012: 123) on Bora.

The term 'Aktionsart' is mainly used to capture lexical properties of verbs which may relate to activities or states, or be bounded or unbounded. Some grammarians employ this term to capture additional facets of non-spatial marking on the verb, including degree, instrument, and manner.

§7.2.4: See further details in Dixon (2012: 26–30) and Chung and Timberlake (1985: 242–3). See Kenesei et al. (1998: 314–15) on Hungarian, Sulkala and Karjalainen (1992: 321–2) on Finnish; Fortescue (1984: 292, 326) on West Greenlandic; Boas and Deloria (1941: 111) on Lakhota; Guillaume (2008: 639, 655) on Cavineña; Olawsky (2006: 503–15) on Urarina. For a discussion of mirativity, see DeLancey (1997), Aikhenvald (2012c) and references there. See Molochieva (2010: 248–50) on Chechen.

§7.2.5: See Aikhenvald (2004b, 2006c, 2012a) and references there, on evidentiality.

§7.2.6: See Dixon (2012: 22–5), Elliott (2000), Mithun (1995) on form and meanings of realis and irrealis; Aikhenvald (2012a: 190–2) on reality status in Amazonian languages; Ekdahl and Grimes (1964: 262) on Terêna; Foley (1991: 238–40), on Yimas; Lichtenberk (1983a: 182–3) on Manam.

§7.3.1: See Dixon (2012: 197–342) for valency-changing derivations; see England (1983: 201, 203), on Mam. See Dixon (2012: 138–96) on general features of reflexives and reciprocals.

§7.3.2: Dixon (2000) outlines the major parameters for causatives; see Cole (1982: 136–40) on Imbabura Quechua. Studies of applicatives include Mithun (2001) and Peterson (2007); discussion of applicatives in Haspelmath et al. (2005) is to be treated with caution. Valency-changing derivations in Amazonian languages are discussed in Aikhenvald (2012a: 226–47). See Weber (1989: 167–70) on Huallaga Quechua, Dixon (1977: 303 ff) on Yidiñ.

§7.4: See Mithun (1984), Aikhenvald (2007b) on typological parameters of noun incorporation; see Li and Thompson (1981: 75–7) on Mandarin Chinese; Velázquez-Castillo (1996: 107, 134–6) on Guaraní; Merlan (1976) on Nahuatl; Dixon (1988: 227) on Boumaa Fijian.

§7.5: See Dixon (1972: 75) on Dyirbal; Benveniste (1971) and Dixon (1979, 2002: 208) on delocutive verbs, Sneddon (1996) on Indonesian; Dixon (2008) on English; Dixon (1988: 184) on Boumaa Fijian; Cole (1982: 180) on Imbabura Quechua, Weber (1989: 164–6) on Huallaga Quechua; Aikhenvald and Dixon (2011a: 232–44) for more detail on meanings and forms of verbalizing affixes.

§7.6.1: See Aikhenvald (2006a), Foley and Olson (1985), Givón (1991), and Durie (1997) on serial verb constructions. See Baxter (1988: 213) on Kristang; Hyslop (2001: 289) on the Lolovoli dialect of North-east Ambae; Bruce (1988: 29) on Alamblak; Lord (1975: 41–2) on Igbo.

§7.6.2: See Heine (1993), Kuteva (2001) on general properties of auxiliaries and their paths of grammaticalization; Aikhenvald and Muysken (2011) on these and other multi-verb constructions in the languages of the Americas; Cole (1982: 133–4) on Quechua; Lehmann (1993: 218–19) on Tamil; Chapman and Derbyshire (1991: 180–4) on Paumarí; Payne and Payne (1990: 414) on Yagua; Sulkala and Karjalainen (1992: 25, 115–16) on Finnish; Dixon (2004a) on Jarawara; Haig (2001: 213) on Kurmanjî; Guillaume (2008: 151–3) on Cavineña.

§7.6.3: See Amha and Dimmendaal (2006), on multi-verb constructions involving converbs in Omotic and Cushitic languages; Genetti (2005), on similar constructions in Tibeto-Burman; Dixon (2006b) and references there on coverbs; Aikhenvald and Muysken (2011) on the languages of the Americas; see Comrie (1976b: 262–3), Dixon (2012: 245) on analytic causatives; Aikhenvald (2003: 458–9) on Tariana.

§7.7: See further observations by Dixon (2010a: 108–10) on the structure of a verb phrase; Weber (1989: 83–4) on Quechua. The relative order of morphemes and its motivation are addressed by Mithun (2000); also see Bybee (1985) for a discussion of the principle of 'relevance' and ordering of morphemes. See Jauncey (2011: 261) on Tamambo.

§7.8: Additional checklists on verbal categories are in Dixon (2012: 189–91, 232–5, 289–90, 336–7). A brief checklist of additional points concerning derivation and noun incorporation is in Aikhenvald (2007b) and in Aikhenvald (2011a).

8

Adjectives and adverbs

Every language has a large open class of nouns. Almost every language has an open class of verbs. Adjectives may be more elusive. In some languages, they form a large open class. Other languages have a small, closed, adjective class. Adjectives may share syntactic and morphological properties with verbs, or with nouns, or with both. They may have features of their own, and be very distinct from other word classes. Semantic types associated with adjectives include dimension, age, value, and colour.

Adjectives typically modify nouns. Adverbs modify verbs, and may overlap with adjectives in their meanings. In the final section, we turn to adverbs, and the viability of 'adverb' as a word class.

8.1 Adjectives: syntactic functions and semantic types

Adjectives perform two major tasks: they state a property, and further specify a noun's referent. Their major syntactic functions are

(i) modifying the head noun in a noun phrase, e.g. *a tall boy*, and
(ii) stating a property, either (a) by serving as a copula complement in a clause, e.g. *The boy is tall*, or (b) by being head of an intransitive predicate.

In 8.1, from Tariana, the adjective 'tall' occupies the intransitive predicate slot, and takes the tense-evidentiality marker.

(8.1) hĭ   walikiri   yenunite-naka
       this young.man tall+NCL.ANIMATE-PRESENT.VISUAL
       'This young man is tall'

Verbs, nouns, adjectives, and members of other word classes can also head intransitive clauses. However, only verbs take a full set of mood, tense, evidentiality, aspect, and modality markers; the rest—including adjectives—may be able to occur with just a subset of these. Adjectives as heads of predicates in Tariana cannot take markers of imperative mood, and of many aspectual categories.

In some languages, adjectives can directly modify the verb. This is the case in some varieties of English, for example *He speaks (real) loud*. To modify a verb in British English, an adjective takes a derivational suffix *-ly* which transforms it into a manner adverb, for example *He speaks (really) loudly*.

In most languages adjectives can modify nouns and serve as copula complements. This is the case in English. In some languages, adjectives have just one of the two major syntactic functions. Adjectives in Hua can only be used as modifiers (that is, their only function is (i)); to be used as copula complements, they have to be verbalized.

Carib languages from South America have a class of words which can be copula complements (like nouns, but unlike verbs), and also modifiers to verbs. To modify a noun, they have to be nominalized. They cover typical adjectival meanings—including dimension, age, value, and colour. In Trio, *pija* 'little' can be used to modify a verb, as in 'do little', and serve as a copula complement, as in 'he is little'. If nominalized, *pija-n* (little-NOMINALIZER) can modify a noun, or just mean 'little something or someone'. That is, these adjectives only have function (ii) but not (i).

An adjective class is recognized on the basis of the syntactic properties just discussed. It is also expected to cover at least some of semantic types found in languages with small, medium-sized, and large adjective classes.

The following four core semantic types are typically associated with large and small adjective classes:

1. DIMENSION—'big', 'small', 'long', 'tall', 'short', 'wide', 'deep', etc.
2. AGE—'new', 'young', 'old', etc.
3. VALUE—'good', 'bad', 'lovely', 'atrocious', 'perfect', 'proper(/real)', etc.
4. COLOUR—'black', 'white', 'red', etc.

Further semantic types tend to be associated with medium-sized and large adjective classes:

5. PHYSICAL PROPERTY—'hard', 'soft', 'heavy', 'wet', 'rough', 'strong', 'clean', 'hot', 'sour', 'round', 'raw, green, unripe', etc. And a subclass referring to corporeal properties, e.g. 'well', 'sick', 'tired', 'dead', 'absent'.
6. HUMAN PROPENSITY—'jealous', 'happy', 'kind', 'clever', 'generous', 'cruel', 'proud', 'ashamed', 'eager', etc.
7. SPEED—'fast, quick', 'slow', etc.

Additional semantic types are associated with large adjective classes in some languages, including:

8. DIFFICULTY—'easy', 'difficult', 'tough', 'hard', 'simple', etc.
9. SIMILARITY—'like', 'unlike', 'similar', 'different (strange)', 'other', etc.
10. QUALIFICATION—'definite', 'true', 'probable', 'possible', 'likely', 'usual', 'normal', 'common', 'correct', 'appropriate', 'sensible', etc.

11. QUANTIFICATION—'all(/whole)', 'many', 'some', 'few', 'only', 'enough', etc.
12. POSITION—'high', 'low', 'near', 'far/distant', 'right', 'left(/strange)', 'northern', etc.

If a language has a small closed class of adjectives, they are likely to cover dimension, age, value, and colour, and also some physical properties. Manambu has a small class of agreeing adjectives consisting of 'small', 'big', and 'good'. The adjective class in Namia, a Papuan language from Sandaun Province, has seven members, covering size ('small', 'tiny', 'huge', 'large', etc.) and value ('bad'). Kamula, a Papuan language from Western Province, has two adjectives of dimension, two of age, two of value, and one of physical property. The adjective class in Kwomtari, a Papuan language from Sandaun Province, consists of twenty members, of which six refer to dimension, two to age, four to value, six to colour, and two to physical properties ('hot' and 'cold'). Larger adjective classes are expected to cover most semantic types.

We saw in §5.6 that adjectives can be divided into grammatical subclasses which correlate with their meanings. Macushi, a Carib language, has two small subclasses of adjectives. One includes DIMENSION, VALUE, PHYSICAL PROPERTY, and SPEED; the other covers DIMENSION, PHYSICAL PROPERTY, QUANTIFICATION (all, few, many), NUMBER (two) and TIME.

Manange, a Tibeto-Burman language from Nepal, also has two adjective classes, both medium-sized. One class, of about thirty members, shares many properties with nouns. The other one, with about fifty-seven members, is verb-like. Noun-like adjectives cover COLOUR, SPEED, and QUANTIFICATION. Verb-like ones cover HUMAN PROPENSITY and DIFFICULTY. Semantic parameters of DIMENSION, AGE, VALUE, PHYS-ICAL PROPERTY, and POSITION are expressed with adjectives from both subclasses.

The two adjective classes in Cavineña differ in a number of ways. Adjectives from a large closed class of 110 to 120 members always occur with a suffix -*da*. They function as copula complements and can modify a verb. Their meanings cover DIMENSION, AGE, VALUE, COLOUR, PHYSICAL PROPERTY, and HUMAN PROPENSITY. Adjectives from a closed class of sixteen members can only function as modifiers within a noun phrase. They cover DIMENSION, AGE, COLOUR, and just some PHYSICAL PROPERTIES.

Semantic types of adjectives may determine their order within a noun phrase. In Finnish, an adjective expressing shape, age, or colour of the head noun is placed closest to it; a dimension adjective will be further away, for example *iso musta koira* 'big black dog'. In Hungarian, an adjective expressing a stable or invariable property will be placed closer to the head noun than an adjective conveying more changeable properties. An age or a size adjective will precede a colour one, for example *új fehér ing* 'new white shirt'.

Adjectives can form a small closed class. This is what makes them special in the first place. Adjectives can be very similar to nouns, or very similar to verbs, or both, or neither.

8.2 How adjectives are special

Adjectives may share all, or some, properties of nouns, and yet retain their special status. Alternatively, they may be like verbs—but never fully identical. In some languages, adjectives have a set of their own categories, distinct from those of nouns, and of verbs. Many grammarians find themselves confronted with a question: 'Does the language I am working on have an adjective class?'. Dixon (2010b: 105–8) lists sixty possible criteria for delineating adjectives. Their careful application will be helpful in solving the 'adjective' puzzle.

8.2.1 When adjectives are 'like' nouns

Adjectives may be able to head a noun phrase, and share grammatical categories with nouns. But the nature of nominal, and of adjectival, categories is distinct.

Genders, noun classes, and number, are intrinsic to a noun. These same categories can be realized, as agreement markers, on adjectives when they modify a noun within a noun phrase. This is what we saw in §6.1 and in §6.2. The Portuguese noun *castelo* 'castle' is recognizable as belonging to the masculine gender because it ends in -*o*, and also because it triggers masculine agreement forms of the definite article *o* and of the adjective *branco* 'white:masculine singular', in *o castelo branco* 'the white castle'. If we form a plural, *castelo-s* 'castles', the forms of agreeing modifiers—including the adjective—will change, to match the noun: *o-s castelo-s branco-s* 'the white castles'. That the noun is the head of the noun phrase is demonstrated by the fact that it determines the gender and number forms of agreeing modifiers. In many languages, including Latin, Russian, and Finnish, adjectives have to take the same case forms as the nouns they modify.

Adjectives refer to qualities, and to properties, which are gradable. In many languages adjectives stand apart from other word classes in being able to form a comparative, or to mark gradation. Comparative and superlative forms in Hungarian and in Turkish can only be formed on adjectives. In Aguaruna, only adjectives can occur with the derivational suffix -*(t)taku* whose meaning is similar to English -*ish*, for example *wíŋka* 'blue', *wiŋká-ttaku* 'pale blue'. The intensifier *ima* means 'more' when used in comparative constructions with adjectives (and can be accompanied by the optional comparative particle *apatakama*).

(8.2) hu oya ima   muunta-i   au-haĩ   (apatakama)
　　　 this pot MORE   big-COPULA.3.DECL that-COMITATIVE (COMPARATIVE)
　　　 'This pot is bigger than that one'

When used with nouns, *ima* means 'only', for example *ima biika-na-kɨ* (INTENSIFIER bean-ACCUSATIVE-RESTRICTIVE) '(I ate) only beans'.

In a few languages, all adjectives and just some nouns have comparative forms. This is the case in Finnish, and also in some Romance languages, such as Portuguese. From the adjective *belo* 'beautiful' one can form a comparative *mais belo* 'more beautiful' and a superlative *belissimo* 'the most beautiful'. And from the noun *amigo* 'friend' one can form a comparative *mais amigo* 'more of a friend' and a superlative *amicíssimo* 'most friendly'.

Adjectives in Turkish are very much like nouns. Besides having their own comparative and superlative forms, adjectives have a few derivational suffixes not used with nouns. Only adjectives can take prefixes, to intensify their meanings, for example *yeni* 'new', *yep-yeni* 'brand-new'.

Adjectives may share some, but not all, categories with nouns. Adjectives in Aguaruna cannot take ablative and genitive cases (which are typical for nouns only). In Tsova-Tush, a North-east Caucasian language, nouns have eight cases (including nominative, dative, ergative/instrumental, allative, and comitative). Adjectives distinguish only two forms—nominative and oblique. Of the eleven cases for Estonian nouns mentioned in Table 6.4, adjectives as modifiers can take only seven: if a noun occurs in the terminative, instrumental-comitative, abessive-privative, or essive case, the adjective takes the genitive form, for example *suur-e kivi-ga* (big-GENITIVE stone-INSTRUMENTAL) 'with a big stone'. In Finnish and in Aguaruna nouns can take possessive affixes, while adjectives cannot.

In many Australian languages, nouns and adjectives are morphologically similar. The differences are subtle. For example, in Yankunytjatjara, the semantic effect of reduplication of an adjective is to 'deintensify' the meaning of the root, for example *pulka* 'big', *pulkapulka* 'biggish'. A reduplicated noun describes something as similar to the referent of the root, for example *ngura* 'camp', *ngurangura* 'a sort of camp, a temporary camp'. A grammatical marker can have a different meaning with nouns and with adjectives. In Yir-Yoront, an Australian language, the modifier *marr* means 'actual, present-day' if used with a noun, and 'very' if used with an adjective.

8.2.2 *When adjectives are 'like' verbs*

Adjectives in a language may appear to be verb-like. They may be able to head an intransitive predicate, and take most verbal markers. And yet they will be likely to stand apart from verbs in a number of ways. They may take fewer morphological indicators: for instance, adjectives will be unlikely to occur with imperative markers. The same morphemes may have different meanings with verbs, and with adjectives. Adjectives, but not verbs, will tend to occur in comparative constructions.

Having verb-like adjectives is a feature of many Oceanic and East Asian languages. In the Lolovoli dialect of North-east Ambae, an Oceanic language, an adjective can head a predicate, just like any verb. Adjectives can occur with the same markers of reality status and aspect; but their meanings differ. The particle *mo* expresses realis with verbs and 'process, in the past or in the present' with adjectives. As expected, adjectives do not form imperatives.

A serial verb construction hardly ever consists of two adjectives. Adjectives, but not verbs, can modify a noun without any special marker. For instance, both the intransitive verb *laka* 'be noisy' and the adjective *garea* 'good' can head a predicate. *Garea* can modify a noun, as in *ngie tangaloi garea* (she/he person good) 'She or he is a good person'. *Laka* cannot: **Ngie tangaloi laka* (she/he person be.noisy) **'She or he is a noisy person'* is ungrammatical.

Adjectives in Longgu, also Oceanic, can function as intransitive predicates. In addition, they can also modify both nouns and verbs. Unlike verbs, they cannot be nominalized. A reduplicated adjective has intensive meaning, for example *meta* 'good', *mwane meta-meta-i* (man good-RED-sg) ' the very good man'. A reduplicated verb has durative meaning 'always', for example *muha* 'be happy', *mwane muha-muha-i* (man-be.happy-RED-sg) 'the always happy man' (not *the very happy man).

All verbs, and all adjectives in Lao, a Southeast Asian language, can occur with markers of irrealis and of progressive aspect. Lao verbs and adjectives are negated in the same way and can both be directly modified by ideophones. But words which express adjectival concepts stand apart from the rest: they can be reduplicated, for example *suung3* 'tall' versus reduplicated form *sungø-suung3* 'tallish'. Reduplication does not apply to active verbs, like *lèèn1* 'run': **lènø-lèèn1* 'running-ish'? is nonsensical. Adjectives can be marked directly by *kua1* 'more than' and intensified by modifiers meaning 'really' and 'rather'; verbs cannot.

Only adjectives can occur in comparative constructions in Korean: this feature sets them apart from verbs. And there are further, more subtle, differences between Korean verbs and verb-like adjectives. The suffix *-élan/-ala* expresses the imperative with verbs. When used with an adjective, this same suffix has exclamatory meaning.

8.2.3 Adjectives in their own right

Adjectives may be distinct from both nouns and verbs. There are several options.

First, adjectives may be in both camps—they can share properties of nouns, and of verbs. In Tashelhit and other Berber languages, adjectives inflect for gender and number as agreement categories in a noun phrase (similar to nouns). If used as heads of intransitive predicate, they inflect for tense, aspect, person, and number of the subject, like verbs.

Secondly, adjectives may share some features of nouns, and some of verbs, and have some of their own as well. Adjectives in Tariana can modify a noun and agree with it in noun class and in number. Agreement markers on adjectives are the same as the ones on nouns themselves, with one exception. Only adjectives have a plural animate marker *-peni*. They can also function as heads of predicates and then take markers of tense, evidentiality, aspect, and mood, except for the imperative mood. Unlike verbs, they cannot form an agentless passive, or a causative.

Adjectives in Aguaruna share some morphological features with nouns (see §8.2.1), and some with verbs. They occur with the same modifiers as verbs, but with a different meaning. The adverb *ʃiiha* means 'well' when modifying a verb:

(8.3)   ʃiiha hapi-ka-ta
        well   pull-INTENSIVE-IMPERATIVE
        'Pull it well!'

The same form means 'very' when it modifies an adjective:

(8.4)   hu-ka   ʃiiha sutahutʃi-i
        PROXIMAL-FOCUS very short-COPULA.3.DECLARATIVE
        'This is very short'

Similarly, the modifier *sintʃi* means 'very' with verbs, and 'strongly' with adjectives.

THIRDLY, adjectives can be unlike any other word class. In Khinalug, a North-east Caucasian language, adjectives have no nominal categories of number, case, or noun class. They also do not have any verbal features, and are thus easily recognizable as a separate word class. Adjectives in English are unlike nouns and verbs. Unlike nouns, they do not take plural suffixes; nor can they occur as heads of NPs (with a few exceptions). Unlike verbs, they do not occur with tense-aspect marking, and cannot head a predicate. Only adjectives may take comparative and superlative marking—either suffixes *-er*, *-est*, or modifiers *more* and *most*. Only adjectives can occur on their own as copula complements, as in *He is big*. A singular noun would require an article or a modifier, for example *He is a student*.

8.2.4 *Why adjectives?*

Adjectives can be elusive: a bit like nouns, a bit like verbs, and bit like no other class. A superficial similarity between nouns and adjectives may be misleading. In his discussion of adjectives and nouns in Turkish, Lewis (2000: 50) remarks that 'the dividing line' between these two classes 'is a thin one, but it is still worth drawing'. Aguaruna adjectives are very much like nouns. And yet a careful grammarian has been able to identify more than ten features that set adjectives apart from nouns, and also from verbs—we saw this in §8.2.1 and §8.2.2. Adjectival concepts in Lao are expressed through verb-like forms which have at least four properties setting them apart from active verbs, as we saw in §8.2.2. A comprehensive grammar has to be as detailed as possible. Attention to detail is what allows us to set the 'property words' apart from whatever other class they may resemble.

There is one more reason why it is important to identify special grammatical features of an adjective class. Empirical investigation shows that there is always a class of words which reflect at least the core semantic adjective types of dimension, age, value, and colour. Identifying such 'property words' as a special class is important for the grammar to find its place within a cross-linguistic typological perspective.

Noun-like adjectives could, at a pinch, be treated as a special, aberrant class of nouns. Verb-like adjectives can be considered a special class of 'adjectival' verbs. A grammarian may opt to discuss adjectives as a separate word class, or as a subclass of nouns or of verbs—this is a matter for them to decide. Enfield (2004b) considers adjectives in Lao as a subclass of stative verbs. Post (2008) provides ten properties for distinguishing adjectives from verbs in Thai (genetically, and typologically, very similar to Lao), and considers them a special word class.

Special adjectivizing derivations offer a strong criterion in favour of adjectives as a separate class. More on this in the following section.

8.3 Making new adjectives

Adjectives can be derived from verbs and from nouns, and also from other word classes. Derived adjectives tend to belong to the semantic types of HUMAN PROPENSITY, SIMILARITY, and PHYSICAL PROPERTY.

Adjectives derived from verbs may relate to a property associated with the action, or with its result, for example Hungarian *viszket* '(to) itch', *visket-ős* 'itchy', Tamambo *mana* 'laugh', *mana-mana* 'friendly', *sale* 'float', *sale-sale* 'light (in weight)', Awa Pit *ii* 'die', *ii-ta* 'dead'. Adjectives can relate to a property of the A/S (subject) or O (object) of the verb, as in English *forget-ful, turn-able, attract-ive* (A/S), *forget-able* (O); Hungarian *olvas* 'read', *olvas-ható* 'readable' (O), and Amele *bebes* 'terrify', *bebes-ec* 'terrifying' (A/S). In English, the suffix *-able* can also refer to location, for example *walk-able, liv-able*. Adjectives of any type may have a special 'privative' or negative counterpart, for example Hungarian *olvas-hatatlan* 'unreadable', *olvas-atlan* 'unread'.

Deverbal adjectives tend to have all the properties characteristic of underived adjectives. Participles, or 'deverbal modifiers', deserve a special mention. In numerous languages, such modifiers can be regularly derived from verbs, and thus can be considered part of the verbal paradigm. These 'participles' tend to have verbal categories which include ASPECT, RELATIVE TENSE, MODALITY, and VALENCY-CHANGING. Their argument structure and marking is the same as that of verbs. Participles can be A/S oriented ('active' participles), S/O oriented ('passive' participles), or have no orientation. 'Resultative' participles are always S/O oriented, for example English *a fallen leaf, a recently recorded song*. In terms of expressing tense and aspect, A/S and S/O oriented participles may display asymmetry. This is the case in Latin:

(8.5)	A/S oriented, 'active' participle	S/O oriented 'passive' participle
present	*scrib-ens* 'writing'	—
past	—	*scrip-tus* 'written'
future	*scrip-turus* 'going to write, about to write'	*scrib-endus* 'to be written'

'Participles' may differ from adjectives in their grammatical properties. In Latin, participles have nominal tense (past, present, and future: cf. the end of §6.6), and adjectives do not. In such instances, participles cannot be considered mere 'deverbal adjectives'. In Hungarian, participles have no comparative forms, and cannot be used with intensifiers or head a predicate. They are then best considered a special subclass of verbs whose major function is marking the predicate of a relative clause.

Adjectives derived from nouns may relate to the material something is made of, for example English *wood-en*; to similarity with a noun, as in English *mann-ish* and Hungarian *könyv* 'book', *könyv-szerű* 'like a book'; or a property and a characteristic, such as English *passion-ate*, *beauti-ful*, or Basque *negar* 'tear', *negar-ti* 'tearful'.

Denominal adjectives may have a 'proprietive' meaning, for example English *hairy*; Hungarian *kazetta* 'cassette', *kazettá-s* 'having cassettes'. The opposite of proprietive is privative, as in Hungarian *könyv* 'book', *könyv-telen* 'book-less'. English has two privative markers which derive adjectives from nouns. One, *-less*, as in *parent-less*, refers to the lack of N as something one would expect and hope to have. The other one, *-free*, as in *dust-free (environment)* and *parent-free (evening)*, conveys the idea that the absence of the noun is somehow welcome or desirable.

Negative adjectives in English can be derived from those adjectives which do not have an antonym: one cannot say **un-little*, or **un-big*, but *un-ready* and *un-satisfactory* are all right, grammatically. English has seven suffixes to form adjectives from proper names or places, or people, for example *Swed-ish*, *Turk-ic*, *Canaan-ite*, *Bengal-i*, *Vienn-ese*, *Newton-ian*, and *Austria-n*. This shows how specific adjectivizing derivations may be.

The same suffix can be used to derive adjectives from nouns, and from verbs, with similar meanings. Examples from English include *-less*, *-able*, *-ful*, and *-y*. In Modern Welsh, the suffix *-gar* derives adjectives with habitual meaning from verbs, for example *ennill* 'to gain', *enillgar* 'lucrative', and from nouns, for example *dialedd* 'vengeance', *dialeddgar* 'vengeful'.

Adjectives may be derived from other word classes. In Egyptian Colloquial Arabic an adjective can be derived from a preposition, for example *fo:ʔ* 'on/up', *fo:ʔami* 'upper'. In Evenki, a Tungusic language, adjectives derived from adverbs have a general meaning 'relating to', for example adverb *tyma:tne* 'in the morning', adjective *tymar* 'pertaining to the morning', adverb *amaski* 'backwards', adjective *amaski-pty* 'former, backward'.

Adjective compounds may consist of an adverb plus an adjective, as in English *evergreen*. Compounds consisting of a noun and an adjective may refer to a property associated with a body or another part, such as English *heart-sick*, *head-strong*, *top-heavy*. They may also involve comparison, for example English *icy-cold* 'cold as ice', *dirt-cheap*, *snow-white*, Estonian *haud-vaikne* (grave-silent) 'silent as a grave'. There may be compounds with other relations between parts, for example English *bomb-happy*, *snow-blind*, or locative compounds, for example *brim-full, world-famous*. Russian has numerous coordinate compound adjectives referring to tinges of colour, for example *sero-goluboj* 'grey-blue'.

Adjectives can be derived from other adjectives. The derivational affix *-ish* in English derives adjectives indicating 'lesser', or 'approximate' quality, for example *blue, bluish, red, reddish*. This suffix can derive adjectives from nouns, for example *nightmarish, feverish, bookish*. Diminutive and augmentative derivations often apply to nouns or to adjectives, for example Portuguese *grande* 'big', *grandão* (big+AUGMENTATIVE) 'very big'.

There are no languages in which all verbs or all nouns are derived from another word class. However, some languages—such as Warekena—have no underived adjectives (here, all adjectives are formed from verbs).

8.4 Beyond adjectives: property concepts through other means

Languages with small and medium-sized adjective classes may express property concepts through other means. Languages with large systems of multiple classifiers (see §6.1.5–6) may lack adjectives of physical property referring to shape. Shape concepts are expressed with classifiers. This is a feature of Tariana, and many Tucanoan and Witoto languages. Dimension can be expressed with augmentative and diminutive marking on nouns (as is the case on Palikur, an Arawak language from Brazil and French Guiana).

Physical property and human propensity terms can be expressed through nouns (something like 'she cleverness' for 'she is clever'), or through verbs (something like 'she clevers'). Speed terms are likely to be associated with the adjective class if the adjective class includes terms for physical property: this is the case in English, Dyirbal, and Samoan. If physical properties are expressed through verbs, then speed is likely to be expressed through adverbs, as is the case in Bemba and Sango. More on this in Dixon (1982: 46–9). In many languages, including Mam and Tariana, numbers and quantification are expressed through a separate closed class. More on this in §9.5.

8.5 Adverbs

Just as an adjective is expected to modify a noun, so 'adverb' typically refers to a word class whose main syntactic function is to modify verbs. The same form can serve both functions, as in some varieties of American English. In their meanings, adverbs overlap with adjectives. Verb modifiers may, however, fall into more than one distinct class of words, in terms of their syntactic behaviour and morphological properties. This is why identifying a single putative class of 'adverbs' may turn out to be far from straightforward.

8.5.1 *Syntactic functions, grammatical categories, and semantic types*

Adverbs typically cover the following semantic groups:

1. MANNER, e.g. *doggedly, anxiously.* This broad category may include value (*well, badly, really*), distance (*far, closely*), speed (*quickly, slowly*) and difficulty (*easily*).
2. SIMILARITY, e.g. *similarly, like;*
3. QUALIFICATION and EVALUATION including EPISTEMIC EXPRESSIONS, e.g. *possibly, probably, eagerly;*
4. QUANTIFICATION, ADDITION, DEGREE, FREQUENCY, and INTENSIFICATION, e.g. *fully, partly, often, very, also;*
5. POSITION and DIRECTION, e.g. *vertically, horizontally, southerly;*
6. LOCATION IN TIME, e.g. *today, yesterday, previously, already, yet.*

The most frequent function of an adverb is to modify a verb, for example *Come quickly.* This function is typical of manner adverbs. In addition to this, adverbs may modify a clause or a sentence, for example *He is also coming* and *He has not come yet.* These are often referred to as sentential adverbs, and may cover quantification, addition, degree, frequency, intensification, and also location in time.

An adverb can modify a noun phrase or its head, for example *Give me only the ripe lemons.* Or an adverb can modify an adjective, as in *I picked the truly ripe lemons.* This is typical of adverbs of value and intensification. An adverb can modify another adverb, as in *She did this rather badly.* This function is typical of adverbs with intensifying semantics, referring to the degree of a property of an adjective.

Adverbs are typically poor in terms of grammatical categories. Some may have comparative and superlative degree (similar to the corresponding adjectives). Usually, only manner adverbs have these, for example Hungarian *lassan* 'slowly' (from *lassú* 'slower'), *lassabban* 'more slowly', *leg-lassabban* 'most slowly'.

Different derivational markers may correspond to different semantic classes of adverbs. Many manner adverbs in Hungarian are formed from adjectives with the modal-essive case *-n/-an/en*, for example *szép* 'nice', *szépen* 'nicely'; a few contain the locative case *-ban*, for example *sutyom-ban* (secret-in) 'secretly'. Adverbs referring to direction may contain directional case markers, for example *elő-ről* 'from the front', *elő-re* 'forward'.

In terms of their structure, grammatical categories, and syntactic functions, the class of adverbs is disparate. Manner adverbs typically stand apart from the rest of 'verbal' modifiers, and can often be treated as a separate word class, with their own morphology. Sentential adverbs may stand apart from other adverbs in terms of their syntactic behaviour, correlations with negation and scope: this is the case with temporal adverbs such as *already* and *yet* in English. This is what makes it hard to identify a valid class of 'adverbs' on a cross-linguistic basis. In many languages, there is not enough evidence for 'adverbs' as a coherent word class. Adverbs may not just be elusive: this class, inherited from traditional grammar, may turn out to be illusory. Manner adverbs are by no means universal. Adjectives can provide manner modification to verbs in Cavineña and in Tariana. Cavineña also has a closed class of four preverbal modifiers meaning 'vigorously', 'immediately', 'startling', and 'properly'.

Languages with numerous epistemic modalities (§7.2.4) may have no epistemic verbal modifiers. Time may be expressed with temporal nouns (a special subclass of nouns—see H under §5.4). Location and direction may be expressed through locational nouns, and locational and directional marking on the verb and in serial verb constructions (see G under §5.4; §7.1, and §7.6.1). In some languages, time words and locationals may form separate closed word classes—see §9.6.

Deictics and question words can occur in the function of obliques, providing locational and temporal specification; these are often best considered as special closed classes, with their own categories (rather than as 'adverbs'). Intensifiers ('very', 'a little') may be a closed class of bound forms, as in Tariana. In many languages, quantifiers form a closed word class (see §9.5). Cavineña has three postverbal quantifiers with the meaning of frequency (*pidya* 'once', *beta* 'twice', and *kimisha* 'three times'). In none of these languages, do the data warrant postulating a special class of 'adverbs'.

Adverbs are said to fulfil an 'adverbial' function—broadly speaking, that of providing modification to the verb, or the clause. Nouns functioning as peripheral or oblique arguments (see §3.9) form what can be referred to as 'adverbial phrases'. Their meanings are similar to 'adverbs'—including time words, locationals, and so on—with corresponding meanings. Compare *I will come today* with *I will come on Tuesday*. Adverbial clauses appear in lieu of a peripheral or an oblique, as in *I will come as soon as I can*. More on these in Chapter 12.

8.5.2 *Making new adverbs*

Derived adverbs are less widespread than derived adjectives, nouns, or verbs. A typical meaning of a derived adverb is 'manner'. In many languages, this sets manner adverbs apart from other verb modifiers. Adverbs derived from adjectives typically refer to the manner in which an action is realized, for example Modern Welsh *cyflym* 'quick', *yn gyflym* 'quickly', and Basque *eder* 'handsome', *ederki* 'well'. In Basque and in Evenki, manner adverbs can be derived from nouns and from verbs, for example Basque *harri* 'a stone', *harri-ka* 'by stoning', *jo* 'to hit', *jo-ka* 'by hitting'; Evenki *ajav-* 'the love', *ajav-ne* 'lovingly', *helinche-* 'to hurry/hasten', *helinche-ne* 'in a hurry'. The ubiquitous prefix *va'a-* in Boumaa Fijian can derive manner adverbs from adjectives and from some nouns, but not from verbs, for example adjective *levu* 'big', *va'a-levu* 'greatly', *Viti* 'Fiji', *va'a-Viti* 'Fijian way', *tuuraga* 'chief', *va'a-tuuraga* 'chiefly'.

Many adjectives in English form a manner adverb by adding *-ly*, meaning 'do it in that way'; for example, *clever-ly*. Adverbs derived from nouns in English may have a broadly directional meaning, for example *home-wards* 'towards home', *clock-wise* 'circular motion in the direction that the hands of a clock move', and *side-ways* 'with the side of an object facing forwards instead of, as would be expected, the front facing forwards'.

In Hungarian and in Finnish, affixes that impart adverbial meanings to nouns and apply productively can be alternatively considered case markers, for example Hungarian suffixes *-ként* 'as, in the quality of' and *-kor* 'at (the hour, time)', for example *orvos* 'doctor', *orvos-ként* 'as a doctor' (e.g. 'work as a doctor'), *négy-kor* 'at four o'clock', Finnish *-sti* 'in the manner of', for example *nopea-sti* 'quickly'. Time words can be components of a compound, for example Hungarian *dél-után* (midday-after) 'in the afternoon', *dél-előtt* (midday-before) 'in the late morning'. Compound adverbs in Estonian tend to have locational meanings, for example *ümber-ringi* (around-round) 'all around', *koha-peal* (spot:GENITIVE-on) 'on the spot'.

Frequency adverbs in Finnish can be derived from number words with specific suffixes: *-isin* is only used with three and four, as in *neli* 'four', *nelisin* 'four at a time', and *-ttain* occurs with other numbers, for example *kaksi* 'two', *kaksittain* 'two at a time'.

Having specific derivations, depending on the meaning of a verb modifier, may provide further criteria for identifying subclasses within a larger class of 'adverbs', or setting 'manner adverbs' apart from other classes. Alternatively, the grammarian may opt to consider each subtype a separate word class.

8.6 Summing up

To define the class of adjectives in a language, one needs to establish the syntactic functions and grammatical categories of adjectives (and compare them with nouns and verbs, as appropriate). For each subclass of adjectives it is important to ascertain whether it is open or closed, and what the semantic parameters are (based on the parameters in §8.1).

Not every language has a grammatically defined word class of 'adverbs'. Manner words can form a separate class. 'Verbal modifiers', with other meanings identified in §8.5, can make up a special word class. When investigating verbal modifiers, one should identify their syntactic functions (whether they modify the verb, or also the clause, a noun or an adjective), their grammatical categories (typically, just comparative and superlative), and derivational properties, if any.

Notes and sources

§8.1: For a general discussion of the properties of adjectives, see Dixon (2004b, 2010b: 62–114) and papers in Dixon and Aikhenvald (2004). Dixon (2010b: 104–8) lists grammatical criteria useful for distinguishing adjectives from nouns, and from verbs. See Haiman (1980: 268–9, 286) on Hua; on adjectival concepts and the corresponding word class in Carib languages, see Derbyshire (1985: 10–15) on Hixkaryana; Carlin (2004: 376–9, 384–7) on Trio; a summary of adjectives in South America is in Aikhenvald (2012a: 139–41).

See Spencer (2008: 59) on Kwomtari; Routamaa (1994), on Kamula; Feldpausch and Feldpausch (1992: 30) on Namia; Abbott (1991: 88, 129–30) on Macushi; Genetti and Hildebrandt (2004) on Manange; Guillaume (2008: 68–9, 73) on Cavineña; Sulkala and Karjalainen (1992: 87), on Finnish; Kenesei et al. (1998: 92–3) on Hungarian.

§8.2.1: See Sulkala and Karjalainen (1992: 204, 339–40) on Finnish; Overall (2008: 146–9) on Aguaruna; Kenesei et al (1998: 189) on Hungarian; Lewis (2000: 50–3) on Turkish; Holisky and Gagua (1994: 171–3) on Tsova-Tush; Kibrik (1994: 381–2) on Khinalug; Viitso (2007: 35) on Estonian; Alpher (1991: 22–6) on Yir-Yoront; Goddard (1983: 144–5) on Yankunytjatjara; Dixon (2002: 67–8) on adjectives in Australian languages; Fabricius (1998: 55, 87–91) on posible differences in the semantics of reduplication in nouns and in adjectives in Australian languages. Note that in some languages, reduplication may have similar meanings for nouns and adjectives, and thus cannot serve to distinguish them. For instance, in Dyirbal reduplication of the full noun always implies plurality of a noun, e.g. *gulgiṟigulgiṟi* 'lots of prettily painted men', and of an adjective, e.g. *midi-midi* 'lots of little ones' (Dixon 1972: 242, 251, Fabricius 1998: 90–1).

§8.2.2: See Hill (1992: 77–9) on Longgu; Enfield (2004b: 334–5) on Lao; Hyslop (2004: 268–73) on North-east Ambae; Sohn (2004) on Korean.

§8.2.3: See Aspinion (1953) on Tashelhit; Aikhenvald (2003: 76) on Tariana; Overall (2008: 144–5) on Aguaruna; Kibrik (1994) on Khinalug; Dixon (2010b: 90) on English.

§8.3: See Aikhenvald (2011a: 271–5) on adjectivization as a word-class-changing derivation; see Dixon (2014) on adjectives in English; Kenesei et al. (1998: 362–3, 366–7) on Hungarian; Jauncey (1997: 11) on Tamambo; Curnow (1997: 11) on Awa Pit; Roberts (1987: 325–6) on Amele; Saltarelli (1988: 260) on Basque; King (1993: 86–9) on Modern Welsh; Abdul-Fetouh (1969: 109) on Egyptian Colloquial Arabic; Nedjalkov (1997: 306) on Evenki. Adjective compounds in English are discussed at some length by Adams (1973: 90–104); also see Aikhenvald (2007b).

§8.5.1: See Dixon (2005: 377–440) on syntactic and other properties of adverbs, with special attention to English; Table 12.1 in Dixon (2005: 383) outlines the functions of adverbs derived from adjectival semantic types. Van der Auwera (2011) focuses on time adverbs in some languages of Europe. See Kenesei et al. (1998: 332, 348–51) on Hungarian; Sulkala and Karjalainen (1992: 349–50) on Finnish; Guillaume (2008: 67) on Cavineña.

§8.5.2: See Saltarelli (1988: 260–1) on Basque; Nedjalkov (1997: 306–7) on Evenki; Sulkala and Karjalainen (1992: 349, 360) on Finnish; Kenesei et al. (1998: 348, 370–1) on Hungarian; Dixon (1988: 109–11, 183–4) on Boumaa Fijian; King (1993: 238) on Modern Welsh; Dixon (2010a: 149–50, 2005: 381–5, 2014) on the formation of adverbs in English.

§8.6: A useful set of thirty parameters for distinguishing adjectives can be found in Dixon (2010b: 104–8).

9

Closed classes

The content, the nature, and the number of closed classes vary across languages. In some languages, adjectives form a small closed class of just a few members, typically with the meanings of dimension, age, value, and colour. Manner adverbs can also form a closed class (see Chapter 8). Verbs form a largish closed class in a few languages in New Guinea, including Kalam and Dumo.

Closed classes cover shifters—personal pronouns, demonstratives, time words, and locationals. Their reference varies according to speech participants, their location, and the time of the event.

Other closed classes may include determiners, articles, interrogatives, indefinites, quantifiers, and number words. Adpositions—that is, prepositions and postpositions—are usually a closed class. Negators, connectives, and discourse markers may form closed classes in their own right.

9.1 Personal pronouns

Every language has a set of personal pronouns, that is, shifters whose reference varies depending on who is talking and who they are talking to.

Any speech act involves two Speech Act Participants (SAP)—the speaker, or 'first person', and the addressee, or 'second person'. Many languages have just these two personal pronouns. Others also have the 'third person' pronoun, to refer to someone who is neither the speaker nor the addressee. The 'third person' pronoun is part of the same paradigm as the SAP forms. It normally can replace a noun. In *The man picked a nut and he cracked it*, *he* replaces *the man*, and *it* replaces *the nut*.

Free, or independent, pronouns are found in every language. Defining features of free pronouns as a separate closed class include person, number, and gender (§9.1.1), and interpersonal relations (§9.1.2). They can head the noun phrase in a core, and often also in oblique, function; we turn to their syntactic and morphological properties in §9.1.3. Possessive pronouns mark the possessor within a noun phrase—see §9.1.4. Reflexive, reciprocal and also logophoric pronouns express the identity of some arguments with each other—see §9.1.5. Bound pronouns, or pronominal affixes, may occur on the predicate signalling core participants (also see §7.1); or they can mark possessor within a possessive noun phrase—see §9.1.6.

9.1.1 *Person, number, and gender in free pronouns*

Person, number, and gender in free pronouns are linked together. The most common number distinctions are (see also §6.2.1):

- (a) singular/plural, where singular refers to one participant, and plural to more than one;
- (b) singular/dual/plural, where dual refers to two participants and plural to more than two;
- (c) singular/dual/paucal/plural, where dual refers to two participants, paucal to a few (and fewer than plural), and plural to many; and
- (d) singular/dual/trial/plural, where dual refers to two participants, trial to just three, and plural to many.

Let us look at some examples. Many languages distinguish three persons and two numbers in their personal pronouns. This is the case in Hungarian as shown in 9.1:

(9.1) | PERSON | SINGULAR | PLURAL |
| --- | --- | --- |
| First | *én* | *mi* |
| Second | *te* | *ti* |
| Third | *ő* | *ő-k* |

Personal pronouns may not be easily parsed into person and number morphemes. In Hungarian, the third person plural pronoun contains the plural marker *-k*. Other pronouns are not analysable. In Cupeño, a Uto-Aztecan language formerly spoken in California, all plural pronouns contain the suffix *-m*. None of the forms is fully regular.

(9.2) | PERSON | SINGULAR | PLURAL |
| --- | --- | --- |
| First | *ne'* | *che-m* |
| Second | *e'* | *e-m* |
| Third | *pe'* | *pe-m* |

Dyirbal distinguishes singular, dual, and plural numbers in personal pronouns. The subject (or A/S) forms in the Mamu dialect are listed in 9.3:

(9.3) | PERSON | SINGULAR | DUAL | PLURAL |
| --- | --- | --- | --- |
| First | *ñaja* | *ñali* | *ñana* |
| Second | *ŋinda* | *ñubala* | *ñuñay* |

Yimas distinguishes four numbers in first and second person pronouns:

(9.4)   PERSON   SINGULAR   DUAL   PAUCAL   PLURAL
        1   *ama*   *kapa*   *paŋkt*   *ipa*
        2   *mi*   *kapwa* *paŋkt*   *ipwa*

Neither Dyirbal nor Yimas have a third person pronoun. One can refer to a third person with a noun phrase, or with a demonstrative. Having no special form for third person reference is a feature of many Australian, Papuan, and North American Indian languages. The third person form in Chipewyan, an Athapaskan language, derives from *ʔeyi déne* 'that person'.

We now turn to further features of personal pronouns.

I. HOW NUMBER CAN INTERACT WITH PERSON. Number distinctions in pronouns can be neutralized depending on person value. English has one form, 'you', to cover singular and plural second person. (The older form of the singular second person pronoun, *thou*, is archaic and hardly used. Some varieties of English employ new formations for 'you plural'—including *you all*, *you-s*, and *you guys*). In Amele one form is used for second and third person dual, and another one for second and third person plural (Table 9.1).

One pronoun for non-singular second and third person is typical of other languages from the New Guinea Highlands. The form *köl/kale* in Kobon, from the same area, refers to all of the dual and plural second and third person pronouns. Chipewyan, an Athapaskan language, has one form for first and second person plural: *si/sị* '1sg', *nën* '2sg', *nhuni/nuxni* '1pl/2pl'.

Dual number may be expressed only in first person pronouns, and not in other persons. Yidiñ has special forms for dual and plural, or non-singular, first person, and only one, non-singular, form for second person (see § 9.5).

TABLE 9.1. Personal pronouns in Amele

PERSON	SINGULAR	DUAL	PLURAL
1st	*ija*	*ele*	*ege*
2nd	*hina*	*ale*	*age*
3rd	*uqa*		

(9.5)   PERSON   SINGULAR   DUAL   NON-SINGULAR
         First   *ŋayu*   *ŋali*   *ŋañji*
         Second   *ñundu*   *ñundu:ba*

Non-singular personal pronouns may have additional meanings. Aguaruna has two first person plural pronouns: *ii* refers to a specific group of people, and *hutii* refers to a non-specific, or more general group.

II. INCLUSIVE AND EXCLUSIVE PRONOUNS. In many languages of North and South America, Australia, and Oceania, first person non-singular 'we' may include, or exclude, other speech act participants. A set of forms called 'inclusive' includes the addressee and refers to 'me and one addressee' (for duals) or 'me and many addressees' (or 'me, and addressee, and non-addressees') for plurals. The 'exclusive' refers to 'me and someone else (not addressee)' for duals, and 'me and many others (non address-ees)' for plurals. This is what we saw in (6.12), for Motuna. Independent pronouns in Tamambo distinguish first person non-singular inclusive ('me and you'), and first person non-singular exclusive (Table 9.2).

Personal pronouns in Longgu distinguish inclusive and exclusive forms in the three non-singular numbers—dual, paucal, and plural (Table 9.3).

Tok Pisin, an English-based Creole and a major lingua franca of Papua New Guinea, distinguishes inclusive and exclusive forms in all three non-singular numbers—dual, trial, and plural (Table 9.4).

TABLE 9.2. Personal pronouns in Tamambo

PERSON/NUMBER	FORM
1st singular	*iau*
2nd singular	*niho*
3rd singular	*nia*
1pl inclusive 'me and others including addressee'	*hinda*
1pl exclusive 'me and others excluding addressee'	*kamam*
2pl	*kamim*
3pl	*nira*

TABLE 9.3. Personal pronouns in Longgu

NUMBER	1ST		2ND	3RD
singular	*nau/na*		*oe*	*ngaia**
	INCLUSIVE	EXCLUSIVE		
dual	*gaoa/ga*	*amerua*	*amurua*	*girua/girurua*
paucal	*golu*	*amelu*	*amolu*	*giraolu*
plural	*gia*	*ami*	*amu*	*gira*

TABLE 9.4. Personal pronouns in Tok Pisin

NUMBER	1ST		2ND	3RD
singular	*mi*		*yu*	*em*
	INCLUSIVE	EXCLUSIVE		
dual	*yu-mi-tu-pela*	*mi-tu-pela*	*yu-tu-pela*	*(em)tu-pela*
trial	*yu-mi-tri-pela*	*mi-tri-pela*	*yu-tri-pela*	*(em)tri-pela*
plural	*yu-mi*	*mi-pela*	*yu-pela*	*ol*

The forms are clearly analysable: they contain *mi* 'I', *tu* 'two; exponent of dual', *yu* 'you', and -*pela*, originally based on English 'fellow' which can be interpreted as a collective marker.

III. MINIMAL VERSUS AUGMENTED NUMBER SYSTEM IN PERSONAL PRONOUNS. Many non-European languages have one form for the two Speech Act Participants—speaker and addressee. The special speaker-plus-addressee forms are one paradigm with the rest of the personal pronouns. The distinctions involved can be described in terms of a distinction between a 'minimal' system versus an 'augmented' system.

This is how it works. Hdi, a Chadic language, has a set of 'minimal' forms referring to one person ('I', 'you (singular)', or 'he/she') or to two people ('me and you') (Table 9.5). A set of augmented forms indicates one or more participants added to the minimal set, that is, 'us', 'you, me, and one or more person', 'you (plural)', and 'they'.

TABLE 9.5. Personal pronouns in Hdi: a minimal/augmented system

PERSON	NUMBER: MINIMAL	NUMBER: AUGMENTED
First	*íí* 'I'	*áŋní* 'we (without second person)'
First + Second	*úú* 'you and me'	*ámú* 'you and me and other(s)'
Second	*kághá* 'he/she'	*kághúní* 'they'
Third	*tsátsí*	*xáxə̀n*

Minimal-augmented systems are widespread in the languages of the Philippines, a number of languages from North and South America (including Carib), Australia, and from the Chadic branch of Afroasiatic.

IV. IMPERSONAL PRONOUNS. Languages may have a pronominal form with generic or impersonal reference, used in general statements. Tariana has a generic pronoun *pha* 'one, people in general'. Its use is comparable to that of non-specific pronominal forms in European languages, for example English *one*, French *on*, and German *man*, or generic nouns, for example Portuguese *a gente*. The exact overtones of impersonal pronouns vary. The impersonal pronoun in French can refer to more than one speech act participant, and even to first person, for example *on y va* 'we are going'. The Tariana impersonal pronoun can have inclusive reference, 'you and me'. 'One' in English can be used to avoid self reference, as in *One suddenly realized that one was being followed*.

V. PRONOUNS AND GENDER. Generally speaking, if a language distinguishes genders in second person pronouns, it will be likely to also distinguish them in third person pronouns. Many Afroasiatic languages distinguish feminine and masculine gender in second and third person singular and plural. A typical system is in Hausa (Table 9.6).

Most frequently, gender is distinguished just in the third person, as in French or Portuguese. Some languages distinguish genders in second, but not first or third person. Minangkabau, a Western Austronesian language from Sumatera in Indonesia, has one form, *(a)den*, for 'I', and one form, *inyo* for 'she, he, and it'. There are two forms for 'you': *waang* or *ang* 'you masculine' and *kau* 'you feminine'.

Having special forms for feminine and masculine genders in first person pronouns is less common. Gala, a Ndu language from the Sepik province in Papua New Guinea, has two genders in the singular free pronouns, but not in the plural or dual (Table 9.7).

TABLE 9.6. Free personal pronouns in Hausa

PERSON	GENDER	SINGULAR	PLURAL
First		nī	mū
Second	feminine	kē	kū
	masculine	kai	
Third	feminine	ita	sū
	masculine	shī	

TABLE 9.7. Personal pronouns in Gala

PERSON/GENDER	SINGULAR	DUAL	PLURAL
1 masculine	wun	æn	nan
1 feminine	ñin		
2 masculine	min, mən	bən	gun
2 feminine	yin		
3 masculine	kəl, kər	(na)bəl	lar, lal
3 feminine	ki		

Table 9.7 reflects a common tendency, across the world's languages. Pronouns tend to distinguish genders in singular number only. This is the case in English and German. It is somewhat unusual to have more gender distinctions in a non-singular than in a singular number. Personal pronouns in Spanish are a case in point (Table 9.8). Note that first and second person plural pronouns are derived from a combination of a personal pronoun and an indefinite adjective *otro* 'other (masculine)', *otra* 'other (feminine)'.

Gender in pronouns may be different from gender in other areas of the grammar. Grammatical gender in English is only expressed in third person singular pronouns *she*, *he*, and *it*.

Pronouns may reflect aspects of reference classification other than gender. In Finnish and Bengali, personal pronouns typically refer only to humans (there are no gender distinctions).

TABLE 9.8. Personal pronouns in Spanish

PERSON/GENDER	SINGULAR	PLURAL
1st person masculine	*yo*	*nosotros*
1st person feminine		*nosotras*
2nd person masculine	*tú, vos*	*vosotros*
2nd person feminine		*vosotras*
3rd person masculine	*él*	*ellos*
3rd person feminine	*ella*	*ellas*

9.1.2 Interpersonal relations in free pronouns

Personal pronouns may reflect societal conventions, hierarchies, and interpersonal relations. In many European and a few non-European languages, plural forms of pronouns indicate respect. These forms are conventionally labelled *T*- and *V*-forms, cf. French *tu* 'you singular; informal' versus *vous* 'you plural; you singular (polite)' (some more examples were mentioned in §7.5). If two people use *T*-forms to each other, they indicate intimacy and social closeness or equality. In contrast, *V*-forms indicate respect and social distance. If one person uses the *T*-form and the other uses the *V*-form, this asymmetry will reflect an imbalance in power or in status: a more powerful, authoritative, or older person has the right to use *T*- and to expect *V*- in return. The second person plural pronoun in Tamambo is also used to express respect to the (singular) addressee, and to talk to someone older than the speaker, or to a person of social esteem, such as a pastor or a chief.

A third person form can also be used to address another person politely. In Italian, the second person singular *tu* implies 'intimacy, familiarity, closeness between speaker and addressee' (Maiden and Robustelli 2007: 460–2). It is also 'used (regrettably) by people who feel that they are in authority and want to stress the importance of their power', 'or to threaten and to show contempt'. In contrast, the third person singular *Lei* implies, 'first and foremost, social distance (non-familiarity) between interlocutors'.

Languages spoken in the highly stratified societies of East and Southeast Asia have elaborate systems of personal pronouns. Their use is determined by the speaker's relationship with, and attitude to, the addressee, and also their relative age and sex. Table 9.9 offers a selection of personal pronouns in Korean.

Level I is the deferential and polite level 'where the addressee, or the third person referent, must be a socially superior adult or a distant (stranger) adult'. The speaker

TABLE 9.9. A selection of personal pronouns in Korean

LEVEL	1ST PERSON		2ND PERSON		3RD PERSON	
	Singular	Plural	Singular	Plural	Singular	Plural
I	*ce/cey*	*ce-huy-(tul)*	*tayk*	*tayk-tul*	D *pwul* D *elun*	D *pwun-tul* D *elun-tul*
II	*na*	*wuli-(tul)*	*tangsin caki*	*tangsin-tul*	D *i* *ku* *ku nye*	D *-tul* D-*tul* *ku nye-tul*
III	*na/nay*	*wuli-(tul)*	*caney*	*caney-tul*	D *salam* *ku*	D *salam-tul* D *-tul*
IV	*na/nay*	*wuli-(tul)*	*ne/ney*	*ne-huy-(tul)*	D *ai/ay*	D *ai/ay-tul*

then uses the 'humble' first person form. Level II is called 'blunt': 'the addressee or the third person referent is generally equal or lower status than the speaker, yet he or she is an adult'. Level III is 'familiar and intimate': the addressee or the third person referent is lower than the speaker, and may not be an adult. Level IV is the 'plain' level (the addressee or the third person can be a child). Some of the third person forms in Table 9.9 are in fact demonstratives (D) (variants appear in one cell).

Not all means of referring to oneself, or to the other person, are included here. A noun phrase can be used in lieu of first person pronoun, for example *pon-kwan* 'I (this office)', *so-in* 'I (small person)' are used in military camps and 'some humble letters'.

Pronouns and terms of interpersonal address in Lao, Thai, and many other languages of East and Southeast Asia tend to form a large, and almost an open-ended class. Personal pronouns in Thai include about twenty-seven first person forms, twenty-two second person forms, and eight third person forms. The basic system of personal pronouns in Lao is given in Table 9.10 (numbers indicate tones). 'Bare' pronoun forms vary regionally, and according to speakers' socio-economic status. They can be rude; and considered as exponents of lower education. If used between close friends, they indicate the warmth of a relationship. Distinctions at the pronominal level are fewer in rural environments, where people would hardly ever have the occasion to use the first and second person formal pronouns.

Lao has many more strategies for personal reference, each for a specific social context. There is a special first person form used by monks when talking to lay people. Some nouns, including kinship terms, occupation or role terms ('teacher', 'monk') and personal names can be used for address, and also for first, second and third person reference.

TABLE 9.10. A selection of personal pronouns in Lao

Number	Level		1st person	2nd person	3rd person
SINGULAR	BARE		*kuu3*	*mùng2*	*man2*
	FAMILIAR		*haw2*	*too3*	*laaw2*
	POLITE		*khòòj5*	*caw4*	*phen1*
	FORMAL		*khaa5-phacaw4*	*thaan1*	*thaan1*
PLURAL	BARE		*phuak4-kuu3*	*suu3*	*khaw3*
	POLITE	INCLUSIVE	*cu-haw2*	*cu-caw4, phuak4-caw4*	*khacaw4*
		EXCLUSIVE	*cu-khòòj5*		

In some Australian languages, non-singular personal pronouns encode kinship relationships of the participants. Lardil has two forms for 'third person dual (them two)'. One, *pi-rri*, refers to 'two people in the same generation level, or two levels apart, for example ego and brother, sister, grandparent, or grandchild', and the other, *rni-inki*, refers to 'two people either in alternate generation levels, or three levels apart, for example ego and parent or child, or great-grandparent, or great-grandchild'. To understand the system of pronouns, one has to have a good grasp of kinship relationships, and of social organization.

9.1.3 *Special features of free personal pronouns*

Personal pronouns can usually be listed exhaustively, as befits a closed class. They tend to be noun-like. Their special morphological and syntactic properties justify treating them as a class on their own.

Pronoun-specific grammatical features include gender, humanness, and number distinctions, and also social relationships, as we saw in the previous section. These are the potential defining features for personal pronouns as a separate word class.

Pronouns may have categories nouns lack. In English, only personal pronouns distinguish genders, and grammatical cases, for example *me*, *him*, *her*. In Spanish only *yo*, 'I', *tú* 'you singular', and *se* 'oneself' have special forms used with prepositions. Instead of *con yo* and *con tú* one uses fused forms, *conmigo* and *contigo*.

Pronouns may have fewer case distinctions than nouns. Pronouns in Tariana do not have locative case. Nouns in the object function take the object case marked by -*nuku* only if they are topical. But pronouns always take the object case marker -*na* if they are in an object function. In Finnish, personal pronouns cannot form a comitative case.

Pronouns may have more number distinctions than nouns. Nouns and demonstratives in Yimas distinguish just singular, dual, and plural numbers (and no paucal). Only personal pronouns have a four-term number system (as we saw in example 9.4).

In Hungarian, the accusative of the first and second person pronouns involves a somewhat irregular form—see (9.6). The nominative case forms (given in 9.1) are repeated here.

(9.6)

PERSON	SG: NOMINATIVE	SG: ACCUSATIVE	PL: NOMINATIVE	PL: ACCUSATIVE
1st	*én*	*engem(et)*	*mi*	*minket, bennünket*
2nd	*te*	*téged(et)*	*ti*	*titeket, benneteket*
3rd	*ő*	*ő-t*	*ő-k*	*ő-k-et*

The accusative of the third person pronouns is formed like that of nouns, with the suffix -*t* attached to the nominative stem. Special pronominal declensions are a feature of Slavic, Baltic, and Balto-Finnic languages.

Nouns in Dyirbal and in Yidiñ have an absolutive-ergative case system, with an opposition between the absolutive case, for S and O, and ergative case, for A. Personal pronouns are drastically different: they distinguish a nominative case for S and A, and an accusative case, for O. This is a typical instance of 'split ergativity' based on the semantics of a noun phrase: more on this in Chapter 10.

Syntactic functions of personal pronouns are restricted, if compared to nouns. Pronouns can hardly ever be possessed in a possessive noun phrase. The modifiers they can occur with are limited, to say the least. Personal pronouns in Ainu and in Manambu cannot take any modifiers at all. Personal pronouns in English cannot be modified by an article. In Lao, personal pronouns stand apart from nouns in a number of ways. Unlike nouns,

(a) personal pronouns cannot be heads of noun phrases with demonstrative modifiers (that is, one cannot say 'this me');

(b) personal pronouns cannot head a possessive construction (one cannot say 'someone's I');

(c) they cannot be complements of the copula verb *pên3*;

(d) they cannot be used in a numeral classifier construction;

(e) they cannot be modified by a relative clause.

In addition, personal pronouns may have special syntactic features. They can be part of a special pronoun elaboration, or 'inclusory', construction. This is found in numerous languages of the Pacific area, and also in a number of European, Mesoamerican, and African languages. In (9.7), from Mwotlap, an Oceanic language from Vanuatu, a third person dual pronoun 'them two', refers to two people: a chief and a woman, who has just been mentioned in the text:

(9.7)   mayanag   kōyō   mo-gom
        chief   3du   PERF-ill
        'The chief and her are ill' (lit. the chief they-two are ill)

Similarly, in Tok Pisin one can say *mitupela Pauline*, literally, 'we two Pauline', meaning 'Pauline and I'. Alternatively, both participants can be specified, as in Manambu *bər ñan asay* (them.two child father) 'the two of them father and child'. An elaboration construction can contain a linker, for example Latvian *mēs ar Jāni* 'Jani and I' (literally, we and Jani). Or one of the components can be marked with the comitative case, as in Hungarian *mi Péter-rel* (we Peter-COMITATIVE) 'Peter and I' (literally 'we with Peter').

Pronoun elaboration constructions form one noun phrase. They constitute a strategy for noun coordination, and are specific to pronouns as a word class.

9.1.4 Possessive pronouns

Personal pronouns may function as possessors within a noun phrase. They are then likely to appear in special possessive forms: these are possessive pronouns. Of the two sets of possessive pronouns in English, one is used as a modifier to a noun, for example *my book*, and the other one as head of a noun phrase, for example *mine* as in *Give him mine* (that is, something belonging to me). The choice of gender in third person singular pronouns is determined by the gender of the possessor, for example *her book* or *his book* (Table 9.11).

TABLE 9.11. Two sets of possessive pronouns in English

PERSON/NUMBER OF POSSESSOR	POSSESSIVE PRONOUN	
	AS MODIFIER	AS NP HEAD
1st singular	*my*	*mine*
2nd singular	*your*	*yours*
3rd singular feminine	*her*	*hers*
masculine	*his*	*his*
neuter	*its*	*its*
1st plural	*our*	*ours*
2nd plural	*your*	*yours*
3rd plural	*their*	*theirs*

Spanish possessive pronouns have two forms. A short form is used as a modifier preceding the head of a noun phrase (pre-head modifier), for example *mi amigo* 'my friend'. A long form can be used as an NP head, and as a modifier following the head of a noun phrase (post-head modifier), for example *un amigo mío* (INDEFINITE.ART-ICLE.MASC.SG friend.MASC my:LONG.FORM.MASC) 'a friend of mine'. All forms agree in number with the possessed noun rather than with the possessor (unlike English). Only those forms which have a masculine form in *-o* agree in gender, again, with the possessed noun, for example *nuestro libro* (our+MASC.SG book) 'our book'.

Possessive forms of personal pronouns are often irregular. In Awa Pit, a Barbacoan language from Ecuador and Colombia, they consist of a pronoun with the possessive enclitic *=pa*; singular pronouns undergo fusion, for example 1sg *na* plus *=pa* results in *ap*, for example *ap pimpul* 'my leg'.

Having possessive pronouns with a special form is not universal. In many languages, including Basque, Turkish, Dyirbal, and Estonian, the genitive form of a personal pronoun is used to mark a pronominal possessor, for example Estonian *minu raamat* 'my book'. There can be bound possessive affixes; more on these in §9.1.6.

9.1.5 Pronouns of argument identity

Pronouns can express argument identity. If an O is the same as A, a language may use a special reflexive pronoun. The reflexive pronoun in English expresses the person, number, and gender of the subject, as in *I hid myself, she hurt herself*. Subject pronouns do not distinguish number in second person while the reflexive ones do, for example *You hurt yourself* versus *You hurt yourselves*. The pronoun *they*, in its relatively new usage as the gender-neutral singular pronoun, has a reflexive correlate *themself*. Reflexive pronouns vary in their structure.

In Hua, a reflexive pronoun consists of the free personal pronoun and the possessive bound pronoun, for example *dgai-'di* 'I myself', lit. 'my I', *kgai-'Ka* 'you yourself', lit. 'your you'. Reflexive pronouns in Hungarian consist of the form *maga-* accompanied by possessive suffixes, for example *maga-m* 'I myself', *maga-d* 'you (singular) yourself', *maga-tok* 'you (plural) yourself'.

Some languages have one reflexive pronoun which does not change for person. The reflexive pronouns in Russian *sebja* 'self', and in Estonian *ise/enda* 'self', are used to mark coreferentiality with any person. The reflexive in Japanese inflects for number, but not for person: *jibun* 'reflexive singular', *jibun-tachi* 'reflexive plural'.

Reflexive pronouns may have an intensive, or 'autoreflexive' function: they emphasize the participation of the subject as the main actor, as in English *he did it himself* or *he himself did it*, or Hungarian *én magam varr-t-am ez-t a zakó-t* (I myself sew-PAST-1sg.DEFINITE this-ACC DEF.ARTICLE jacket-ACC) 'I sewed this jacket myself'. Or intensive pronouns may form a special set, as in Basque where they do not have a reflexive meaning, for example *neu* 'I myself', *heu* 'you (intimate) yourself', *geu* 'he or she himself or herself'.

Reciprocal pronouns can mark the actions done to one another. Hungarian has one reciprocal pronoun, *egymás*, regularly marked for case, as in *ők szeret-ik egymás-t* (they love-3pl each.other-ACC) 'they love each other'. Reciprocal pronouns can consist of two words, as in English *each other*, *one another* or Estonian *teine teise* 'each other' and *üks teise* 'one another'.

Reflexive and reciprocal pronouns may express interpersonal relations. Korean has an elaborate system of level distinctions in personal pronouns, as we saw in Table 9.9. The choice of a third person reflexive form depends on the social standing and age of the referent. The neutral form *caki* is used for people of all ages; the deferential form *tangsin* is used to refer to adult social superiors, and the plain form *ce* is used for social inferiors, children, and animals. The reflexive form *casin* is used for first, second, and also third person.

This is by no means universal. Personal pronouns in Lao have a number of social status distinctions (see Table 9.10). However, the reflexive marker *too3* 'body, self' and the intensive marker *qêêng3* 'self, on one's own' do not reflect social status.

A reflexive or a reciprocal pronoun may function as an argument within a clause, and also as a possessor within a noun phrase. The reflexive pronoun *dodoc* in Amele has the two functions. In English, the reflexive forms in *-self* cannot function as possessives: *own* is used to mark a possessor coreferential with the subject, for example *John washed his own (John's) clothes*. Some languages have just one form for reflexive and for reciprocal; this is the case in many Romance languages.

Reflexive and reciprocal pronouns may be based on a noun; most frequently, a body part term 'head', 'body', or 'bone'. Hdi utilizes the word *vghá* 'body' in the object function, both as a reflexive and as a reciprocal. Hausa, also Chadic, indicates reflexive with the noun *kâi* 'head' followed by a bound genitive pronoun, for example *kâi-nā* 'I myself', lit. 'my head'. Reciprocals are indicated by the word *jūnā* 'other' also accompanied by a bound genitive pronoun. Despite the clear link between a reflexive or a reciprocal and a noun, their behaviour may justify considering them a closed subclass.

There may be further types of pronouns indicating identity of participants. In many African languages, 'logophoric' pronouns indicate that the subject of a speech clause in a complex sentence is the same as one of the participants in the reporting clause.

This is how it works in Mupun, a Chadic language from Nigeria. A non-logophoric pronoun *wu* 'he' is used in the reporting clause, 'he said'. If the same pronoun is used in the speech clause, it means that the third person pronoun refers to someone else:

(9.8)   wu   sat   nə   wu   nas   an
          he:non.logophoric   say   COMPL   he:non.logophoric   beat   I
          'He$_i$ said that he$_j$ (someone else than he$_i$) beat me'

Using a logophoric pronoun in the speech clause means that 'saying' was done by the same person as the one who did the 'beating':

(9.9)   wu   sat   nə   ɗi   nas   an
        he:non.logophoric   say   COMPL   he:logophoric   beat   I
        'He$_i$ said that he$_i$ (same person) beat me'

Reflexive, reciprocal, and logophoric pronouns may be part of a closed class of personal pronouns. Or they may be considered separate closed subclasses in their own right. Enfield (2007: 317) remarks that the reciprocal and collaborative marker *kan3* (and its variants) in Lao 'does not belong in a larger form class', forming a class on its own.

9.1.6 *Bound pronouns*

So far we have focused on independent free personal pronouns. In many languages, an argument of the verb can be signalled on the verb itself with bound pronouns. As we saw in §7.1, these may express core arguments. They can also mark the nominal possessor and argument identity (including reflexives and reciprocals). If a language has obligatory bound pronouns, a sentence may just consist of a verb with the bound pronoun, as in Manambu:

(9.10a)   ya-kna-ñən
          come-FUT-2sg.feminine
          'You (woman) will come'

The free pronoun can optionally be added, to emphasize the identity of the subject:

(9.10b)   ñən   ya-kna-ñən
          you.feminine   come-FUT-2sg.feminine
          'You (woman; not someone else) will come'

Bound pronouns are often similar to free pronouns in their form. In Manambu the bound form *-ñən* 'you feminine' is segmentally the same as the free personal pronoun. In Warekena, free pronouns consist of a combination of bound personal pronominal prefix with the suffix *-ya*, for example *nu-tapa* (1sg-walk) 'I am walking', *nu-ya* 'I'.

Bound pronouns in Romance languages are clitics. They have special rules for their ordering before the verb. For instance, in French, first and second person dative clitic pronouns precede the object clitic pronouns, for example *je te le donne* (I to.you it.OBJECT give) 'I give it to you'. Third person dative clitic pronouns follow the object, as in *je le lui donne* (I it.OBJECT to.him give) 'I give it to him'.

Bound pronouns may differ from free pronouns in numerous ways. They never head a noun phrase. They always have a fixed position within the verb or verb phrase.

They always constitute a closed grammatical system—this is in contrast to personal pronouns which can arguably be a large open set (as in the languages of East and Southeast Asia).

Bound pronouns may have categories free pronouns lack. Pronominal prefixes in Caddo, a Caddoan language from Oklahoma, distinguish four persons: besides first, second, and third person, there is an additional 'fourth person', similar to English 'one' in its function. It is used to refer to someone whose identity is unknown. Or their identity may be known, but the speaker may wish not to draw attention to them. An example is in (9.11).

(9.11) yi-t-hayas=ʔnih-ah
        IMPERS-AGENT-DATIVE=pay-PERFECTIVE
        'One has paid him'

This same prefix can be used to refer to a less important character in a story. Until recently, it was obligatory for Caddo speakers to use such impersonal, or 'defocusing' prefixes in addressing one's in-laws.

Bound pronouns can combine a number of functions. In Arawak languages of South America and in Mayan languages, the same set of bound pronouns can be used to mark the possessor on a noun, and the subject (A/S) on the verb. In Tupi-Guaraní and Carib languages the same set marks the possessor and the S/O on the verb. It is logical to discuss bound pronouns in the same section of the grammar as free pronouns, due to a close conceptual, and often formal, connection between these.

Free pronouns can be obligatory, as they are in English. In languages with bound pronouns, free pronouns tend to be used less often—only in special contexts, where one participant has to be contrasted to the other, as in Hungarian, and in Spanish. Independent pronouns in Tamambo are used sparingly—to introduce a new participant or to topicalize a participant, to emphasize the participation of a known referent in discourse, or to indicate the person and number of the subject of a non-verbal clause. If a language is rich in bound pronouns, it will be less so in free pronouns.

9.2 Demonstratives

Demonstratives are a class of shifters which refer (often by pointing) to some person, or some thing, other than speaker or addressee. Every language has a closed class of demonstratives. We distinguish three types.

(a) NOMINAL DEMONSTRATIVES can occur in an NP with a noun or a pronoun (e.g. '[this stone] is hot') and, in most languages, can make up a complete NP (e.g. '[this] is hot').

(b) LOCAL ADVERBIAL DEMONSTRATIVES occur either alone (e.g. 'put it <u>here</u>') or with a noun taking local marking (e.g. 'put it (on the table) <u>there</u>').

(c) VERBAL DEMONSTRATIVES 'do it like this' (sometimes with an accompanying mimicking action) can occur as the only verb in a predicate, or together with a lexical verb.

Types (a) and (b) are found in every language. Type (c) is relatively rare.

The terms demonstrative and deictic are almost synonymous. Some grammarians use the term 'demonstrative' for nominal demonstratives, and 'deictic' as a cover term for the whole macro-class.

9.2.1 *The meanings of demonstratives*

Demonstratives centre around the two speech act participants—the Speaker and the Addressee. The meanings of nominal and adverbial demonstratives cover:

(i) distance to or from the speaker, and sometimes also to or from the addressee;
(ii) visibility by the speaker, and sometimes also by the addressee;
(iii) height, stance, and direction, with respect to the speaker, or to the addressee.

Many languages have a two-term demonstrative system, where 'this' (close to speaker) contrasts with 'that (far from speaker)', as in English and in Alamblak, a Papuan language:

(9.12) *ind-ar-r* (DEMONSTRATIVE-close-masc.sg) 'this (one)'
        ind-ur-r (DEMONSTRATIVE-far-masc.sg) 'that (one)'

A language may have a three-term system. This would include another term referring to mid-distance, as in Quechua:

(9.13) *kay*   'this (one) here' (proximal)
        chay   'that one there' (mid-distance)
        taqay 'that one over there, far' (distal)

Longgu, an Oceanic language, distinguishes four degrees of distance in its demonstratives:

(9.14) *nene*   'this: proximal'
        nina   'that: medial'
        ninaina 'that over there'
        nihou   'that a long way over there'

TABLE 9.12. **Demonstratives in Palikur**

	in speaker's hand	near to speaker and to addressee	far from speaker and near addressee or vice versa	far from both, visible	very far from both, not visible
masc	*ner*	*ner*	*nop*	*netra*	*nere*
fem	*no*	*no*	*nop*	*notra*	*nore*
neut	*inin*	*ini*	*nop*	*inetra*	*inere*

Demonstratives may combine reference to the relative distance of the object from the speaker, the addressee, and the object's visibility. Palikur, an Arawak language from Brazil and French Guiana, has five sets of demonstratives: 'in speaker's hand', 'near to speaker and to addressee', 'far from speaker and near addressee or vice versa', 'far from both, visible', and 'very far from both, and not visible'. Each distinguishes three genders: masculine, feminine, and neuter (Table 9.12).

If a language is spoken in a hilly area, demonstratives may encode relative height, stance, and direction (uphill, downhill, and also upriver, downriver, etc.). This is known as 'topographic' deixis. Lak, a North-east Caucasian language, has five demonstratives, which include topographic members:

(9.15)   *va*   'this close to speaker'
          mu   'this close to hearer'
          ta   'that far from both speaker and hearer'
          qa   'the one higher than the speaker'
          ga   'the one lower than the speaker'

Height and direction in demonstratives may be integrated with visibility, as in Hua (Table 9.13).

The spatial reference of demonstratives can be extended to temporal reference, for example *this year, that year*. Demonstratives may have overtones of endearment and familiarity. Cavineña has three demonstratives: *riya* 'near speaker', *tume* 'there, near or familiar to addressee', *yume* 'over there, not near or not familiar to speaker or addressee'.

Demonstratives in English can have emotional and attitudinal overtones. As Zandvoort (1975: 148) put it, 'the kind of feeling implied (affection, vexation, contempt, disgust, etc.) depends on the situation'. Both *this* and *that* may carry either a positive or a negative overtone. One can say *I can't stand that/this mother-in-law of yours* (negative), *These/those modern poets publish a lot* (could be positive or negative), *This headache is killing me* (negative).

TABLE 9.13. Demonstratives in Hua

LEVEL WITH SPEAKER		UPHILL	DOWNHILL
close to speaker	*ma*		
close to hearer	*na*	*buga*	*muna*
neutral as to distance	*ora*		
visible, distal	*bura*	*biga*	*mina*
non-visible, distal	*bira*		

Local adverbial demonstratives point to a place—unlike nominal ones which point to an object. In English, local adverbial demonstratives *here* and *there* parallel *this* and *that* in terms of spatial relations. Local adverbial demonstratives are often derived from nominal ones; they may have more distinctions, as in Indonesian:

(9.16) NOMINAL DEMONSTRATIVES   LOCAL ADVERBIAL DEMONSTRATIVES
    ini 'this: near speaker'   *s-ini* 'here: near speaker'
    itu 'that: not near speaker'   *s-itu* 'there: mid-distance from speaker'
                                     sana 'there: far from speaker'

Local adverbial demonstratives may also have fewer distinctions than nominal ones. Longgu has just two adverbial demonstratives, *ine* 'here' and *ina* 'there'.

Verbal demonstratives, or deictic verbs, are essentially a closed subclass of verbs which involve deictic reference to the action. They can be discussed jointly with verbs, and mentioned again in the section on demonstratives as a closed class.

In Mapuche, the major indigenous language of Chile, the verb *fa-* and its derived forms mean 'do/be/become like this (proximal)', and *fe-* means 'do/be/become like that (distal)'. Compare *fa-nte-* 'be big like this' and *fe-nte-* 'be big like that':

(9.17) iñché ñi tasa eymi mi   tasa **fa-nte-n-üy**
      I   my cup you.sg your.sg cup be.like.this-'much'-VERB-INDICATIVE
      'My cup is as big as your cup here'

(9.18) iñché ñi tasa eymi mi   tasa **fe-nte-n-üy**
      I   my cup you.sg your.sg cup be.like.that-'much'-VERB-INDICATIVE
      'My cup is as big as your cup over there'

Further types of demonstratives may include manner demonstratives, for example Ainu *taa* 'this way', *too* 'that way', or Finnish *näin* 'in this way', *noin* 'in that way'. In English, an angler may demonstrate the size of a catch either by holding his hands wide apart and saying *It was this big* or *It was so big*, or else holding up a number of fingers and saying *They were this many* or *They were so many*. It appears that *so* has deictic reference as an alternative to *this* in contexts like this.

In terms of their syntactic and morphological features, demonstratives may constitute a rather divergent class of words. Each of the subclasses of demonstratives may show similarities with other word classes: a nominal demonstrative may be somewhat similar to an adjective, and an adverbial demonstrative may be similar to an adverb. Alternatively, a grammarian may opt to consider nominal and adverbial demonstratives as separate closed classes.

9.2.2 What demonstratives can do

Nominal demonstratives can have a number of grammatical categories which they may, or may not, share with nouns or adjectives. In Yimas, demonstratives are similar to nouns in that they distinguish singular, dual, and plural numbers (we can recall, from (9.4), that pronouns also have paucal number). In Finnish, demonstrative pronouns lack abessive and instructive singular case forms. Mandan Siouan and Guaicuruan languages have a special set of classifiers used just with demonstratives.

In terms of their syntactic functions, nominal demonstratives may be able to:

1. make up a complete NP, as in *This is hot*;
2. occur in an NP as a modifier with a noun or a personal pronoun, as in *This stone is hot*;
3. occupy the copula complement slot, as in *The fact is this*.

Further functions of demonstratives may include anaphora, to refer to something earlier in the text. One can anaphorically refer to a participant, and substitute the reference to a participant with an anaphoric mention. This is 'substitution anaphora', as in (9.19). Note that in English demonstratives can be used for substitution anaphora only with inanimate referents (third person pronouns will be used otherwise).

(9.19)   John brought <u>a cake</u>, and <u>that</u> [substitution anaphora] tasted good.

One can anaphorically refer to a stretch of text, as in (9.20). This is 'textual anaphora'.

(9.20)   <u>John came in late</u>, and <u>this</u> [textual anaphora] annoyed everyone.

Cataphora is the opposite of anaphora—its function is to refer to something later in the text. An example of substitution cataphora is in (9.21), and of textual cataphora is in (9.22).

(9.21) <u>These</u> are the choices: either publish or perish

(9.22) I will tell you <u>this</u>: all the money is going to be cut.

Many languages employ one form for these functions. Third person pronouns and nominal demonstratives can be used anaphorically, and cataphorically in English, for example *He sang loudly. It annoyed me.* In some languages, demonstratives used for deixis may not be used for anaphora. Demonstratives in Tamambo are a case in point; there is instead a special anaphoric-only form *mwende*. Demonstratives *nii4* 'this' and *nan4* 'that' in Lao can only be used as modifiers within a noun phrase, but not as heads of noun phrases.

Table 9.14 illustrates the syntactic functions of nominal demonstratives in English.

We can recall, from §6.7, that nominal demonstratives tend to have a special place within the noun phrase structure: they occur on its edges. When establishing the status of nominal demonstratives as a closed class, it is essential to determine their special morphological, and syntactic, properties and functions.

Local and manner adverbial demonstratives generally function as non-inflecting modifiers to verbs. They may have deictic functions, and may also be used anaphorically. Verbal demonstratives can express textual anaphora, as in Mapuche:

(9.23) fa-le-wma   iñché

   DEICTIC.VERB.become.like.this-STATIVE-COMPLETIVE.VERBAL.NOUN   I

   'This is how I was' (referring to what has been said before)

TABLE 9.14. **Properties of nominal demonstratives in English**

FUNCTION	PROXIMAL *this*	DISTAL *that*	EXAMPLE
1. Can make up a whole NP	yes	yes	*this is me; let me tell you this*
2. Can occur in an NP with a noun	yes	yes	*this man*
3. Can occur with other modifiers in the leftmost position in an NP	yes	yes	*these two big fat men*
4. Substitution anaphora	yes	yes	Example 9.19
5. Substitution cataphora	yes	yes	Example 9.21
6. Textual anaphora	yes	yes	Example 9.20
7. Textual cataphora	yes		Example 9.22

A note on terminology. The term 'pronoun' is sometimes used to refer to members of numerous closed classes used as heads of noun phrases and as modifiers within them. Hence terms like 'demonstrative pronouns', 'indefinite pronouns', 'negative pronouns', and so on. Personal pronouns whose reference changes depending on the person are very different from demonstratives and other closed classes used to replace nouns. Consequently, we set the latter apart from other closed classes by not referring to them as 'pronouns'. Demonstrative determiners are sometimes referred to as 'demonstrative adjectives'. This is misleading, since demonstratives are usually different from adjectives in their morphological and syntactic functions: for instance, unlike adjectives, they cannot be used in comparative constructions.

9.3 Articles and noun markers

Articles typically cover definiteness and specificity (see §6.5). They always form a closed class. French and German have definite and indefinite articles; these distinguish genders in the singular number, for example French *le* 'masculine singular definite', *un* 'masculine singular indefinite', *la* 'feminine singular definite', *une* 'feminine singular indefinite', *les* 'plural definite', *des* 'plural indefinite'. In Hungarian, a Ugric language with a system of definite and indefinite articles, these do not inflect for number or for gender.

The rules of article use vary. In Hungarian, entities mentioned in discourse for the first time, and copula complements, appear without an article, for example *diák vagyok* (student be.1sg) 'I am a student'. In English and in many Romance languages an indefinite article is used then. Articles can vary, across languages, in how they can occur together with modifiers within a noun phrase. Definite articles can co-occur with possessive pronouns in Italian and Portuguese, but not in French or English. Compare Portuguese *o meu sapato* (DEFINITE.ARTICLE.MASC.SG my.MASCULINE.SINGULAR shoe) 'the shoe of mine' and English *my shoe* (not *the my shoe).

Articles may combine reference to the noun's syntactic function and its definiteness or specificity. Tamambo has two articles: the definite article *na* and the indefinite *te*, both used just for the direct object.

Articles can be enclitics, as in Longgu, where a noun with a specific referent is marked by a singular clitic =*i* or the plural clitic =*gi*. Nouns with generic reference are not marked. Articles may be postposed or preposed to the noun phrase. In Maṽea, an Oceanic language from Vanuatu, the preposed article *le* marks specific nouns, the postposed form *aite* is used for indefinite nouns, and [*te* NOUN PHRASE *aite*] is a way of marking indefinite and non-specific noun phrases. Definite noun phrases are left unmarked.

In many Oceanic languages, noun markers form a closed class (these are sometimes misleadingly called articles: see §6.5, for some examples from Fijian). The Lolovoli dialect of North-east Ambae has seven markers which combine reference to the type of noun, and also its specificity and syntactic function. Of these, *a* marks a noun in the S/A function; *na* marks a noun in the O function; *lo* marks a noun in the locative function; a proper name in any function can be accompanied by the noun marker *i*. There is a plural human marker *re* and a collective human *ire* meaning 'all'. The indefinite *tea* can be used with any noun.

Noun markers in Dyirbal form a closed class of four items. They show the location of the referent, its case function, and its gender. The most common marker begins with *ba-*, meaning 'there and visible'. It also has a default function, used when distance and visibility are not relevant, for example *balan ḍugumbil* (NOUN.MARKER.fem.absolutive woman) 'woman', *bayi yara* (NOUN.MARKER.masc.absolutive man) 'man'. Noun markers have the same case system as do nouns; their forms are somewhat irregular.

Many languages lack articles and noun markers. If they have been identified, the grammarian will need to outline their semantic, syntactic, and also discourse functions, together with their special morphological features.

9.4 Interrogatives and the like

Every language has questions, or interrogative clauses, as a separate clause type. A polar question seeks confirmation of information with regard to the whole clause. Polar questions in English are expressed with special intonation, and also the reversal of the subject and the first word within the auxiliary, for example *Did John come on time?* The answer can be *yes* or *no*; hence an alternative term for polar questions as 'yes/no' questions. This term is European-centred, and is better avoided: quite a few indigenous languages spoken outside Europe simply do not have words for 'yes' or 'no'. Confirmation or lack thereof is done through other means (more on this in Chapter 11).

In some languages, polar questions are marked with an affix to a verb, for example Huallaga Quechua *-chu* and Aguaruna *-ka*. Polar questions can be marked with an independent non-inflecting word, for example Estonian *kas* and Cavineña *are*. A polar question marker is usually best treated as a closed class on its own. In Estonian and in Cavineña the polar question marker occupies clause-initial position—this is what sets it apart from other non-inflecting elements. Content interrogatives or interrogative words (see §9.4.1), indefinites, inflected markers of relative clauses, and even some determiners are traditionally referred to as interrogative, indefinite, and relative pronouns. This reflects their use as 'pro-forms' which can replace nouns.

9.4.1 Interrogative words

A content question seeks information about a constituent within a clause. Content questions include interrogative words. Typical interrogatives are 'who?', 'what?', 'which?', 'how many/how much?', 'why?', 'how?', 'where?', and 'when?'. Some languages have an interrogative verb 'do what?'.

The interrogatives tend to form a natural class: they occur in questions as a clause type. Interrogative words in Tariana, Jarawara, and Aguaruna occur together with a special interrogative mood marker on verbs within questions. Content interrogative words in English tend to occupy the sentence-initial position.

Interrogatives may share other features. In Tariana, all of them contain the formative *ku/kw-*, for example *kwaka* 'what?', *kwana* 'who?' (both noun-like), *kuite* 'which?' (which has a special set of noun class markers and thus stands apart from adjectives and demonstratives), *kwemaka* 'when?' (time word), *kwe* 'how, why?' (manner adverb). In Aguaruna, *wahĩ* 'what?' (pronoun-like), *wahu-pa* 'how many, how much?' (quantifier), *wahuka* 'how?' (adverb), and *wahu-ti* 'when?' (time word) share a formative *wah*. English interrogatives share the formative *wh-* —hence the highly English-centred term '*wh*-words' or even '*wh*-questions', used by some in lieu of 'content questions'.

In one sense, interrogatives can be said to form a macro-class, since they share some syntactic features. On a closer look, they are usually split across classes. Interrogatives in many languages do not form one word class in terms of their morphological categories and syntactic functions. Each of them may pattern with another word class. 'Who?' and 'What?' may share properties with nouns, or with nominal demonstratives and personal pronouns. 'Which?' may behave similarly to an adjective; and 'How many/how much?' may be indistinguishable from quantifiers.

In Longgu, *tai* 'what thing, what sort of thing?', *te* 'who?', and *eve* 'where?' are noun-like; *vita* 'how many?' is a quantifier, *angiuta* is an adnominal modifier as a separate closed subclass, and *ata* 'what?' and *awade* 'how?' are verbs. Tamambo has one interrogative verb *siva* 'do what?'.

The pronouns *ki* 'who?' and *mi* 'what?' in Hungarian are noun-like: they inflect for number and case. Interrogative modifiers also used as heads of NPs include *melyik* 'which one?', *hányadik* 'which one (in terms of ordinal number)?', *milyen* 'what kind?', *hány* 'how many?', *mekkora* 'which size?'. When used as heads of NPs they can inflect for case, but not for number. Locational interrogatives *hol* 'where?', *honnan* 'from where?', and *hová/hova* 'to where?' are adverbs.

Interrogatives in Dyirbal share similarities with different word classes: *miña* 'what' is noun-like in that it refers to nouns (with non-human referents). There is an interrogative member of the adjective class *miñañ* 'how many?'. The form *waña* 'who?' is similar to personal pronouns in that it follows a nominative-accusative pattern in its inflection. A set of interrogative forms correspond to noun markers; these are used to enquire about the location of the referent:

(9.24)   wuñjiñ   yara   miyanda-ñu
          INTERROGATIVE.NOMINATIVE.MASC   man   laugh-PRESENT
          'Where is the man that is laughing?'

Interrogative words may have special forms for human, and for non-human referents, independently of whether the language has genders or classifiers elsewhere. Uralic languages typically have no noun classes, or classifiers of other types. The distinction between the human interrogative 'who?' (**ki*) and the non-human 'what'? (**mikä, *mi*) goes back to proto-Uralic. Igbo has different forms for 'who?' and 'what?'; there are no other animacy distinctions.

9.4.2 *Indefinites*

Interrogative words may have an indefinite sense. Jamul Tiipay, a Yuman language, has three forms which can be used 'with interrogative force in questions and with indefinite force in commands': *me'a* 'where, somewhere', *me'ap* 'who, someone', *maayiich* 'what, something, anything'. They inflect for cases, similarly to nouns. Interrogative-indefinite verbs (a subclass of verbs) include *ch-i* 'to say what?, to say something', *ma 'wi* 'to do how?, to do what?, to do somehow, to do something', *mu 'yu* 'to be how?, to be somehow', *mu 'ui-i* 'to be/do why?, to be/do for some reason'. In addition, questions contain a special interrogative suffix. The same form *maayiich* means 'what?' in (9.25) and 'something' in (9.26).

(9.25) maayiich-pe-m   gaayiin   aakatt-chu
        what-DEM-INSTR   chicken   cut-QUESTION
        'What did he use to cut up the chicken?'

(9.26) maayiich   we-nyally
        something   3person-swallow
        'He swallowed something'

Indefinite forms may be derived from interrogatives, for example Hungarian *vala-mi* (INDEFINITE-what) 'something', *vala-ki* (INDEFINITE-who) 'someone', and Estonian *keegi* 'somebody' (from *kes* 'who?'), and *miski* 'something' (from *mis* 'what').

Indefinites tend to be spread across different word classes. For instance, English *some* and *any* are indefinite determiners which can modify a noun, for example *some milk*, or head an NP, for example *Do you want some?* By combining them with the interrogative locational, and manner adverb, one obtains locationals, *somewhere* and *anywhere*, and adverbs *somehow* and *anyhow*.

9.4.3 *Negative and relative words*

Indefinites can be the basis for negatives. In Estonian, indefinites acquire negative connotations in negative clauses. They may also be negated with a special negator *mitte*, for example *mitte keegi ei mängi malet* (NEGATIVE SOMEONE/nobody NEG play chess:PART) 'nobody plays chess'. In Russian, negative pronouns are derived from interrogatives with a negative prefix, for example *ni-kto* 'no-one' from *kto* 'who?'.

A relative clause is a modifier to a head noun within a noun phrase (we return to this clause type in §11.2 and §12.2.1). A relative clause construction may involve a relative marker, sometimes referred to as a 'relative pronoun'. In English, different forms of an interrogative correspond to the function of the common argument in the relative clause: *who* is used for human subject, *whom* for human participant in other functions, *which* is used for non-human referents, *where* for location, and *when* for time. It is interesting to note that in standard English *what* cannot be used as a relative pronoun. In Finnish, *joka* 'which' refers to a human referent, and *mikä* 'that' (same as the interrogative 'what?') to a non-human one. The relative adverb *jolloin* means 'when' and the adjective *jollainen* means 'which, such as'. In Hungarian, relative pronouns are derived from interrogatives by compounding with the erstwhile demonstrative *a*, for example *ki* 'who?', *aki* 'who, which', *mi* 'what?', *ami* 'which', *hol* 'where?', *ahol* 'where', *hány* 'how much?', *ahány* 'how much'.

Relative 'pronouns' may have different forms depending on animacy and syntactic function of the common argument shared by the relative clause and the main clause. This is what sets them apart from unchangeable 'relative clause markers' (see §9.6).

9.4.4 *Determiners of further kinds*

Further semantic groups of determiners may include:

- universal determiners, such as English *all* and *both*;
- distributive determiners, such as English *each* and *every*;
- disjunctive determiners, such as English *either* and *neither*;
- alternative determiners, such as English *other* and *another.*

Each of these may have their own syntactic and morphological features. In Aguaruna, the alternative determiner *tikitʃi* 'another, other' shares most properties with demonstratives. Unlike demonstratives, it does not agree in case with a noun it modifies; and it can be modified by a demonstrative, for example *nu tikitʃi* (anaphoric another) 'those other(s)'. This justifies putting it into a special closed class.

Tariana has a general indefinite determiner *pa-* 'one, another, someone, anyone', and a distributive individualizer *napada* 'each, every': these occur with different subsets of classifiers, and each constitute a closed class. Traditional grammar applies the term 'pronoun' to all of these.

Semantic types associated with adjectives may include SIMILARITY, covering the indefinite 'other', and QUANTIFICATION ('all/whole', 'many', 'some', 'few', 'only', 'enough', etc.) (as we can recall from §8.1). If these meanings are expressed with adjectives, a language may or may not have a closed class of items associated with any of these.

9.5 Quantifiers and number words

Meanings to do with quantification can be expressed in every language. In many languages, quantifiers form a separate closed word class. Their major syntactic function is to modify an NP head. Aguaruna has a closed class of nine quantifiers including *aʃi* 'all', *matʃik* 'a little, a little while', *biti* 'full', *dikasi* 'a little, few', *dukapi* 'enough, a lot', *himaituk* 'half', *kuwaʃata* 'many, much', *mai* 'both', *uhumak* 'a little'. All of them may precede or follow the NP head, but do not take case markers and cannot head an NP. They can also modify verbs. Quantifiers may include number words.

Quantifiers in English can be divided into 'paucal' quantifiers (*a little, a few, several*) and 'degree' quantifiers (*little, few, much, many*). Only the latter are gradable. They are shown in (9.27).

(9.27) QUANTIFIERS FOR COUNT NOUNS   QUANTIFIERS FOR NON-COUNT NOUNS
     He made [many mistakes]   *Has he got [much money]?*
     He made [more mistakes than you]   *Has he got [more money than you]?*
     He made [(the) most mistakes]   *Has he got [(the) most money]?*
     He made [few mistakes]   *He has got [little money]*
     He made [fewer mistakes than you]   *He has got [less money than you]*
     He made [(the) fewest mistakes]   *He has got [(the) least money]*

English distinguishes quantifiers used with count nouns and with non-count nouns (the same quantifier is used for both in other languages, including Lao and Aguaruna). *Many* and *few* occur with the plural form of the NP head, while *much* and *little* occur with the singular form. Noun phrases are in square brackets.

Number words can be similar to quantifiers in terms of their syntactic and morphological properties. In Longgu, number words and quantifiers can be heads of predicate, of NPs and modifiers within noun phrases. Aguaruna has a closed set of ten native number words. Similarly to quantifiers, they can occur before and after the head of an NP, and can modify a verb. Unlike quantifiers, they take case agreement with the head noun in a noun phrase.

In Tariana, both quantifiers and number words can occur with numeral classifiers; they take somewhat different sets of classifier morphemes. If a language has numeral classifiers (see §6.1.3), this is a strong criterion in favour of number words forming a special word class.

Number words are a special class in many languages, especially Semitic, Indo-European, and Oceanic. In Saaroa, an Austronesian language from Taiwan, and in Jarawara, number words are a subclass of verbs. Typical subtypes of number words include cardinal numbers, ordinal numbers, and also fractions. Different number words may belong to different word classes. In Gurr-Goni, an Australian language, number 'one' is an adjective, and 'two' is a noun (Rebecca Green, p.c.).

The majority of Amazonian languages have underived forms for 'one' to 'three' (more rarely, 'four'). Aguaruna is no exception to this. Three native numbers *makitʃiki* 'one', *himaha* 'two', and *kampaatuma* 'three' stand apart from other number words in that they can undergo reduplication, to convey the meaning of 'number each', for example *hima himaha* 'two each'. They can also take the iterative suffix -*a* meaning 'times', as in *makitʃki-a* 'once'. Numbers higher than three are conventionalized descriptions of fingers used in counting: the term for 'four' translates as 'finger used to paint with annatto (traditional paint)'; 'five' as 'finished hand', 'six' as 'one added to a hand' and so on.

Are number words universal? Is counting a universal practice? Hale (1975) suggested that Warlpiri and other Australian Aboriginal languages originally had no number words as such; the erstwhile determiners with quantitative meanings were later reinterpreted as number words under the impact of Western culture. In a number of Amazonian languages, 'one' is related to 'be alone', and 'two' to 'be a pair'. The lack of original cultural practice of counting would explain the scarcity of large numeral systems as a special class in Amazonia and in Australia. More on this in Chapter 14.

In languages with large sets of number words—including Indo-European, Semitic, and languages of Southeast Asia and Mesoamerica—one can count ad infinitum. Nevertheless, 'number words' can be considered a closed class: the set of roots used for numbers is always limited.

9.6 Closed classes of further kinds

Each subtype of modifiers to verbs, including manner modifiers, locations, and time words, may form a closed subclass of its own. Manner modifiers (or adverbs) and time words in Tariana each constitute a largish but closed class. Syntactically, they function as verb modifiers, and can head the predicate. Manner adverbs have special derivational affixes, and cannot take any other markers. In contrast, time words, for example *upitha* 'in the old days', *desu* 'tomorrow', *ikasu* 'today', can take some of the nominal cases.

Functions of a noun phrase within a clause can be indicated by special independent grammatical words. If these are preposed to the head noun, they are called 'PREPOSITIONS', for example English *on the ball*. If they come after the noun, they are called POSTPOSITIONS, for example Hungarian *dél útan* (midday after) 'after midday'. A cover term for prepositions and postpositions is 'ADPOSITIONS'. Some languages have both prepositions and postpositions. The adposition *pärast* in Estonian means 'because' if postposed to a noun (which has to occur in the genitive case), for example *sõja pärast* (war:GENITIVE.SG because) 'because of the war', and 'after' if preceding a noun (which then occurs in the partitive case), for example *pärast sõda* (after war:PARTITIVE.SG after) 'after the war'. Adpositions normally occur just in noun phrases. In some languages, they can also link clauses, for example English *She had a hard time [after the death of her husband]* and *She had a hard time [after her husband died]*. In Tamambo, they cannot take affixes, or be reduplicated to derive other forms.

Adpositions can fall into different subclasses. Longgu has five simple prepositions which take no special marking (*i* 'at', *vu* 'towards', *ni* 'for, to', *mi* 'as far as (place)', *mai* 'from'), one noun-like preposition *ta-* 'location at' which takes possessive suffixes; and five verbal-like prepositions which take object suffixes. Tariana has a closed set of thirty-four postpositions and one preposition. Postpositions divide into eight classes depending on whether they can occur with bound pronominal prefixes and case markers.

A language may have a closed class of CONNECTIVES, or CONJUNCTIONS, whose function is to link clauses or noun phrases. The same set of connectives is used to coordinate noun phrases and clauses in Tamambo, including *mai/mana* 'and, with', *tene* 'or', and *ne* 'but'. There is another set of connectives which mark the semantic link between a main and a subordinate clause, for example *matan(i)* 'because', *mwe* 'in order to, that', and *are* 'if'. Manambu has one clause connective *alək* 'this is why', and two connectives for noun phrase linking, *wa* 'and' and *o* 'or' (a loan from Tok Pisin, the local lingua franca). Connectives typically have no grammatical categories of their own. Non-inflected INTERROGATIVE MARKERS in polar questions often form a special closed class (see §9.4). Relative clauses can be signalled by an unchangeable RELATIVE MARKER, for example *še* or *ašer* in Hebrew.

DISCOURSE PARTICLES may form a separate class. In Tamambo these include *te* 'eh, you know, to elicit acquiescence from the addressee', *ro* 'thus, so that's it' and *si* 'just'. Topic markers in Lao attach to a noun phrase, marking it as a topic, and form a class on their own. They are transparently related to demonstratives, for example *niø* 'general topic, *nii4* 'proximal demonstrative', *hanø* 'distal topic', from *han5* 'distal demonstrative'.

Depending on their function, and distribution, there may be many more classes of invariable grammatical words, under the umbrella term of 'particle'. Lao has a large set of sentence-final particles marking questions, illocutionary force, commands, and

TABLE 9.15. Imperative particles in Lakhota

MEANINGS	WOMAN SPEAKING	MAN SPEAKING
Command	*na*	singular addressee *yo'*, *wo'*
Seeking permission	singular addressee *ye'*, *we'* plural addressee *pe'*	plural addressee *po'*
Mild request (please)	singular addressee *ye'* plural addressee *pi ye'*	

speakers' source of knowledge and attitude to it. Imperative particles in Lakhota, a Siouan language from the USA, vary depending on whether they mark a command or a request, and whether the speaker is a man or a woman (see Table 9.15).

We saw in §6.1 that noun classifiers, numeral classifiers, and possessive classifiers can be independent grammatical words. Then, they typically each form a special closed class. Lao has a few dozen numeral classifiers postposed to the noun plus number word. The classifier construction is in square brackets (numbers indicate tones). See example (9.28).

(9.28)   kuu3   sùù4   [paa3   sòòng3   too3]
         I   buy   fish   two   NUM.CL.ANIMATE
         'I bought two fish'

NEGATION MARKERS may form a closed class of independent words. The marker of negation *bòò1* in Lao occupies a slot of its own in the verb phrase. The negator *te* in Tamambo appears in the same slot as some aspectual markers, and is related to the negative verb *tete*. Nevertheless, it is not a verb. Independent negators *ma:* 'declarative negator', *akəs* 'declarative habitual negator', *ata* 'desiderative negator', and *tukwa* 'prohibitive' in Manambu form a closed, and heterogenous subclass. They occur with different verb forms; all of them appear before the verb, except *ma:*, which can occur before the verb in present and past tenses, and after the verb in the future.

Further closed classes may include PROFORMS, which are used instead of another form. The 'hesitation' proform *naa* in Aguaruna is used if one cannot recall the exact noun. Unlike a noun, the proform cannot be modified. PRO-CLAUSES, or PRO-SENTENCES, form a class on their own, for example Manambu *ayei* 'yes', *ma:* 'no', Yankunytjatjara *uwa* 'yes', *wanyu* 'just let', Tariana *haw* 'yes', *ne* 'emphatic no', *hãida* 'I don't know'.

Every language has INTERJECTIONS which express surprise, pain, and many other reactions. They may form a small closed class. Interjections in Longgu form a small class and include *eo* 'OK', *gase!* 'disbelief and amazement', *iiii* 'to express admiration and surprise, used only by women', and *ni* 'said with rising intonation to get confirmation or agreement'. In others, they appear to constitute a larger class, open to loans, as in Cavineña. Interjections tend to contain unusual sounds and syllable structures (see §4.1.5) and can occur in limited functions (for instance, only as modifiers to verbs). They can hardly ever take any derivational markers.

We can recall, from §5.8, that IDEOPHONES, or EXPRESSIVES, can form a large open class. They are sound-symbolic: their phonological form resembles the sound or impression associated with the action or with the referent. Large and potentially open classes of expressives are a typical feature of African, Southeast Asian, South American, and Papuan languages. They may contain unusual sounds, reduplication, and even triplication patterns, for example Paumarí *giririririniki* 'sound made by water snake', Macushi *tîren tîren tîren* 'sound of spoons and plates'. Expressives in Lao usually consist of two rhyming syllables, both equally stressed and having the same tone, for example *quj1-luj1* 'fat, tubby' (e.g. a chubby baby), *qòòt5-sòòt5* 'of a place, completely silent'. Their only function is to modify verbs. Expressives in Macushi can modify verbs, or occur as complements of the verb 'say' to express sounds made, for example *tîko tîko taa* (sound.of.bubbling say) 'bubble'. They can function as arguments of verbs and take a limited amount of derivation, both in Macushi and in general. Expressives can be considered together with closed classes, since they always stand apart from the rest of the language in terms of their phonological make-up and limited grammatical categories and functions.

There may be further, language specific, closed classes. Tariana has a locative deictic *ñhaka* 'right here' which cannot take any morphological markers and can only modify a verb. The more detailed the grammar is, the more of these will be identified.

9.7 Summing up: a statement of closed classes

Every language has closed classes, but they may be rather diverse. Personal pronouns, demonstratives and interrogative words are found in every language. Quantifiers, number words, and determiners of all sorts may form classes on their own; or they

TABLE 9.16. A selection of closed word classes in Manambu: a comparison

	HEAD OF NP	MODIFIER		CASE MARKING	OVERT NUMBER AND GENDER
		prehead	posthead		
Personal pronouns	yes	yes	no	yes	no
Demonstratives	yes	yes	no	yes (not all)	yes
Indefinite *nəkə-* 'another, other'	rare	yes	no	yes	yes
Indefinite *nəwək* 'another one'	yes	no	no	no	no
Quantifiers	yes	yes	yes	no	no
Number words 1–4	yes	yes	yes	no	no
Number words higher than 4	yes	no	yes	yes	no

may be part of a larger class. Each class has to be defined based on its syntactic and morphological features, and semantic content.

An example of a comparative summary statement of a selection of closed classes in Manambu is in Table 9.16. Six classes are contrasted in terms of whether they can occur as heads of noun phrases or as modifiers before or after the head, whether they can take case marking, and whether they can be marked for gender and number.

Members of small classes (up to two dozen members) can be listed exhaustively. Umbrella terms—such as 'particle'—are best used with caution. 'Particle' may refer to any class of words which have no special morphological categories; but these can be very different in terms of their syntactic behaviour. Using 'one term for all' may obscure the distinctions between diverse classes which may also include negators, connectives, and discourse markers.

Notes and sources

§9.1: Basic distinctions in personal pronouns are discussed by Dixon (2010b: 189–223); Bhat (2004) is generally reliable; see Dixon (2010b: 257–8) for an appraisal of other sources, in particular those claiming that free pronouns are absent in some languages where in fact they exist, such as Acoma. The term 'hearer' is sometimes used interchangeably with 'addressee' but hardly is felicitous since it encompasses anyone who may hear the speech act, and not be a speech participant.

§9.1.1: See Hill (2005: 233) on Cupeño; Mithun (1999: 69–78) on person, number, and gender in pronouns in North American Indian languages; Cook (2004: 94–5) on Chipewyan; Foley (1991: 111–14) on Yimas; Roberts (1987: 208) on Amele; Davies (1981: 154) on Kobon. Some general features of pronouns in Amazonian languages are discussed in Aikhenvald (2012a: 141–52); see Dixon (2002) on pronouns in Australian languages.

See Dixon (1977: 168) on Yidiñ; Dixon (1972: 50) on Dyirbal; Overall (2008: 155–6) on Aguaruna; Jauncey (2011: 88) on Tamambo; Hill (1992: 91) on Longgu; Verhaar (1995) on Tok Pisin; Frajzyngier (2002: 84) on Hdi; Payne and Huddleston (2002: 426–7) on English 'one'; Aikhenvald (2012a: 143–6) on impersonal pronouns in Amazonian languages.

Impersonal pronouns are sometimes referred to as 'fourth person'; however, this term is used in other meanings, e.g. reflexives (see, for instance, Mithun 1999: 76).

Correlations between person and gender are discussed in Aikhenvald (2000: 252–5). See Newman (2000: 477) on Hausa, Marnita (1996: 64) on Minangkabau; Corominas (1954: 523) on Spanish; Aikhenvald (2008: 592) on Gala. On further correlations between person, number, and gender see Aikhenvald (2000: 254–5).

Aikhenvald (2000: 70–7, 369) offers more on the gender differences in pronouns, and in other word classes, across the languages of the world.

§9.1.2: See Maiden and Robustelli (2007: 460–5) on Italian; Shibatani (2006) on hon-
orifics; Aikhenvald (2010: 219–32); Coates (2003: 33–4) on the pragmatics of *T*- and
V- forms, and Clyne, Norrby, and Warren (2009) on address systems in modern
European languages; Jauncey (2011: 92) on Tamambo. See Sohn (1994: 283–8) on
Korean; Goddard (2005: 19–22) on the languages of East and Southeast Asia; Enfield
(2007: 77–82 and p.c.) on Lao.

The pragmatic motivations for polite and higher-status overtones of second and
third person plural are discussed in Brown and Levinson (1987: 199–200).

See Hale (1966) and Dixon (1980: 276) on Lardil; further details and references
on kinship-based pronouns are in Dixon (1989: 255, 2002: 283–4).

§9.1.3: See Kenesei et al. (1998: 260–1) on Hungarian; Butt and Benjamin (2004: 134–6)
on Spanish; Sulkala and Karjalainen (1992: 271) on Finnish; Dixon (1972: 49–50) on
Dyirbal; Dixon (1977: 168) on Yidiñ; Tamura (2000: 47) on Ainu; Enfield (2007: 78)
on Lao; Jauncey (2011: 88–9) on Tamambo.

On pronoun elaboration, or the 'inclusory', construction, see Lichtenberk (2000),
Dixon (1988: 157–61), Bril (2004: 527), and especially Dixon (2010b: 207); see Kenesei et al. (1998: 269–70) on Hungarian. The term 'inclusory' is confusing because of
its superficial similarity to the term 'inclusive', and the fact that 'inclusory' constructions are typically based on exclusive pronouns.

§9.1.4: See Dixon (2005: 20) on English; Butt and Benjamin (2004: 93–100) on Spanish;
Curnow (1997) on Awa Pit.

§9.1.5: See Kenesei et al. (1998: 271–3) on Hungarian, Hualde and de Urbina (2003: 152)
on Basque; Viitso (2007: 46–7) on Estonian; Frajzyngier (1993: 107–11) on Mupun.
We can recall, from §7.3, that reflexives meaning 'do something to oneself' and
reciprocals meaning 'do something to each other' may be marked through verbal
affixes. See Dixon (2012: 140–5) and references there on the pronominal strategy of
expressing reflexive, and reciprocal meanings. See Haiman (1980: 225, 369–70) on
Hua; Roberts (1987: 122–31) on Amele; Sohn (1994: 148–9) on Korean; Frajzyngier
(2002: 195–8) on Hdi; Heine (2000) and Heine and Kuteva (2001: 406–7) on the
development of reciprocals and reflexives from body part terms in African languages; Newman (2000: 522–30, 482) on Hausa; Enfield (2007: 319, 333) on Lao; Iwasaki
and Ingkaphirom (2005: 55) on Thai; Hinds (1986: 114–16) on Japanese.

§9.1.6: See Dixon (2010b: 210–23) on the properties of bound pronouns; Aikhenvald
(2012a: 176–7), Aikhenvald (2013a: 42–3) on multifunctional bound pronouns in
Amazonian and other languages; Chafe (1990) on Caddo.

§9.2.1: See Dixon (2010b: 223–46) for a general discussion of demonstratives and further references. See Bruce (1985: 81) on Alamblak; Weber (1989: 38) on Quechua;
Hill (1992: 81, 96–7) on Longgu; Aikhenvald and Green (2011) on Palikur; Murkelinskij (1967: 497) on Lak; Haiman (1980: 258) on Hua; Guillaume (2008: 616)
on Cavineña; Sneddon (1996: 160, 189) on Indonesian; Smeets (1989: 424–5, 2008:

504–5) on Mapuche; Tamura (2000) on Ainu; Sohn (1994: 296–7) on Korean; Diessel (1999) for further features of demonstratives.

Additional perceptual meanings in demonstratives include audibility, as in Santali and in Dyirbal (see Aikhenvald 2004a, and references there). The semantic extensions of these demonstratives are parallel to those in evidentiality systems: the visual demonstrative can refer to 'what is evident', while the auditive one may also refer to smell, taste, and feeling.

§9.2.2: See Dixon (2010b: 247–57) on functions of demonstratives; Jauncey (2011: 93–4) on Tamambo; Enfield (2007: 99–100) on Lao; Smeets (1989: 424–5, 2008: 504–5) on Mapuche.

§9.3: See Kenesei et al. (1998: 257–60) on Hungarian; Hyslop (2001: 98) on the Lolovoli dialect of North-east Ambae; Guérin (2007) on Mav̈ea; Dixon (1972: 44–8; forthcoming) on Dyirbal.

§9.4: See Collinder (1965: 138) on proto-Uralic. See Dixon (2010b: 400–33) and references there on interrogatives; Dixon (1972: 49–53) on Dyirbal; Overall (2008: 182–3) on Aguaruna; Hill (1992: 104) on Longgu; Kenesei et al. (1998: 268–9, 278–81) on Hungarian; Viitso (2007: 50–1) on Estonian; Jauncey (2011: 95–6, 255) on Tamambo. See Dixon (2012: 401–4) on indefinites and interrogatives in other languages; Dixon (2002: 328–35) on indefinite-interrogatives in Australian languages; Miller (2001: 174–8) on Jamul Tiipay. Some information on indefinites in European languages can be found in Haspelmath (1997). See Payne and Huddleston (2002) on determiners in English; Overall (2008: 162) on Aguaruna; Aikhenvald (2003: 214–15) on Tariana.

See Dixon (2010b: 329, 344–5, 363–4) on 'relative pronouns'; Sulkala and Karjalainen (1992: 286–7) on Finnish; Kenesei et al. (1998: 28–1) on Hungarian. See Sulkala and Karjalainen (1992: 287), for the term 'relative words'.

§9.5: See Overall (2008: 165–7) on Aguaruna; Enfield (2007: 104–11) on Lao; Payne and Huddleston (2002: 392–6) on English; Hill (1992: 83) on Longgu; Aikhenvald (2000: 100–20) on the use of numeral classifiers with number words and quantifiers; Aikhenvald (2012a: 350–60) on counting and number words in Amazonian languages; Dixon (2012: 71–80) on number words in general.

§9.6: See Jauncey (2011: 96–7, 106–9) on Tamambo; Hill (1992: 101–5) on Longgu; Aikhenvald (2003: 222–33) on Tariana; Aikhenvald (2011c) on adpositions as clause linkers; Enfield (2007: 100–1, 41–71, 119–56, 300–2) on Lao; Boas and Deloria (1941: 111–12) on Lakhota; Overall (2008: 184–5) on Aguaruna; Goddard (1983: 36) on Yankunytjatjara; Guillaume (2008: 86–9) on Cavineña; Abbott (1991: 149–51) on Macushi; Chapman and Derbyshire (1991: 350–1) on Paumarí.

10

Who does what to whom: grammatical relations

Grammatical relations between participants are crucial for understanding how each language works. We start with a snap-shot of core grammatical relations, transitivity, and marking the participants. We then briefly address the types of systems, and touch upon the syntactic categories of 'subject' and 'object'.

10.1 Core grammatical relations and transitivity

In every language, a clause consists of a predicate (which typically relates to a verb) and a number of arguments. 'Core' arguments must be either stated or understood from context. 'Peripheral' (or 'oblique') arguments are optional (they are also called adjuncts).

In §3.9, we outlined the two main clause structures across the languages of the world. One is 'intransitive', with one core argument—'intransitive subject', nicknamed 'S'. The other one is 'transitive', with two core arguments: these are 'transitive subject', nicknamed 'A', and 'transitive object', nicknamed 'O'.

Languages can group these in different ways: we thus obtain nominative-accusative and absolutive-ergative patterns. Or there can be a mixture of the two. Copula clauses and verbless clauses represent further clause types—see Chapter 11.

A transitive clause may also have a further core argument, 'E' (short for Extension to core), additional to its O. Verbs with three core arguments are called ditransitive. Typical ditransitive verbs include 'give', 'borrow', 'lend', 'bestow (a name upon someone)', 'show', and 'tell'.

An intransitive clause may also have an additional obligatory argument (also nicknamed 'E') whose properties are different from those of an O of a transitive clause (see §3.9). In some cases, E looks very similar to O. An E can be marked similarly to O. In Quechua and in Aguaruna the E (recipient) and the O take the same case form. Syntactic tests may help distinguish these arguments—see §10.9.

The transitivity of the clause is determined by the number of participants the situation (that is, the predicate of the clause) involves. Some verbs and the situations they describe always involve more than one participant. These include verbs of physical affect—'kill', 'hit', 'strike'. In a rather impressionistic way, they can be referred to as 'highly' transitive.

Verbs of corporeal actions—'laugh', 'cry', or 'excrete'—can be considered 'less transitive', in that they do not have to involve a second participant. Verbal concepts which do not presuppose a participant being affected are likely to be coded as intransitive verbs in some languages. The reporting verb, 'say', is transitive in English, Tariana, Jarawara, and ditransitive in Dolakha Newar. It is intransitive in Urarina, Dyirbal, Samoan, and Yup'ik Eskimo.

The notion of 'argument structure' captures the number, and the expression of core arguments. The exact semantic roles and meanings of A, S, O, and E vary, depending on verb type. An 'A'—the subject of a transitive verb—is likely to be the controller or initiator of the activity. It can be the 'perceiver' with verbs of perception; or the 'giver' with verbs of transaction, including 'give'.

An 'O' is the second argument of a transitive clause. Its semantic roles range from the entity affected by the actions of the A, to the thing given, or to something perceived, and so on. An 'S' is the sole participant of an intransitive clause. It can have a multiplicity of semantic roles, including the 'mover' in motion verbs such as 'run', the 'one in the state of something' in verbs of state such as 'be hungry' or 'be rich', and so on. An 'E' includes beneficiary, recipient, and also location, for example English verb *put* (something somewhere).

Two further types of clause are the copula clause and the verbless clause (see §3.9). A copula clause requires two arguments—the copula subject (CS) and the copula complement (CC). Verbless clauses are somewhat similar to copula clauses. Their arguments are the verbless clause subject (VCS) and the verbless clause complement (VCC). VCS and CCS tend to be similar to each other, and to A/S. Copula complement (CC) and verbless clause complement (VCC) tend to share features—see §10.8.

10.2 How to mark grammatical relations

Every language has some mechanism for distinguishing A and O within a transitive clause. The sole argument of an intransitive verb—S—might be expected to be marked in a third, different way. But this is in fact very uncommon. A rare example comes from Waŋkumara, an extinct language from Australia. The case marker *-ani* is used for S, *-andru* is used for A, and *-aṇa* is used for O (if they are expressed through nouns). Waŋkumara pronouns also have different forms for A, S, and O. For example, the first person pronoun 'I' is *ŋani* if it is in S function, *ŋaṭu* in A and *ŋaṇa* if in O function.

A and O occur in a different clause type from S. Grammars tend to operate economically, and either

(i) mark S in the same way as A, resulting in a NOMINATIVE-ACCUSATIVE SYSTEM ('ACCUSATIVE', for short), or

(ii) mark S in the same way as O, resulting in an ABSOLUTIVE-ERGATIVE SYSTEM ('ERGATIVE', for short).

Grammatical relations can be expressed through case markers (see examples (6.20)–(6.21), from Turkish and Dyirbal, and more below), and adpositions. Case markers are bound morphemes, while adpositions (that is, prepositions and postpositions) are free morphemes, which typically form a closed class in their own right. Some languages have bound pronouns on the verbs marking A/S (as in Latin: see examples (7.1)–(7.2), or A/S and O (as in Manambu: see examples (7.3)–(7.4)), or just A (as in Paumarí, see example (7.5)).

The order of constituents within a clause can distinguish A, S, and O. English has strict constituent orders: AVO and SV. Both A and S occur before the V(erb), and O occurs after it. This pattern of constituent order is 'accusative'. If A appears on the different side of the verb from both S and O, S and O are grouped together, and we obtain 'ergative' constituent order. This is the case in Päri, a Western Nilotic language, which has SV and OVA orders.

Labels 'morphological ergativity' and 'morphological accusativity' are fully appropriate when only case inflections are involved. They are less adequate if a language employs other mechanisms for marking the core arguments' functions, including bound pronouns and constituent order (which is a syntactic matter). The best practice is to refer to an 'accusative' system and an 'ergative' system for *core argument marking in general*.

Many languages combine the two basic types of core argument marking—accusative and ergative—in one of several ways. These combinations are known as 'split' systems, the topic of §10.5.

10.3 Nominative-accusative systems

Nominative-accusative systems group together A and S. These are marked with nominative case. O is marked differently, with the accusative case. In most languages, the nominative case is expressed with zero—that is, it is morphologically unmarked. Examples (6.20a–b), from Turkish, illustrate this principle. In (10.1), from Quechua, the S of the clause ('child') is marked with zero. This is the nominative case:

(10.1) Wamra   puñu-n
        child:NOM sleep-3person
        'Child sleeps'

In (10.2), 'child' is the object marked with -*ta* (the accusative case). The A, Juan, remains unmarked as befits the nominative case:

(10.2) Hwan   wamra-ta   puñu-chi-n
        Juan   child-ACC   sleep-CAUS-3person
        'Juan makes the child sleep'

Grammatical relations in Quechua are also expressed through verbal cross-referencing on the verb, also on a nominative-accusative basis (the third person suffix in (10.1)–(10.2) marks S and A). The formally unmarked nominative case is the citation form of a noun.

In a few languages, the A and S acquire formal marking, and the O is formally unmarked. This is known as 'marked nominative systems' (since Dixon 1994: 63–7). Such systems are attested in three branches of Afroasiatic—numerous Omotic and Cushitic languages from Ethiopia, and Berber languages across North Africa—and in genetically unrelated Nilotic languages, spoken in East Africa. Yuman languages, from California, also have a 'marked nominative' system. In Jamul Tiipay, from this family, the S and the A noun phrases are marked with-*ch* and O is not marked. This unmarked form is also used for citation.

Accusative case forms may have other uses. The accusative case in Quechua can also indicate direction and endpoint, for example *punta-ta chaya-r* (peak-ACC arrive-ADVERBIAL) 'arrive at the peak'. It can also mark length of time, or a point in time, as in *mirkulis taarri-ta* (Wednesday evening-ACC) 'on Wednesday evening'. In Latin, the accusative case also expresses direction, for example *Roma-m* 'to Rome', and time, as in *mult-os ann-os* 'many years'. It is also used in exclamations—in one of his famous speeches against Catilina, Marcus Tullius Cicero exclaimed *Heu me miser-um!* (oh I:ACC miserable:ACC) 'O miserable me!'

10.4 Absolutive-ergative systems

Absolutive-ergative systems group together S and O. These appear in a form known as 'absolutive'. A is marked with the ergative case. The absolutive is typically formally unmarked, and is the citation form of the noun.

Consider (10.3) and (10.4), from Avar, a North-east Caucasian language from Daghestan. The A ('father') in (10.4) is marked with the ergative case. The S (male child, or 'boy') in (10.3) and the O (female child, or girl) in (10.4) have no segmental case marking, as is expected for the absolutive (also see example (6.21), from Dyirbal).

(10.3) w-as   w-ekér-ula
        MASC-child.ABS   MASC-run-PRESENT
        'The boy (male child) runs'

(10.4) Inssu-cca   j-as   j-écc-ula
        father(masc)-ERG FEM-child.ABS FEM-praise-PRESENT
        'Father praises the girl (female child)'

In a few languages, ergative and absolutive are both marked on nouns: Kaluli, a Papuan language, has the ergative case -ɛ, for A, and absolutive case -ɔ, for S and O. Ergative and absolutive forms of personal pronouns may also both be marked. Matses, a Panoan language, uses the ergative case marker -*n* and the absolutive case Ø for nouns. Pronouns have distinct non-analysable forms for A and S/O. 'You', the O in (10.5), is marked with absolutive case:

(10.5) debi-n$_A$ mibi$_O$ kues-o-ş h
        Davy-ERG$_A$ 2.ABS$_O$ hit-PAST-3person.A/S
        'Davy hit you'

The S, 'you', in (10.6), is marked just like the O in (10.5):

(10.6) mibi$_S$ ush-o-k
        2.ABS$_S$ sleep-PAST-INDIC.1/2.personA/S
        'You slept'

In (10.7), 'you' is the A of the transitive clause. It is expressed with a special ergative form:

(10.7) debi-Ø$_O$ mimbi$_A$ kues-o-k
        Davy-ABS$_O$ 2.ERG$_A$ hit-PAST-INDIC.1/2person.A/S
        'You hit Davy'

Not every part of Matses grammar is morphologically ergative. Examples (10.5)–(10.7) show that the bound pronoun on the verb marks A and S (the 'subject': see §10.9). That is, bound pronouns on the verb itself reflect the nominative-accusative pattern, while the case marking on nouns and on independent personal pronouns is absolutive-ergative. More on this in §10.5.

Forms superficially similar to ergative case in Matses have instrumental meaning (however, they express an oblique, and not a core, grammatical relation). In Epena Pedee and other Choco languages of Colombia the same form is used for the ergative case, and also for instruments, reason, or cause and movement away from the source. In Dyirbal nouns marked with the ergative -*ŋgu* and those marked with its look-alike instrumental show different syntactic behaviour (see §6.4, and examples (6.24)–(6.25) there). 'Case syncretisms' of this kind are interesting for a diachronic study of a language. However, in a synchronic grammar, similarity in form is not enough to claim similarity in function.

10.5 Split ergative systems

About a quarter of the languages of the world are absolutive-ergative. Most of these languages have some nominative-accusative characteristics as well. This mixture of two types of core argument marking is known as 'split ergativity'. This is usually based on some grammatical and semantic parameters. Split ergativity can be determined by the meaning of the noun phrase, in agreement with the 'Nominal hierarchy' (§10.5.1), by the meaning of the verb (§10.5.2), by tense and aspect (§10.5.3), or by combinations of several factors (§10.5.4).

10.5.1 *The meaning of a noun phrase and the Nominal hierarchy*

In quite a few languages, nouns operate on an absolutive-ergative principle, and personal pronouns have nominative-accusative case marking. This is the case in Dyirbal (see §9.1.3). In (10.8) (repeated from 6.21), 'man' is the O marked with the absolutive case. 'Woman' is the A and is marked with the ergative case:

(10.8)   [bayi   yara]$_O$ [baŋgun   yibi-ŋgu]$_A$
         NOM.MARKER:masc   man:ABS   NOM.MARKER:fem   woman-ERGATIVE
         balga-n
         hit-PAST
         'The woman hit the man'

If A, S, and O are expressed with pronouns, the marking changes. The same form of the pronoun 'I', *ŋaja*, is used for the S in the intransitive (10.9) and for A in transitive (10.10).

(10.9)   ŋaja$_S$ bani-ñu
         I:NOM   come-PAST
         'I came (here)'

(10.10)   ŋaja$_A$ [bayi   yara]$_O$ balga-n
          I:NOM   NOM.MARKER:masc   man:ABS   hit-PAST
          'I hit a man'

In (10.11), a different form of the pronoun 'I' is used for an O. This is an accusative form:

(10.11)   ŋayguna$_O$ [baŋgun   yibi-ŋgu]$_A$ balga-n
          I:ACC   NOM.MARKER:fem   woman-ERG   hit-PAST
          'A woman hit me'

The principle behind split ergative marking based on the meaning of a noun phrase reflects a general principle: a participant in an unusual role may acquire special marking, and a participant in an expected role does not have to. The first person singular, 'I', is the quintessential A (the 'agent', the 'perceiver', the 'donor', and so on). 'I' is more likely to appear as A than as O. When it does appear in O function, it will be marked. Next most likely A is a second person ('you'). Third person pronouns, demonstratives, human, animate, and inanimate nouns are less likely to be 'A'. Many verbs typically have a human noun in their A function (e.g. 'think', 'believe', 'tell'); for others, A tends to be human or animate ('bite', 'strike', 'see', 'hear'). There is more variety with regard to O. An inanimate noun can be O of most verbs.

The Nominal Hierarchy reflects our expectations as to which participants are more likely to appear in A than in O function (Figure 10.1).

Participants at the left end of this hierarchy are more likely to be in A function and have agentive properties. Those at the right end are more likely to be in O or S function; they can be conceived of as less agentive and less A-like. In Dixon's (1994) words:

it is plainly most natural and economical to 'mark' a participant when it is in an unaccustomed role. That is, we would expect that a case-marking language might provide morphological marking of an NP from the right-hand side of the hierarchy when it is in A function, and of an NP from the leftmost end when in O function (as an alternative to providing ergative marking for *all* A NPs, of whatever semantic type [as in Matses—A. Y. A.], or accusative marking for *all* O NPs [as in Quechua—A. Y. A.]). (Dixon 1994: 85)

Marking an O, as in Quechua or in Latin, implies a nominative-accusative system; this principle of marking extends from left to right within the hierarchy. Marking an A, as in Matses or in Dyirbal, means having an absolutive-ergative system; and this extends from right to left. This is why nominative-accusative marking is more likely to be used with personal pronouns. In contrast, absolutive-ergative marking is more likely to occur with inanimate nouns.

We saw in the previous section (examples 10.5–10.7) that in Matses free arguments have an absolutive-ergative system, and bound pronouns are nominative-accusative. In many languages bound pronouns have developed from free pronouns. A 'bound' versus 'free' split may be considered a subtype of the split discussed here. If bound pronouns mark grammatical relations in a different way from free NPs, they are likely to follow the nominative-accusative principle even if free NPs follow the absolutive-ergative pattern.

1st and 2nd p pronouns	Demonstratives 3rd p pronouns	Proper nouns	Human	Animate	Common nouns Inanimate

←--

more likely to be in A than O function

FIGURE 10.1 Nominal hierarchy and split ergativity. (Dixon 1994: 85)

10.5.2 *The meaning of a verb*

In a number of languages, some intransitive verbs mark their S in the same way as A. These verbs typically express volitional and controlled actions, and are called Sa (or active) verbs. They typically include verbs of motion such as 'walk', 'run', 'jump', and other volitional verbs such as 'talk', 'sing'. Other verbs mark their S in the same way as O. These verbs are usually non-controlled, non-volitional, and refer to states. They are called So, and include verbs such as 'be sick', 'hiccup', and 'weep'. Such system is known as 'split-S'.

Warekena of Xié has a set of prefixed bound pronouns which refer to the A of transitive verbs. Bound pronominal enclitics mark the O of transitive verbs, as in (10.12):

(10.12)   pi-yutʃia-mia=yu
          2sgA-kill-PERF=3sg.femO
          'You killed her'

The only argument (S) of Warekena intransitive verbs of motion, volitional verbs, and a few others, including the verb 'die', is expressed with the prefixes. These are Sa verbs:

(10.13)   pi-tapapa-mia
          2sgSa-walk-PERF
          'You walked'

The S argument of verbs of state which denote non-volitional and non-controllable processes—such as 'be sick', 'be dirty', 'be well', 'be dry', 'dawn'—is marked with enclitics, just like the O (in 10.12):

(10.14)   anetua=yu
          be.well=3sg.fSo
          'She is well'

This kind of argument marking is typical for most Arawak languages. The exact choice of semantic parameters for Sa and So is language-specific. For instance, in Hidatsa, a Siouan language, volitional and controlled verbs such as 'follow', 'run', and 'talk' belong to the Sa class. This class also includes the verbs 'have the hiccups', 'die', and 'forget'. The So class includes non-volitional verbs 'yawn', 'fall down', and 'cry', and as well as volitional 'stand up', 'roll over', and 'dress up'.

Alternatively, intransitive verbs may have the option of marking their S either as A or as O, with a difference in meaning. Baniwa, an Arawak language, marks A/Sa with prefixes, and O/So with enclitics, just like Warekena. So, *ri-kapa-ni* (3sg.nfAsee-3sg. nfO) means 'he sees him', and *ri-emhani* (3sg.nfSa-walk) means 'he walks'. The So of stative verbs is expressed with enclitics, for example *hape-ka-ni* (cold-DECL-3sg.nfSo) 'he is cold'.

In Baniwa, the S of a number of verbs can be marked as Sa or as So. When one of such verbs is marked as Sa, the verb has a controlled meaning, as in *ridza-ka* (3sg.nfA/Sa+weep-DECL) 'he is weeping'. And when such a verb is marked as So, the meaning does not imply control—the same verb *-idza* 'cry' will refer to a natural phenomenon, rain: *idza-ni* (weep-3sg.nfO/So) 'it is raining'. Verbal prefixes in Baniwa also mark the A of a transtive verb, and suffixes mark the O.

This is known as a fluid-S system. A most spectacular instance has been described for Tsova-Tush (or Batsbi), a North-east Caucasian language. Here, grammatical relations are marked with cases: absolutive for O and ergative for A:

(10.15) k'nat-ev   bader   dah"   dapx-diễ
         boy-ERG   child:ABS VERBAL.PARTICLE undress-AOR:3person
         'The boy undressed the child'

The S of an intransitive verb can be marked with ergative if the S is 'a human participant to whom is ascribed volition and conscious (mindful) control with respect to the situation denoted by the verb'. The choice depends on 'the responsibility or activeness of the subject'. In (10.16), the S fell down because of their own fault:

(10.16) as   wože
         1sg:ERG   fell
         'I fell' (it was my own fault that I fell down)

The S of the intransitive verb is marked as absolutive if no fault or volition is involved. In (10.17), 'I' fell without this being my fault:

(10.17) so   wože
         1sg:ABS   fell
         'I fell' (no implication that it was my fault)

Verbs referring to activities that must be controlled ('walk', 'wander', 'talk', 'think') are used only with the ergative, Sa, marking. Verbs referring to activities which cannot be controlled—such as 'tremble', 'be afraid', 'be hungry'—can only take an absolutive S. The majority of verbs may be used as both Sa and So (as in 10.16–10.17), with a difference in meaning.

For example, *ʔopdalar* 'come to be hidden' is used as an So verb if the subject 'comes to be hidden, not because of anything she herself does, but because something moves in front of her. Ergative marking must convey a situation in which the subject does something which results in becoming hidden, such as moving behind a barrier'

(Holisky 1987: 111). Some verbs, such as 'die', are unlikely to be used as Sa: the consult-ant insisted that this is because 'no one ever wants to die'. However, if a distraught lover throws herself into a river to commit suicide, her death could be reported using the Sa marking with 'die': dying can then be viewed as volitional.

10.5.3 Tense and aspect

An absolutive-ergative system may be used in clauses marked by past tense and perfect aspect, with nominative-accusative being used everywhere else. Examples of this type are found in many Iranian and Indic languages. In Hindi and Rājāstanī, an absolutive-ergative system is restricted to perfective aspect. In Kashmiri, Pamir languages, and Middle Persian, absolutive-ergative marking is restricted to past tenses. In (10.18), from Kashmiri, the A ('Mohan') is marked with the ergative case in the past tense. The verb takes an agreement marker referring to O ('the clothes').

(10.18)   mohn-an$_A$ chəl'$_O$ palav
          Mohan-ERG   washed:OBJECT.CASE   clothes:masc.pl
          'Mohan washed the clothes'

And in (10.19), cast in the future tense, the A is marked with the nominative case which is also used for marking S, in (10.20):

(10.19)   su$_A$ pari   kita:b$_O$
          he:NOM   read:FUT   book:OBJECT.CASE
          'He will read a book'

(10.20)   su$_S$ thok   seṭha:
          he:NOM   tired   lot
          'He is very tired'

What is the motivation behind this split? Completed actions and actions in the past can be conceived of as being oriented towards what happened to the O. Then, the A acquires the marking—and we get an ergative system. Actions cast in the present, future, or imperfective focus on who did, does, or will be doing it—A or S: we then have to mark the O, and the system is nominative-accusative.

10.5.4 Split patterns with more than one factor at play

More than just one factor may condition the distribution of absolutive-ergative and nominative-accusative patterns. Island Carib and Garifuna are typical of Arawak lan-guages: the S of stative verbs is marked just like O, and the S of active intransitive verbs is marked like A. In addition to this split-S pattern, an absolutive-ergative pattern is attested in the past tense and perfect aspect, while a nominative-accusative system is consistently used in the imperfective and the future. This is an example of how a split based on the verb's meaning can combine with a split based on tense-aspect. Shokleng, a Jê language from southern Brazil, marks grammatical relations in an absolutive-ergative manner in the resultative aspect. It follows the nominative-accusative pattern if the action is continuing and not completed. But this only applies to main clauses. All dependent clauses follow the absolutive-ergative principle.

Can languages combine three or more sets of factors determining the distribution of nominative-accusative and absolutive-ergative patterns? And are there any further potential factors conditioning the distribution? We leave these questions to future investigations.

10.6 'Non-canonically' marked arguments

The ways in which grammatical relations are marked may correlate with the semantic roles of A, S, and O. An A, as the actor and the agent of a verb of affect, for example 'hit' or 'break', can exercise full control and be volitional. We saw in (10.4) that this type of A in Avar is marked with the ergative case. The A of a perception verb, the 'perceiver', exercises less control, and is perceived as less volitional. In Avar, such an A is be marked with the locative case:

(10.21)   ínssu-da$_{\text{A:PERCEIVER}}$ j-as$_\text{O}$ j-ix-ula
           father-LOCATIVE   FEM-child FEM-see-PRESENT
           'Father sees the girl (female child)'

In Avar, A of a verb of feeling and emotion is marked with the dative case. This type of A is also not volitional and not controlled, but its semantic role is different from that in (10.21):

(10.22)   ínssu-je$_{\text{A:EXPERIENCER}}$ j-as$_\text{O}$ j-óɬ'-ula
           father-DATIVE   FEM-child FEM-love-PRESENT
           'Father loves the child'

This pattern—typical for North-east Caucasian languages—offers a reason for considering verbs of feeling and emotion as grammatically defined subclasses of verbs (see §5.5.2).

The degree of A's control over the situation can be expressed through case marking. In Punjabi, an Indo-Aryan language, if perception is controlled, the A is marked with the nominative case: 'listen' in (10.23) is a controlled activity.

(10.23)   Tusïï$_{\text{A:CONTROLLED}}$ shor$_\text{O}$ suṇiaa
           you:NOM   noise:MASC.SG listen:PAST:MASC.SG
           'You listened to the noise'

'Hearing' something—unlike 'listening to something' is not controlled. The A of 'hear' is expressed with an oblique case accompanied by the dative marker in (10.24).

(10.24) [Tuàà   nüü]$_{\text{A:NON.CONTROLLED}}$ shor$_{\text{O}}$ sunaaii dittaa
         you:OBL   DATIVE   noise:MASC.SG hear   give:PAST:MASC.SG
         'You heard the noise'

The unusual, or 'non-canonically marked', A, of verbs of perception, volition, desire, and physical states usually share syntactic features with canonically marked A and S. More on this in §10.8.

10.7 Case marking, definiteness, and topicality

In many languages, case marking may correlate with the role of the participant. In numerous Tibeto-Burman, Australian, and Papuan languages, the A or S can be marked for case if the argument exercises control over the activity or performs it of their own accord. In Yawuru, an Australian language, the volitional A and S are marked with the suffix -*ni(m)*. Non-volitional A and S are unmarked.

In Tariana, the A, and also the S, are unmarked for case if they are not in contrastive focus to another participant, as in (10.25a):

(10.25a) ñamu$_{\text{A}}$ nawiki$_{\text{O}}$ di-hña-pidana
          evil.spirit person   3sg.nf-eat-REMOTE.PAST.REPORTED
          'The evil spirit ate people'

If the A (or S) is contrasted to something else, it takes the case-marker -*ne* 'focused A/S':

(10.25b) ñamu-ne$_{\text{A}}$ nawiki$_{\text{O}}$ di-hña-pidana
          evil.spirit-FOC.A/S person   3sg.nf-eat-REMOTE.PAST.REPORTED
          'The evil spirit ate people' (in contrast to other dangerous entities who did not)

The O of transitive verbs may be marked only if specific. In Spanish, the preposition *a* marks specific animate Os. Compare:

(10.26) Deseo   [un   empleado]$_{\text{O}}$
         want.1sgPRESENT an:MASC.SG employee:MASC.SG
         'I want an employee' [Anyone will do]

(10.27) Deseo   [a   un   empleado]$_{\text{O}}$
         want.1sgPRESENT OBJECT.MARKER an:MASC.SG employee:MASC.SG
         'I want an employee' [a specific one, but I cannot think of his/her name for the moment]

Marking Os differently depending on their definiteness, specificity, and topicality is also known as 'differential case marking'.

Differential case marking can interrelate with the semantics of the noun phrase, in agreement with the principle captured by the Nominal Hierarchy in Figure 10.1. In Tariana, and many related languages, personal pronouns are always marked for case if in O function. Nouns in O function are only marked if specific and topical. Example (10.28) means 'the evil spirit ate a specific person':

(10.28) ñamu$_A$ nawiki-nuku$_O$ di-hña-pidana
         evil.spirit person-SPECIFIC.OBJECT   3sg.nf-eat-REMOTE.PAST.REPORTED
         'The evil spirit ate a specific person'

Tariana combines semantic marking of A and S, and differential marking of O based on specificity.

The marking of subject (A/S) and of object (O) in Wolaitta, an Omotic language from Ethiopia, correlates with the definiteness of a noun. Any noun (definite or indefinite) is morphologically marked for nominative case (in A/S function). An indefinite O is unmarked. This indefinite O is also the citation form. The system is typical of a marked nominative language (a rather uncommon pattern: see §10.3).

In (10.29), from Wolaitta, A and O are indefinite. A ('a dog') takes the marked nominative case, and O ('a boy') is in the unmarked form used for the accusative case and for citation:

(10.29) kan-í$_A$ na?á$_O$ dagant-iísi
         dog-INDEF.NOM   child:masc.sg.INDEF.UNMARKED.ACC scare-3sg.masc.PERF
         'A dog scared a boy'

If the O is definite, it acquires special accusative case marking. A definite A and a definite S will also be marked. In (10.30), 'the father' is marked with accusative case because it is definite; and 'the boy', in A function, is marked with the definite nominative case suffix since it is definite:

(10.30) na?á-y$_A$?aawá-a$_O$ laat-iísi
         boy-masc.sg.DEF.NOM   father-masc.sg.DEF.ACC   inherited-3sg.masc.PERF
         'The boy inherited (the goods of) the father'

In (10.31), the definite marked nominative form of 'the boy' is in S function:

(10.31) na?á-y$_S$ gupp-eési
         boy-masc.sg.DEF.NOM   jump-3sg.masc.IMPERFECTIVE
         'The boy jumps'

And in (10.32), the definite (and thus marked) accusative form of 'the boy' is in O function:

(10.32)   kaná-y$_A$ naʔá-a$_O$ dagant-iísi
          dog-masc.sg.DEF.NOM boy-masc.sg.DEF.ACC scare-3sg.masc.PERF
          'The dog scared the boy'

That is, definite nouns distinguish A/S and O (both of which are marked). The marked nominative system (with the accusative unmarked) is restricted to indefinite nouns.

Cross-linguistically, definite, specific, and topical arguments tend to be more formally marked than their indefinite, non-specific, and less topical counterparts. The writer of a grammar may have to take these issues up again in chapters dealing with discourse and the pragmatics of communication—see Chapter 13.

10.8 Arguments of copula clauses and of verbless clauses

Copula clauses can be considered a minor type of clause, compared to the ubiquitous transitive and intransitive clauses. Not every language has copula clauses. A copula, or a copula verb, differs from other verbs in one important respect. A copula has a relational meaning: unlike any other verb, it serves to establish the relationship between the Copula Subject (CS) and the Copula Complement (CC). In contrast, other verbs—which describe a state, or an action—have their own referential meaning. Thus, the copula verb 'be' in English may express an identity relationship between the CS and the CC, for example *This woman is a teacher*, or attribution, for example *This woman is tall*, or location, for example *The cat is in the garden*, or possession, for example *This house is Mary's*. Change of state ('becoming something, or someone') is also often expressed with a copula verb. In some languages, a copula verb may occur with just one argument, the Copula subject, producing an existential reading, as in Latin *Deus est* (God is) 'God exists'.

Some or all of the semantic relations expressed through copulas may be achieved through apposition. We then obtain a verbless clause. This will also have two arguments—a Verbless Clause Subject (VCS) and a Verbless Clause Complement (VCC). Verbless clauses in Tariana take tense-evidentiality markers but only some aspect markers. They express:

- identity, as in *Hī tʃiāli nuri-naka* (this:ANIMATE man 1sg:son-PRESENT.VIS) 'this man is my son',
- attribution, as in *hī tʃiāli hanu-ite-naka* (this:ANIMATE man big-NCL:ANIMATE-PRESENT.VIS) 'this man is tall', and
- possession, as in *hīnu-ite-naka* (this:ANIMATE 1sg-POSSESSIVE:CL.ANIMATE-PRESENT.VIS) 'this (one) is mine'.

In Manambu, verbless clauses express identity, and do not distinguish tense (unlike copula and other clauses), for example *wun ma:m* (I elder sibling) 'I am an elder sibling'. In a few languages, a clause can consist of just the VCS. Exclamatory, optative, and some descriptive clauses in Russian may consist just of a VCS, for example *Kakaya radostj!* 'What joy!', *Toljko by zdorovje!* 'Only if (there was) health!', *Dom, ulica, fonarj, apteka* '(There is) a house, a street, a streetlight, a pharmacy'.

Copula verbs usually constitute a separate subclass of verbs (see §5.5). They may have restricted morphological possibilities. They can hardly ever be passivized. In many languages, including Hebrew, a copula cannot be causativized. Copula verbs in Manambu do not occur with directional markers (see §5.5). In terms of their historical development, copula verbs often come from positional verbs, for example *kumpa-* 'sit' in Jiwarli and neighbouring languages in the north-west of Western Australia, *estar* in Spanish and Portuguese, from the Latin verb *stāre* 'stand', or verbs of motion, for example *yi-* 'be, become' in Manambu from the verb *yi-* 'go'. In many languages, copula clauses and verbless clauses cannot form commands, or occur in dependent clauses. These are some of their characteristic features, to which we turn in Chapter 11.

Synchronically, the same form can co-exist in its function of positional or motion verb and its copula function. They can be distinguished by the number, and types of arguments they take: for example *yi-* 'go' in Manambu can occur with an oblique in the allative case, and *yi-* as copula can only occur with the formally unmarked copula complement. Copula verbs can develop into auxiliary and support verbs (see §7.6.2–3).

A copula may be omitted if the relationship is clear from the context. In Hungarian, the copula is omitted in clauses referring to identity and attribution in the present tense if the CS is third person, but not under other circumstances. Then, a verbless clause can be considered a subtype of copula clause.

The grammatical relations of CS and VCS tend to be marked in the same way as S. In the majority of nominative-accusative languages, CS and VCS are expressed with the formally unmarked nominative case. They are expressed with the formally unmarked absolutive in absolutive-ergative languages, such as Cavineña and Chukchi, a Chukotko-Kamchatkan language from the north-east of Russia.

The Copula Complement (CC) and the Verbless Clause Complement (VCC) are typically expressed with a formally unmarked case: the nominative in nominative-accusative systems and the absolutive in absolutive-ergative systems, such as Chukchi and Cavineña. Guillaume (2008: 96) notes that, in Cavineña, despite the fact that the CC and the VCC superficially resemble an O of a transitive clause (both are marked as absolutive), 'there are many differences. Unlike absolutive [S/O—A.Y.A.] arguments, the CC cannot be represented by a bound pronoun, (and) cannot be omitted'. A CC normally occurs preposed to the copula predicate, unlike the O which follows the verb.

In marked nominative languages (§10.3), CS and VCS may be expressed with the formally unmarked accusative case (this is the case in Berber languages, Wolaitta,

Jamul Tiipay, and other Yuman languages), or with the nominative case (as in Oromo, a Cushitic language).

The CC and the VCC may have their own, special marking. In Chukchi, the CC can appear in the 'equative' case, meaning 'in the quality of'. The CC in Estonian can be marked with the nominative case. Then, the relationship of identity between the CS and the CC is understood to be permanent, as in (10.33).

(10.33)   Ta   on   õpetaja
          she/he is   teacher:NOM
          'He or she is a teacher'

The CC can be marked with the essive case. Then, the CS is identical to a CC only temporarily:

(10.34)   Ta   on   siin   õpetaja-na
          she/he is   here   teacher-ESSIVE
          'He or she is here (in his temporary capacity of) a teacher'

In Kamaiurá, VCS and VCC are expressed with the formally unmarked 'nuclear' case used for citation if the VCC expresses a permanent characteristic of the VCS. In (10.33), my uncle is the chief forever:

(10.35)   je=tutyr-a   morerekwar-a
          1sg=uncle-NUCLEAR   chief-NUCLEAR
          'My uncle is the chief'

If the VCC is expressed with the attributive case -*am*, CS is only temporarily identical with VCC. In (10.36), my uncle was chief for just some time, and is no longer chief:

(10.36)   je=tutyr-a   rak   morerekwar-am
          1sg=uncle-NUCLEAR   ATTESTED.EVID   chief-ATTRIBUTIVE
          'My uncle was (in the capacity of) a chief'

CS and VCS typically behave like other 'subjects'—see §10.9. CC and VCC hardly ever share syntactic features with arguments of other types. We turn to the meanings of copula and verbless clauses, and their special features, in §11.1.

10.9 Capturing argument structure

Grammatical relations can be changed, by removing, adding, or rearranging arguments. We can recall, from §7.3, the most common argument (or valency) reducing derivations are passive and antipassive (see Boxes 7.1–7.2). The most common valency-increasing derivations are causatives (Box 7.3) and applicative (Box 7.4).

The three major grammatical relations, A, S, and O, can be grouped with regard to their morphological marking, and also syntactic properties. A and S arguments can be captured under the umbrella notion of 'subject', based on the following syntactic features:

(i) canonical imperative sentences always involve the speaker commanding the addressee, which has to be an S or an A;
(ii) verbs of ability ('can'), attempt ('try'), 'begin', 'finish', and 'want' typically trigger identity of A and S;
(iii) serial verbs in most languages share A and S (§7.6.1);
(iv) in most languages, 'switch reference' in clause linking indicates identity of A and S (see Chapter 12).

These properties may help identify non-canonically marked A and S as similar to other, canonical, A and S.

The idea of 'accusative' and 'ergative' alignment originated in the morphological marking of core arguments. The notions can be further extended to the syntactic level, dealing with the constraints on the building up of complex sentences in terms of the treatment of core arguments. If two clauses—in a coordinate or subordinate relationship—require for a certain purpose a common argument which is in S or A function in each, the language may be said to have 'accusative syntax'. This applies to English. In contrast, in Dyirbal and other syntactically ergative languages, a common argument has to be in S or O function. We return to accusative and ergative treatment, or 'alignment', of core arguments, in Chapter 12.

The category of O can be syntactically defined in terms of being the potential target of the passive. If a language has constructions where two arguments look like O in their morphological marking, only one of them may be the target of the passive. In (7.18), from Imbabura Quechua, only the former A ('Maria') has all the syntactic properties of an O. 'Maria' (but not José) can become the S of a newly derived passive. A/S and O can differ in terms of forming relative clauses, and nominalizations. In Ute, a Uto-Aztecan language, the O that has a full set of object properties has to immediately follow the verb.

In many languages, the Copula Subject and the Verbless Clause Subject are marked in the same way as S. In Yuman and many Berber languages with marked nominative systems, CS and VCS are expressed with formally unmarked accusative case (also used as citation form); Copula and Verbless Clause Complements are expressed with marked nominative case. In Oromo and a number of other Cushitic languages, CS and VCS take the nominative case, and CC and VCC—accusative case. Case marking, semantics, and syntactic properties of arguments justify treating copula and verbless clauses separately from other clause types. More on this in Chapter 11.

10.10 Concluding remarks

Here are a few points, particularly relevant for understanding grammatical relations. Transitivity classes of verbs are to be established on a language-specific basis, with special attention to the marking of different semantic roles captured by A, S, O, and also E. If the language has unusual, non-canonically marked arguments, it is essential to show how they relate to the more canonically marked ones in terms of their syntactic behaviour.

A further question is: how do core arguments of copula clauses and verbless clauses compare to A, S, and O? In analysing changes in grammatical relations, special attention should to be paid to the 'derived' S of passives and antipassives (see §7.3). If the language allows causativization of transitive verbs, treatment of—and behaviour of—the erstwhile A and O are topics for special scrutiny. Grammatical features of 'subjects' and 'objects' help establish the status of A, S, and O independently of how they may be marked.

WARNING: It is a serious error to equate A with agent—A (transitive subject) is a nickname for a syntactic function which can encompass many semantic roles, of which agent is just one. Another one is 'perceiver', as in *I hear the thunder clap*. Following the same principle, O (transitive object) is not necessarily a 'Patient'—the syntactic category of O encompasses an array of semantic types, including patient (the entity affected by the action), thing perceived, something given or transferred, something liked and so on. It is important not to confuse semantic roles (which are potentially unlimited in number) and syntactic functions which are restricted in each grammar.

Notes and sources

§10.1: A preliminary semantic approach to transitivity is in Hopper and Thompson (1980); see a discussion of further parameters, including volitionality and control on the part of the A/S argument in Dixon (2010b: 142–7). The lack of ergative case marking on the subject of 'say' indicates that it is intransitive in Eskimo: see Munro (1982: 304–5) and Aikhenvald (2011a) on transitivity of speech verbs; see Dixon (2005: 102–205) on semantic verb types, and Onishi (2001) on transitivity and argument marking for verbs of different types. Dixon (1994) offers a general perspective on grammatical relations, with special focus on absolutive-ergative systems. Also see §5.5.1, on transitivity classes of verbs. See Blake (2001) on differentiating between case markers and adpositions.

§10.2: Dixon (1994: 40–52), Aikhenvald and Dixon (2011c: 144–6) and Aikhenvald (2012a: 200–2) summarize the principles of marking grammatical relations. See McDonald and Wurm (1979: 16, 22, 28) on Waŋkumara; other examples of tripartite marking are in Dixon (1994: 40–1; 2002: 299–314, 347–51, 516–20). See Andersen (1988) on Päri.

§10.3: Dixon (1994: 62–9, 2010b: 119–23) discusses markedness in nominative-accusative systems; see Chapter 13 of Dixon (2010b) for a discussion of differences in marking grammatical relations with case and with bound pronouns on verbs. König (2008) is a comprehensive study of marked nominative systems in African languages. Some grammars use the term 'absolute', or 'absolutive' for the formally unmarked accusative case (which is misleading, in view of the traditional use of the term 'absolutive' in absolutive-ergative systems). See Weber (1989: 175–84) on Quechua; Miller (2001: 153–5) on Jamul Tiipay; Amha (2012) on Omotic languages.

§10.4: See Ebeling (1966: 77) on Avar; Fleck (2006) on Matses; Aikhenvald (2012a: 207–9) for absolutive-ergative systems in Amazonian languages; Schieffelin (1985) on Kaluli; Harms (1994: 65) on Epena Pedee.

§10.5: Dixon (1994: 70–110) offers a full account of 'split' ergative systems.

§10.5.1: See Dixon (1994: 83–94; 1972: 130–5; p.c.) on the nominal hierarchy, split ergativity based on the semantics of NPs, and on Dyirbal. The idea of the Nominal Hierarchy goes back to Silverstein (1976). Special cases of split ergativity in Amazonian languages are discussed in Aikhenvald (2012a: 210–12). See Dixon (1994: 94–7), for a discussion of 'bound' versus 'free' split.

§10.5.2: See Dixon (1994: 72–8) on split-S and fluid-S systems, and further references there; Mithun (1991) on semantic parameters relevant for distinguishing Sa and So in North American Indian languages; Aikhenvald (2012a: 212–14) on Amazonian languages including Warekena. See Holisky (1987: 104–5, 111) on Tsova-Tush (note that she calls 'absolutive' nominative); Aikhenvald (1995b) on Baniwa. Split-S and fluid-S systems are known under a variety of other terms, including 'active-stative', 'agent-patient' and 'split-intransitive'.

§10.5.3: See Dixon (1994: 100) and references there; Aikhenvald (2012a: 214–16) on Amazonian languages; Wali and Koul (1997: 152–3) on Kashmiri.

§10.5.4: See Taylor (1977: 46–51; 1956); Aikhenvald (2012a: 216–17). Also see Dixon (1994: 211); and Aikhenvald (2012a: 219–22) for some discourse-dependent ergative splits.

§10.6: See Ebeling (1966: 77) on Avar; Onishi (2001: 28–9) on Punjabi and other Indo-Aryan languages. See the papers in Aikhenvald, Dixon, and Onishi (2001) for further instances of non-canonical argument marking, and Dixon (2010b: 147–52) for a summary. Onishi (2001) offers an in-depth discussion of their semantics, and marking.

§10.7: See Dixon (1994: 28–35) on semantic marking of A and S, and examples of Tibeto-Burman and Papuan languages; Dixon (2002: 132–3) on Australian languages; Hosokawa (1991: 254) on Yawuru; Aikhenvald (2003: 141–3) on Tariana. The concept of 'differential case marking' and the relevant semantic distinctions were introduced by Bossong (1991), see also Blake (2001: 120). See Amha (2012: 489–93 and p.c.) on Wolaitta and other Omotic languages.

§10.8: See Dixon (2010b: 160–84) on copula and verbless clauses. See Shvedova (1970: 560ff) on this and other clause types in Russian; the third example in the text is a quote from a famous poem by Alexander Blok. See Austin (1998) on the verb 'sit' as a copula in a number of languages from Western Australia. More instances of grammaticalization of motion and positional verbs into copulas are in Heine and Kuteva (2002). See Guillaume (2008: 94–7) on Cavineña, Dunn (1999: 310–11) on Chukchi; Kossmann (2012) and references there on Berber languages; Miller (2001: 155) on Jamul Tiipay; Mithun (1999) on Yuman languages; Owens (1985) on Oromo. Ainu (Tamura 2000: 50–1) is among the few languages which mark CS and CVS differently from A and S. See Erelt (2007: 97–8) on Estonian (and a snap-shot of cases in Estonian in Table 6.4); see Seki (2000: 111–12, 161–2) on Kamaiurá.

§10.9: See Dixon (1994: 131–42) on the universal features of 'subject', including control in reflexives and reciprocals (§7.4). The notion of pivot is discussed in Dixon (1994: 8–18, 14–81, 2012: 197–205) and Aikhenvald and Dixon (2011c: 148–50). Grammatical relations in copula clauses and verbless clauses are discussed in Dixon (2010b: 166–70). See Cole (1982: 136–7) on Imbabura Quechua.

Clause and sentence types

The clause is the basic unit which describes an activity, a property, a state, or a relationship. Clauses can be classified according to the three groups of related features:

I. INTERNAL STRUCTURE, INCLUDING NUMBER AND ROLES OF PARTICIPANTS AND TYPE OF PREDICATE. In terms of their internal structure, clauses can be transitive, ditransitive, intransitive, or extended intransitive. Further types are copula clauses and verbless clauses—see §11.1.

II. SYNTACTIC FUNCTION. A clause which forms a sentence on its own, that is, can be used as a complete utterance is a 'main clause'. Dependent clauses cannot form sentences on their own. They have a function with respect to the main clause within a sentence—see §11.2.

III. PRAGMATIC FUNCTION, OR TYPES OF SPEECH ACTS. A main clause—a sentence in itself—reflects a speech act: a statement, a command, or a question—see §11.3.

Clause types differ from each other in their grammatical properties. The full set of categories of non-spatial setting (tense, aspect, and mood, etc.) is typically marked in declarative main clauses. A main clause expresses absolute tense. A dependent clause is likely to express 'relative tense'—that is, the time with respect to another event or state. The principle of relative tense is reflected in 'back-shifting' in English complement clauses. A speech report like *He said: 'I went home early'* can be recast with a complement clause as *He said that he had gone home early*, using the past-in-the past form known as 'past perfect'. Dependent clauses hardly ever contain imperative forms (commands and questions can be embedded in complex sentences as types of complement clauses: see §11.3.2). Every language has negation (or 'polarity') as a clausal category—see §11.4.

11.1 Internal structure of clauses and clause types

Transitive and intransitive clauses, and the ways their participants are marked, were discussed in §10.1–10.7. Copula clauses and verbless clauses are neither transitive nor intransitive (see §10.8 and §3.9). A relational meaning of 'possession' ('having' and 'belonging') can be expressed with a number of different clause types: see §11.1.3. A variety of clause types may express comparison; see §11.1.4.

11.1.1 Copula clauses

Copula clauses consist of a Copula Subject (CS), copula verb in the predicate slot, and Copula Complement. As we saw in §10.9, the Copula Subject (CS) is typically marked like A/S in nominative-accusative languages, and like S/O in absolutive-ergative languages. In terms of its behaviour, it generally aligns with S (the intransitive subject). The Copula Complement (CC) can be marked differently from A, S, O, and CS (as we saw in §10.8). For instance, in Manambu the CC can never be expressed with bound pronouns, while A, S, O, and CS can. Copula clauses typically have the following relational meanings:

   (i)   Attribution, with an adjective in the CC slot, as in *The house is big*.
  (ii)   Identity, with a noun in the CC slot, as in *This house is a king's palace*.
 (iii)   Location and existence, with a noun accompanied by an adposition or an affix in the CC slot, e.g. *The car is in the garage*.
 (iv)   Benefaction, with a noun accompanied by an adposition or an affix in the CC slot, e.g. *These flowers are for me*.
  (v)   Possession, with a possessive phrase in the CC slot, e.g. *These flowers are mine*.
 (vi)   Change of state, with a noun or an adjective in the CC slot, e.g. *He became a teacher*.

In some languages, a copula verb can occur with just one argument, CS, with an existential meaning, as in Latin *sum* 'I am, I exist'. The verb 'be' in Latin can also be used with a CC, in all of the meanings typical of a copula clause. The existential marker *ʔum* in Hakha Lai, a Tibeto-Burman language, is used only in existential clauses, with one argument. If a CC is present, the copula verb *sii* is required. In Tschangla, also Tibeto-Burman, copula clauses containing *cha* express location, attribution, and also existence; clauses with *gila* express identity. Locative and existential copula clauses may have possessive meanings—we turn to these in §11.1.3.

The nature of the CC may vary across languages. In English, a complement clause (see §11.2) can occupy the CC slot of a copula clause with the meaning of attribution, as in *The fact is that we have won the game*. A locational clause can occupy the CC slot with the meaning of location, as in *This house is where we live*.

The choice of copulas may depend on the type of relationship. Kham, a Tibeto-Burman language, employs the copula *li-/le-* in existential clauses and in clauses denoting location, possession, and attribution of current and temporary properties. The copula *ta-* expresses change of state ('become') and general properties. Two copulas in Spanish and Portuguese are *ser*, to express permanent properties, and *estar*, to express temporary ones. The choice of a copula may depend on the meaning of the Copula Subject. Manambu has a copula verb *na-* with the CS referring to natural phenomena, for example seasons, a copula *tay-* with CS referring to temperature and climate, for example 'cold' and 'hot'; a copula *yasa-* with CS referring to physical states, for example hunger and thirst, and a copula *yæy-* with CS referring to smells.

In many languages, copulas are a special subclass of verbs: they cannot be causativized, or form an imperative (this is the case in Manambu and Tariana; see also §5.5). In other languages, a copula is a separate, non-inflecting, word class, for example Japanese *da*.

Copula clauses can have a negative counterpart. The negative copula *sede* in Tariana is used for location, existence, and possession, to replace the copula *alia*. The copula *alia* can also express identity, attribution, and benefaction; in these meanings it is negated with the verbal suffix *-kade*.

11.1.2 Verbless clauses

Verbless clauses consist of a Verbless Clause Subject and Verbless Clause Complement in apposition. In a number of languages, some or all of the meanings expressed through copula clauses can be expressed through verbless clauses. In Kham, the relationship of identity is expressed through a verbless clause:

(11.1)   ao-rə$_{\text{VCS}}$ ŋa-zaː-rə$_{\text{VCC}}$
          this-PL   1sg-child-PL
          'These are my children'

When a verbless clause expressing identity is negated, a negative copula has to be used:

(11.2)   ao-rə$_{\text{VCS}}$ ŋa-zaː-rə$_{\text{VCC}}$ maːhkə
          this-PL   1sg-child-PL   NEGATIVE.COPULA
          'These are not my children'

Verbless declarative clauses in Wolaitta express relations of identity and attribution, as in (11.3). As in many marked nominative languages, the Verbless Clause Subject (VCS), 'cattle', is marked with the nominative case, and the Verbless Clause Complement (VCC) is expressed with the formally unmarked accusative case (this is also the citation form):

(11.3)   méhé$_{\text{VCS}}$ miiššá$_{\text{VCC}}$
          cattle:NOM   money:ACC
          'Cattle is money' (that is, cattle is valuable)

To express location and benefaction, the copula marker *-a* is used:

(11.4)   hagé$_{\text{CS}}$ [maná-ss]$_{\text{CC}}$-a$_{\text{COPULA}}$
          this:MASC.SG.NOM   Mana-DAT-COPULA
          'This is for Mana'

Another copula is used in interrogative clauses of identity, and attribution:

(11.5)   hanná_{CS}   [zalʔ-ánc]_{CC}-ee_{COPULA}
          this:FEM.NOM   trade-NOMINALIZER-COP.INTER
          'Is this one (feminine) a trader?'

Generally, verbless clauses tend to have fewer morphological possibilities than clauses of other types. In Wolaitta and Tariana, they may not occur with the full set of tenses and aspects. In Manambu they take no aspect or tense markers. In many languages, verbless clauses do not form commands. To be used as dependent clauses, verbless clauses may have to be rephrased with a verb as their predicate.

11.1.3 *Possession within a clause*

Marking possession in a clause may involve a verb of ownership 'have', or 'belong'. This is typically a transitive verb. Its A (subject) is Possessor, and its O is the Possessed noun. We mentioned in §5.5 that in some languages the verb 'have' may be unusual in terms of its features. In Tariana, the verb 'have' cannot combine with any morphological derivations—causative, reciprocal, or passive. In Tamambo -*noha* 'have' is the only transitive verb which cannot occur with any tense or aspect marker. Verbs of possession often do not form imperatives. This is so in Harar Oromo, Amharic, and Tariana.

If the Possessed noun is the subject, and the Possessor an oblique, we obtain belong-type verbs. A 'have' construction is 'about' the Possessor, *John has a red car.* A 'belong'-construction is about the Possessed noun, for example *The red car belongs to John.* That is, the distinction is pragmatically-based. In *have*-constructions, the Possessor is usually definite, and the Possessed noun may be indefinite. In *belong*-constructions, the Possessed noun is typically definite, while the Possessor may be indefinite.

In many Indo-European languages *have*- and *belong*-constructions involve verbs. In Estonian, Colloquial Welsh, and a number of Slavic and Baltic languages, the equivalent of a *have*-construction is a copula clause. The reverse, 'belong to', can be expressed with a verb. This is the case in Estonian:

(11.6)   Jaanil   on   auto
          Jaan:ADESSIVE   is   car
          'Jaan has a car', lit. 'To Jaan is a car'

(11.7)   [See auto]_S   kuulub   Jaanile
          this car   belong.3sgPRESENT   Jaan:ALLATIVE
          'This car belongs to Jaan'

The Possessor within a possessive copula clause in Estonian is marked with the adessive case (meaning 'onto something'). This is known as a Locational schema of possessive marking. In Yimas, it is marked as 'accompaniment'—an example of a Comitative schema.

(11.8)   yampaŋ   kantk-n   amayak
         head.CLASS.VI.sg   with-1sg   COP.1sg
         'I have a head (lit. I am with head)'

In Hungarian, the possessor takes the dative case, similar to a beneficiary, or a goal. This is an example of a Goal schema of possessive marking.

(11.9)   nek-em   van   macskám
         DATIVE-1sgPOSS   exists   cat+1sgPOSS
         'I have (my) cat' (lit. For me my cat exists)

An intransitive verb 'exist' can also be used to express possession. A possessive noun phrase is then its only argument. In Jarawara both the copula *ama-* 'be' and the intransitive verb *-wata-* 'exist' can be used this way:

(11.10)   okoto   ama-ke
          1sgPOSS+daughter   be-DECL.fem
          'I have a daughter' (lit. my daughter is)

Another option for expressing possessive relationships is a verbless clause with a topicalized Possessor. This 'Topic schema' is used in North-east Ambae if the Possessor has to be expressed with a free pronoun or noun phrase.

(11.11)   [Ngie,]$_{TOP}$ vale-na   gai-rue
          3sg   house-3sgPOSSESSOR   NUM.CL-two
          S/he has two houses (lit. S/he, her/his houses two)

This is reminiscent of topic prominent clauses, typical for languages of Southeast Asia (we return to these in §13.1.1, and especially example (13.4)).

Possession can be expressed in other ways. West Greenlandic has derivational suffixes *-qar-* 'have' and *-qi-* 'have as', added to the Possessed noun. The Possessor is expressed with a bound pronoun:

(11.12)   aningassa-ati-qar-punga
          money-ALIENABLE-HAVE-1sgPOSSESSOR:INDICATIVE
          'I have (some) money'

The prefix *ka-* on a noun marks predicative possession in Tariana and in many other Arawak languages. The way of saying 'John has a wife' in (11.13) is similar to colloquial English 'I am monied' as an alternative to 'I have money'.

(11.13)   Juse   ka-sa-do-pidaka
           José   POSS/ATTRIB-spouse-FEM-RECENT.PAST.REPORTED
           'José has a wife (lit. is spoused)'

Different predicative constructions within one language may correlate with different types of possessed nouns, possessive relationships, and possessors. The choice of derivational suffixes for expressing predicative possession in West Greenlandic depends on what type of thing one possesses, for example *-gig-* 'have a good (something)', *-lug-/-lup-* 'have a bad (something)', *-kit-* 'have a small (something)' and *-tu-* 'have much/a big (something)'.

Or different possessive constructions can be employed, reflecting the same categorization of nouns as in possessive NPs. In Koyukon, the verb *-t'aanh* 'have' is used with alienably possessed nouns. With kinship nouns, which are inalienably possessed, possession is indicated with the verb 'be'. Along similar lines, in Jarawara the verb *-kiha* 'have' can only be used with alienably possessed nouns, for example 'I have two dogs'. Kinship possession is expressed with a copula or an existential clause (as in (11.10)), 'My daughter is'/'My daughter exists' meaning 'I have a daughter'.

Why so? Verbless clauses and copula clauses are essentially used for time-stable relationships. Thus, they are expected to cover whole–part and kinship relations. Verbal clauses may correlate with the agency of the 'owner', and allow variation in terms of time-stability and temporality of possession. The intrinsic semantics of clause types underlies a cross-linguistic tendency to use 'have' with less intimate, less stable, and more alienable possession.

11.1.4 Comparative constructions

Comparison may be expressed with a variety of clause types. A comparative construction involves contrasting items (people, things, actions, or states) in terms of how similar or different they are. Monoclausal comparatives can be realized through copula clauses or verbless clauses; other options include intransitive and transitive clauses.

A prototypical comparative scheme involves:

(i)   'comparee', that is, who or what is being compared;
(ii) 'parameter of comparison', that is, property in terms of which comparison is made;
(iii) 'standard of comparison', that is, who or what the comparee is being compared with.

For instance, in *Jane is more assiduous than her sister*, *Jane* is the comparee, *assiduous* is parameter of comparison, and *her sister* is 'standard of comparison'. The mark of the comparative construction is *than*. In English, the parameter takes a further comparative marker, *more*, or the suffix *-er*. Comparative constructions may help determine word class. (If this is so, it may be sensible to discuss them jointly with word classes.) In many languages, adjectives stand apart from other word classes in that they have special comparative forms (as we saw in §8.2.1–3).

The parameter of comparison can be a copula complement, as in English, or a verbless clause complement, as in Manambu. The standard of comparison may be marked in the same way as a core argument, or an oblique. In Basque it takes the absolutive case. In Estonian the standard of comparison is marked with the elative case ('from'), and in Hungarian it requires adessive case ('at'). The standard of comparison may be considered a grammatical relation in its own right, different from A, S, O, and any of the obliques.

In a number of languages, the standard of comparison is implicit and cannot be overtly expressed within a comparative clause. In Manambu, the marker of comparison *-pək* can be attached to adjectives of size or value (which form a small subclass of adjectives). One can say *kə ñan nəma-pək-al* (this.feminine.sg child big-COMPARATIVE-3sg.fem.PRED) 'This girl is bigger'. The standard of comparison cannot be included in the same clause—it is usually either clear from the context, or is stated separately in another clause.

Comparative constructions can also be expressed through an extended intransitive clause. In many African languages, a comparative clause follows the schema 'X surpasses Z' at X-ness', as in Hausa (Heine and Kuteva 2001: 405–6 focus on the pan-African character of this comparative scheme):

(11.14) naa fi   Muusaa wàayoo
         I   surpass Moses   cleverness
         'I am cleverer than Moses' (lit. I surpass Moses in cleverness)

A comparative can be expressed through a serial verb construction (see §7.6.1), typically, with the verb 'exceed', or 'surpass', combining with a verb which denotes the parameter of comparison, as in Mupun, and many other African languages, within a transitive or an intransitive clause.

Comparison may involve superiority, that is, being 'more' than something else. There can also be comparative of inferiority—being 'less'. Comparison may reflect equality, for example *Jane is as assiduous as her sister*. A further option is a superlative: *Jane is the most assiduous girl (in the class/in Cairns/in the nation)*. Each of these meanings can be expressed with a variety of clause types.

A comparative construction can be used to compare two clauses, for example English *Jack makes cakes better than Jane prepares the steak*. In Hungarian, comparing two clauses involves two markers of comparative, *mint* 'than' and *amilyen* 'what, which', in addition to a comparative marker on the adverb:

(11.15)   Anna   gyors-abb-an   olvas,
          Anna   fast-COMPARATIVE-ADVERB   read.3sgPRESENT.INDEF
          mint   amilyen   gyors-an   Péter olvas
          than   which   fast-adverb Peter read.3sgPRESENT.INDEF
          'Anna reads faster than Peter does' (lit. Anna reads faster than which fast
          Peter reads)

Comparison of two predicates involves markers *inkább* 'rather' and *mint* 'than':

(11.16)   Anna   inkább   írja,   mint olvassa
          Anna   rather   write.3sgPRESENT.DEF   than write.3sgPRESENT.DEF
          a   könyv-ek-et
          DEF.ART book-PL-ACC
          'Anna writes rather than reads books' (lit. Anna rather writes than reads books)

Some languages do not have a special comparative construction. Two clauses can be
juxtaposed to express comparison. In Warekena, to say 'This dog is bigger than that
one' one says 'This dog is big, that dog is small'. The fact that in some languages comparatives are unusual, and perhaps avoided, may correlate with the social and cultural
organization of their speakers; we return to these in §14.4.6.

11.2 Clauses and their syntactic functions

A main clause forms a complete utterance and is equivalent to a sentence. A main
clause distinguishes the maximum number of categories, including speech acts.
Dependent clauses (which may be referred to as 'subordinate' clauses) form part of a
sentence and have a function within the main clause, or with respect to it.

COMPLEMENT CLAUSES fill an argument slot in another clause. In *I heard [that Brazil
beat France at soccer]*, a *that*-complement clause occupies the slot of a transitive object,
O. In *[That Brazil beat France] does not surprise me*, a *that*-complement clause occupies
the slot of a transitive subject, A.

RELATIVE CLAUSES modify the head of a noun phrase (which plays the role of an
argument or an oblique within another clause), for example *I cursed the architect [who
designed an inappropriate building]*.

ADVERBIAL CLAUSES may occupy the slot of an oblique, as for example, a temporal
clause in *[After he had planned to write a book]*, *he failed to do so*.

A non-main, or 'dependent', clause is usually said to be 'embedded' within the main
clause. Any clause type can be used in the main clause. In some languages, verbless
clauses may not be used in dependent clauses (as we saw in §11.1.2). Dependent clauses
may differ in terms of (a) which linkers and verbal forms are used; (b) expression of

grammatical relations; (c) the order of constituents; (d) their placement with regard to the main clause; (e) the semantic relationship between the main and the dependent clause. Main and dependent clauses may be negated differently—we return to this in §11.4.

Two or more main clauses can be coordinated, to form a complex sentence, for example [*I asked John to write a book*] [*but he declined*]. The two clauses have the same status.

Dependent clauses can be combined with a main clause through clause chaining. Then, (a) one clause is 'main' in the sense that it bears all the tense, aspect, mood, and speech act modification; and (b) other clause(s) are dependent on it. But they cannot be considered complement clauses or embedded subordinate clause(s)—they are neither an argument, nor an oblique within the main clause. Such co-dependent clauses can be marked for relative tense, and often for person of the subject as the same or different from that of the main, or controlling, clause. These co-dependent clauses are also called 'medial clauses'. The main clause is then known as the 'final clause'.

In (11.17), from Manambu, the main, or the final, clause 'she went off' is marked for tense, and person, gender, and number of the subject. The gender, number, and person of the subject are also marked on the dependent clause. This clause also takes a morpheme (-*k*) indicating that its subject is different from that of the main clause, and that the action happened prior to that of the main clause, or in connection with it, or might have been the reason for it:

(11.17) [a-di   jəb   kur-də-k]
         DEM.DIST-pl   design   make-3sg.masc-COMPLETED.DS
         ata   ya:l
         then   go+3sg.femPAST.TENSE
         'After he had made those designs (or as he made those designs; or because he made those designs), she went off'

A language may not have a special clause type for a complement clause function. Then, another construction is used instead. Dependent clauses in languages with clause-chaining can be used in lieu of complement clauses, as 'complementation' strategies. In Manambu, a co-dependent clause can be used this way, just like a complement clause would be used in another language:

(11.18) [a-di   jəb   kur-də-k]   və-tua
         DEM.DIST-pl   design make-3sg.masc-COMPLETED.DS   see-1sgPAST
         'I saw him make these designs' (lit. He having made these designs, I saw)

We return to the types of dependent clauses, and clause linking in Chapter 12.

11.3 Speech acts and sentence types

The three major speech acts are statements, commands, and questions. They correspond to three kinds of independent clause types (and thus sentence types). Each of these is marked with a choice from the mood system—declarative, imperative, and interrogative (see §7.2.1). The range of possible speech acts (and thus potential clause types) in any language may go beyond these. Expressing surprise or exasperation may require an 'exclamatory' clause.

The three major sentence types have their own phonological, morphological, and syntactic properties. They may be associated with distinct intonation contours. A rising intonation may be a feature of a question, and a level intonation that of a statement. In Motuna, a Papuan language from Bougainville, a command has a sharp falling intonation. And in English, 'an imperative used to convey an authoritative command is likely to be uttered with a low fall' (Davies 1986: 59).

Constituent order may correlate with sentence type. In English, subject-verb-object order is what we find in statements: *I have written a paper.* If I make this into a question, the first word of the auxiliary comes first: *Have I written a paper?* And in a command, the subject (second person 'you') can be omitted: *Write a paper!*

One clause type can cover several speech acts. A declarative or an interrogative sentence can be used as a command. A notice *No animals are allowed* is a way of commanding not to bring animals in. *Why don't you come inside* implies an invitation, or even a command, and hardly requires an answer. We turn to such versatile sentences in §11.3.4.

11.3.1 Imperatives and commands

Canonical imperatives are commands addressed to a singular second person. In some languages, commanding expressions can be addressed to someone other than the addressee. These 'noncanonical imperatives' include commands directed to first person ('me' or 'us'), and are sometimes referred to as 'hortatives'. There may also be commands to third person (which are sometimes referred to as 'jussives'). Special categories of imperatives include distance in space ('do here' versus 'do there') and distance in time ('do immediately' versus 'do later'), and politeness (as we saw in §7.2.1).

Imperative clauses can be special in a number of ways. Every verb, and every type of predicate, can be used in a statement. Imperatives can typically be formed on any transitive verb, and a goodly portion of intransitive verbs. But imperatives of verbs which encode potentially uncontrollable actions are often avoided. In English, the command *Hiccup!* is pragmatically odd. In a number of languages—such as Seneca, an Iroquoian language, Nivkh, a Paleo-Siberian isolate, and Tariana, from north-west Amazonia—such a command is simply ungrammatical. In English, commands cannot be formed on modal verbs: one can hardly say *Need!* or *Can!*

Some languages do not have a dedicated imperative paradigm. Another verbal category is then 'co-opted' to express a command. Example (11.19), from Ngala-kan, an Australian language, has two meanings—that of a statement in the present tense and that of a command. The two can be differentiated by the context, and by intonation:

(11.19)   ŋiñ-waken   ṛere-ka?
          2sg-return.PRESENT   camp-ALLATIVE
          (a) 'Go home!' or (b) 'You are going home'

The main meaning of an imperative sentence is a 'command', or 'directive' speech act. In a language with just one imperative form, the imperative form can have further meanings. In English, the imperative can be used for orders, commands, demands, for example *Get out of my way!*; requests, pleas, or entreaties, as in *Please, help me tidy up!*; advice and recommendations, as in *Keep your options open!*; instructions, as in *Insert a cassette as illustrated with its labelled side facing you*; invitations, as in *Come over and see my new kitten*; and permissions, as in *Take as many as you like.*

The exact interpretation of an imperative form depends on numerous factors, often hard to capture. While orders imply telling someone else what to do, requests involve asking someone to do something, with an option for the addressee not to comply (though the assumption often is that they are likely to). The 'asking' rather than 'telling' or 'ordering' overtone is commonly signalled by additional means: *please, kindly*, an interrogative tag, or a performative parenthetical such as *I beg you.*

Imperatives can be negated differently from declaratives. Negative imperatives (also known as prohibitives) may be marked with a variety of morphological means, including affixes and clitics. There may be fewer grammatical distinctions in prohibitives than in imperatives: in Maale prohibitives do not distinguish politeness, while positive imperatives do. Tariana (7.12a–7.12c) has several positive imperative forms, but only one negative imperative.

Forming an imperative in Latin involves using the verb's root; this is the shortest and the simplest form in the language. Not so with prohibitives. A prohibitive consists of an auxiliary construction with the imperative form of the negative verb *nolle* 'not want, be unwilling, refuse' followed by an infinitive. Archimedes is reported to have said (11.20) to a Roman soldier who, despite being given orders not to, ended up killing the famous geometer during the conquest of Syracuse.

(11.20)   Noli   tangere   circulos   meos
          not.want.2sgIMPV   touch.INF   circle.ACC.PL   my.ACC.PL
          'Don't touch my circles'

Prohibitives may differ from positive imperatives in their intonation, and in the order of constituents. In English, the subject of a prohibitive—if present—commonly follows the verb. Example (11.22) is judged less felicitous than (11.21):

(11.21) Don't you open the door—judged felicitous
(11.22) You don't open the door—judged less felicitous

These, and similar, properties may suggest that—at least in some languages—the prohibitive can be considered a special sentence type, distinct from a positive command.

11.3.2 *Interrogatives*

Interrogative sentences come in two varieties. CONTENT INTERROGATIVES feature a content interrogative word. In English these are *who, what, which, where, when, why,* and *how*. The label 'wh- words' is sometimes used for the content question words in English since all except *how* begin with *wh-*. This English-centric label is best avoided for languages other than English. The function of content interrogatives is to seek information from the addressee (see §9.4.1 on interrogative words and their word class membership).

Sets of interrogative words can be small. Ashéninca Perené, a Campa Arawak language from Peru, has *niNka* 'who', and a general interrogative word *tsika* in terms of which all other interrogative concepts are expressed. Ewe, a Kwa language from Ghana, marks content questions by placing a particle *ka* at the end of a noun phrase: 'person *ka*' is 'who', 'thing *ka*' is 'what' and so on. The form *néne* 'how many, how much' can be placed after any noun. (In Ewe, polar questions are marked by the particle *à* at the end of a clause). This is one of the most economical systems in the world. There may also be morphological marking of a clause as a content question, and/or a distinctive intonation pattern.

In numerous languages, including Mupun, Tamil, Japanese, Swahili, Chinese, and Manambu, an interrogative word within a content question remains in the same place as in a corresponding statement. In other languages, including English, Romanian, and Hausa, an interrogative word occurs at the beginning of the question.

POLAR INTERROGATIVES seek confirmation or disagreement rather than information. They are sometimes called 'yes/no questions'. This general label is not accurate since quite a few languages (especially outside Europe) lack words for 'yes' and 'no'. As Dixon (2012: 377) puts it, the term 'polar interrogative' 'should not be taken to imply that there are only two possible answers to a question seeking confirmation, these being polar opposites. In fact, there is a range of perfectly legitimate and commonly occurring answers, including "not really", "so they say", "not sure", "I believe so", and "it's not clear".

Polar questions can be marked by a wide variety of means: a distinctive constituent order, change in intonation or pitch, a tag, a polar question particle, a special verb form (interrogative mood), some other special morphological or phonological feature, or a combination of several of these.

Forming a polar question in English involves reversing the order of the subject constituent and the first word of the auxiliary, if there is one in addition to rising intonation, as in *Can your brother speak German*? If there is no auxiliary, it has to be supplied, for example *Does your brother speak German*? In many other languages, including Russian, Portuguese, and Manambu, forming a polar question does not involve change in constituent order.

In many languages, a polar question can be shown simply by intonation (typically, but not invariably, final rising intonation). Some languages have—in addition to intonation, or instead of it—a special interrogative affix or particle. Questions in Sanuma, a Yanomami language, are marked by the absence of sentence-final glottal stop (used in non-interrogative sentences). In Estonian, a polar question is marked with a question particle in the sentence-initial position:

(11.23)   Kas   sa   tuled?
           INTERROGATIVE you.sg come.PRESENT.2sg
           'Are you coming?'

Different types of polar questions may depend on the kinds of answers expected, or the attitude of the questioner or of the questioned. In Mupun, a Chadic language, polar questions can be marked by one of the three suffixes on the last word of the sentence, depending on the presupposition and attitude of the speaker: *-e* is neutral in that it does not carry any specific attitude of the speaker towards the truth of the proposition; *-a* indicates that the speaker is looking for confirmation of what they believe is true; and suffix *-o/-wo* is used to seek a confirmation of an unexpected proposition, and also to express surprise, and disbelief.

Questions that do not require responses and do not seek information or confirmation are known as 'rhetorical' questions. A prime example is the famous opening sentence of Marcus Tullius Cicero's first speech against Catilina, *Quo usque tandem abutere, Catilina, patientia nostra?* 'How long, Catilina, will you abuse our patience?' There is here a difference between the interrogative form of the sentence (cast as a content question) and the speaker's intention: to make the point about Catilina abusing our patience rather than asking him when he is going to stop. In Koasati, a Muskogean language from Louisiana, rhetorical questions acquire a special segmental mark (the tag *-háʔwá*).

A polar or content question can be embedded as an interrogative complement clause, as in *I know [where the money is]*. This is sometimes called an 'indirect question'. Similarly, a command can be embedded, as in *I told John [that he should not go to the Southern Highlands]*. This is referred to as an 'indirect command', and is also a type of complement clause. Once embedded, both commands and questions no longer have a special status as independent 'sentence types'.

11.3.3 *Exclamations*

Exclamatory sentences, or exclamations, can be recognized as a minor sentence type (they are used less often than other types). Exclamations express surprise and unexpected or otherwise remarkable information. They may be elliptical and consist just of interjections, as in *Oh dear!*, *Boy!*, or *Ouch!*

Exclamatory sentences can have their own grammatical properties. In Tariana and neighbouring East Tucanoan languages, exclamations are one-word utterances pronounced with higher than normal pitch and no tense-evidentiality specifications. Exclamations may be marked just with a special morpheme. In Chrau, a sentence-final particle *o'n* expresses bewilderment and surprise. Exclamations typically have a special intonation contour.

Exclamations may have the same structure as other sentence types; one constituent can acquire special pitch or emphatic stress. Each of the following exclamations, from French, has the form of another sentence type—the declarative in *Elle est BELLE!* 'She is beautiful!', and the interrogative in *Est-elle BELLE!* 'Is she beautiful!' and *N'est-elle pas BELLE!* 'Isn't she beautiful!'. (The constituents emphasized are in capital letters).

Exclamations *Qu'elle est BELLE!* and *Comme elle est BELLE!* do not share their syntactic structure and intonation with any other sentence type. The expressions *quelle chance!* (lit. 'what luck') and *quel génie!* (lit. 'what genius') can only occur in exclamations. Both contain an interrogative pronoun, but cannot undergo the inversion of subject and object as would be normal for a question. Example (11.24a) is grammatical, and (11.24b) is not (unless it is understood as a question and pronounced with the appropriate intonation):

(11.24a)   Quelle chance tu   as   eue!
           what   luck   you   have had
           'What luck you have had!'

(11.24b)   ?Quelle chance as   tu   eue!
           what   luck   have   you   had
           'What luck have you had?'
           *'What luck you have had!'

A similar principle applies to English: *How very tall he is!* is grammatical as an exclamation, but cannot be understood as a question. An exclamation which does look like a question is not a question because it cannot be answered, and does not have a question intonation. *Boy, is syntax easy!* and *What beautiful legs she has!* are not questions: they do not have question intonation, and do not require an answer. They cannot be negated: **How easy syntax isn't!* and **What beautiful legs she doesn't have!* are not acceptable.

11.3.4 *Versatile sentence types*

One sentence type can be used instead of another one to achieve a special effect. An imperative may sound too embarrassingly imperious and thus face-threatening. An essentially non-imperative form is then co-opted, in order to 'save face' or to avoid direct confrontation, to comply with existing hierarchies, social relationships, and etiquette, or to provide a more nuanced way of conveying directions. Such 'command strategies' may convey a meaning a straightforward imperative may lack.

In many languages, interrogatives can be used in lieu of directives. Their exact meanings depend on the context and the intonation. *Could you please close the window?* (said with a friendly intonation) shows interrogative form but has the pragmatic function of a polite command. And *Will you be quiet!*, said in a harsh and annoyed tone, also has interrogative form but is very much a command (which is why I have written it with an exclamation mark rather than a question mark). Reason questions as directives have opposite polarity to what is being requested: *Why don't you sweep the floor* is a command to sweep the floor and not a question asking for a reason; it would not be appropriate to respond to it by saying *Because I am too busy dusting the books*.

Statements can have the pragmatic force of a directive, or a request. In Colloquial English, any statement may be interpreted as a directive, given the right context. A statement *It is cold in here* can be understood as a request or suggestion to close the window, and saying *There is no milk left* is interpretable as a request, or even an order, to go and get more milk. A statement cast in future form is understood as a stern command in English: *You will do it right now* sounds almost like a threat.

Not so in other languages. This is how Cowell (2007: 57) describes the difference between future statements as directives in English and Arapaho, an Algonquian language of Oklahoma: 'Whereas in English use of the future tense as an imperative tends to constitute a very strong and peremptory command, emphasising the authority of the speaker ("you *will* go to school today, young man!"), in Arapaho the use of the future often makes the utterance not really a command at all, but instead a recognition of the strong authority of the other person, who cannot be commanded, or prevented from acting, but only deferred to'.

Free-standing dependent clauses appear as directives in many Indo-European languages. Performative constructions (such as *I order you to do X*) are a common way of phrasing suggestions, invitations, and directives of other sorts. In many languages of the world, the performative part, or the main clause, may be ellipsed. The result is what looks like a syntactically incomplete sentence. The effect of incompleteness—result of an ellipsis—can be associated with the lesser force of a command or a request as a potentially threatening act. An *if*-clause can occur on its own, as a polite directive, usually a request. In Modern English, an isolated *if*-clause in its directive function 'allows the speaker to express that he/she is not assuming the performance of the act requested of the hearer; the hearer has an option'. A doctor could say to a patient: *If you'd like to get dressed now.* An isolated *if*-clause will have the intonational properties of a complete declarative sentence. The ellipsed material cannot be easily recovered. This is an instance of 'desubordination': an erstwhile dependent clause now used as a sentence in its own right. This may be considered a special sentence type: it has some features of a dependent clause, the intonation of a statement, and the function of a request.

There are many other command strategies. Verbless directives in English are common in written notices, such as *Smoking prohibited, No visitors beyond this point,* or *No alcohol.* Verbless constructions are also commonly used in spoken language to indicate what is being ordered or asked for, for example *Two black coffees, please; Two adults, please* (as a shorthand for 'I request admission for two adults'); *Single to Manchester* (booking transport). Abbreviated commands such as *Forward! On your feet! Faster! Left, right! At the double! To the left!* are a feature of the language of the military: they have brusque overtones and presuppose immediate compliance.

Just as questions do not necessarily seek information, imperative forms may not express directive speech acts. When an imperative form is included in the first clause of a complex sentence, its most common interpretation in English is as a conditional. The sentence *Ask him about his business deals and he quickly changes the subject* is understood as 'If you ask him about his business deals he quickly changes the subject'. An idiomatic expression of surprise can take the form of a command, such as *Stone the crows!*

In many languages of the world, imperative forms may be used as tokens of politeness, in saying 'hello' and 'goodbye', and in expressions of good will, and of annoyance. Expressions such as *Take care* or *Fare thee well* are prime examples. They are tokens of speech etiquette—a kind of social glue which helps interlocutors acknowledge each other's presence. They do not command anything, and are conventionalized to varying extents. Yet using them correctly is a sine qua non for successful interaction within a community.

Imperatives may be reinterpreted as discourse markers and attention-getting devices: they may then lose their status as verbal forms altogether. The Italian form *Guarda!* 'Look!' is often used in discourse as a means of permitting the speaker to break into a conversation, implying that they have something extremely important to say which would require immediate attention. Then, such forms no longer serve to 'command'—they are imperative sentences in their form, but not in their function.

The ways in which different sentence types are used in each language are closely intertwined with existing practices and cultural conventions. Just as imperatives may not be appropriate to use in some circumstances (for instance, addressing someone older than oneself), asking questions to seek information may be awkward. This is the case in many Amazonian and Australian Aboriginal societies. Other linguistic strategies are used instead: for instance, making a relevant statement about something the person already knows and thus volunteering information first. If I wonder how many children someone has, I first tell them about myself and my family, and they may then volunteer similar information in response.

Cultural practices and attitudes provide additional motivation for the ways in which different sentence types can replace one another; in other words, a full outline of the pragmatics of sentence types in a given language is bound to include an 'ethnography of communication'. We return to this in Chapter 13.

11.4 Negation as a clausal category

All languages make a choice between positive and negative main clauses. The positive polarity is always unmarked, and the negative is always marked. In verbal clauses, negation tends to be associated with the verb. And if the verb is negated, so is the whole clause. Negation may be expressed with a negative word, typically, an unchangeable 'particle', for example Portuguese *não* or Manambu *ma:*. Or it can be marked with an affix on the verb, for example Tucano *-ti-*, for example *apê-ti-mi* (play-NEG-PRESENT. VISUAL.3sg.masc) 'he is not playing'. Negation can be expressed simultaneously by two forms: clausal negation in Tariana is shown by prefix *ma-* and suffix *-kade*, as in *ma-manika-kade-naka* (NEG-play-NEG-PRESENT.VISUAL) '(he) is not playing'. A verb in Tariana can only contain one prefix; so, person, number, and gender of the subject argument (normally marked by a personal prefix) is not marked under negation. Person, number, and gender are thus not distinguished in negative clauses.

Clausal negation may involve an auxiliary construction, as in Finnish (see §7.6.2), or English *I do not know*. In Spanish, a sentence can contain one negative marker, as in *nunca viene* 'he/she never comes'. Or it can contain two negatives, with the same meaning and only a stylistic difference, as in *no viene nunca* 'he/she never comes'. If a negative form follows the verb, a negative will also precede the verb, as in *nadie dijo nada* 'no one said anything', literally, 'nobody said nothing'. In Italian, if a negative pronoun follows the verb, the verb has to be preceded by the negator *non*, as in *Non vidi niente* 'I didn't see anything'. And if it precedes the verb, the negator *non* is not used, for example *niente vidi* 'I didn't see anything'.

Clause types can be differentiated by their negation. In Akkadian, all non-main clauses use the negation marker *lā*, and the main clauses generally use the negation *ul*. Manambu employs the negator *ma:* in independent main clauses, and the suffix *-ma:r-* in all dependent clauses. We saw in §11.1.1 that in Kham a negative copula is used to negate verbless clauses. Clauses with verbs as predicates employ the negative prefix *ma-* in the declarative, and *ta-* in the imperative forms.

Prohibitive, or negative imperative, clauses are often marked differently from positive imperatives. For example, Manambu has one imperative marked with a prefix, and three prohibitive suffixes *-tukwa* 'neutral prohibitive, *-way* and *-wayik*. Prohibitives in Latin are markedly different from positive imperatives (as we saw in (11.20), and §7.2.1).

What makes negative clauses special is that they often distinguish fewer meanings than their positive counterparts. In Koegu, a Surmic (Nilotic) language from Ethiopia, the distinction between perfective and imperfective aspect is expressed only in positive, but not in negative clauses. Estonian distinguishes three persons and two numbers on verbs in positive polarity. In negative clauses there is a single form covering all persons and numbers. This is shown in 11.25, for the verb *tulema* 'to come':

(11.25)   positive   negative

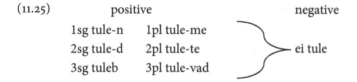

    1sg tule-n   1pl tule-me
    2sg tule-d   2pl tule-te   ei tule
    3sg tuleb   3pl tule-vad

Negation can vary in its scope. Besides negation with a clausal, or sentential, scope, a language may have the option to negate a constituent separately. In English *Not many students passed* can be contrasted to *Many students did not pass*. We saw in §9.4.3 that there can be special negative pronouns (sometimes derived from interrogatives). In Estonian they contain a nominal negator *mitte*. A cross-linguistically established feature of serial verb constructions (as a single predicate) is that their components cannot be negated separately (§7.6.1). This is one of their features as single predicates. We saw in §6.6 that derivational affixes can produce new nouns with negative meanings, for example English *non-entity*. Many languages have a negative pro-clause 'no' which may form a separate closed class (see §9.6). Different properties of negative clauses may justify considering them a special type.

11.5 Concluding remarks

When investigating clause types, it is vital to distinguish their classification by

(a) their internal structure,
(b) their syntactic function, and
(c) their pragmatic functions and speech acts.

When investigating copula and verbless clauses, one needs to establish which semantic relationships are covered by which clause type, paying special attention to existence, location, possession, attribution, identity, and benefaction.

In discussing clauses in terms of their syntactic function, it is important to ascertain the differences between main clauses and dependent clauses of varied types (including complement clauses, relative clauses, and subordinate clauses). Different sentence types—statements, questions, and commands—may be distinguished through the form of the verb, constituent order, and intonation. A fascinating issue is the possibility of using various clause types in directive functions, and the cultural requirements and limitations on the use of questions and commands.

Notes and sources

§11.1.1: The link between existence, possession, and location was nicely captured by Clark (1978). See Peterson (2003: 424) on Hakha Lai; Andvik (2003: 448) on Tschangla; Aikhenvald (2008: 82) on Manambu; Butt and Benjamin (2004: 423) on Spanish; Shibatani (1990: 304–5, 369–70) on Japanese; Watters (2002: 215–19) on Kham. There may be further, language-specific clause types; for instance, an argument can be made for the presentational construction *there is* . . . (see Dixon 2010b: 160), and expressions of wishes and desires in German (Altmann 1993) as separate types.

§11.1.2: See §10.3, §10.7 and Amha (2007) on Wolaitta; Aikhenvald (2010: 152) on restrictions on imperatives of copula and verbless clauses.

§11.1.3: See Dixon (2010b: 299), Heine (1997a: 20–1, 48–9) and Aikhenvald (2013a: 27–36) on possessive relationships in clauses, and the motivation behind the use of different clause types. *Have*-type constructions are also known as H-possession, and *belong*-type ones as B-possession (see Heine 1997a: 29–31). See Viitso (2007: 94) on Estonian; Heine (1997a: 50–60) on various schemata of possession marking; Foley (1991: 305) on Yimas; Dixon (2004a: 381) on Jarawara; Hyslop (2001: 369) on the Lolovoli dialect of North-east Ambae; Fortescue (1984: 171–2) on West Greenlandic; Thompson (1996: 668–9) on Koyukon.

§11.1.4: See Dixon (2012: 344–75) and references there for a general perspective on comparatives; Quirk et al. (1985: 1127–46) for an incisive analysis of comparatives in English. See Saltarelli (1988: 128–9) on Basque; Frajzyngier (1993: 246–7) on Mupun; Aikhenvald (2006d: 32) on serial verb constructions with comparative meanings; Kenesei et al. (1998: 151–3) on Hungarian.

§11.3.1: See Aikhenvald (2010: 150–3) on imperatives, and restrictions on their formation; Onishi (1994) on Motuna; Merlan (1983: 101–2) on Ngalakan; Quirk et al. (1985: 830), Davies (1986), and Huddleston (2002: 929–31)on English; Amha (2001: 155–7) on Maale; Löfstedt (1966: 12–20) on Latin; Aikhenvald (2010: 190–2) and references there on prohibitives.

§11.3.2: See Frajzyngier (1993: 359–66) on Mupun; Mihas (2010: 175–81) on Campa; Ameka (1991: 53–4) on Ewe; Kimball (1991: 301–2, 423–8, 431, 230–2) on Koasati. Dixon (2012: 376–433) presents an in-depth overview of interrogative sentence types; also see König and Siemund (2007) and Sadock and Zwicky (1985); Borgman (1990: 67) on Yanomami.

§11.3.3: See Aikhenvald (forthcoming-a), McCawley (1973), Elliott (1974), and Zanuttini and Portner (2003), on exclamatory sentences; Thomas (1971) on Chrau.

§11.3.4: See Huddleston (2002: 939–40), Comrie (1984); and Aikhenvald (2010: 257–65) on non-imperative forms in command functions. See Brown and Levinson (1987:

227) on incomplete sentences as avoidance strategies; Stirling (1998: 281) on isolated *if*-clauses and their status in English; Vallauri (2004: 210–11) on similar phenomena in Italian, Finnish, and Japanese; see Huddleston (2002: 942) and Quirk et al. (1985: 842–3) on verbless directives in English; see Brown and Levinson (1987: 99ff) on commands in greetings; Waltereit (2002) and references there on attention-getting markers based on imperative forms.

§11.4: Types and complexity of marking negation vary more than any other category across languages. See Payne (1985) and Dixon (2012: 89–137) on basic principles of negation; Deutscher (2009) on Akkadian; Watters (2002: 96–7, 311–10) on Kham; Butt and Benjamin (2004: 344–6) on Spanish; Maiden and Robustelli (2007: 407–8) on Italian. See Dimmendaal (1998: 68) on Surmic languages, and further examples of dependencies between negation and other categories in Dixon (2012: 128–9) and Aikhenvald and Dixon (2011b: 170–205).

12

Complex sentences and clause linking

A sentence consists of at least one main clause. We start with coordination of two or more clauses of the same status: see §12.1. We then turn to relative clauses (§12.2.1), complement clauses (§12.2.2), adverbial clauses (§12.2.3), and chains of clauses connected through switch reference (§12.3). Ellipsis and syntactic pivot are important principles in combining clauses (§12.4). Sentences containing speech reports stand apart from the rest (§12.5). In the final section (§12.6) we turn to other features of the sentence as a whole.

12.1 Coordinated clauses

Any main clause can be used on its own (see also §3.11 and §11.2). A complex sentence can consist of several main clauses. In (12.1), from Kham, two main clauses are juxtaposed to each other, without any conjunction, to express a warning: that is, the second clause states a 'possible consequence' of non-compliance with the first one (see §12.6).

(12.1) nə-tə   ta-ba-ni,   [nə-pa-ya]
        there-ON PROHIB-go-2sg:IMPV 2sg-fall-FUT
        'Don't go up there, you will (or might) fall'

Main clauses can be also linked with coordinating conjunctions. The English conjunction *but* expresses contrast, for example *John has been studying German for many years, but he does not speak it well*. The conjunction *and* expresses 'addition', as in *Mary peeled the potatoes and John cooked the meat*. It can be used if the action of one clause follows that of the other, as in *Mary lent me her car, and* (or: *and then) John complained about it*.

Coordination involves linking clauses of the same status. That is, two or more non-main clauses can be coordinated in the same way as two or more main clauses. Coordinating conjunctions may also be used to link noun phrases. This is the case in English (but not in some other languages, as we saw in §9.6). Noun phrases can also be coordinated with elaboration, or inclusory constructions (see §9.1.3), and adpositions and cases meaning 'with'.

12.2 Dependent clauses

The major types of dependent clauses are relative clauses, complement clauses, adverbial clauses, and co-dependent clauses which form clause chains.

12.2.1 Relative clauses

A relative clause (RC) is a dependent clause which has an argument in common (CA, or common argument) with the main clause (MC), or matrix clause, and which provides specification to the CA. There are two main kinds of relative clause.

A RESTRICTIVE relative clause provides information about the Common Argument specifying, or restricting, its reference. A typical example is English *The waiter [who sang a comic song]RC was sacked*. The restaurant had a number of waiters, and the relative clause helps single out the unfortunate one who lost his job.

A NON-RESTRICTIVE relative clause provides background information on a Common Argument which has already been fully identified. For instance, I have only one son, and so a relative clause in the following example only supplies extra information on what he does: *My son, who is a musician, has built another guitar.*

Some languages, including Tariana and Fijian, have only restrictive relative clauses. In English, a non-restrictive relative clause is traditionally set off by commas (in writing) and by special intonation (in speech). There may be grammatical differences between the two types. In a restrictive relative clause in English, *who* can be substituted for *that*: one can say *The waiter [that sang a comic song]RC was sacked*. Not so in a non-restrictive relative clause. Restrictive relative clauses can be 'stacked': it is possible to say *The man [who was laughing]RC [who you pointed out to me]RC was arrested*. But one cannot say **Bill, who was laughing, who you pointed out to me, was arrested*. In Amele, a Papuan language, only a non-restrictive relative clause can be shifted to the end of the sentence; restrictive and non-restrictive relative clauses differ in their intonation pattern.

Relative clauses vary in terms of (i) the nature of the Common Argument, (ii) its syntactic functions in RC and in MC, and (iii) where it is stated.

(I) THE NATURE OF THE COMMON ARGUMENT. In terms of their functions, relative clauses are modifiers to a noun head. In every language the head of a noun phrase can be a common noun. In many languages, it can also be a proper noun, a personal pronoun, and a demonstrative (as we saw in §6.7). Which one of these can be modified by a relative clause and thus be the CA is a major question. For instance, in English a pronoun can be a CA, for example *You, who voted for me, will get the best jobs*. In Tariana and in Dolakha Newar only a noun can.

(II) THE SYNTACTIC FUNCTIONS OF THE CA. The CA is shared by the MC and RC, and will thus have a syntactic function within both. In some languages, including English, the CA can be in any function in each clause.

This is not the case in other languages. In Dyirbal, the CA has to be in S or O function in the RC. In the MC, it can be in any of the core functions (A, S, O) or in dative, instrumental, or locative (but not allative or ablative) functions. In Warekena, a CA can be in S or O function in either MC or RC; or a locative or an instrumental oblique in the MC can be co-referential with O or S in the RC. Notably, a CA cannot be in A function in either clause. To understand how relative clauses work in a language, one needs to systematically examine the functions of the Common Argument in both clauses.

In their seminal work on 'Noun phrase accessibility hierarchy', Keenan and Comrie (1977, 1979) outlined a hierarchy of the possible functions of the CA in the RC. In some languages, such as Malagasy, the CA can only be in subject (A/S) function in the Relative Clause. In Welsh, an O can also be a CA. Tamil and Korean add 'obliques' to possible CAs. In French, a CA can also be possessor. That is, if a language can have an oblique as a CA, it will also have an O as a CA. And if CA can be possessor in a noun phrase, it can also be an oblique and an O. See further details on later work in Dixon (2010b: 320–1).

(III) WHERE THE CA IS STATED. The Common Argument can appear within the RC, within the MC, within both, or within neither. Or it can be omitted from an RC, creating a gap, as in Mangguer, a Mongolic language. The CA can be shown by a relative pronoun in the RC and a noun in the MC, as in English and in Standard Portuguese in (12.2):

(12.2) A   moça [que eu encontrei   alí]$_{RC}$
        ART.DEF.fem.sg girl   that I enountered.PAST.1sg there
        foi   embora
        go.PAST.3sg away
        'The girl whom I met there went away'

In (12.3), from Colloquial Brazilian Portuguese, the CA is shown by a pronoun within the RC, and a noun within the MC:

(12.3) [Eu   tenho   uma   amiga]$_{MC}$
        I   have.PRES.1sg ART.INDEF.fem.sg friend:fem.sg
        [que ela   é   ótima]$_{RC}$
        that she   is   the.best.fem.sg
        'I have a friend who (she) is the best'

In Kobon, the Common Argument can be stated in the RC:

(12.4) [ñi   pai pak-öp]$_{RC}$ [Ø   yad nöŋ-bin]$_{MC}$
        boy   girl hit-PERF.3sg   CA   1sg perceive-PERF.1sg
        'I know the boy who hit the girl' or 'I know the girl whom the boy hit'

This sentence is ambiguous: it can have either of the meanings shown in the gloss to (12.4). To make it clear, the CA will have to be stated in both clauses—as in (12.5).

(12.5) [ñi (u)   pai pak-öp]$_{RC}$ [ñi (u)   yad nöŋ-bin]$_{MC}$
        boy (that) girl hit-PERF.3sg   boy (that) 1sg perceive-PERF.1sg
        'I know the boy whom the girl hit'

Alternatively, a CA may not be stated in either of the clauses. Example (12.6) comes from a text in Yidiñ: here, the established topic 'I' was stated earlier, and is not repeated:

(12.6) Ø$_A$ Ø$_O$ wawa:l [Ø$_S$ guwa ŋañja:-da   ñina-ñunda]$_{RC}$
        1sg something see:PAST something west creek-LOC sit-RELATIVE
        '[I] saw [something] [which] was sitting by the creek over to the west'

Further features of relative clauses include (iv) their marking; (v) their position within the sentence; and (vi) the expression of clausal categories within them.

(IV) MARKING A RELATIVE CLAUSE. A relative clause can be marked with relative words (or relative pronouns), as in English and many European languages (see §9.4.3). Another option is relativizing markers (that is, uninflected 'particles'). Relativizers *še* and *ašer* in Hebrew come at the beginning of an RC. The relative clause marker *de* in Mandarin Chinese occurs at the end of an RC. (This morpheme is also used in possessive constructions and as a nominalizer.) The relative clause marker *ya* in Tok Pisin appears twice—once at the beginning of the RC and once at its end, as in (12.7):

(12.7) Yu   lukim dispela [ya kon wantaim muruk   i   sanap long em ya]$_{RC}$
        you:sg see   this   REL corn with/and cassowary PRED stand to   it REL
        'Did you see the one that has corn and cassowaries on it?'

The predicate of a relative clause may take a special marker. In Tariana, the predicate of a relative clause takes the prefix *ka-* (which replaces person prefixes). The same prefix is used for predicative possession (see example (11.13), 'José is spoused'). In Dyirbal, the relative clause markers *-ŋu* and *-mi* also indicate possession (on nouns). In Karajá, a Macro-Jê language from Brazil, a relative clause is marked by shifting stress of the verb to the last syllable.

A special type of relative clause, called the co-relative construction, involves a relative pronoun in the RC and a demonstrative, or a personal pronoun, in the MC. Such clauses (also known as cor(r)elatives) are a feature of many Indo-Aryan, Dravidian, and Tibeto-Burman languages. In Marathi, an Indo-Aryan language, the RC contains a relative marker *dzo*, and the MC contains a corresponding marker *to*.

(12.8)   [dzo mulgā kāl   ālā]_{RC}   [to   uttam   tSitrakār   āhe]_{MC}
         REL boy   yesterday come-PAST-3masc.sg CORR excellent painter   is
         'The boy who had come yesterday is an excellent painter'

The literal translation is something like 'which boy had come yesterday, that boy is an excellent painter'.

(V) POSITION WITHIN THE SENTENCE. A relative clause may occupy a special position within a sentence. In Manambu, the RC always precedes the CA, and has a fixed position in the sentence (no other clause does). A relative clause in English follows the CA.

(VI) EXPRESSION OF CLAUSAL CATEGORIES. A relative clause may differ from other clauses in non-spatial setting and polarity. Relative clauses in Manambu share all the tense–aspect specifications with the main clause, but are negated differently. In Tariana, relative clauses have their own relative tense system (different from that of the main clause), indicating whether the event of the RC is simultaneous with, preceding or following that of the MC. Each of these features can be used to recognize a relative clause as a special clause type.

An aside on terminology. By analogy with the structure of a noun phrase, the CA is sometimes referred to as 'head' of a relative clause. Relative clauses with no CA stated are referred to as 'headless' relative clauses. If the CA is stated in the RC, it may be referred to as 'internally headed'. And if the CA appears within the MC, it is called 'externally headed'. These terms are self-explanatory. However, they ought to be used with some caution: they can hardly be applicable to situations whereby CA has to be stated in both RC and MC, and they are problematic with regard to co-relative structures. Some linguists call relative clauses 'adjectival clauses', since relative clauses are modifiers, and thus somewhat 'adjective'-like. This is misleading—adjectives are a word class defined on morphological and syntactic grounds (as we saw in Chapter 8), and relative clauses are full clauses of their own kind.

A relative clause can have further meanings. In a classic article, Hale (1976: 80) describes a type of adjoined clause in Warlpiri, an Australian language. This clause can be interpreted as a relative clause modifying the NP, or as an 'adverbial clause' with temporal or concomitant action meaning. Example 12.9 can be interpreted in either way:

(12.9)   Natjulu-ḷu kapiṇa maliki ḷuwa-ṇi,   [katjiɸŋki
         I-ERG   AUX   dog   shoot-NONPAST COMPLEMENTIZER:AUX
         yaḷki-ṇi   njuntu]_{ADJOINED.CLAUSE}
         bite-NONPAST you
         (a) 'I will shoot the dog if/when it bites you'
         (b) 'I will shoot the dog that bites you/that is going to bite you'

'Adjoined' clauses of this kind are a feature of many Australian languages.

A relative clause must be distinguished from a noun phrase with a participle. A relative clause is a type of clause which must be able to include core arguments and obliques. A participle is a verb form used as a modifier within a noun phrase, as in English *the singing waiter* or, in a compound, *the comic-song-singing waiter* (compare this with *The waiter [who sang a comic song]*$_{RC}$ *was sacked*). Many Tibeto-Burman languages and languages from South America have an all-purpose nominalization employed in any dependent clause. These alternatives to relative clauses as a special type are known as 'relativization strategies'.

12.2.2 *Complement clauses*

An argument of a verb can always be expressed with a noun phrase. Many languages have a distinct clause type which can occupy an argument slot. This is a complement clause (CoCl). Typically, complement clauses function as O arguments of verbs of perception, cognition, and speech. They can also function as S, and even as A, arguments.

In terms of their MEANINGS, complement clauses can be of three types.

(i) FACT COMPLEMENT CLAUSES generally refer to the fact that something took place. They are typically similar in structure to a main clause, and share all the tense–aspect specifications with it. They tend to be marked with a complementizer. In English, a fact complement clause with the complementizer *that* can occupy the O slot, as in *I think [(that) Brazil beat France last night]*$_{CoCl:O}$. The complementizer can be omitted (which is why it is in brackets). It can also occupy an S slot, as in *[That Brazil beat France]*$_{CoCl:O}$ *came as no surprise*, and the A slot, as in *[That Brazil did not beat France]*$_{CoCl:A}$ *stunned everyone*. Then, the complementizer cannot be left out.

(ii) ACTIVITY COMPLEMENT CLAUSES generally refer to an on-going activity. These tend to have some similarity to a noun phrase (rather than a full clause), and their subject (A/S) may be marked differently from that of the main clause. There are typically fewer tense–aspect specifications available. Activity complement clauses in English are marked with the -*ing* form of the verb, and their subject is marked in the same way as the Possessor, for example *[Mary's singing]*$_{CoCl:S}$ *is getting on my nerves*.

(iii) POTENTIAL COMPLEMENT CLAUSES typically refer to the potential of the subject of the complement clause to undertake the activity. This type shares few features with a main clause. The verb tends to occur in a special dependent form (sometimes called 'infinitive'), and generally lacks the tense–aspect specifications available in a main clause. An example of a potential complement clause in English is *I want [you to come here]*$_{CoCl:O}$.

Verbs of perception in English can occur with more than one type of complement clause. Example (12.10a), with the optional complementizer, refers to the fact of Brazil's beating France (say, at soccer) which the speaker ('I') knows from a verbal report. Sentence (12.10b), where the predicate of the complement clause is marked with the suffix

-*ing*, refers to an activity, or a process, which the speaker knows because they physically heard what was happening.

(12.10a)   I heard [(that) Brazil beat France]$_{CoCl:O}$—fact, known through verbal report

(12.10b)   I heard [Brazil('s) beating France]$_{CoCl:O}$—activity, known through physical hearing

The choice of a complement clause here also reflects information source; this is the essence of an evidentiality strategy (mentioned in §7.2.5). The A of the complement clause ('Brazil') is marked differently in (12.10a) and (12.10b): in (12.10a) it is marked in the same way as in a main clause. In (12.10b), it optionally takes the possessive-like suffix *'s*.

A complement clause may be marked with a complementizer (typically, at the beginning of the clause), for example *that* in English, *daß* in Standard German, and *as* in Pennsylvania German. There may be special marking on the verb, such as -*ing* in English or -*ka* in Tariana. We can recall, from §9.1.5, that 'logophoric pronouns' in many African languages indicate that the subject of a complement clause (especially that of a speech verb) is, or is not, the same as one of the participants in the main clause (examples 9.8–9.9 from Mupun illustrated this).

A complement clause can occupy a specific position within the main clause (also known as the 'matrix' clause). In English and German, it is the same as that of the corresponding NP in that slot. In Tariana, a complement clause of verbs of perception and cognition always comes before the matrix clause:

(12.11)   [di-uka-ka]$_{CoCL:O}$ nu-ka-na
          3sg.nf-arrive-COMPL.CL   1sg-see-REMOTE.PAST.VIS
          'I saw that he arrived'

This is one of the special properties of complement clauses in the language which sets them apart from all other clause types. Adverbial clauses in Tariana can either precede or follow the main clause.

Verbs of different semantic types may require different types of complement clauses. In Pennsylvania German, verbs of cognition such as *denke* 'think', *meene* 'mean', and *glawe* 'believe' take fact complement clauses marked with the complementizer *as* 'that'.

(12.12)   ich   glaab   net   [as   ich   noch   elter   waar]$_{CoCl:O}$
          I   think   not   that   I   still   older   was
          'I don't think that I was any older'

If they have a potential meaning, that is, refer to a projected activity or event, they are marked with *fer* 'for, so that':

(12.13)   ich   hab   gedenkt   [fer   in   schteddel   geh]$_{CoCl:O}$
          I   have   thought   for   in   town   go
          'I thought of going into town'

Verbs of perception *sehne* 'see', *haere* 'hear', and *rieche* 'smell' may take formally unmarked, juxtaposed complement clauses to express activity:

(12.14)   ich   hab   noch   niemand   ghaert   [sage]$_{CoCl:O}$
      I   have   yet   no.one   heard   say
      'I haven't yet heard anyone saying [. . .]'

They take complement clauses with the complementizer *as* if they express a fact—that is, the fact of knowledge about something that has occurred:

(12.15)   ich   hab's   g'schpiert   [as   er   uffgricht   waere   is]$_{CoCl:O}$
      I   have.it   sensed   that   he   excited   become   is
      'I sensed that he became excited'

Verbs of speech such as *sage* 'say' can only take complement clauses marked with *as*.

Complement clauses vary in terms of what CORE FUNCTIONS they can have within the main clause. English, German, and many European languages have no restrictions: a complement clause can be in A, S, CS, or CC function. In Modern Hebrew, a complement clause can be in any function other than the A (transitive subject). A complement clause in Akkadian can only be in O, S, or CS function, and in Tariana it can only be an O (as we saw in (12.11)).

Complement clauses may stand apart from other clause types in terms of verbal categories. In most languages of the world, including Tariana and Matses, evidentiality is not expressed in complement clauses (or any other non-main clauses). The activity complement clauses marked with *-ing* and potential clauses marked with *to* in English may not include modal verbs such as *can*, *must*, or *will*.

Activity and potential complement clauses may have restrictions on whether they have the same or a different subject as the main clause. In White Hmong, a complement clause with potential meaning (marked with the complementizer *kom*) can be used only if its subject is different from that of the main clause:

(12.16)   kuv   ntuas   [kom   Li$_S$ mus]$_{CoCl:O}$
      I   advise   COMPLEMENTIZER   Li   go
      'I advised Li to go'

A constituent shared by the main clause and the complement clause can acquire the form required by the predicate of the main clause, rather than by the predicate of the complement clause. In (12.17), from Dolakha Newar, the verb 'see' takes its O in the dative case. The S of the complement clause ('she') takes the dative case, because the clause it is in occupies the O slot of the matrix clause with 'see' as the predicate:

(12.17) cilā=n$_A$ ninpatti [āmta   kho-en   coŋ-gu]$_{CoCL:O}$ khon-ai
         goat=ERG daily   3sgDATIVE cry-PARTICIPLE stay-NOMZ=COMPL see-3sg.PRES
         'The goat sees her (lit. for her) cry every day'

This is known as 'raising'. Whether or not 'raising' is involved in complement clause constructions in English such as *Mary persuaded John to kill Fred* is a matter of debate (some discussion and references can be found in Dixon 2010b: 388–9).

We can recall, from §11.3.2, that a polar or a content question can be used as an interrogative complement clause, also known as 'indirect question'. In English and in many other languages such complement clauses contain interrogative pronouns, as in *I know [who came yesterday]*. A command can also be rephrased as a type of complement clause (especially in speech reports), as in *I told John that he should not go to town*, or *I told John not to go to town*.

Not all languages have bona fide complement clauses. Another clause type, or kind of construction, may then be used, as a strategy, with verbs of perception, cognition, liking, and so on. The choice of complementation strategy depends on the type of verb in the main clause. This is the essence of 'complementation strategy'. The verbs 'believe' and 'dream' in Tariana can only take an activity nominalization in lieu of a complement clause (in O function) (rather than a complement clause). An example is at (12.18):

(12.18) pi-uka-nipe-nuku   tapulisa-mahka   nuha
         2sg-arrive-NOMZ-TOPICAL.O dream-RECENT.PAST.NONVISUAL I
         'I dreamt of your coming; I dreamt that you had come'

A *-ka* complement clause (as illustrated in (12.11)) cannot be used here.

In Akkadian, the verb 'know' cannot take a complement clause. The way of saying 'I know that my neighbour stole a cow' is to juxtapose two clauses: 'my neighbour stole a cow, I know (this)'. If a content question appears in the O slot of a speech verb, a complement clause cannot be used either: a relative clause will be used instead: the way of saying 'don't you know what he did to me?' is 'don't you know that which he did to me?'. In Dolakha Newar, the complementizer *-khā* is only used in complement clauses in O function of verbs of perception and utterance; nominalizations as complementation strategies are used with other verbs in other functions.

In Manambu and in many other Papuan languages with clause chaining, a co-dependent clause is used in the O slot of perception verbs—something we saw in (11.18). (Incidentally, this is a piece of evidence in favour of verbs of perception as a separate subclass of verbs.)

12.2.3 Adverbial clauses and clause chaining

Adverbial clauses occupy the slot of an oblique constituent within the main clause. They can express time, location, condition, consequence, manner, cause, result, and purpose. An adverbial clause can be marked by a connective. The English sentence *Buy your ticket as soon as you reach the station* contains a connective *as soon as*. Connectives typically form a closed class. Content interrogatives, such as English *when*, can also mark an adverbial clause: *When you get to the station, do not forget to buy a ticket*. In a number of languages, including English, adpositions can link clauses. In *I always have coffee before noon*, the preposition *before* marks the oblique noun phrase with temporal meaning. And in the sentence *I always have coffee [before I go to work]*, the same form *before* links two clauses (also see §9.6).

Special verbal forms can be used in adverbial clauses. In English, temporal adverbial clauses whose predicate is marked with *-ing* can occur with a number of connectives, including *after, before,* and *once*, as in *Once having made a promise, you should keep it.* Temporal adverbial clauses containing verbal forms in *-ed* can be introduced with connectives *as soon as, once, till,* and *when,* for example *When washed, the garment may shrink.* The predicate of conditional clauses in Manambu is marked with the suffix *-ga:y.*

In many languages, nominal case markers on nouns are employed as clause connectives on verbs. All the eleven cases in Kham mark adverbial clauses: for instance locative case 'at' marks a temporal adverbial clause, the elative case 'away from' marks a conditional clause (further details are in Watters 2009: 101–2). Example (12.19) illustrates the locative case as a marker of the temporal adverbial clause:

(12.19) [ŋa-pã:-zya-kə]ₜₑₘₚₒᵣₐₗ.cₗₐᵤₛₑ   zə,   hu-ke
1sg-speak-CONTINUOUS-LOCATIVE EMPHATIC come-PERFECTIVE
'While I was speaking, he came'

Adverbial clauses may have further special features. In many languages they do not distinguish evidentiality, or include questions and commands. In Manambu they take a non-main clause negator *-ma:r-* (most main clauses are negated with *ma:*).

Clauses with the meaning of 'condition' may show further complexities. POSSIBLE CONDITION—which may come true—may be expressed differently from COUNTERFACTUAL CONDITION. In English, possible condition is expressed by using the present tense form of the verb in the adverbial clause (marked with *if*) and a future form in the matrix clause:

(12.20)   If it rains, we will postpone the trip—POSSIBLE CONDITION

Impossible, or counterfactual condition, is expressed by a 'past-in-the-past' form in the *if*-clause, and a potential past form in the matrix clause:

(12.21)   If it had rained, we would have postponed the trip—COUNTERFACTUAL
CONDITION

In Kham, the elative ('away from') suffix on the verb marks a possible condition; for counterfactual condition, the same suffix is attached to the copula 'be, become' (and the lexical verb is nominalized). In Akkadian, the connective *šumma* 'if' marks possible condition; to express counterfactual condition, the irrealis particle *-man* is added to *šumma*. However, many languages, including Aguaruna, have only possible condition, and no counterfactual.

We can recall, from §11.2, that in many Papuan languages of New Guinea, dependent, or non-main, clauses are combined in a 'clause chain', forming a complex sentence. The predicate of the dependent clauses takes an affix: this expresses relative tense (with respect to the main clause, or the following or preceding clause), and the identity of their subject (A/S)—whether it is the same or different. This is the essence of switch reference—the topic of the next section.

A dependent clause typically expresses fewer categories than a main clause. Questions and commands cannot usually occur as dependent clauses. Dependent clauses can mark an action or state concomitant or simultaneous with that of the main clause. They can also be interpreted as expressing condition, cause, and result. They can be used as complementation strategies (see §11.2, and examples 11.17–11.18). A typical example is in (12.22), from Amele:

(12.22) [Ija Malolo uqa=na ka jic   ana-g   onbo=nu
         1sg Malolo 3sg=of car road mother-3sgPOSS there=for
         sum-udi]$_{DEP.CL(SS)}$ [bi-bil-igin] $_{DEP.CL(DS)}$ [ne-ce-b]$_{DEP.CL(DS)}$
         wait-3sgDIRECT.OBJECT(SS) DUR-sit-1sgSIM.DS   come.down-DS-3sg
         [tobo-co-min]$_{DEP.CL(DS)}$ [bel-ow-an]$_{FINAL.CL}$
         climb.up-DS-1sg   go-1du-YESTERDAY.PAST
         'As I waited there yesterday on the main road (lit. mother road) for Malolo's
         car he came down and I climbed in and off we went' (literally, I waiting
         sitting for Malolo's car on the mother road, he coming down, me climbing
         up, we went)

Grammarians vary in how they analyse such dependent, or 'co-dependent', clauses. Such clauses may be interpreted as occupying a core, or an oblique slot. They always have some semantic connection with each other and with the main, or final clause. But the exact meaning depends on the context.

An alternative to clause chains are sequences of special verbal forms—termed converbs or participles—used exclusively in dependent clauses, to express additional, or concomitant actions. Example (12.23), from Dolakha Newar, shows a chain of converbs typical for a Tibeto-Burman language.

(12.23) [kāsi   oŋ-an]   [jal-ai   ju-en]
         Kāsi   go-CONVERB burn-BORROWED.VERB be-CONVERB
         citrāŋga bicitrāŋga   sit-a
         Citrāŋga Bicitrāŋga   die-3sgpast
         'Going to Kāsi, and burning (committing self-immolation),
         CitrāŋNga and Bicitrāŋga died'

Such chains can be very long. Their major function is backgrounding concomitant actions and foregrounding the main ones; we return to this in Chapter 13.

12.3 Switch reference

Canonical switch reference is a category of the verb of the dependent clause indicating whether the subject is the same as that of the main clause, or different. Switch reference is often associated with clause chaining. One clause can be considered 'main' in the sense that it bears all tense, aspect, and mood specifications. Other clauses are dependent: they can be marked for the person of the subject and the tense relative to that of the main clause.

In many languages with switch reference, the marker for Same Subject (SS) is an invariable morpheme. The Different Subject (DS) form distinguishes the person and sometimes also the number of the subject. This is what we saw in (11.17), for Manambu. In other languages, person is distinguished for both SS and DS forms. This is what we saw in (12.22), from Amele.

In a number of languages of South America, different clause-linking enclitics are used depending on whether the subjects of the dependent and the main clause are the same, or different. In (12.24), from Tariana, the subject of the dependent clause is the same as that of the main clause. The two are linked with the clitic -*hyume* 'after, because, as':

(12.24)   [di-kama-hyume]$_{\text{DEP.CL.(SS)}}$ [tuki   di-ñami-pidana]$_{\text{MAIN.CL}}$
          3sg.nf-get.drunk-AFTER   almost/little 3sg.nf-die-REMOTE.PAST.REPORTED
          'As he got drunk, he almost died'

In (12.25), also from Tariana, the subject of the dependent clause is different from that of the main clause. The two are linked with the clitic -*nisawa* 'after, because, as':

(12.25)   [di-kama-nisawa]$_{\text{DEP.CL.(DS)}}$ [di-sa-do   di-na
          3sg.nf-get.drunk-AFTER   3sg.nf-spouse-FEM 3sg.nf-OBJ
          du-kwisa-pidana]$_{\text{MAIN.CL}}$
          3sg.f-scold-REMOTE.PAST.REPORTED
          'As he got drunk, his wife scolded him'

In each case, the dependent clause does not distinguish tense, or evidentiality, unlike the main clause. In Maxakalí and a few other Macro-Jê languages of Brazil, switch reference is expressed though independent connectives.

In all these instances, switch reference allows us to establish the identity of the 'subject'. In other words, switch reference is a strong test for subjecthood—that is, a syntactic unit which covers the A and the S. In languages of the Panoan family and in Aguaruna, all from South America, switch reference markers are chosen depending on whether the subjects of the dependent and the main clause are identical, or whether the subject—A or S—of one clause is identical to the object of the other. These languages are unique in this respect.

Clause chaining is a powerful device for keeping track of participants and their actions. We return to this in Chapter 13.

12.4 Ellipsis and pivots

If a sentence includes the same argument more than once, the second instance may be ellipsed if it is clear from the context. Ellipsis may create reduced sentences. A teenager could answer a question *Where are you going?* with a curt *Nowhere.* In Basque, the verb of a second coordinated clause can be left out since it is clear from the context:

(12.26) Gu-re   herri-ko   mutil-ak   trakets-ak   d-i-ra
         we-GEN   village-REL   boy-PL:ABS   clumsy-PL.ABS   3ABS-PRESENT-be
         neska-k   ordea   iaio-ak   Ø
         girl-PL.ABS however   agile-PL.ABS (are)
         'The boys in our village are clumsy, the girls, however, Ø agile'

Languages vary as to how much ellipsis is permitted, and what can be ellipsed. In German, the auxiliary verb may be omitted from the second clause if it is the same as in the first clause (Juliane Böttger, p.c.):

(12.27) Die   Frau   hatte   gearbeitet und der
         ART.DEF.fem.sg   woman   had   worked   and ART.DEF.masc.sg
         Mann   Ø   geschlafen
         man   (had)   slept
         'The woman had worked and the man (had) slept'

Some speakers of Standard German reject this kind of ellipsis as incorrect. In Standard English, this would not be grammatical. In Chapter 13, we will return to ellipsis and how it can be used in discourse.

If two clauses within a complex sentence have an argument in common, a syntactic pivot may determine which co-referential participants within a sentence can be ellipsed, and which cannot. In languages with 'accusative' pivot, the shared argument can be omitted from the second clause *only* if it is in S or A function in each clause.

In the following four examples, *John* is in S or A function in each and can either be replaced by a pronoun or omitted from the second clause (shown here by placing the pronoun in parentheses). The common arguments are underlined.

(12.28)
<u>John</u>$_S$ laughed and (<u>he</u>$_S$) sat down   <u>John</u>$_A$ saw Mary$_O$ and (<u>he</u>$_A$) patted Fido$_O$
<u>John</u>$_S$ laughed and (<u>he</u>$_A$) patted Fido$_O$ <u>John</u>$_A$ patted Fido$_O$ and (<u>he</u>$_S$) sat down

When the shared argument is not in a pivot function (S or A) in each clause, it cannot be omitted from the second clause. There are no parentheses around the pronouns in (12.29) because they cannot be omitted if the meaning is to be preserved.

(12.29)
<u>John</u>$_S$ laughed and Mary$_A$ heard <u>him</u>$_O$ <u>John</u>$_A$ patted Fido$_O$ and Mary$_A$ watched <u>him</u>$_O$
<u>Mary</u>$_A$ saw John$_O$ and <u>he</u>$_S$ sat down   <u>Mary</u>$_A$ saw <u>John</u>$_O$ and <u>he</u>$_A$ patted Fido$_O$
<u>Mary</u>$_A$ saw John$_O$ and Fido$_A$ bit <u>him</u>$_O$

One could omit the pronoun from three of these sentences but the meaning would then be changed. For example, *Mary saw John and sat down* implies that it was Mary, and not John, who sat down. **Mary saw John and Fido bit* is ungrammatical. The second clause can be transformed into a passive, and then the ellipsis of the newly arisen S will be acceptable: *Mary saw John and was bitten by Fido*.

Some languages combine S and O as pivot functions. They have an 'ergative' pivot. In Dyirbal, two clauses may only be coordinated if they share an argument which is in S or O function in each. If one of the arguments is in A function, then the antipassive derivation must be applied (this derivation was mentioned in §7.3.1, and in examples 6.24–6.25, from Dyirbal).

In (12.30) 'woman' is in S function, and is marked with absolutive case.

(12.30)   [balan   yibi]$_S$ miyanda-nyu
          NOUN.MARKER.FEM woman:ABS laugh-PAST
          'A woman laughed'

In (12.31), 'woman' is in O function, and 'man' is in A function (marked with the ergative case):

(12.31)   [balan   yibi]$_O$ [baŋgul   yara-ŋgu]$_A$
          NOUN.MARKER.FEM:ABS woman:ABS NOUN.MARKER.MASC:ERG man-ERG
          bura-n
          see-PAST
          'A man saw a woman'

These two clauses can only be combined into one sentence if they share an argument which is in S or O function in each clause. The occurrence of that Noun Phrase in the second clause can be omitted. The two options are (12.32) and (12.33):

(12.32) [balan   yibi]$_O$ [baŋgul   yara-ŋgu]$_A$
         NOUN.MARKER.FEM:ABS woman:ABS NOUN.MARKER.MASC:ERG man-ERG
         bura-n,   Ø   miyanda-nyu]
         see-PAST (woman=O/S) laugh-PAST
         'A man saw a woman (and) Ø (=woman) laughed'

This example cannot possibly be understood as *'A man saw a woman and laughed'.

(12.33) [balan   yibi]$_O$ miyanda-nyu
         NOUN.MARKER.FEM:ABS woman:ABS laugh-PAST
         [baŋgul   yara-ŋgu]$_A$ Ø   bura-n
         NOUN.MARKER.MASC:ERG man-ERG   woman=S/O see-PAST
         'Woman laughed and was seen (by man)', literally, 'Woman laughed,
         (and) man saw Ø (=woman)'

This example cannot mean *'Woman laughed and saw man'.

To say 'A man saw a woman and laughed', one needs to form an antipassive of the transitive verb 'see' (adding the suffix *-ŋa-)*. This is shown in (12.34).

(12.34) [bayi   yara   bural-ŋa-nyu
         NOUN.MARKER.MASC:ABS man:ABS   see-ANTIPASSIVE-PAST
         bagun   yibi-gu],   Ø   [miyanda-nyu]
         NOUN.MARKER.FEM:DAT woman-DAT man (S) laugh-PAST
         'A man saw a woman (and) Ø (=man) laughed'

This places the erstwhile A argument into S (a pivot function) and converts the original O into a peripheral argument (marked by dative case), which can either be included or omitted.

Not every language has pivot restrictions. In Tariana, a shared core argument in any function can be omitted from the second clause if recoverable from the context.

Syntactic pivot is the essence of inter-clausal, or syntactic, ergativity or accusativity. Pivot restrictions offer a strong criterion in favour of a syntactic unity for A/S (in languages with accusative pivots), and S/O (in languages with ergative pivots). A pivot provides a further building block for organizing discourse: it is what a stretch of discourse is about, that is, its topic. We return to this in Chapter 13.

12.5 Reporting what someone else has said

In every language one can report someone else's speech. The speaker can use their own words, recasting the original speech, within an 'indirect' speech construction. Or the other person can be quoted 'directly', just as they spoke.

A speech report situation involves at least two speakers—the 'author' of the original speech, and the 'reporter'. A speech report construction contains: (i) the speech report content, (ii) the reporting marker, or 'quote framer', and (iii) a linker between these. In a direct speech construction, the speech report content corresponds exactly (or more or less so), to what the original author of the speech report content said. In (12.35) the direct speech report—marked with quotes in the written language—is postposed to the reporting verb 'say'.

(12.35)   He said: 'I needed more money yesterday'

There is no overt link between the two. Alternatively, the report may be converted into 'indirect speech', without using the original speaker's words. The author's speech is 'adapted' to the 'perspective' of the reporter, and the speech report is cast as a complement clause. Look at (12.36):

(12.36)   He said (that) he had needed more money the previous day

Here, the person who made the pronouncement was someone other than the author. Hence, the original 'I' is changed to 'he'. And since the pronouncement was prior to the report, *needed* is 'back-shifted' to the 'past perfect', or past with respect to the past, *had needed*. The time adverb *yesterday* is changed to *the previous day*. The complementizer *that* is an optional marker of a syntactic link between the reporting clause and the speech report content.

A reporting marker is often a verb of speech, or an expression 'be like' or 'do like', or a combination of both. An intonation break, or a complementizer, typically mark the link between the reporting marker and the speech report. Many Australian, Papuan, and South American languages have only direct speech reports.

Verbs of speech which occur with speech reports can effectively go beyond simply 'speaking' into expressing cognition, desire, and intention. As Munro (1982: 316) put it, 'the meaning of "say" must . . . go beyond the idea of simply communicating facts by uttering words, and must probably include at some level a recognition of the general human reaction to speech as a characteristic indicator of personality and intention'.

In Dolakha Newar a direct quote construction is used to express hope, thought, and fear. This is how one says 'He was afraid the dog would bite':

(12.37)   [ām [khicā=n ŋyā-eu]_{Speech.report} haŋ-an   gyāt-a
           3sg dog=ERG bite-3sgFUT   say-PARTICIPLE fear-3sgPAST
           Literally: 'Saying "the dog will bite", he feared'

This kind of construction, and its whole array of meanings, is a property shared by numerous South Asian, and Papuan languages. A direct speech construction may express desire, cause, purpose, and intention. For instance, a sentence like 'The cat wants or intends to eat the duckling' is rendered into Manambu as 'The cat says: "I will eat the duckling"'.

Direct speech reports vary in their syntactic functions. In Dolakha Newar and Jarawara, they are similar to complement clauses. In other languages, including Manambu and Cahuilla (a Uto-Aztecan language), they can be considered obliques.

Using direct speech reports makes the text polyphonous and the description more vivid—it is a powerful stylistic device, often exploited in narratives.

12.6 Putting a sentence together

We have seen that, within a complex sentence, a relative clause modifies a noun phrase. A complement clause is an argument of the predicate of the main clause; we described their types, and marking, in §§12.3–12.4. Clauses of other kinds can be combined into one sentence. The main types of semantic relationships are listed in Table 12.1.

Most of these relations can be expressed by putting together two main clauses, via coordination. Or one clause can be marked as dependent, or adverbial. For example, a causal relationship in English can be expressed by coordinating two main clauses, as in *John has been studying Japanese all his life, therefore he speaks the language very well*. Or this can be achieved through framing the 'cause', or reason, as a non-main, adverbial clause: *Because John has been studying Japanese all his life, he speaks the language very well*. We can recall, from (12.1), that putting two main clauses one after the other in Kham is a way of expressing warning, or possible consequences. Juxtaposed clauses in Kham can also express contrast of two events—see (12.38):

(12.38) [ŋa: zihm-da   ŋa-ba-ke],   [ol te   ma-ba-e]
         I   house-ALL 1sg-go-PERFECTIVE he FOC NEG-go-IMPERV
         'I went to the house, (but) he (in contrast) didn't go'

The focus marker in the second clause corroborates the contrastive reading.

The point to remember is: different techniques of clause linking may correspond to different semantic relations between clauses, depending on the language. The semantic relations may be inferred from the context. The marking can be polysemous. For instance, possible condition and temporal succession may be expressed in the same way. In investigating semantic relations between clauses within a sentence, one can look at the major types of relations and their expression. Or one may opt to first determine the types of marking and clause types, and then map them onto the semantic types.

How to recognize a sentence? This is far from trivial. In European languages with a written tradition, a sentence can be defined as the material that comes between two

TABLE 12.1. Semantic types of clause linking

Meanings of clause linking	Exemplified by markers in English

Temporal
  Temporal succession
  Relative time
  Conditional
	
	and, then, and then
	after, before, when, since, until, while
	if (. . . then)

Consequence
  Cause
  Result
  Purpose
	
	because, therefore
	(and) so
	in order that, (in order) (for) to

Possible consequence, warning	in case, lest

Addition
  Unordered addition
  Same-event addition
  Elaboration
  Contrast
	
	and
	and, moreover
	<apposition>
	but, although

Alternatives
  Disjunction
  Rejection
  Suggestion
	
	or
	instead of
	rather than

Manner
  Real
  Hypothetical
	
	like, in the way that
	as if (like)

full stops (or 'periods'). For spoken languages, and languages for which writing has been introduced just recently, one has to rely on other clues. In many South American languages, the final syllable of a sentence is nasalized (more details are in Aikhenvald 1996). In languages with clause chaining, the final clause (which bears most grammatical information) signals the end of a sentence. There can also be intonational clues. In Manambu, the predicate of each dependent clause within a clause chain has raising intonation; this is not the case with the final clause.

None of these clues is watertight. A string of clauses may be divided into sentences in several ways, depending on what the speaker wants to say, how they pause, and how the rest of the discourse is organized. To complicate matters, in actual narratives and conversations one enounters incomplete sentences. A noun phrase, or part of a verb phrase, can form a sentence on its own. In English, if one is asked *Are you coming or going?*, the answer may well be an elliptical *Coming*. In Manambu, a question 'When did you take these pictures?' may warrant an answer 'As I was going off': this contains a dependent clause without a final clause. Languages vary in how much reduction, or ellipsis, is permitted and how much is conventional. We turn to this in Chapter 13.

We can recall that a dependent clause can be used on its own, as a result of 'desubordination' (see §11.3.4). In English and a number of other European languages, a desubordinated *if*-clause can express a request, or a mild command. A doctor may say to a patient: *If you could open your mouth now*. In Manambu a same-subject dependent clause can be used as a curt command.

Indirect speech reports can occur on their own, if the reporting clause introducing indirect speech is omitted and left implicit. According to Quirk et al. (1985: 1032), it is 'only the back-shift of the verb, together with equivalent shifts in personal pronouns, demonstratives, and time and place references, that signals the fact that the words are being reported, rather than being in direct speech.' In (12.39), the italicized verbs are backshifted to the past tense. This is how we know that we are dealing with a desubordinated speech report.

(12.39)   'So that *was* their plan, *was* it? He well *knew* their tricks, and *would show* them a thing or two before he *was* finished. Thank goodness he *had been* alerted, and that there *were* still a few honest people in the world!'.

Sentence types, including desubordinated speech reports and clauses, can be manipulated to achieve special stylistic and discourse effects. Their choice and their expression may correlate with speech genres, and speakers' proficiency. These are the topics for our next chapter.

12.7 Concluding remarks

We will now summarize some of the points raised in this chapter.

It is useful to start with an overview of complex sentences in the language. Coordinating clauses of the same status (main or non-main) may involve simple juxtaposition, or linkers. For each linker, it is important to specify whether it can also be used to coordinate constituents other than clauses (for instance, noun phrases).

To understand how relative clauses work, one needs to determine what types of Common Arguments are allowed—that is, if a relative clause can modify a noun, or another type of constituent, such as personal pronoun or a demonstrative. A discussion of relative clauses will also include a careful examination of the roles of the Common Argument in the RC and in the MC, and where it is stated. The position of the RC with regard to the MC and the expression of clausal categories (tense, aspect, mood, negation, and so on) may also define the RC as a special clause type. A language may employ participles, or nominalizations, in lieu of relative clauses as 'relativization strategies'.

For complement clauses, it is essential to determine which functions they can occur in (A, S, O, CC, CS), how they are marked, what position they occupy with respect to the main clause, and whether they have any other special features, in terms of the expression of tense, aspect, evidentiality, and so on. Complement-clause-taking verbs may belong to various semantic classes, including perception, cognition, and speech. Most languages have complementation strategies: their forms and functions, and the verb types they occur with deserve special attention.

Adverbial clauses may require special connectives (note that nominal case markers and adpositions may be used as adverbial clause markers). They may also have other special features, including the expression of non-spatial setting. A language can have a general category of dependent clauses linked into a clause chain. If clause chains have switch reference, one needs to explore the nature of the same subject and the different subject, and their marking, and also the meanings and discourse effects of clause chains.

In most languages with switch reference, this operates in terms of S and A as one syntactic category. Some languages have syntactic pivot—either nominative (S/A), or ergative (S/O)—in clause combining. For any language, one needs to investigate whether it is possible to delete one of co-referential A, S, and O in combined clauses within one sentence, to ascertain whether any pivot restrictions are at work.

In approaching speech reports, the main task is to determine what constructions are in use. And if the language distinguishes between direct and indirect speech, what are the properties of each of these? They may include shift in person, spatial and temporal deixis, or changes in mood and modality. There may be a special way of rephrasing indirect commands, and questions. Direct speech reports may, or may not, be comparable to complement clauses. They may have additional meanings going beyond a speech act—a direct speech report may be a way of expressing a wish, an intention, or even a reason.

Investigating semantic connections between various clauses which form a sentence can be done in two ways. One can start with semantics, and attach a form to each type of meaning (of the ones outlined in Table 12.1, and perhaps other, language-specific ones). The other alternative is to outline the forms first and then investigate what semantic types they correlate with. I personally prefer the latter.

A final question to ask is: how to determine the limits of a sentence in a language? Any intonational cues need to be investigated. We also have to determine how much ellipsis is possible; and whether dependent clauses, and indirect speech reports occur on their own as a result of 'desubordination'. This will add a historical perspective to an essentially synchronic grammar.

Notes and sources

§12.1: See Watters (2009: 112–14) on Kham; further observations on coordination are in Haspelmath (2004) and papers there.

§12.2.1: See Dixon (2010b: 313–69) and references therein on relative clauses; Andrews (2007) for a discussion of relative clauses in English; Aikhenvald (1998) on Wareke-na; Slater (2002: 233–5) on Mangguer; Davies (1981: 30ff) on Kobon; Roberts (1987: 49–50) on Amele; Dixon (1977: 328) on Yidiñ; Li and Thompson (1981: 113–23, 623) and Luo (2013) on Mandarin Chinese; Verhaar (1995: 215) on Tok Pisin; Dixon (2010b: 340–2) on Dyirbal; Aikhenvald (2008: 468–75) on Manambu; Aikhenvald (2003: 537) on Tariana; Ribeiro (2006) on Karajá; Pandharipande (1997: 81–3) on Marathi.

Participles as alternatives to relative clauses are a prominent feature of Indo-European and Balto-Finnic languages. See Sulkala and Karjalainen (1992: 46–8) and Sands (2012) on complement clauses and complementation strategies in Finnish.

§12.2.2: See Dixon (2006a, 2010b: 370–421; 2010a: 128–31) on general properties of complement clauses, and further discussion of complementation in English; Bur-ridge (2006a) on Pennsylvania German (the interlinear glossing given by Burridge has been preserved here); Genetti (2006) on Dolakha Newar; Deutscher (2006) on Akkadian; Jarkey (2006: 124–6) on White Hmong; de Vries (2013) on Korowai. Complement clauses containing a verbal form which can also be used as a nomi-nalization are sometimes referred to as clausal nominalizations. This is somewhat misleading: such usage blurs the boundaries between deverbal derivation and dif-ferent clause types.

§12.2.3: An incisive discussion of adverbial clauses in English is in Quirk et al. (1985: 1069–126); see Thompson and Longacre (1985), and Dixon (2009) and references there on semantic types of adverbial clauses and their marking. A comprehensive account of adpositions and case-markers used for clause-linking is in Aikhenvald (2011c).

See Roberts (1997: 103–5) on clause chaining in general, and in Amele; Genetti (2005) on clause chaining expressed through converbal (or participial) forms; Wat-ters (2009) on backgrounding in clause chains in Kham.

§12.3: A useful discussion of switch reference in Papuan languages is in Roberts (1997); earlier studies include Haiman and Munro (1983) and papers there. See Aikhenvald (2012a: 338–46) and references there on switch reference in Amazonian languages, and a brief discussion of unusual switch reference in Panoan languages.

An alternative and useful name for dependent clauses in clause chains marked for switch reference is 'marking clause'. The 'main' clause is then called 'controlling clause': it typically controls the choice of the same or of a different subject. A further alternative is to call the 'main' clause a 'final' clause, and the dependent clause a 'medial' clause. This is the option followed in Papuan linguistics.

§12.4: See Haspelmath (2004) on coordination and ellipsis in general, and an example from German similar to (12.27); See Saltarelli (1988: 90) on Basque; Haspelmath (2004) and Dixon (2010a: 133) on ellipsis in complex sentences; see Dixon (1994), and Aikhenvald and Dixon (2011c) on the notion of pivot.

§12.5: See Aikhenvald (2011b) and references there on direct, indirect, and semi-direct speech reports, with a special focus on Papuan languages; see Adelaar (1990) on polysemous speech report constructions in Andean languages of South America; and further examples in Aikhenvald (2012a: 348–9). See Genetti (2006: 149) on Dolakha Newar; Saxena (1988) on South Asian languages.

§12.6: A further semantic distinction within complex sentences is between a Focal clause and a Supporting clause. The Focal clause will refer to the major activity or state. The Supporting clause will provide information additional to that in the Focal clause. It may specify the time frame, or the consequence of the Focal clause. See Dixon (2009) on these issues, and on the semantic relationships in clause linking. Some principles of desubordination are addressed in Aikhenvald (2010: 275–80, 343–4).

13

Language in context

We now come to a further question: How are the grammatical structures of a language used in actual discourse, and in communication? This takes us to discourse-pragmatic organization, or information structure. We start with the concepts of topic, and focus (§13.1). We then turn to linking sentences to shape a narrative (§13.2), before looking at communication, speech formulae, and different genres of stories in §13.3.

Ideally, a reference grammar will touch upon areas of lexical meanings considered interesting, or unusual, by the author. No language is 'primitive': but languages do vary in their domains of lexical wealth—see §13.4.

13.1 Information structure

Information structure reflects the organization of a sentence, a stretch of text, or a whole narrative. The topic is what the stretch of text is about. A participant or part of a sentence can be contrasted to another part; we are then dealing with 'focus'. Any participant can be more, or less, important. They can be contrasted to someone else, foregrounded or backgrounded, newly introduced or old and remembered from past experience. Each of these can be expressed through constituent order, special markers, and grammatical categories such as case and passives or applicatives.

13.1.1 To mark a topic

A 'topic' is what a stretch of discourse, or a sentence, is about. Within a sentence, its counterpart is 'comment', that is, what is said about the topic. For example, in the first sentence in (13.1), *John* is the topic, and the fact that he is the manager is comment; John is then referred to as *he* with a personal pronoun in an anaphoric function:

(13.1)　John$_{\text{TOPIC}}$ is the manager$_{\text{COMMENT}}$. He is the boss here.

A topic can be marked in a number of ways. In many languages, it tends to come first— that is, to be placed at the beginning of the sentence. We can recall, from §10.7, that definite, specific, and topical arguments tend to be more formally marked than their indefinite, non-specific, and less topical counterparts. Many languages have special morphemes (clitics, or affixes) marking topics, such as Japanese *-wa*, Korean *-nun*, and Ainu *anak(ne)*. The sentence (13.2), from Japanese, is about John:

(13.2)   John   wa   gakusei   desu
         John   TOP   student   COPULA
         '(Speaking of John) (he) is a student'

In many instances, including (13.1) and (13.2), the topic is also the grammatical subject. However, subject and topic do not have to always coincide.

Topic markers in Lao are similar to demonstratives (this was mentioned in §9.6). A topic tends to appear at the beginning of a sentence, in agreement with a general tendency to put topical participants upfront. Example (13.3) comes from a joke about a man who never learned how to read. He receives a letter, but can't understand what it says. He had noticed before that his neighbour puts on spectacles every time he reads a letter. So the man goes to a shop and buys spectacles. But when he comes back home with his new spectacles, he realizes that he is still unable to read the letter. He then goes back to the shop to complain. In (13.3), numbers mark tones.

(13.3)   [vèèn1-taa3   caw4   niØ]$_{TOPIC}$ qaan1   nangsùù3   bòØ   daj4
         glass-eye   2sgPOSS   TOPIC   read   writing   NEG   CAN
         '(With) the spectacles (of) yours$_{TOPIC}$, (I'm) unable to read'

The noun phrase 'your spectacles' is marked with the general topic marker *niØ*: it indicates that this is what the stretch of text is centred on.

Many languages have further grammatical means to show whether or not the people or objects within a sentence are important to the surrounding discourse. If they are, they will come up again and again in a text, or in a conversation which would centre around them.

The passive construction in English is a case in point. In the sentence *John was hit by a car*, *John* (the S of the passive) is the topic—this is why 'he' was put into the S function, and the erstwhile A of the verb *hit*, *the car*, put into an oblique slot. We expect the subsequent conversation to revolve around John. A reaction we expect would be *Oh no! Is he OK?* And a reaction like *Oh no! I hope the car is OK!* would sound rather odd. That is, the passive construction is used when the former object of a passivized verb (now its intransitive subject) is the topic, and the former subject of the transitive verb (now an oblique) is not.

In languages with differential marking of subjects and objects, an object or a subject takes a special marker for case if it is topical or definite (as we saw in §10.7). In these instances, case (that is, grammatical function of a noun phrase) reflects the information structure. An argument which has acquired the S function through passive or antipassive derivation (§7.3) or been brought into O function by applying applicative derivation (§12.4, §7.3.2) is likely to be a topic of a stretch of discourse.

In many languages with bound pronouns (see §9.1.1) free pronouns are used sparingly: their main function is to mark information structure. In Tamambo, free pronouns introduce, or topicalize a participant. They can also emphasize the participation of a known referent in discourse.

Many languages have strategies for 'topicalization'. Then, the topic is moved to a special position, often to the left of the clause. A topic may then take a marker, and is often separated from the rest of the sentence with a pause. In English, an unstressed noun phrase moved to the left of a clause and preceded by *as for* or *concerning* is used to reactivate or reintroduce a topic into the discourse. But if *as for* or *concerning* are followed by a stressed noun phrase, the effect is that of contrast, as in *Mary said she wouldn't help, but as for me, I'm willing*.

Topicalization may be expressed through a biclausal 'clefted' construction. In English *It was my sister whom he married*, the topicalized noun phrase *my sister* is a copula complement of the verb *be* followed by a relative clause.

'Left-dislocation' of a topic has an additional effect—that of focusing on the participant, and signalling them as special, as in *My sister, he married her after all.*

Getting a full understanding of pragmatic functions of markers, and of constructions, may be a challenging task. Two sentences may refer to the same situation (and thus have the same meaning in terms of semantics), but differ in their information structure. *John was hit by a car* and *A car hit John* describe the same unfortunate event. In Tariana, two sentences *Tʃinu-nuku nu-ka-ka* (dog-TOPICAL.NONSUBJECT 1sg-see-REC.PAST.VISUAL) and *Tʃinu nu-ka-ka* (dog 1sg-see-REC.PAST.VISUAL) 'mean' the same thing: that I saw a dog. The difference is subtle: the first sentence implies that the dog will be what we are going to talk about, that is, the topic of our discourse. This is why it is marked with the special case for topical non-subject. In the second sentence, the dog (unmarked for case) is peripheral to what we are talking about—in all likelihood, we will never mention it again.

The pragmatic differences can only be disclosed by an analyst who will look beyond a sentence taken out of context, notwithstanding the fact that a linguistically naïve consultant may claim that the two sentences 'mean' the same. If a language has a flexible constituent order, it is more than likely that the order of subject, object, and verb will be determined by what you are talking about (the topic), what you want to contrast to something else (the focus), and how your discourse is structured. Remember: everything in a language is there for a reason. Our task as grammarians is to understand the motivation for what may appear 'freely' interchangeable forms, or ways of saying things.

Many isolating languages of East Asia are sometimes referred to as 'topic-prominent'. This term reflects the sheer frequency of topic-comment structures, many of them used as regular ways of expressing some clause types. In Mandarin Chinese, if the Possessor and the Possessee have a close, or 'part–whole' relationship, the

'Possessor' will be set apart from the attributive clause as the topic. A typical example is at (13.4). The example has two readings—an attributive in (a) and a possessive in (b). Its literal translation will be 'Elephants, noses are long'.

(13.4) xiàng   bízi   cháng
        elephant   nose   long
        (a) 'Elephants' noses are long'
        (b) 'Elephants have long noses'

A conventionalized, or grammaticalized, topicalization strategy is the essence of a Topic schema as an option for expressing possessive relationships in some languages. We can recall, from §11.1.3, that such a 'Topic schema' is used in the Lolovoli dialect of Northeast Ambae if the Possessor has to be expressed with a free pronoun or noun phrase (see also example (11.11)). This involves a verbless clause with a topicalized Possessor.

(13.5) [Garivi   ngihie,]$_{TOP}$ golo-na   qaravu
        rat   that   tail-3sgPOSSESSOR   long
        'That rat has a long tail' (lit. 'That rat [PAUSE], its tail is long')

The topic is set apart from the rest of the sentence by a pause (marked here with a comma). Conventionalized, or grammaticalized, topicalization techniques can be used in other functions. Content questions in French frequently involve a construction similar to topicalization, as in *Qui est-ce qui aime Jean?* 'Who loves Jean?' (literally, Who is it who loves Jean?). In Manambu, content questions frequently involve contrastive focus marking on the question word—this takes us to our next point.

13.1.2 *Topic, focus, and contrast*

A noun phrase can be introduced into a stretch of discourse as a future topic. Once established, it will be definite and specific. We can recall, from §6.5, that definiteness and specificity are discourse categories: they can only be established within a context larger than one clause or sentence. A 'definite' participant is the one always identifiable within the context of discourse. Dependence on discourse context sets definiteness and specificity apart from other nominal categories. A topic can also be generic, that is, it may refer to a class of entities and not to any individual member of the class. In (13.6), from Mandarin Chinese, a generic noun phrase is the topic—the class of 'cats' is what we are talking about:

(13.6) māo$_{TOP}$ xǐhuān   hē   niú   nǎi
        cat   like   drink   cow   milk
        'Cats like to drink milk'

Classifiers can only be used with specific topics, and not with generic ones. This high-lights possible discourse overtones of classifiers (see §6.1.6): if the use of classifier in a language appears to be 'optional', it is likely that the reason may be related to discourse.

A stretch of discourse can contain more than one topic—an older one, and a newer one. An older backgrounded topic can be called semi-active: the referent has been mentioned before in the discourse, but was backgrounded ('deactivated') due to inter-vening discourse material. Inactive referents are in a person's long-term memory, and may need accentuation (by sentence stress) in order to be re-introduced in the dis-course and thus become reactivated. A reactivated topic may acquire a special marker. In (13.7), from Manambu, 'John' was the topic of a previous stretch of discourse; but since he had gone away to the river, the conversation switched to one of his children. As John is coming back, the conversation returns to him, and he is 'reintroduced' as a reactivated topic, with a special pronoun:

(13.7) John   ada   bu
        John   REACTIVATED.TOPIC.masc.sg   already
        vara-na-d
        come-ACTION.FOCUS-3masc.sg.SUBJ
        'John (we were talking about him before and are talking about him again) is coming already'

A contrastive participant, or action, will be foregrounded, or highlighted. In English, this involves contrastive stress, for example *Pete did the washing up YESTERDAY* (and not today), or *PETE* (not Mary) *did the washing up*. Contrastive participants may take a special focus marker. For instance, Urarina has a clitic *=te* which attaches to focused and foregrounded participants. Classifiers (see §6.1.3) may be used if the noun is in focus. In a number of Tibeto-Burman, Australian, Papuan, and South American languages, the A or S can be marked for case if the argument exercises control over the activity or is in focus and has to be contrasted to other participants (see §10.7). In Tamambo, Spanish, and Hungarian, free pronouns are used to mark those participants which are in focus or have to be highlighted.

In Lao, a relative clause is one of the means for expressing contrastive focus. The 'rel-ativized' argument is the subject of the copula verb *pên3*, modified by a relative clause:

(13.8) qaaj4   khòòj5   pên3   [phu   khaa5 kaj]RELATIVE.CLAUSE
        elder.brother   1sgPOSS COPULA   MALE.HUMAN   kill   chicken
        'My (elder) brother is (the) one (who) killed a chicken'

In Manambu, any constituent can be put in contrastive focus. This involves marking a noun phrase or the predicate as if it were a non-verbal predicate, with a special set of cross-referencing markers. In (13.9), the subject ('bad men') is focused on:

(13.9) kuprapə du-adi   dəkəm   vya-dana-d
        bad   man-3pl.NONVERBAL.CLAUSE   he+ACC   kill-3pl.SUBJ-3sg.masc.O
        'It was the bad men (who) killed him'

Focused constructions are often used in answers to content questions. Example (13.9) is an answer to a question: 'Who killed the little boy?'

A language can distinguish different degrees of contrast in its focus marking. The clitic =*dya* in Cavineña expresses mild contrastive focus, giving one constituent a bit more prominence compared to others. The clitic =*bakwe* is used in contrastive statements which go against expectations, and set a participant apart from others. In (13.10), the speaker has arrived by plane at the Araona village, and the pilot (in contrast to the speaker) went on to Ixiamas:

(13.10) Piloto=bakwe   kueti-kware   Ixiama=ju
         pilot=CONTRASTIVE.FOCUS   pass-REMOTE.PAST   Ixiamas=LOCATIVE
         'The pilot (in contrast to the speaker) continued (lit. passed) to Ixiamas'

Another way of bringing a participant back into discourse is through additional clarification at the end of a sentence, known as 'afterthought'. Afterthoughts are typically separated by a pause from the main sentence. For instance, one can say in English *He annoys me, that man*: here 'that man' is an afterthought—to specify the referent of the pronoun.

13.1.3 *Topics, participants, and pivots*

What kinds of participants are more likely to be topics? In a seminal study, Du Bois (1987) noted two universal tendencies, to do with how participants function in discourse. These tendencies have come to be known under the label 'preferred argument structure'.

First, he pointed out that the topic of a stretch of discourse tended to be a noun phrase in a subject, A or S, function. His second finding was that 'arguments comprising new information appear preferentially in the S or O roles, but not in the A role' (1987: 805). Once introduced as a new topic, a participant will become topically established. These tendencies offer discourse motivation for a syntactic link between S and O, on the one hand, and a link between A and S, on the other hand.

In Lao, introducing a participant for the first time involves a presentational construction with the intransitive verb *mii2* 'there is': a new participant, which is a future topic, is in the S function. Or a new participant can be introduced as an O or as an oblique argument (following Du Bois' (1987) predictions). If the participant's initial mention is not completely new, it can be introduced as a topic at the beginning of the sentence, set apart from the rest of a clause by a pause, and then followed by a pronoun in the subject (S) slot. This is a description of a video clip the speaker has just watched.

(13.11) lot1   man2   lèèn1 kiaw4   paj3 haa3 toØ-nii4
       vehicle 3p.pronoun run   encircle go   seek INAN-DEM
       '(The/a) car, it runs around going toward this thing'

A topic tends to be the common argument running through a stretch of text. If established and recoverable from the context, it can be omitted. We saw in §12.4 how pivot restrictions may determine the omission of identical arguments in adjacent clauses. If two clauses within a complex sentence have an argument in common, a syntactic pivot may determine which coreferential participants within a sentence can be ellipsed, and which cannot. In languages with 'accusative' pivot, such as English, the shared argument can be omitted from the second clause *only* if it is in S or A function in each clause. Then, A and S will be treated as coreferential. In languages with 'ergative' pivot, such as Dyirbal, the shared argument can be omitted *only* if it is in S or O function. That is, S and O will be coreferential—something we saw in (12.32)–(12.33).

In many languages any of the core arguments and obliques can be ellipsed, if recoverable from the context. Such languages do not have pivot restrictions. 'Referents of the understood subjects' of the verbs in (13.12), from Lao, 'could be anything at all which makes sense' (Enfield 2007: 166):

(13.12) phen1 cap2 namØ-kòòn4   vaang1 saj1
       3p   grab CLASS.TERM:LIQUID-chunk   place   put
       phùùn4 lèkaØ   pùaj1
       floor   LINKER   melt
       'S/he grabbed some ice and placed it on the ground and it melted'

In real story-telling and real communication 'this openness of reference is hardly as problematic as it might first seem, thanks to the ample constraints on information which context provides. Without such concrete contextual information, listeners' interpretations will appeal to common expectations, both from argument structure . . . and cultural logic. We are highly likely to read the 'zero' subject of *pùaj1* 'melt' as referring to ice mentioned in the previous clause' (Enfield 2007: 166)

To track participants in a narrative, or a conversation, in an isolating language like Lao or Mandarin Chinese one needs to rely on the context. If a language has bound pronouns on the verb, these help keep track of who did what to whom. In Urarina, subject inflection on verbs does the job. In languages with gender distinctions, such as Manambu and Tariana, gender markers help establish the identity of participants. So do classifiers in their various environments. In Tariana, once a referent—for instance, a house—is introduced into discourse, it can be referred to with just a classifier (on a numeral, a demonstrative, or in a possessive construction).

The principles behind tracking referents and ultimately understanding how a story, or a conversation, unfolds, can only be understood if the grammarian is working with real texts and embraces the language as it is, rather than relying on translation and elicitation. Once a participant has been established in discourse, they may not have to be mentioned again. Many grammarians note that it is not easy to find natural examples of two noun phrases occurring in one clause—one of them will be likely to be omitted as a topic recoverable from the context, or replaced with a pronoun or another referent-tracking device. This obviously makes the task of establishing a 'basic' constituent order in a clause an unproductive and artificial exercise.

Switch reference within clause chains is another means of keeping track of who did what. We can recall, from §12.2.3 and §11.2, that switch reference in clause chaining in Papuan and most South American languages operates on the 'same subject' principle.

Clause chaining may have another function—backgrounding some actions and their participants and foregrounding others. In many languages, non-main clauses set the scene, or provide a background, for the main action expressed through a main clause. In Tibeto-Burman languages Galo and Kham, clauses containing nominalized verbs express backgrounded actions, which are important only for creating a backdrop for more important events described within main clauses in a narrative. A further way of formulating an 'aside' will be a parenthetical expression.

13.1.4 'Asides' or parentheticals

Speakers and stories vary in how they flow, and what information is presented as main, and what as subsidiary. Expressing one's attitude, opinion, or even information source, can be done with a parenthetical expression, as Trask (1993: 199) puts it, 'a word, phrase, or sentence which interrupts a sentence and which bears no syntactic relation to that sentence at the point of interruption'. European languages tend to have a plethora of parentheticals, such as English *I think, I suppose*, Spanish *parece*, Italian *sembra*; and French *dit-on* and *paraît-il*.

A parenthetical construction in English 'can parallel any kind of sentence which includes a THAT complement clause coming after the verb' (Dixon 2005: 234). A parenthetical may consist of a subject and verb, and also an object, and provides a comment on the clause. It may expresses opinion (*I think*) or information source (*I am told* or *I suspect*). Adverbs and adjectives may be used in parentheticals. Parentheticals may occupy the same syntactic position as sentential adverbs, with a similar semantic effect:

(13.13a)   She will, regrettably, have to sell her car
(13.13b)   She will, I regret, have to sell her car

An adverb and a verb may have different meanings when used as parentheticals. In *The King will, it is correct, enter by the front door*, the parenthetical with an adjective indicates that this is a correct statement of what the King will do. But in *The King will, correctly, enter by the front door*, with the corresponding parenthetical adverb, the King will act in a correct manner.

Parentheticals contain additional and backgrounded information. They are separated from the sentence where they are inserted by a short pause or an intonation break
(or a comma, in written language). Parentheticals help qualify the utterance in terms
of the speaker's viewpoint and attitude. They may express hedging; their meanings and
functions are sometimes similar to modality markers.

In languages with pervasive clause chaining, non-main clauses often reflect backgrounded and less relevant information: this reduces the need for parenthetical
expressions. However, they do exist. The ubiquitous phrase *nu-a-ka nhua* (1sg-say-
subordinator I) 'as I am saying' in Tariana can mean something like 'I think' or 'I am
saying' in English. (This expression is also used as a pause-filler, to allow the speaker
to buy time while thinking what they are going to say next.)

13.2 Putting sentences together

Every sentence is embedded within the context in which it is produced. Speakers take
turns in taking part in conversations. Each language will have a range of techniques
and conventions for organizing stories. Some repetition may be involved in structuring one's narrative, to keep track of what is happening—see §13.2.1. Some parts can be
left out without creating a misunderstanding—this is the essence of ellipsis in §13.2.2.

13.2.1 Linking sentences: recapitulation, repetition, and 'bridging'

Sentence-linking devices serve to ensure the flow of the talk. Linking sentences
can be done through connectives (see §9.6). Another commonly used technique
involves repetition of the last final verb of a chain as a dependent clause within the
following clause chain. This is known as 'bridging' repetition. A typical example is
(13.14), from Kombai, from the Awyu-Dumut family in New Guinea. Repeated verbs
are in bold face:

(13.14)   [Kha-negena]   [refe   fe
          go.3sg.non.future-until:DS   year   one
          büwene-n-a]   **khumolei]**
          finished-3sg.non.future-trans.sound-DS   die.3sg.NON.FUTURE
          [Khumolei-n-a]   [ifamano]
          die.3sg.NON.FUTURE-trans.sound-DS   bury.3pl.NON.FUTURE
          'It went on during one year and then he died. He died and they buried him'
          (literally, it **having gone**, one year **having finished**, he died, he **having died**,
          they buried him)

The function of bridging linkage is to mark discourse continuity. Reiterating the same
verb explicitly expresses the fact that sentences are part and parcel of the same topic
chain, and one episode or paragraph. Once the bridging chain stops, we expect the

story to turn to a different topic or a different subplot. This is often signalled by a pause between chains, or a connective, such as *ata* in (13.15), from Manambu:

(13.15) [Də kənawur dəpu-kabakəm ra-d],   [rə-də-k],
         he up.here inside-cave+LOC sit-3sg.masc.SUBJ sit-3sg.masc-DS
         [kray-də-də   as   ada
         bring-3sg.masc.SUBJ-3sg.masc.O dog REACT.TOP.masc.sg
         saula-da-d],   [**saula-də-k**],
         bark.inside-3sg.masc.SUBJ-3sg.masc.O bark.inside-3sg.masc-DS
         [o,   bal-ad,   **wa-d**],
         oh, pig-3sg.masc.NOM say-3sg.masc.SUBJ
         [**wa-ku**], [vya-k   yi-də-l],
         say-SS   hit-INTENTION go-3sg.masc.SUBJ-3sg.fem.TIME
         [ata və-də-d   a-də   du-a:m]
         then see-3sg.masc.SUBJ-3sg.masc.O that-masc.sg man-ACC
         'He (a fugitive) sat inside a cave, he **having sat** (there), the dog brought in
         (by the hunter) **barked inside** (the cave), he **having barked**, (the hunter)
         said 'Oh, it is a pig', he **having said** (this), he was going to hit (the fugitive),
         then he saw that it was that man.'

After this, the story turns to the fate of 'that man'—the fugitive. Bridging repetition allows the audience to keep track of who did what to whom (especially through the use of same subject or different subject markers).

To signal the end of a subplot, many languages use a recapitulating phrase, 'having done so'. This is a feature of many South American languages, including Aguaruna, Tariana, and Tucano. In a typical Tariana story, the speaker would tell the audience how he went out early, fished, went round a lake, and then

(13.16) [kay nu-ni] [dekina   nu-dia   nu-maɾa
         thus 1sg-do afternoon 1sg-return 1sg-go.down
         nu-nu-na-pita   nu-ya-dapana-se]
         1sg-come-REM.P.VIS-AGAIN   1sg-POSS-CL:HOUSE-LOC
         'Having done this, I returned to my home downriver'

To introduce a new participant, or to foreground a backgrounded participant, one may opt to repeat a constituent from a previous sentence. This device is known as constituent overlay. Example (13.17) is a typical beginning of a story in Tariana. The newly introduced participant—a man—is someone whom women do not like.

(13.17) paita   tʃiãli-pidana   ina: meninite-pidana
         one+CL:ANIM man-REM.P.REP women not.loved-REM.P.REP
         ina: meninite-pidana   diha
         women not.loved-REM.P.REP   he
         'There was a man, he was not loved by women, not loved by women was he'

Throughout a conversation, each interlocutor may have a way of marking their turn.
In Manambu, this is done through the connective *aw* 'so' or a general noun *ma:gw*
'whatever'. If a speaker wants to tell a longer story, or to interrupt someone with
something they consider important, they typically use first person imperative of the
verb 'speak', *wau?* 'May I talk, let me talk?'. To mark that the interlocutor is engaged
with the conversation, or listening to a story, they will interpolate a brief *Akan aka*
'this is how it is'.

Tariana and the neighbouring Tucanoan languages share a 'conversation sustainer'
question–response pattern. This is the most common strategy of showing a listener's
participation in conversational interaction.

When A (speaker) tells a story, B (listener) is expected to give feedback, after just
about every sentence, by repeating the predicate (or the last verb within a serial verb
construction) accompanied by an interrogative evidential. These pseudo-questions do
not have question intonation. This is how it works in Tucano:

(13.18) A ɨ̃   niî-ami
            OK   say-REC.P.VIS.3sg.nf
            'He said, OK'

         B niî-a-ti
            say-REC.P-INTERROGATIVE
            'He said it?'

Such interactions have little meaning per se, but they have an important function—
they show that speaker A is being heard, and the conversation can go on.

13.2.2 Ellipsis

A participant, or a part of a story, does not have to be repeated. We saw in (9.19)–(9.20)
that demonstratives can refer to something or someone already mentioned in what
is known as 'anaphoric' use. Throughout a narrative, or a conversation, some participants, or even actions, can be left out, or 'ellipsed', if understood from the context.

Languages vary in how much ellipsis is allowed. In some, a noun phrase on its own
can constitute a reduced sentence. Dixon (2010a: 133) describes how Yidiñ, an Australian language, favours being explicit—a reply to a question must be a full clause. So,
an answer to 'What are you going out for?' will be stated in full as 'I'm going to hunt

wallabies'. Dyirbal, Yidiñ's neighbour to the south, follows a different strategy—a more economical reply will be preferred. Thus, a question 'What are you going out for?' may receive a one-word response, for instance, *Barrgan-gu* (wallaby-DATIVE), 'for walla-bies'. Dyirbal has a higher proportion of reduced sentences than Yidiñ.

In many European languages verbless constructions are commonly used in spoken language to indicate what is being ordered or asked for, for example *Two beers, please*; *Two adults, please* (as a shorthand for 'I request admission for two adults). Curt one-word commands are often a feature of special genres. In commands such as *Forward! On your feet! Faster! Left, right! At the double! At ease!* the verb of motion is understood. In English, one single adjective can function as a directive, as in *Careful*! ['Be careful'], *Quiet*! ['Be quiet!]. So can a noun, for example *Silence in court!* Saying *Fora!* 'Out!' in Portuguese or *Välja* 'Out!' in Estonian is a curt command, to be obeyed immediately. Such commands in European languages are not uncommon in the language of the military.

One-word commands in Manambu consist of nouns marked for case. Saying *diya:k!* (excrement+LK+DATIVE/AVERSIVE) 'for (fear of) excrement' was a warning for some-one walking on a path and not looking, for fear of stepping onto a dog's excrement.

The amount of ellipsis, and thus the frequency of reduced sentences, may depend on speech genre. In Manambu being elaborate and precise in one's speech is a highly appreciated skill for story tellers and traditional orators. But in day-to-day life, com-munication is highly elliptical. One-word responses are frequent. For example, if I ask a speaker 'Where do you live?', she is likely to just say *Wun ka:d* 'I am this one', literally 'I this.masc.sg', rather than saying 'I live in this house here'. To produce a curt command to be performed immediately, speakers often use a dependent clause on its own. For example, a command to pray before a meal is phrased as *Məl kusə-ku!*, literally, 'Having closed eyes!' There is thus an iconic correlation between the brevity of the expression and its curtness and abruptness.

13.3 To use the language

The ways in which communication proceeds depends on speech practices, and speech genres. We start with speech formulae, and some patterns of what can be called 'phatic communication'.

13.3.1 *Speech formulae, greetings, and farewells*

Learning how to maintain a conversation and interact in a language is fun—and will help a grammarian understand how language is used. In many small tribal languages, there is no quick and easy way of saying 'hello' or 'goodbye'. Asking 'Have you come?' and receiving a reply 'I have come' is a typical greeting among the Tariana and the Yam-inahua (a Panoan group in Peru). A morning greeting among the Arawak-speaking Guajiro in Colombia and Venezuela is a question 'How was your dream?'.

The verb 'go' is often used in departure formulas. Among the Manambu, if I want to leave, I may signal this by saying 'I am now going to leave you' and wait for my companions to say *Yara ma:y* (well go.IMPERATIVE) 'Go well!'. I will reply to this using an imperative of the verb 'stay': *Yara adakw!* (well stay.IMPERATIVE) 'Stay well'.

Greetings may relate to what people are doing. When one goes to the river in the morning to bathe, a normal greeting among the Manambu will be 'Are you going to bathe?' The answer will be 'I am going to bathe'; to which the first speaker will reply 'you go well'. If you pass someone on the road in a Manambu-speaking village, you may greet them saying: *yara kwa:n a-nay* (well stay+SEQ IMPV-play) 'Staying well, play!' If they are working, a proper thing to say is: *yara kwan yawi akur* (well stay+SEQ work IMPV+do) 'Staying well, do work'.

If one is sitting in a house and wants to greet a passer-by, one would use a second-person imperative, encouraging them to move on in the direction they are already going. The direction could follow the course of the Sepik river (the major orientation point). Sentence (13.19) would be used if the person's direction of movement follows the river upstream, and (13.20) if the person's direction of movement follows the river downstream.

(13.19) maya   a-war
         go.IMPV+VOC   IMPV-go.up
         'Off you go upstream'

(13.20) maya   adi:d
         go.IMPV+VOC   go.down.IMPV
         'Off you go downstream'

Such phatic interaction may appear tedious and obsequious—but this is what people do, to different degrees, the world over. In standard Australian English, if I want to ask a workman when he is going to send me an estimate for a job he has undertaken to do, I will ring him up and first engage in an apparently meaningless conversation:

(13.21) Me: Hi, Cameron. How are you going?
         Cameron: Hi, mate. Pretty good, yourself?
         Me: Not too bad. It's a nice day today, isn't it. Oh, by the way—remember the estimate you promised?

If I get straight to the point, I will be rude—and may not get the information I am after.

Greetings and speech formulae are not just curious facts; they often reflect traditional attitudes and precautions. A common greeting in Jarawara, an Arawá language from southern Amazonia, is *ifa ama-ti?* (specifier.fem be-2sgCOPULA.SUBJECT)

'Is it you?' (lit. are you the specified one?). This means 'is it your spirit in your body'—and not absent—something that might happen during a period of trance, or if an evil spirit had invaded your body. A typical response will be: *(ee) ifa ama o-ke* (yes specifier.fem be 1sgCOPULA.SUBJECT-DECLARATIVE.fem) '(Yes), it is me'. The addressee is reassured—they are indeed talking to a real person and not to an evil spirit in disguise.

The traditional Manambu address and greeting rituals used to be rather elaborate. Every Manambu clan owns a set of totems and special address terms. In greeting and farewelling people, it is customary to use the appropriate term belonging to their father's clan, and also to their mother's clan: this used to be a way of thwarting evil spirits. This practice is gradually dying out. As befits a society with a classificatory kinship system (mentioned in Chapter 2), everyone's relationship to everyone else in the Manambu area is defined through kinship links. People tend to address each other by using kinship terms. Among the Nungon of Morobe Province, using a person's proper name to address them is plainly rude.

It often comes as a surprise to journalists and naïve language learners that the overwhelming majority of small languages of Amazonia, New Guinea, Oceania, and Africa simply do not have any way of saying 'thank you' and 'please'. In languages of Amazonia and New Guinea, there are no simply one-way words to express gratitude. Giving and receiving do not require verbal acknowledgement—gifts are traditionally exchanged based on reciprocal relations and networks of obligations and debts. Nowadays, some languages borrow terms like 'thank you' or 'please' from the local lingua franca. The way one answers a question in the positive or in the negative may also not be an easy matter—many indigenous languages do not have a word for 'yes' or 'no'. To express agreement or disagreement, one might have to repeat the clause one agrees, or disagrees, with.

13.3.2 *Speech genres and story-telling*

A comprehensive grammar will take account of the ways in which stories are told, and of special grammatical and other features of different genres.

Traditional stories usually begin, and end, in a particular way. In many European languages a folk tale will start with an introductory *once upon a time*. Estonian folk tales start with an expression *Elanud kord . . ,* literally, 'there is reported to have lived once . . .' An ancestral myth in Tariana would open with the time word *walikasu* 'at the beginning, back in the old days'. Such a start sets the scene for the story to come, and also gives the audience a sneak preview into the genre to be expected.

A formula will also conclude a story. In Tariana, any story (a folk tale, a myth, or a narrative dealing with a historical event) would end in a verbless clause with the adverb *kida* or *kaida* 'finished, ready', or the possessed noun *kewhidana*, literally 'its head'. A speaker may add to this a verbal clause *di-sisa-naka* (3sg.nf-finish-PRES.VIS) 'it is finished'. A typical ending of a tale in Manambu is rather imaginative: for many people it translates as 'the story goes back to its base'; for some, it is 'the story enters an enclosure'—as if, when told, the story was let out of where it is kept, and when it is finished, it goes back to its resting place. For a real-life narrative, a speaker would just say 'it is finished'.

Different speech genres may have their distinct features—both grammatical and lexical. A grammaticalized marker of information source (that is, an evidential) is often chosen depending on the genre of a story (see §7.2.5). Traditional stories passed on from one generation to the next are typically cast in reported evidential. In a language with many evidential choices, an autobiography is likely to be narrated using a visual evidential. In Tariana, one talks about one's dreams using non-visual evidential.

Different speech registers—or politeness levels whose choice depends on the relationship between a speaker and an addressee—may have special grammatical features. This is the case in Japanese and Korean. Ponapean, an Oceanic language, has a different set of possessive classifiers whose choice depends on the status of the possessor and the speech register—whether common, honorific (humiliative or 'exalted'), or royal.

The language of songs is often different from the day-to-day language. Among the Yagua of north-eastern Peru, the ancestral *ñá* songs are sung in an archaic language not intelligible to anyone who is not a shaman or a master of chants. A special language in magic chants is used among the Kuna, a Chibchan-speaking group in Panama. The style involves special lexicon, and grammatical markers not employed in the everyday language. In Dyirbal, about one-third of the 820 words in the recorded songs are not found in any other genres. Only in songs can a suffix—for instance, a case marker—be omitted to fit in with the rhythm.

Men and women often speak differently—their intonation and pitch may vary, and they may choose different ways of saying things. Japanese has a number of first person pronouns used exclusively by men, and another set used exclusively by women. These differences can be manipulated: a female professor may switch to 'male' language as a token of her status. This is not always welcomed by more traditional people, and branded as 'tasteless' language use. A number of expressions in Japanese are used by women only: for instance, a woman would say *ka sira* 'I wonder', while a man would say *ká né/ná* (but might use *ka sira* when speaking to a woman).

In a number of North American Indian languages, male and female varieties have systematic phonological and grammatical differences. This was first described by Sapir, in his grammar of Yana, a language of northern California. Forms used by men are longer than those used by women: where a man would say *'ina* 'tree, stick' a woman would say *'i^h*. To form a question, men would add an enclitic =*n*, for example *'au'asi=n* 'Is there fire?', while women would lengthen the final vowel: *'au'asi:* 'Is there fire?'

In many Australian and South American languages, the relationship with one's in-laws requires special behaviour, and special language use. The avoidance style may have the same phonology and grammar, but different lexicon. The avoidance speech style called *Jalnguy* was used in the traditional Dyirbal-speaking society. One of its characteristics was one-to-many relationship: one word in Jalnguy would correspond to several in the day-to-day style Guwal. So, one Jalŋuy term *jijan* will refer to any kind of lizard or goanna and correspond to a dozen specific forms in Guwal.

A Kalapalo speaker from the Xingu region of northern Brazil will never touch an in-law, or look at them. They will never address them directly, or utter their name. Moreover, a word similar to their name will also be avoided. For example, one man's brother-in-law was called *Tafitse*, 'Macaw'. And when talking about a macaw, the man would always describe it as 'an object made from the one with blue tail feathers'.

Personal names may be special in many ways. We saw in Chapter 5 that they form a special subclass of nouns in terms of their grammatical features. In many cultures, personal names are believed to have a special power. Among the Malagasy of Madagascar who speak a Western Austronesian language, whenever a common word forms the name or part of the name of the chief of the tribe, it becomes sacred and may no longer be used. The Kambaata women from Ethiopia never utter the first name of their senior in-laws after marriage, and avoid any word starting with the same syllable (or even the same consonant) as their names. Suppose a woman's father-in-law is called Tiráago. Then, instead of *timá* 'enset (type of banana) dish left over from dinner and eaten in the morning' she will use the form *ginjirá* 'left over from dinner eaten in the morning'. Another woman's mother-in-law is called *Caa'mmíse*: the woman never utters words with initial *ca* or *caa*. Having to avoid a name creates motivation of name replacement—and thus change in the lexicon. This takes us to our next section.

13.4 Issues in semantics and features of lexicon

Grammatical meanings, and the semantic content of various word classes, are at the heart of any comprehensive reference grammar. Once all, or most, phonological, morphological, syntactic, and pragmatic issues have been addressed, a grammar writer may choose to have a close look at some particularly striking features of the lexicon, and lexical semantics of a language. A special chapter on lexicon may start with an overview of the etymological make-up of the lexicon. Many languages contain numerous loans from their neighbours. The semantic fields covered by loans and principles of code-switching can be included in the chapter dealing with the language's semantic organization.

A language can display an amazing wealth and diversity in some semantic fields. Jarawara has four verbs of 'eating', depending on the nature of action: -*kaba*- means 'eat where a lot of chewing is involved (used of meat, fish, sweet corn, yams, manioc, biscuits, etc.), *jome -na-* 'eat where little or no chewing is needed, e.g. eating an orange or banana' (also used for swallowing a pill), *komo -na-* 'eating which involves spitting out seeds', and *bako -na-* 'eating by sucking' (e.g. watermelon, cashew fruit). Tariana has numerous verbs which cover feeling, thinking, remembering, and other mental processes.

Languages vary in how much detail can be expressed in their lexicon, both nominal and verbal. Manambu, like many other Papuan languages, lacks verbs for certain notions—such as 'want, desire, covet'. This is expressed with the desiderative or optative suffix. There is no special root meaning 'refuse', or 'refute'—the only way of saying this is *ma: wa-*, lit. 'say no'. The notion of 'agree, accept' is expressed through *ya:kya wa-*, 'say OK'.

In other semantic fields, Manambu is highly specific. To properly say 'carry', one needs to know the manner in which the action was performed: if something is carried on the head the term is *tiya-*; if it is carried hanging from a shoulder, it is *kalu-*; if one carries a big bundle in one's arms, it is *tapu-*, and carrying under the arm is referred to as *səkət-*. If the object is carried with hands and arms but is not too big, the appropriate term is *yata-*. On the other hand, Manambu has numerous verbs with a general meaning, including *kə-* 'consume (eat, drink, and smoke)', *sə-* 'put, plant', and *kur-* 'get'. And the generic verb, *kar-/kra-* 'bring, carry' does allow the speaker to remain vague as to the manner in which the object was carried.

A fair degree of specificity is notable in most word classes in the language. Names are considered an item of wealth in traditional Manambu culture; so it is little wonder that different types of 'names' are distinguished lexically: *ap-a-sə*, literally 'bone name', refers to the person's main name they are known by; *ta:y-sə* (before-name) is another term for the name which was given first; and *səgliak* is a term for any additional name. Time words are another area of high precision: with respect to *nəbəl* 'today', one distinguishes two terms for future: *sər* 'tomorrow' and *mu* 'the day after tomorrow', and five for the past: *na:l* 'yesterday', *nagəs* 'the day before yesterday', *dəbəña* 'three days before today', *pasəta:kw* 'four days before today' and *wakənay* 'five days before today, remote past'. But if one chooses not to be precise, one may just say *nagəs* to refer to the recent past, and *wakənay* or *ta:y, ta:yir* 'before' to say 'a long time ago'. This is a major feature of the Manambu lexicon: one can be highly specific, or choose to go for a rather general term.

Amazonia is renowned for its diversity in plants, and in animals. This is reflected in the vocabulary of every Amazonian language. Over 40 per cent of the lexicon I have gathered for Tariana are botanical and zoological terms. General terms reflect what is considered most useful, or most important. The Tariana have general terms for *itʃiri* 'game (typically mammals)', *kepiria* 'birds', and *kuphe* 'fish'. The term *katanapiri* covers most invertebrates (without any further differentiation), and *mawari* 'snake (in general)' can also be applied to worms.

The organization of the lexicon may hold the clue of why the language is the way it is, taking us to the next chapter.

13.5 Envoi

Discourse, or pragmatic, motivation may lie behind any seemingly free variation in the use of any language structure. 'Free' constituent order may be a chimera: a topic will tend to be placed upfront, and less important items will follow it. If a classifier, or gender agreement, is optional, in all likelihood, there will be subtle and hard-to-capture pragmatic differences between seemingly 'synonymous' expressions.

Notes and sources

§13.1.1: See Chafe (1976), Li and Thompson (1981: 85–7), Radetzky (2003) and Dixon (2010a: 174–5) on properties and functions of topics; Li and Thompson (1976) on subject prominent and topic prominent languages; Li and Thompson (1981: 92–3; 129–30) on Mandarin Chinese; further examples are in Luo (2013: 196–8). See Hyslop (2001: 269) for Ambae; Grevisse (1986: 642–53) on the structure of interrogative clauses in French. Useful discussion and definitions of parameters relevant to information structure are in Lambrecht (1994) and Cruse (2006). See Shibatani (1990: 262–80) for an incisive discussion of topic constructions and various aspects of information structure in Japanese, Korean, and Ainu; Ochs et al. (1976: 381) on the expression of topics in English; Enfield (2007: 102) on Lao; Jauncey (2011: 88–91) on Tamambo.

§13.1.2: See Li and Thompson (1981) on Mandarin Chinese; Enfield (2007: 116) on Lao; Olawsky (2006: 697–702) on Urarina; Guillaume (2008: 665–6) on Cavineña; Jauncey (2011: 88) on Tamambo; Butt and Benjamin (2004: 130–1) on Spanish; Kenesei et al. (1998: 263) on Hungarian. Further readings on topic and its overtones include Chafe (1976 and 1994).

§13.1.3: See Du Bois (1987) and Genetti and Crain (2003) on preferred argument structure; a further summary in Aikhenvald and Dixon (2011a: 165–8). Dixon (2012: 198–205) discusses the relationship between topic and pivot in clause-combining. See Enfield (2007: 162, 166) on Lao, Olawsky (2006: 849–56) on Urarina. Arguments against the universal applicability of the 'basic' constituent order were given by Mithun (1987); see also Gildea (2000) for a reappraisal of the concept in the analysis of natural languages not based on elicitation, and Enfield (2007: 272–7) on the pragmatic basis of constituent order in Lao; Watters (2009) on Kham; Post (2009) on Galo.

§13.1.4: Urmson (1952) is the classic study of parentheticals. Dixon (2005: 233–8) provides a typological framework and an in-depth study of parentheticals in English, in terms of their form and their function; other studies include Kaltenböck et al. (2011) and Dehé and Kavalova (2007). See Aikhenvald (2003: 583–4) on Tariana.

§13.2: Texts can be organized in thematic units, sometimes referred to as 'paragraphs': see, for example, Farr (1999) and Chafe (1987).

§13.2.1: 'Bridging' repetition (see Dixon 2009) is also known as 'head-tail' or 'tail-head' linkage; for a perspective from Papuan languages and further references, see de Vries (2005). See de Vries (2005: 364) on Kombai; Aikhenvald (2003: 577–83) on Tariana, Aikhenvald (2008: 544–5) and fieldnotes on Manambu, and Overall (2009: 173–4) on Aguaruna. In his analysis of sentence and clause linking Galo, Post (2009: 94) focuses on marking discourse continuity as a major function of bridging repetition. See Aikhenvald (2002b: 125) and references there on the conversation sustainer pattern in Tariana, Tucano, and East Tucanoan languages.

§13.2.2: See Aikhenvald (2010: 280–2) and references there on ellipsis in commands.

§13.3.1: See Aikhenvald (2012a: 369-74) and references there on greetings and farewells in Amazonian languages; Dixon (2004a: 370, 564–5) on Jarawara; Sarvasy (forthcoming) on Nungon; Aikhenvald (2008: 584–90) on Manambu; Künnap (1992) on Estonian.

§13.3.2: See Chaumeuil (1993) on Yagua; Sherzer (1990: 243–50) on Kuna; further examples of special styles in Amazonian languages are discussed in Aikhenvald (2012a: 365–9); Dixon and Koch (1996) on Dyirbal songs and their linguistic features; further discussion, and examples of different speech styles in various ritual practices across the world can be found in Senft and Basso (2009). A summary of features of ceremonial speech genres in North American Indian languages is in Mithun (1999: 291–92). See Shibatani (1990) and Martin (1975) on Japanese, Sohn (1994) on Korean, and Keating (1997) on Ponapean.

See Martin (1975: 936–7), Shibamoto (1987), and Okamoto (1995) on female and male speech in Japanese. See Sapir (1929) on Yana; Mithun (1999: 276–80) on North American Indian languages; Aikhenvald (2012a: 374–5) for a summary of male and female languages in South America. See Dixon (1980: 59–65 and 2002: 91–5) on mother-in-law style in Aboriginal Australia; Aikhenvald (2012a: 362–5) on taboos and avoidance style in Amazonian languages, and Basso (2007) on Kalapalo; Treis (2005) on name taboos among the Kambaata and other Cushitic-speaking groups in Ethiopia, and Simons (1982) and Holzknecht (1987) on name taboos in the Austronesian world, including Malagasy. *Hlonipa* is the name of a similar avoidance among the Nguni and the Southern Sotho of Southern Africa: alongside avoiding the names of the father-in-law and other male affines, a Nguni woman may not mention words with the same root or root syllables: see Herbert (1990).

§13.4: See Dixon (2004a) on Jarawara, Aikhenvald (2003) on Tariana, Aikhenvald (2008) on Manambu.

14

Why is a language the way it is?

One language may be similar to another because the two are genetically related and have a shared origin. Or they can be similar in some ways because they are spoken next to each other, and there is contact between the speakers. The physical environment may be mirrored in the grammar of a language. The grammar may also reflect social and cultural features. These may include the lifestyle, beliefs, and attitudes of those who speak it.

The question 'why is a language the way it is' is most fascinating. And it is most elusive. We will never be able to explain everything. It can be even harder to predict what features a language will develop and why.

14.1 Shared origins

Most languages (all save for a few 'isolates') are known to belong to one genetic family. The languages in a family go back to a common 'proto-language'. This would have had a number of mutually intelligible dialects. As dialects move out of contiguity with each other, and inter-group communication is reduced, they will steadily diverge until mutual intelligibility is lost and they may be considered distinct languages. Two speech communities, which originally spoke dialects of a single language, may then form separate tribes, or nations, each with its own laws and customs. Each will pride itself on having its own language, and may strive to increase linguistic differences from the erstwhile co-dialect. Besides the naturally-developed and purposely-contrived differences, there will remain many points of similarity.

The reason why English and German share many forms, many grammatical categories and constructions lies in the fact that they belong to the Germanic branch of the Indo-European family of languages (see also Table 2.1). In §2.3.2, we mentioned common origins, and those similarities between languages which are due to their shared ancestry.

Further to this: related languages may develop along similar lines; they 'will pass through the same or strikingly similar phases': this 'parallelism in drift' (Sapir 1921: 171–2) accounts for additional similarities between related languages, even for those 'long disconnected'.

Wosera and Manambu belong to the Ndu language family in Papua New Guinea. Both languages have developed directional markers on verbs. Each of these grammaticalized from a combination of the verb *sə-* 'put, plant' and an inherently directional motion verb, such as 'go down', 'go inside', 'go up', 'go across', and so on. Consider (14.1):

(14.1)	MANAMBU	WOSERA
	yakə-sə-da-	*yat-sa-da*
	throw-put-go.down	throw-put-go.down
	'throw down'	'throw down'
	yakə-sə-wula-	*yat-sa-wula*
	throw-put-enter	throw-put-enter
	'throw inside or away	'throw inside'
	from the Sepik River	
	and towards the shore'.	

These two related languages are not mutually intelligible and are not in contact. They have developed in a similar way following the principle of 'parallelism in drift'.

A reference grammar may contain a snapshot of features the language shares with its established relatives. Those features which are markedly different may well be due to influence from surrounding languages.

14.2 Language contact

Each language community (save for a very few confined to a distant island or an inaccessible mountain valley) is in contact with other communities, speaking different languages. The communities will interact, through trade, shared festivals and rituals, inter-marriage, and maybe wars. Through all this, their languages also interact. They may come to sound more similar. They may borrow some vocabulary. Some grammatical features of the languages may also converge. However, the speech communities will still constitute separate political groups, and their languages will remain distinct. That is, despite a degree of convergence, they will still maintain significant differences, so as not to be mutually intelligible.

When speakers of a language interact, they borrow forms and meanings. How much they borrow depends on cultural and social factors, including the degree of knowledge of each other's languages, and speakers' sense of purism.

The introductory chapter of a reference grammar is the place to mention which other language groups the language is in contact with. Later on, in one of the final chapters, a grammarian may choose to focus on those patterns in the language which are clearly due to contact with others.

14.2.1 *What to borrow and how*

Borrowing forms is one of the primary effects of language contact. Some borrowed forms are easy to recognize as being 'foreign'. A person can be said to experience *angst* or *schadenfreude*; a language may have *ablaut*, and a country can be said to engage in *realpolitik*. What we have here, in italics, are lexical borrowings: they are words from one language (German) adopted into another (English).

If something is really 'cool', an English-speaking youth could refer to it as *über-cool*. The root 'cool' is English. But the prefix *über* is German; it means 'super'. This word contains a grammatical borrowing. The preposition *via* 'by way of' comes from the Latin word *viā* (ablative singular of the noun *via* 'road, channel, course', literally meaning 'from the road, by the road'). Lexical, and grammatical forms can be borrowed directly.

A borrowing can penetrate a language through an intermediary. After South America was colonized by the Spanish and the Portuguese, many words from local languages made their way into English through the intermediaries of these two languages. The words *jaguar*, *tapir*, and *jacaranda* are a legacy of the now extinct Tupinambá language, from South America, which came into English through the intermediary of Portuguese. The word *hammock* was borrowed into English about 1555 from Spanish, which acquired it from Taino, an Arawak language spoken on the island of Hispaniola. The Taino were the first group encountered by Columbus. The form *hamaca* found in Taino was inherited from the proto-Arawak language: it survives in related languages. All these words were borrowed to describe new items (for instance, a hammock, or a hanging bed), for which Spanish (and English) had no word of their own.

An alternative to directly borrowing a form is lexical calquing. A new word is created by translating morpheme-by-morpheme from a source language. For instance, the German *Ein-druck* 'impression' (literally, 'in-press') has been calqued from Latin *im-pressio*, where each morpheme is translated from Latin into German. The term for 'roof' in Nigerian Arabic translates literally as 'the head of the house': this is how speakers of the surrounding Chadic languages refer to a roof. Lexical calquing creates similarity in structure, and not so much in form.

There can also be a grammatical calque. A passive construction in Mandarin Chinese originally used to convey a negative, 'adverse' meaning; this construction largely lost this overtone as a result of pervasive translations from Indo-European languages (English and Russian) into Mandarin Chinese.

Phonemes and sounds can also be borrowed. Imagine a language spoken in a geographical area surrounded by languages of a different genetic affiliation, and a long way away from related languages. Such a language is likely to develop features atypical for the family it belongs to but shared with its neighbours. Features of this kind are most likely to be due to language contact. This is how Armenian, an Indo-European language, has developed glottalized consonants, due to intensive contact with non-Indo-European languages in the Caucasus. Such consonants are absent from other

Indo-European languages. The contact explains why Armenian sounds different from its genetic relatives.

Once a foreign form is borrowed, it often assimilates to the phonological patterns of the recipient language. The words *spaghetti* and *gelato* have both been borrowed into English from Italian. But they have been assimilated to the phonological patterns of English: they sound just like any English word would. Words that have been perfectly integrated into the phonological and morphological systems of the language can be difficult to identify as borrowings. It takes a linguist to detect that the English words *cherries*, *very*, and *beauty* are in fact loans, from Old Norman French *cherise*, Old French *verai, varai, vrai*, and Old French *bealte, beaute, biaute* respectively.

By contrast, unassimilated loans stand apart from native words in their phonological make-up. In Mazateco, an Oto-Manguean language from Mexico, all voiceless stops become voiced after nasals; thus we never find the sequence [nt], only [nd]. However, in some Spanish loans, among them *siento* (from Spanish *ciento*), a frequently used word for 'one hundred', one does find the native Spanish sequence [nt]. Mazateco has been described as having two 'coexistent phonemic systems'—one native, and one for loans (this was mentioned in §4.1.5).

Loans may retain morphological features of the source language. For example, some Latin borrowings into English require the Latin plural, for example, *colloquium* (sg.) versus *colloquia* (pl.), whereas others allow either the Latin plural or the English plural, for example, *syllabus* (sg.) can be pluralized either as *syllabuses* or *syllabi* (pl). Still other borrowed Latin nouns are fully assimilated into the English morphological system and take only the English plural, for example, *diplomas* as opposed to the original Latin *diplomata*.

If one language is significantly different from its proven genetic relatives, language contact is the 'usual suspect'. Cantonese has classifiers in possessive constructions. This feature is atypical for most Sinitic languages, and may well be due to contact with Miao-Yao-speaking groups.

Some types of forms are more resistant to borrowing than others, but no linguistic feature is entirely 'borrowing-proof'. Number words tend not to be borrowed in Indo-European and Afroasiatic languages, so some linguists have considered number words to be a category resistant to borrowing. However, the importance of numbers in trade and commerce has led to frequent borrowing of numbers in many languages of the world. In Chamorro, the major indigenous language of Guam, all the original numbers were replaced by borrowings from Spanish.

Personal pronouns are not immune to borrowing, although this is not frequent. English forms *they, their, them* were borrowed from Scandinavian, replacing the old English *hie, hiera, him* respectively. Many native American languages have borrowed conjunctions and discourse markers from Spanish. In Tojolabal, a Mayan language spoken in Mexico, conjunctions *y* 'and', *pero* 'but', *porque* 'because', and discourse markers *pues* 'well' and *bueno* 'well' all come from Spanish.

A prefix, a suffix, or a grammatical element can be borrowed. We saw above how the German prefix *über* and the Latin preposition *via* have made their way into English. There are also many suffixes in English of French origin—including *-ment*, as in *develop-ment*, and *-age*, as in *out-age*. A Spanish diminutive *-tu* is used with native words in Bolivian Quechua: one says *rumi-tu* (stone[Quechua]-diminutive[Spanish]). And the Spanish plural suffix *-s* can appear on native nouns together with the native plural marker *-kuna*: *runa-s-kuna* means 'men', where *runa* is the native Quechua word for 'man', *-s* is a Spanish plural suffix, and *-kuna* 'plural' comes from Quechua.

Easily separable forms with clear boundaries are easier to borrow than forms which are fused, or which involve complex morphophonological alternations. Conversely, it is harder to borrow forms if they have to be incorporated into morphologically complex paradigms. For example, Mohawk, an Iroquoian language, does not borrow verbs, 'due to the fact that the obligatory affixes on verbs are especially complex'. This means that 'the particular structure of Mohawk . . . acts as a restriction impeding the borrowing of foreign words' (Bonvillain 1978: 32).

Some grammatical and other features spread from one language to the next because they are especially important for communication. Having obligatory marking of information source—that is, 'evidentiality'—in one's language often correlates with a requirement to be precise. As a consequence, evidential meanings tend to be shared by neighbouring groups. Hardman (1986: 133) reports how difficult it is for Aymara speakers to imagine how one can speak a language which does not mark the information source. She and her colleagues had to 'adjust their English' and always specify how they knew things, so as not to upset their Aymara-speaking friends. In §14.4.5, we turn to how evidentiality reflects principles of communication.

Language attitudes of speakers often determine whether loan forms are acceptable or not. In many languages, 'foreign' importations are limited, as a token of unacceptable language-mixing. Speakers of many unrelated languages within the Vaupés River Basin linguistic area have a strong cultural inhibition against 'language-mixing'. This is viewed in terms of foreign morphemes and unlawful 'insertion' of borrowed words from a different language into one's speech. Those who violate the principle of 'keeping languages strictly apart' and commit the 'crime' of mixing their languages by introducing lexical and grammatical loans are ridiculed as incompetent and sloppy. Once speakers are conscious of the foreign material in their lexicon—or grammar—they can try and get rid of it. This is what has happened in the history of various literary languages, including Hungarian, Finnish, and Estonian.

Language contact reflects the speakers' history, their language attitudes, and social interactions. What it also reflects is the political status of each group. A minor language is more likely to borrow forms from a dominant one than the other way round. This is why we find many loans from Spanish in Mesoamerican and South American languages, and just a handful of loans from indigenous languages into a local variety of Spanish.

14.2.2 *Linguistic areas*

Borrowings and structural similarities may extend over all or most of the languages in a geographical region, no matter whether they are related or not. We then get large-scale linguistic diffusion, defining the region as a linguistic area (or a Sprachbund). Languages may remain different in many of their forms, but their structures will converge towards a similar prototype.

A linguistic area is a geographically delimited region which will include languages from at least two language families, or different subgroups of the same family. Languages will share a number of significant traits (most of which are not found in languages from these families or subgroups which lie outside the area). Diffusion within an area can be unilateral (when it proceeds from one source) or multilateral (when it involves several sources).

A very well-studied linguistic area is found on the Balkan peninsula and its environs. All the languages belonging to the Balkans linguistic area are Indo-European, but from different sub-groups. The three Slavic languages are Serbo-Croatian, Bulgarian, and Macedonian; there is also Romanian (a Romance language), Greek, and Albanian. Some scholars add to this Romani (the language of the Gypsies, from the Indo-Aryan group of Indo-European) and Turkish, an unrelated Turkic language. Salient features of the languages of the Balkans are:

   (i)   a central vowel *ɨ* or *ə* (absent from Greek and Macedonian);
  (ii) dative and genitive case fall together;
 (iii) postposed articles (absent from Greek);
 (iv) periphrastic future with an auxiliary corresponding to 'want' or 'have' (absent from Bulgarian and Macedonian);
  (v) periphrastic perfect (with an auxiliary verb corresponding to 'have');
 (vi) absence of infinitives (languages have a construction 'I want that I go' rather than 'I want to go');
(vii) use of a pronoun copy of an animate object so that the object is marked twice.

Languages which comprise the linguistic area of the multilingual Vaupés River Basin in Brazil and Colombia belong to genetically unrelated Tucanoan and Arawak families. The area is characterized by obligatory societal multilingualism, based on the principle of linguistic exogamy: one can only marry someone who speaks a different language.

The main features of the area are:

  (i) nasalization as a prosodic feature;
 (ii) four to five evidentials marking the way in which the speaker has acquired the information (whether seen, heard, inferred, assumed, or learnt from someone else);

   (iii) numerous classifiers used with demonstratives, number words, and in posses-
          sive constructions;
   (iv) small systems of genders;
   (v) nominative-accusative profile;
   (vi) one locative case covering all of direction ('to'), location ('in, at'), and source
          ('from');
   (vii) numerous identical formations, e.g. 'father of goods' = 'rich man'.

None of these individual properties is restricted to the Vaupés area. The way in which
they occur together is unique: this is why this constellation of features is area-specific.

In a situation of intensive language contact within an area, gradual convergence of
languages may result in almost complete structural isomorphism. Then, the grammar
and the semantics of one language are almost fully replicated in another. An example comes from two languages spoken within the Vaupés River Basin linguistic area.
Example (14.2) is from Tariana, an Arawak language, and (14.3) is from Tucano, an East
Tucanoan language in constant contact with Tariana. Examples come from traditional
stories involving a female cannibal. None of the morphemes are cognate.

TARIANA
(14.2)   nese pa:ma   di-na
            then one+NUMERAL.CLASSIFIER.FEMININE 3sg.nf-OBJECT
            du-yana-sita-pidana
            3sg.f-cook-ALREADY-REMOTE.PAST.REPORTED
            'She had reportedly cooked him already' (reportedly, a long time ago)

TUCANO
(14.3)   tiĩta ni'kó!   kɨɨ-re
            then one+NUMERAL.CLASSIFIER.FEMININE he-OBJECT
            do'á-toha-po'
            cook-ALREADY-REMOTE.PAST.REPORTED.3sg.fem
            'She had reportedly cooked him already'

Linguistic convergence does not always result in the creation of identical grammars.
It is also not the case that categories in language contact always match. Languages in
contact often maintain their distinct typological profiles. We can see this in the two
examples. Tucano continues to have just suffixes, and Tariana maintains both suffixes
and prefixes. However, Tariana has developed a complex system of evidentials under
Tucano influence. No other Arawak language related to Tariana has a system like
this one.

Language contact can partly explain why a language is different from its genetic relatives. If a language is in contact with another one, it may adopt new structures, and become more complex. But once a language becomes endangered and starts losing ground to a dominant neighbour, it may become impoverished. An obsolescent language may be inundated with loans and calques from a dominant language, and lose its own grammatical structures and unique profile.

14.3 Physical environment

The lexicon of a language reflects the environment in which it is spoken. This may include a wealth of names for mammals, plants, and other life forms. Grammar may also reflect some aspects of the environment. Lowland Amazonian languages with large classifier systems have different classifiers for palms and for other trees.

If a language is spoken in a hilly area, demonstratives may encode 'topographic deixis'—that is, the relative height, stance, and direction (see §9.2). Demonstratives in Lak, a North-east Caucasian language spoken in a mountainous terrain, have special forms for something at the same level as the speaker, or higher or lower than the speaker (see example (9.15)). In Hua, from the Highlands of New Guinea, demonstratives show whether the object being pointed at is uphill or downhill (see Table 9.13).

Dyirbal is spoken in a mountainous rainforest area of northeast Australia, with many rivers. Locational suffixes (added to article-like noun markers) express directions upriver and downriver, and uphill and downhill. The hilly area along the Sepik River is where speakers of Manambu reside. The language has five topographic demonstratives: there are special forms for 'upriver/uphill', 'downriver/downhill', 'away from the river', 'across the river', and 'off the river'. Similar, but not identical, directional markers are used with verbs. They cover 'upriver/uphill', 'downriver/downhill', 'away from the river', 'across the river away from the speaker', 'across the river towards the speaker', 'off the river or inside', 'sideways away from the speaker' and 'sideways towards the speaker'.

Other languages from the same Ndu family are spoken in a similar environment. None of them have topographic deixis in demonstratives, and only some have directionals on verbs. A feature within a language may be explained through correlation with the environment. But the environment can never fully predict what we are likely to find when confronted with an unknown language.

14.4 Social structures, lifestyle, and beliefs

As Enfield (2004a) puts it,

Grammar is thick with cultural meaning. Encoded in the semantics of grammar we find cultural values and ideas, we find clues about the social structures which speakers maintain, we find evidence, both historically relevant and otherwise, of the social organisation of speech communities. (Enfield 2004a: 3)

Some linguistic categories show eye-catching correlations with cultural values, social hierarchies and their conceptualization. Reference classification devices—genders, and classifiers of different types—echo social stereotypes, and the status of men and women. Marking possession often correlates with values, and attitudes towards ownership. Interpersonal relations and the structure of the society may be a key to understanding how speakers use pronouns and address forms, phrase questions, and get one another to do something. The expression of information source mirrors a cultural requirement 'to be precise'.

14.4.1 Genders and social stereotypes

Masculine and feminine genders may unambiguously reflect cultural stereotypes, and attitudes towards the roles of males and females. Take the use of third person pronouns in English. Up until recently, the masculine pronoun *he* was used as a generic term for any human being, no matter what sex. Recently, with the rise of equal rights for women, this usage has been branded as 'sexist'. A common convention is to use the unmarked generic pronoun 'they'—with a singular reference. We now have a new reflexive pronoun—'themselves' based on plural 'they', but used to refer to one person (a man or a woman). If I don't want to specify whether an author I am criticizing is male or female (or if I don't know), I will say 'The author ought to ask themselves what audience they are writing for'. Cultural pressure against what was conceived as 'male chauvinism'—reflected in pronominal usage—resulted in semantic change. This shows, in a nutshell, that a study of putative correlations between (a) beliefs, mental attitudes, and behavioural conventions and (b) linguistic phenomena could be potentially rewarding.

In a fascinating study of sex roles as revealed through gender reference, Mathiot and Roberts (1979) show how role images of males and females are realized in the use of personal pronouns. The use of the pronouns *he* and *she* to refer to inanimates in American English reflects a number of stereotyped features. These are part of the inherent image and role image American men and women have of themselves, and of each other. A beautiful flower was consistently referred to as 'she', and an ugly cactus as 'he'.

In a few New Guinea languages with masculine and feminine genders, the masculine is associated with culturally important roles, and the feminine with insignificant things, as in Manambu and numerous other Ndu languages. These societies are famous for the dominance of their male cults, and special power of male knowledge by and large denied to women.

Iroquoian languages have two genders: masculine is formally and functionally marked, and feminine is functionally unmarked. Feminine will be used if we do not know whether we are dealing with a man or a woman, if we are talking about human beings in general, or about a mixed group of people. Chafe (2004) describes sex roles and traditional practices in Northern Iroquoian societies (including the Huron, the Seneca, and also the Onondaga):

Sex roles were distributed in Iroquois society in such a way that men were conspicuous, often even flamboyant, and invested with decision-making powers, whereas women stayed in the background, a position from which they nevertheless exerted considerable influence on what men did. Women were neither unimportant nor undervalued. On the contrary, they were responsible for keeping life going, both from day to day and from generation to generation. The importance of women in Iroquoian culture has been emphasised by the anthropologist Cara Richards, who went so far as to exclaim, 'If you must be born a woman, try to be an Onondaga'. (Chafe 2004: 105)

According to Richards (1974: 401), the 'relatively high status of Iroquois women' was reflected in the matrilineal descent, and also the fact that land belonged to women, and women were the ones who appointed the chiefs. The men 'stood out as highly visible figures against this essentially female background'. This seems to fit in with the idea of associating females 'with undifferentiated people in general' (Chafe 2004: 106).

But things turn out to be less simple if one looks further afield. In Jarawara, masculine is the functionally marked gender. It is used to talk about human males (and other referents assigned to masculine gender). The functionally unmarked choice—feminine, or 'non-masculine'—is used for reference to human females (and referents belonging to the feminine gender), and also when we do not know what gender someone belongs to. This, however, does not at all imply that women are better treated, or are higher in status than men: an important woman will be referred to with masculine gender—as if she were promoted to the status of an honorary 'male'. The higher 'male' status is echoed by gender choice.

14.4.2 *Culture, lifestyle, and values in reference classification*

Larger systems of genders, and classifiers of various kinds, often reflect some aspects of culture. North Amazonian languages spoken by people who live along big rivers have a special classifier for 'canoes'. Fulfulde, a West Atlantic language from Senegal, has a special gender for cows—this may well be seen as a consequence of the importance of cattle in the Fulfulde culture. Japanese and Korean have classifiers for books and written documents. Vernacular Amazonian languages do not have such classifiers, since they lacked these artefacts.

Seemingly strange meanings of a gender class can be understood through the cultural underpinnings, and mythological associations. In Fulfulde society, 'cows' are the centrepoint of wealth and of ceremonial life. Once the linguist realizes that, it will come as no surprise that 'ceremonies' (which present an occasion to transfer property rights to items of wealth) will be included in the same class as 'cows'. We can recall, from §6.1, that in Dyirbal, an Australian language, birds are classed as feminine by mythological association since women's souls are believed to enter birds after death.

The composition of a classifier can change due to technological innovations. In Thai, *khan*, a classifier for objects with handles, once applied to bicycles, was later extended to all vehicles, according to their similarity of function. The influx of new items of material culture resulted in the creation of new classifiers. In Thai, some of these new classifiers are loanwords themselves, for example *chut* (from English *suit*), which is used to refer to dresses and Western style suits, as well as to pyjamas and bathing suits. Others are of Thai origin. For instance, *lawt* 'tube' came to be used as a classifier for test tubes, light bulbs, and drinking straws, and *rian* 'coin' is used colloquially for counting dollars.

The use of classifiers can be affected by conscious actions. The most remarkable example comes from Thai. King Mongkut issued a royal order in 1854 whereby 'noble' animals such as elephants and horses should be counted without any classifier; the classifier *tua* could only be used for animals of a 'lower' status. The royal vocabulary replaced the classifier *khày* 'egg'—which had developed associations with testes—with *fo':ng* 'water bubbles'.

Classifiers in possessive constructions often mirror cultural practices and values. This takes us to our next section.

14.4.3 Possession

Possessive patterns reflect lifestyle and attitudes. Possessive meanings and possessive structures change when cultural practices, and attitudes, undergo transformations. As a consequence, possession is highly amenable to contact-induced change. One can often detect the impact of new, changing, values of foreign provenance in the ways one marks possession.

Meanings of possessive classifiers may correlate with what the speakers of a language do. In Cahuilla, a Uto-Aztecan language, a possessive classifier for 'pet' cannot be used with some animals, like feral cats.

Possessive classifiers in Ponapean reflect traditional beliefs and the kinship system. More precisely, with a culturally important notion of *mana* which describes 'the sacred and dangerous power which flows from the deities through the chiefs to the people'; '*mana* flows matrilineally to descendants within chiefly clans', and consequently the 'belief that *mana* extends to possessions makes possessive constructions a meaningful category' in distinguishing between honorific, status-lowering, and common speech registers. Consequently, in Ponapean maternal—and not paternal—relatives have specific classifiers (e.g. *wahwah* 'man's sister's child'). The honorific general classifier, *sapwellime*, is composed of *sapwe* 'land' and *lime* 'hand, arm': this can be explained by a strong cultural link between high status and land ownership. In contrast, the all-purpose possessive classifier in humiliative speech, *tungoal*, means 'food, eating', and this correlates with the link between low status and food, or nourishment as the product of the land.

Possessive classifiers in Oceanic languages reflect aspects of culture. Fijian dialects of Eastern Viti Levu have a classifier for an object which the Possessor contributes 'as a customary obligation—a mat or pig for presentation at a feast, a house being built for a chief, or a spade to be used in a communal garden project'. This same marker (*loga-/laga-*) is also used as a relational classifier for totems in part of northeast Viti Levu.

Possession and its expression may reflect attitudes to what one may, and may not, own (see §6.3.1). In many Amazonian languages, objects of the natural world which exist without human intervention—including 'sun', 'forest', and 'water'—cannot be possessed, and are not used in possessive constructions.

Newly acquired cultural practices may influence the ways people talk about possessions. Traditionally, in the Siouan language Dakota 'natural objects like land, water, animals including the dog but excepting the horse cannot take the possessive pronoun, because under aboriginal conditions they could not be exclusive property of anyone' (Boas and Deloria 1941: 128). But 'at present the cattle on large ranches are considered as property and not as food. Therefore they are expressed as separable property by the prefix *t'a*'.

The Nanti, a Campa-speaking group in Peruvian Amazonia, did not used to consider land itself as being 'ownable'. Recently, the Nanti have been confronted with land disputes and land rights—and as a consequence, their speech practices have changed: one can now 'own' land. In West Greenlandic, the scope of the temporary possession marker *-ut(i)* 'appears to have been extended in use in recent years to include the notion of legal ownership (or other forms of formally or tacitly recognized possession)'.

14.4.4 *Personal pronouns, questions, and commands*

Relationships between people, and established hierarchies, are often reflected in personal pronouns. We can recall, from §9.1.2, how singular and non-singular pronominal forms may express politeness, respect, and deference. Many languages of Southeast Asia have large and elaborate systems of pronouns and address terms. Some are highly specialized, and can only be understood if one has some knowledge of the culture, religion, and social stratification. For instance, the first person pronoun *àattàmaa* in Thai is used by a Buddhist monk when speaking to a non-intimate layman or a lower-ranking monk. The second person pronoun *fàabàat* is used by a commoner when speaking to lower-ranking royalty.

In a number of Australian Aboriginal languages, personal pronouns reflect kinship relationships between people. The Arabana of South Australia were divided into two moieties. Back in the old days, marrying someone from the same moiety was 'like marrying your own sister' (Hercus 1994: 12). This restriction got somewhat relaxed as the traditional conventions fell into disuse. Personal pronouns reflect these relationships. For instance, the first person dual pronoun *alantha* 'we two' will be used if you and I belong to the same moiety. If we belong to different moieties, the form is *alakiya*.

Commands and directive speech acts also reflect relationships between people. A bare imperative form (see §7.2.1) may be considered too 'abrupt'. Another way of

framing a command, or an entreaty, may be used in order to sound 'nice', and to maintain the rules of etiquette, following societal requirements.

Imperative forms, and constraints on their use, may depend on how people are
related to each other. Yankunytjatjara, an Australian language, has a strict avoidance
relationship between a man and his parents-in-law. A mother-in-law's or father-in-
law's requests for food cannot be addressed directly at the son-in-law, and has to be
done through an intermediary. Even the intermediary's speech cannot contain a direct
command; it may be relayed using the quotative particle *kunyu* without any direct
command, or reference to asking, saying 'Your father-in-law says food-*kunyu*'.

Among the Arapaho of Oklahoma, it is only appropriate to use a direct imperative
to a child or a younger person who is expected to immediately comply. In interactions with older and respected people, one uses indirect imperative, as a token of
consideration.

This reflects a general tendency to avoid threatening and confronting situations, and
imposing one's own authority if unwarranted. Asking questions to seek information
is dispreferred in many Amazonian and Australian Aboriginal societies. Questions
are intrusive—information is volunteered rather than directly requested. This makes
communication smooth and minimally threatening.

Different languages classify human relationships in different ways. East Asian languages have highly sophisticated systems of 'honorification', reflecting social relationships between people. Korean distinguishes six levels of honorifics in statements,
questions and commands: plain, intimate, familiar, blunt, polite, and deferential. Rigid
social stratification and hierarchies help explain why a language may display extraor-
dinary complexity in pronouns, terms of address and ways of framing communication.

14.4.5 'To be precise': information source and attitudes to information

Information source is part of grammar in quite a few languages across the globe. Many
of the languages with grammatical information source, known as 'evidentiality', are
spoken by small communities. Being 'precise' as to how one knows what one is talking about is obligatory. Those who do not obey the requirement of being precise are
not to be trusted.

In the context of Amazonian societies, the requirement to be precise in one's information sources may be related to the common belief that there is an explicit cause—most
often, sorcery—for everything that happens. So as not to be blamed for something that
in fact they had no responsibility for, speakers are careful always to be as precise as possible about how they know things. If they are not, they run the danger of being accused
of sorcery, or just deemed unreliable. Those who have evidentials in their languages
complain that languages without evidentials—Portuguese and Spanish included—are
somehow deficient and inadequate. Hence the perception of 'white people'—those out-
siders who do not have information markers in their speech—as 'liars'.

The history of interactions between Indians and the White colonizers has been marked by conflict, bloodshed, and misunderstanding. In many South American countries, Indians are still considered the lowest of the low. Indians reciprocate: the White people have enviable resources and they are rich. But they are not to be relied on because of how they talk. When Indians speak contact languages—Spanish and Portuguese, they often try to say what is crucial in their mother tongues. A most important thing to say is 'how you know things'. Those who omit to say this are dangerous liars, unless they are not quite right in their head.

A missionary comes and starts preaching. He states that Adam ate the apple in the Garden of Eden—and uses visual or 'personal knowledge' evidential. An Aymara, a Tucano, or a Tariana speaker, looks at him suspiciously: has he really seen it? Could he have been present in the Garden of Eden? Or is he telling a lie?

A Peace Corps volunteer, reading from a book, states as personal knowledge that certain seeds yield good crops. An Aymara speaker looks at him with suspicion: 'he cannot possibly have seen this—is he trying to deceive us?' Those who come into Jaqi (Aymara) communities from outside and 'state as personal knowledge . . . facts which they know only through language (e.g. things they have read in books) are immediately categorized as cads, as people who behave more like animals than humans and, therefore, ought to be treated like animals, specifically, through the loss of linguistic interchange' (Hardman 1986: 133). The Aymara concern for a precise data source often results in misunderstandings and cultural 'clashes'. Miracle and Yapita Moya (1981: 53) mention incredulous responses of the Aymara to statements in some written texts like 'Columbus discovered America'; 'was the author actually there' to see? They react with incredulity to 'new (unseen) ideas' such as astronauts visiting the moon. This creates an image of socio-cultural conservatism. And, as a result, some Western writers see the Aymara as 'negative, unimaginative, suspicious, and sceptical'. Disregard for obligatory marking of information source in preparing information booklets on agriculture in Aymara led to their rejection by the people. A language-teaching primer prepared by a German linguistic team in 1980 suffered the same fate for the same reason.

Every Aymara child is taught two important proverbs: 'Seeing, one can say: "I have seen", without seeing one must not say I have seen' and 'Seeing, speak; without seeing, don't speak'. They reflect the paramount importance of vision as information source.

Attitudes towards information source among speakers of other languages with evidentials are similar. In a similar vein, McLendon (2003) reports the atttitudes of speakers of Eastern Pomo, a language with numerous evidentials:

Eastern Pomo speakers from whom I have learned Eastern Pomo since 1959, remembered that when they were children their grandparents constantly reminded them to be careful how they spoke. They were told to be especially careful to speak well to, and about, other people, because if they didn't the person spoken about, or to, might be offended and try to 'poison' them, that is, use ritual or other means to bring them misfortune, illness, or even death. Evidentials which distinguish non-visual sensory experience, inference, memory, and knowledge seem a useful means of speaking with care, asserting only what one has evidence for, and making one's evidence clear. (McLendon 2003: 113)

In Tariana and the surrounding Tucanoan languages information source in questions reflects the information source of the addressee. The cultural constraints on asking too many questions, and relatively low frequency of questions in everyday interaction, can be related to restrictions on taking for granted the other person's information source (if you get it wrong, you may be accused of sorcery).

Australian Aboriginal communities value explicitness. One should be as specific as possible in identification and in description. When R. M. W. Dixon enquired how to say in Dyirbal 'I know where the money is hidden', he was told that details had to be provided. One could say 'I saw where the money is hidden' or 'My father told me where the money is hidden'. In this language there is no verb 'to know'; it would simply be too vague. Only a few Australian languages have grammatical marking for information source. In others, this is achieved by lexical means.

It is definitely not the case that once you have evidentials in your language you have to be precise. In some languages with a small evidential system there may be a non-firsthand term which lacks the 'precision' of information source. There is no indication that many languages with just a reported evidential—such as Basque or Estonian—have a requirement to be 'precise'. Having evidentiality in the language does not mean that speakers have to be more truthful—one can very well tell a lie using a wrong evidential, or wrong information, on purpose. Similarly, having obligatory tense in your language does not make you more punctual.

A requirement to be precise correlates with the value placed by the community on a particular type of knowledge (which may be restricted). If something was seen, heard, inferred, and also assumed, the 'visual' source is likely to be the first option in a 'hierarchy' of evidential choices. Visual perception is the most 'valuable' source, and also the most trustworthy.

In many languages with evidentials, it is a feature which speakers are prepared to discuss. An evidential can be 'rephrased' with a verb of perception which roughly corresponds to its meaning. Being a 'good' speaker—proficient and 'correct' in one's evidential choice—is equated to a being a reliable citizen in numerous Amazonian societies. The requirement to be precise, and the importance of expressing oneself well, appear to be a major motivation for having evidentials in one's language. As Eberhard (2009) puts it,

The avoidance of being wrong is intrinsically related to the avoidance of losing face. The entire Mamaindê evidentiality system, then, may have the larger social function of providing the speaker with a way to avoid losing face within a society where one's words are connected to one's character. (Eberhard 2009: 469)

Epistemological expressions (which subsume evidentials) tell us something about the speech community. They may be used to show power, authority, and agency. An omniscient shaman 'sees' everything. That his special knowledge can be cast in visual evidential highlights his power and authority.

Being specific as to one's information source appears to correlate with the size of a community. In a small community everyone keeps an eye on everyone else, and the more precise one is in indicating how information was acquired, the less the danger of gossip, accusation, and so on. No wonder that most languages with highly complex evidential systems are spoken by small communities. On the other hand, why is it that some languages spoken in small closed communities have only a reported evidential? Fortescue (2003) is also convincing when he speculates that

> presumably life in very small, scattered Arctic communities, where everyone is likely to know of everyone else's doings and where rumours spread easily, is such as to make being VAGUE [emphasis mine] about one's source of information . . . a generally sensible strategy. (Fortescue 2003: 301)

At present, all that can be suggested is that some communities in some areas—for instance, in the Amazonian area, and those in the adjoining Andean region—in some way share a common set of beliefs, mental attitudes, and behavioural conventions, as well as discourse genres; and that these are compatible with the independent development of evidential systems with their requirement to be as precise and as specific as possible about information source. This could help explain why evidentiality has independently evolved in at least six (possibly, more) places in Amazonia, and also why it is so susceptible to being diffused through language contact.

14.4.6 *Attitudes, beliefs, and practices through grammar*

Attitudes to future and beliefs may shape further parts of the grammar. The Mennonite Anabaptists in Canada are fully committed to the subordination of their own will to the will of God. So, the people—who speak Pennsylvania German—do not feel comfortable talking about the future: this to them sounds arrogant. Instead of saying 'I will come', they would use a more tentative expression, such as 'I figure on coming', 'I plan on coming', 'I am supposed to come', or 'I am counting on coming'. The verb *zehle* 'count' can in fact be used for predictions. *Es zehlt gedanst waerre*, literally, 'it counts to be dancing', means 'There will be dancing'. But no matter how grammaticalized the verb is as a future marker, it does retain some of its former sense of 'counting on'. What explains the rather unusual grammaticalization path from 'counting' to 'future' is the attitudes, and the beliefs of the speakers.

Other attempts have been made to relate cultural and cognitive patterns to other grammatical categories. Amazonian languages are known for a special grammatical category of 'frustrative', with the meaning of 'I want to but I can't'. At the end of an incisive account of this category in Amahuaca and other Panoan languages, Sparing-Chávez (2003: 12) attempts to provide a culture-specific correlate for this category in the Amahuaca society: 'The Amahuaca people are shame-oriented and it seems to me that the frustrative helps them to save face by covering up their own shortcomings. They blame others, natural forces, or circumstances. It also helps them to express disagreement or carefully accuse someone without having face-to-face confrontation.'

The lack of large indigenous systems of number words in many Amazonian and Australian languages may well reflect the absence of counting as a cultural practice. We can recall, from §9.5, that in many minority languages of Amazonia number words form a very small class—typically, 'one', 'two', 'three', and then 'many'. In all likelihood, they traditionally did not have any counting routine. Forms nowadays translated as 'one', 'two', and 'three' may not have been used for enumeration. 'One' would have meant '(be) alone', 'two' would refer to '(be) a pair', and 'three' to 'a few'.

These meanings are still there in a few languages. For instance, in Kwaza, an isolate from Amazonia, the number word 'one', *tei-*, also means 'be one, alone', 'two', *aky-*, means 'to be two, company', and three, *e'mã*, means 'one more, again; without companion'. Hixkaryana, a Carib language, has only three number words—*towenyxa* 'one, alone, singly', *asako* 'two, a couple or so', and *osorwano* 'three, a few'. Jarawara, an Arawá language from Southern Amazonia, is likely not to have had any conventionalized number words as such, before contact with Europeans. Dixon (2012: 75–6) hypothesizes that there were two verbs, *-ohari(ha)-* 'be alone, be the only (one/thing)'—as in 'I'm going alone'—and *-fama-* 'be a pair, be a couple with'—as in 'These two men's names are a pair' (that is, 'These two men have the same name'). After contact, *-ohari(ha)-* and *-fama-* must have acquired additional meanings: their meanings were extended to 'be one' and 'be two', in the same semantic set as *terei -na-* 'be three', *tee-na* 'be ten' and other borrowed number words.

Along similar lines, Kenneth L. Hale (1975) suggested that Warlpiri and other Australian Aboriginal languages originally lacked number words as a separate class. Determiners with quantitative meanings were reinterpreted as number words under the impact of Western culture. That is, the absence of a cultural practice may partly determine the stucture, and the composition, of a word class.

The notion of competition, and thus comparison, is intrinsic to many societies. Competition can relate to any activity—including procuring enemies' heads, and also sports. There is then an appropriate set of lexemes, to do with 'winning', 'losing', competing, and so on. Small and egalitarian societies—such as the Makú-speaking groups and Jarawara in Amazonia—did not have traditional competitions or winning, and thus lack words to express these notions. We can recall, from §11.1.4, that some minority languages hardly use comparative constructions. Many of them are spoken by communities in which there is little in terms of institutionalized competition.

These explanations are tantalizing: they seem to allow us to have a sneaky glimpse of what makes the language the way it is. But how far can we go?

14.5 The question 'why?': explanation and prediction

The question 'why is a language the way it is?' does not warrant a single answer. When we look for extralinguistic explanations for linguistic categories, we should avoid the danger of being circular. Do Tucano or Quechua have an elaborate system of evidentials because of a cultural requirement to be precise about one's information source lest one is accused of sorcery? Or is the explanation the other way round?

Language is not some kind of independent algebraic-type system. It only has existence as a tool through which its community of users interact with each other and with the world around them. In keeping with this, external factors may be partly responsible for language change. A group moves into a new region and has to acquire names for plants, animals, and perhaps also types of geographical and other features which they had never seen before.

Further factors may include attitudes to the use of one's own and others' languages, types of political organization, economic practices—such as methods of food production—and socio-cultural attitudes of all kinds. If inter-group marriage is encouraged, a woman who goes to live in the husband's community will naturally learn that language but may also transmit her own tongue to children, so that the language of the next generation bears a substratum of her language.

These factors may allow us to explain some things. But we will hardly ever be able to precisely predict which way a language will develop.

Let's get back to genders, classifiers, and their meanings. Gender systems rarely encode information about the function of an object. This is why one hardly ever finds correlations between functional aspects of material and spiritual culture and the semantics of genders assigned to inanimates. Australian languages, with a special gender encompassing 'non-flesh food', are a notable exception to this.

The predictive power of these correlations is, however, rather limited. It is quite understandable that classifier languages spoken in hunter-and-gatherer societies (as in Aboriginal Australia) with their heavy reliance on vegetable food growing in the bush, would have a special classifier for non-flesh food. However, classifier languages—such as Dâw or Nambiquara—spoken within other hunter-and-gatherer societies in other parts of the world do not have such a class.

Human categorization, as a sort of 'social' function, is likely to correlate with social structure. Animacy and sex, when extended metaphorically, are often influenced by social stereotypes and beliefs. In quite a few cases we can explain what social, cultural, or even environmental parameter a classifier correlates with, in a given society. But we will never be able to fully predict the ways in which non-linguistic parameters would be reflected in the grammar of a language. The example of the lack of a vegetable-food class outside Australia was mentioned above. One would expect Japanese, a language with a well-developed system of honorifics, to have a well-developed system of classifiers reflecting different social statuses—just like Korean. However, unlike Korean, Japanese has just one honorific classifier (*mei*).

These words of caution should not discourage the grammarian from seeking extra-linguistic and other motivation for the emergence of language structures. On the contrary: the more we learn about the shaping of grammatical structures, the more tantalizing the clues that lie ahead. Revealing interactions between the language, and the world, will make the grammar come alive.

Notes and sources

§14.1. See Aikhenvald (2008: 377–407) on Manambu; Wilson (1980: 63–5); Kundama et al. (2006: 132) on Ambulas/Wosera.

§14.2.1. For the etymologies mentioned here, see Barnhart (2008: 1202), Corominas (1954: 83); Gastambide Arrillaga (1990: 15), Aikhenvald (2014) and Aikhenvald (2012a: 63–8) for words of Amazonian origin in English. Forms cognate to Taino *hamaca* are attested in Maipure *amaca*, Piapoco *amàca*, Tariana, Yucuna *hamaca*, Waurá *amaca* (see Aikhenvald forthcoming-b); see Topping (1973: 166–9) on Chamorro. See Owens (1996) on Nigerian Arabic; see Li and Thompson (1981: 496–7), Chao (1968: 703) on Mandarin Chinese. See Chirikba (2008) on how Armenian was influenced by other languages; see Fries and Pike (1949) and §4.1.5 on Mazateco; see Matthews (2007) on contact-induced patterns in Cantonese. See Campbell (1997: 340), and Baugh (1957: 120, 194) on borrowing personal pronouns in English. Brody (1995) provides further examples of borrowed discourse markers; see Appel and Muysken (2005: 172–3) for Spanish borrowings in Quechua. See Aikhenvald (2002b: 5–6) on the Vaupés River Basin linguistic area; see Fodor (1984), and Tauli (1984) on puristic tendencies in European languages.

§14.2.2. See Aikhenvald (2006a) and references there on the definitions of linguistic areas. A concise summary of Balkans as a linguistic area is in Friedman (2006). Similarities between Australian languages were systematically accounted for by areal diffusion and contact by Dixon (2002). Long-standing language contact between Indo-Aryan and Dravidian languages in the village of Kupwar in India have also resulted in extreme convergence; see Gumperz and Wilson (1971), and also Nadkarni (1975) and Emeneau (1956) on India as a linguistic area. See Aikhenvald (2002b and 2006a) on the Vaupés River Basin Linguistic area.

§14.3. See Aikhenvald (2008: 201–22, 385–406) on Manambu; Dixon (2010a: 15–17) for topographic deixis in Australian languages including Dyirbal. Many attempts to establish a straightforward connection between grammar and physical environment sound at best dubious. For instance, it has been suggested that those people who live in damp areas will 'select sounds requiring minimal lip opening', or that those people who live in mountainous areas will develop 'sounds characterised by large expanse of air from enlarged thoracic capacity' (see Brosnahan 1961: 19; and further examples in Dixon 1994: 214–15). Such crack-pot suggestions have thrown some doubt over the very idea of correlating environment and language structure.

§14.4. The interested reader will find further studies of possible correlations between cultural and linguistic patterns in papers in Enfield (2004), Mathiot (1979), Trudgill (2011), Storch (2011) and Dixon (2012: 434–54).

§14.4.1. See the informative survey in Baron (1986: 193–5), and further cross-linguistic studies in Aikhenvald (2012a, 2013a). See Chafe (1967: 13–16) on feminine as a functionally unmarked gender in Seneca; Chafe (2004: 99–107) on the expression of feminine and masculine gender in Iroquoian, Caddoan, and other North American Indian languages; Dixon (2004a: 186–7) on Jarawara; Aikhenvald (2000, 2013a) on social correlates of meanings of genders in New Guinea and other areas.

§14.4.2. See Breedveld (1995: 70–1) on Fulfulde; Juntanamalaga (1988: 320–1) on Thai; Adams (1989: 63) on how the Khmer Rouge revolution affected the social order, terms of address, and honorific classifiers.

§14.4.3. See Seiler (1977: 306) on Cahuilla; Keating (1997: 249, 253, 264) on Ponapean; Carpenter (1986: 18–19) on Thai; Geraghty (2000: 246) on Fijian; Aikhenvald (2012a: 169–70) on possession in Amazonian languages, and Michael (2013) on Nanti.

§14.4.4. See Iwasaki and Ingkaphirom (2005: 49) on Thai; Hercus (1994: 116–18) on Arabana, Dixon (2002: 283–4) for an overview of kinship-determined pronouns in Australian languages; Goddard (1983: 306–7) on Yankunytjatjara; Cowell (2007) on Arapaho, Aikhenvald (2010: 303–12; 219–23) on interpersonal relationships in imperatives; Sohn (1994: 9–10) on Korean.

§14.4.5. See Aikhenvald (2004a, 2004b, 2004c) for a summary of cultural conventions and evidentials, and the papers in Aikhenvald and Dixon (2014). Weber (1986: 138) discusses Quechua cultural postulates which point in the same direction. See Silver and Miller (1997: 36) and especially Hardman (1986: 133–5) on Aymara; Aikhenvald (2003: 311–19) on Tariana. See Eberhard (2009: 468), on Mamaindê, and Aikhenvald (2012a: 272–8) on other Amazonian languages.

§14.4.6. See Burridge (2004: 223–6) on Pennsylvania German. See Aikhenvald (2012a: 353–60) on counting practices in Amazonia; van der Voort (2004: 214–18) on Kwaza; Derbyshire (1985: 1) on Hixkaryana.

§14.5. See Downing (1996: 157) on Japanese classifiers.

15

How to create a grammar
and how to read one

Putting a grammar together is a considerable and rewarding task, as the grammarian unveils the structures of a previously undescribed or poorly understood language. An ideal reference grammar will combine comprehensive descriptions of the facts of the language with their analysis, justified, and argued for. Describing a language is inseparable from interpreting it, and thus analysing it, in a particular framework, with a judicious choice of terms and their explanation.

15.1 Putting a grammar together

The order of the chapters in this book roughly reflects the conventional presentation of information within a reference grammar. One is expected to proceed from the social and cultural setting of the language to its phonetic and phonological make-up, and from then on to its basic building units. That is, most grammars discuss morphological features before embarking on syntax, and only then go on to features of discourse, interaction, and issues in semantics.

15.1.1 What goes into a grammar

A grammar should reflect the society, and make the language—and the culture—of its speakers come alive, through judicious choice of examples and background explanation. Ideally, a grammar writer needs to show how language and culture are intertwined. A grammar should include a selection of texts of varied genres (about 30 printed pages), and a vocabulary. Examples from texts can be referred to in various sections of the grammar, as an addition to other specific illustrative examples. This cross-referencing will help keep the grammar to a manageable size, and link the texts with the points made in the body of the book.

A number of hints as to how to organize a grammar were given in §1.7.4. The principles of organization and cross-referencing (including numbering of examples and glossing) are to be clearly stated in a special section on conventions (this section may also include abbreviations). This same section may contain an outline of the structure of the grammar and justification for how chapters are ordered. Alternatively, the discussion of the structure of the book can be placed at the end of the first chapter. For instance, if you decide to discuss grammatical relations before any other aspect of grammar, this needs to be explicitly stated.

An introduction, or the first chapter of a grammar, is expected to address the whereabouts of the language, its genetic relatives, and its neighbours. This chapter should also include as many cultural and societal features of the people as is reasonable, and relevant for understanding the grammar. The introductory chapter also requires a typological profile of the language: this can be thought of as a road-map for the whole book, helping readers to see what they will encounter within the grammar.

A chapter on the phonology and phonetics should ideally follow the introductory chapter. This chapter lays out the significant sounds of the language. It is conventional to start with segmental phonology, and then proceed to syllable structure and suprasegmental features. From then on a grammar writer is expected to discuss the structure of the phonological word (a grammar would be incomplete if one does not), and how it relates to the grammatical word. There may be a separate chapter on phonological and morphophonological processes. Alternatively, these may be included in the chapter on phonology.

However, the exact order of presentation is dictated by the logic of a language. One can discuss syllable structure before segmental phonology, but will need to offer justification for this.

A chapter on word classes is absolutely necessary in every grammar. It needs to discuss the open and closed classes in the language, with a summary justification of each, and a summary statement of their morphological and syntactic features (and also phonological and semantic properties, if relevant). Within the word class chapter, the description of each word class may be presented as a summary, with more detailed discussions to follow in separate chapters (if there is appropriate complexity to justify this). For instance, the chapter on word classes may simply list categories of nouns and of verbs. These can then be addressed separately, according a chapter to each. Some grammar writers choose to have one summary chapter for open classes, and a separate one for closed classes. The exact choice—how much to include where—depends on the demands of the language.

Derivations which change word class may serve as a criterion for distinguishing them. It is then logical to discuss word-class changing derivations in a word class chapter.

Typical categories of nouns include reference classification—genders (sometimes called noun classes) and classifiers of various types, number, possession classes, case, and definiteness and specificity. There may be some noun-specific derivations which do change word class, and some which do not. New nouns may be formed through compounding. For each type of compound, it is crucial to ascertain whether it forms one phonological word, and whether it can be proved that it forms one grammatical word (and thus is a compound and not a noun phrase).

A grammar has to contain a statement of the structure of a noun phrase. This can be included in a chapter on word classes, or in a special chapter on noun categories, or put later on in a chapter dealing with syntactic structures. Or the grammar writer may choose to have a special chapter on how a noun phrase is organized.

There is no limit on the number of chapters you might want to have in the grammar. A grammar with many short chapters is more user-friendly than one with a small number of lengthy chapters.

Typical verbal categories include non-spatial setting (including modality, tense, aspect, evidentiality, and reality status), valency-changing derivations, and also noun incorporation. Verbs can be derived from other word classes; or new verbs may be formed from other verbs. A section on the structure of verbal word and verbal phrase can be separate, or included as part of a general chapter on verbs.

Multi-verb constructions—including serial verb constructions, and constructions with auxiliary verbs and support verbs—may warrant a separate chapter each. Or they may be included into a more general chapter on verbs.

A grammar may warrant a special chapter on adjectives and various types of verbal modifiers ('adverbs'). Closed classes—including personal pronouns, demonstratives, articles, interrogatives, indefinites, and adpositions (prepositions and postpositions)— may warrant a separate chapter each, depending on the complexity of the system. Or there may be one chapter dealing with all of these. Interrogatives and indefinites often span a variety of word classes: they can be noun-like, adjective-like, or verb-like. It is still advisable to consider them together rather than splitting them across other chapters, to facilitate discussion of interrogative clauses in a later chapter.

A statement of clause types and sentence types is absolutely vital in every grammar. It will address the classification of clauses:

(a) in terms of the type of predicate (e.g. copula clauses, verbless clauses, transitive and intransitive clauses);
(b) in terms of their syntactic functions (e.g. main clauses, relative clauses, complement clauses, and adverbial clauses);
(c) in terms of the speech act they reflect (that is, declarative, interrogative and imperative, and also exclamative).

Clause linking, complex clauses, and discourse parameters should each be addressed in separate chapters. Some grammarians choose to include a special chapter on the effects of language contact. There may be a chapter on the language's history and putative developments from the proto-language, and a chapter—or a section—on some striking features of lexical semantics and semantic fields.

Some categories and issues may not be confined to just one chapter. Take grammatical relations. These may be expressed by case, by bound pronouns on verbs, and also through constituent order. Grammatical relations are also relevant for clause types. The question of 'where do I discuss grammatical relations?' may be a source of concern for a grammar writer. There is no single answer to it. A grammarian may choose to have a special chapter dealing with grammatical relations in the language, pulling it all together. Or they may discuss them together with clause types, leaving some of the discussion for a section on cases or bound pronouns on verbs. One must of course avoid repetition between chapters. But a grammar is one book and one unified whole. Cross-referencing between chapters will help create a general picture.

Every language has clausal negation. Negation can be marked on the verb, or it can be marked with an independent form not attached to any particular word class. In some languages, a constituent (for instance, a noun phrase) can be negated. The structure of a language may warrant a discussion of negation in a separate chapter, or in a chapter dealing with verbal categories. Or it may be appropriately discussed in several chapters. Where it is addressed depends on what works best for the language. A good subject index will draw all the relevant instances together.

Many languages have morphemes with a number of functions. The same set of morphemes can be used as case markers on nouns and as clause-linking devices, as in Kham (something we saw in §12.2.3). It appears logical to discuss their case-marking function both in the chapter on noun categories and in the chapter on grammatical relations. These discussions should be accompanied with brief mention of their polyfunctionality, and cross-references to the chapter dealing with clause linking techniques. Their clause-linking functions can be analysed in that chapter (again, with mention of polyfunctionality and cross-references to where the case functions are described). Efficient cross-referencing and brief summaries will help avoid unnecessary repetition. A further aid for readers could be to have a list of affixes at the end of the grammar, accompanied with translations, glosses, and references to where they are discussed.

Drafts of the introduction, of a chapter on phonology, and one on word classes are usually prepared at an early stage of grammatical analysis. They may have to be refined and even rewritten as the analysis proceeds. This is because in the process of grammatical analysis one often finds additional features. For example, while analysing relative clauses, one may discover a new intonation pattern. This will be added to the chapter on phonology. Additional criteria for word classes might be discovered while analysing clause types. As a consequence, some of the initial chapters often have to be finalized after all the other chapters have been written (as was mentioned in Chapters 2 and 5).

15.1.2 *Synchrony meets diachrony*

A reference grammar is primarily synchronic—the language is analysed as it is at a given point in time. How much information on other, related or neighbouring, languages to include in a grammar depends on how relevant it is, and how much is known.

Tariana, the only Arawak language spoken in the multilingual linguistic area of the Vaupés River Basin, has undergone significant influence from neighbouring languages. A grammar of Tariana would have been incomplete without mention of contact-induced changes, how the language differs from its genetic relatives. and what has been inherited from the proto-language. Anong, a Tibeto-Burman language spoken in Thailand, has undergone restructuring under the influence of Thai; this makes Anong look different from its Tibeto-Burman relatives. A chapter on contact-induced changes in the Anong grammar (Sun and Liu 2009) is more than welcome.

In his grammar of Jarawara, an Arawá language from southern Amazonia, Dixon (2004a) includes comparison of Jarawara with other languages of the family in just a few instances. His grammar has a special chapter on the prehistory of Jarawara which 'recapitulates some of the unusual and apparently irregular features of Jarawara grammar, and suggests a diachronic scenario' with a tentative explanation (2004a: 566). For instance, obligatorily possessed nouns, feminine *tame* 'her foot' and masculine *teme* 'his foot', are, at present, distinguished only by the vowel in their first syllable. Historically, they have derived from proto-Arawá **tama-ni* 'her foot' and **teme-ni* 'his foot' respectively. This chapter is a step towards explaining 'why' Jarawara has developed the way it has.

In many languages one can see the effects of historical processes, such as reanalysis and grammaticalization. In Hup, a Makú language from north-west Amazonia, many verbal roots have become grammatical morphemes with aspectual meanings. In her grammar, Epps (2008: 149–57) explicitly discusses grammaticalization processes, so as to make clear the 'architecture' of grammatical words in Hup. Such discussion can be made in a separate section, or, if relevant, in a section dealing with a particular morpheme.

Adding a historical diachronic facet to a synchronic description may shed some light on the reasons why a form, or a construction, has come about, and how this may have happened. The processes of grammaticalization and reanalysis take place gradually over some time. Incomplete grammaticalization may create additional issues, both for the analysis, and for its presentation in a grammar.

15.1.3 *Analysis, presentation, and argumentation*

A reference grammar is a product of linguistic analysis. However, the way in which one proceeds as analyst, and the way one presents the analysis in a grammar, do not have to coincide. It took me a while to realize that Manambu has a phonological process of rhotic dissimilation. According to this process, the second of two rhotics in adjacent syllables undergo dissimilation in the word-final syllable (which does not contain a long vowel). The majority of examples involve the suffix *-(V)r* 'allative/instrumental' added to a stem ending in *r*. In these instances, the suffix undergoes dissimilation *r → l*, as in *jagər* 'garfish', allative *jagrəl* 'to a garfish'; *ar* 'lake', allative *aral* 'to a lake'. I first heard the form *aral* 'to a lake' from an elderly speaker who was discussing her fishing expedition on a lake the following day. I wrote the form down as a curious fact, and then started paying attention to other similar forms. I soon found out that this dissimilation also applies to loans, for example *kar* 'car', *karal* 'to a car'. Then I discovered that the process does not apply if the last syllable contains a long vowel, as in *kwarəb* 'jungle', allative *kwarbá:r* 'to a jungle'. Later on, I realized that many urban speakers of Manambu, including my main teacher of the language, do use forms like *arar* 'to a lake', instead of *aral*, and violate the principle of rhotic dissimilation.

A reader of my Manambu grammar will have no idea of how this process was discovered. All I present in the book is the result. I do draw readers' attention to interspeaker variation—such as the fact that even some older speakers who live outside the Manambu-speaking villages may occasionally lose rhotic dissimilation. Such variation is how Manambu is currently spoken, and has to be reflected in the grammar.

A grammar writer should indeed include as much information on individual variation as appropriate, and include a measure of explanation. Some variants can be particularly favoured by older people. There may be gender-specific variation: some forms may be used by women, others by men. If two constructions appear to be interchangeable, and speakers say that they 'mean the same thing', the difference between the two may be pragmatic.

REMEMBER: One can never explain everything in a language. But saying that some forms are in 'free' variation is the grammarian's last resort.

The special beauty of grammar writing lies in exploring various analytical options, and offering arguments in favour and against them. For example, sequences of vocalic segments in a language may be analysed as one vocalic nucleus (a diphthong), or as several (a vowel sequence) (see §4.1.3). Box 4.1 contains some suggestions of how to go about distinguishing a complex segment from a unitary one. When one faces such an issue, it is advisable to explicitly discuss the options, and the advantages of each. In his comprehensive grammar of Cavineña, Antoine Guillaume (2008: 32–5) excels in offering alternative analyses of complex consonantal segments *ty, dy, ts, ch, ny*, and *kw*. He concludes that they are best considered as unitary segments, since (a) speakers always pronounce them together at the onset of a syllable, (b) the language does not allow consonant clusters, and (c) if a CV is reduplicated, the whole complex consonant is reduplicated, as if it were one unit (e.g. *jikwi-* 'cut off', *jikwi-kwi=sha* 'cut off many times', and not **jikwi-wi=sha*).

Languages tend to develop gradually. In the synchronic state of a given language, a process of grammaticalization may turn out to be incomplete, and still in process. Motion verbs as minor verbs within serial verb constructions (discussed in §7.6.1) may gradually develop into directional prepositions (this process, pervasive in Oceanic languages, was discussed at length by Durie 1988, Lichtenberk 2008: 465–6, and other scholars in that field). The forms may still retain some verbal features: for instance, in Toqabaqita they take object affixes. These in-between forms can be analysed as exceptional prepositions, or as defective verbs. In some languages they may be more verbal than in others. A comprehensive grammar should discuss their verbal and prepositional features, and the degree and direction of grammaticalization.

We can recall, from §7.1, that Cavineña has a set of eight directional and postural suffixes, including *-jara* 'lie, be in lying position', *-ani* 'sit, be in sitting position', *-neti/-nitya* 'stand, be in standing position', *-sikwa* 'direction of going away'. All of them, except *-sikwa*, occur as independent verbs. Guillaume (2008: 320) notes that postural and directional markers could well be analysed as serialized verbs rather than suffixes. He chooses to analyse them as suffixes because the directional *-sikwa* cannot be used as an independent verb. This allows the analyst to treat them all in the same way.

The question of explanation—'why' the language is the way it is—may warrant a special chapter. Or it may be most effective to distribute explanatory ideas and hypotheses throughout the grammar. A well-constructed subject index (de rigueur in a comprehensive grammar) will help pull it all together.

15.1.4 *Making the most of language examples*

Every statement one makes in a reference grammar has to be proved—that is, corroborated by illustrative examples. To illustrate a point, one may start with a simple example. For instance, to illustrate a reciprocal construction, a short sentence like 'They fought each other' will be useful. If you want to explicitly say what kind of construction does not exist, you may just occasionally include a starred, or an ungrammatical, example of what one cannot say.

Ideally, there should always be an example from a real-life narrative or a conversation. Perfect examples are those which do not just illustrate a grammatical phenomenon, but also reflect something about the speakers' culture, social conventions, and lore. The people who speak the language should come alive through the examples in a grammar.

In order to make the analysis transparent and easy to follow, it is advisable to put multiword constituents in brackets, indicating their syntactic functions with a subscript. This includes stating whether a noun phrase is in A (transitive subject), S (intransitive subject), or O (the transitive object) function.

A grammar needs to contain an appropriate number of examples (to keep it to a reasonable size). It is best to give one or two illustrative examples for each phenomenon one wishes to illustrate, and avoid scores of similar examples which will bore the reader.

However, a word of caution is in order. Textual examples can be long, hard to parse, and contain more points than the grammar writer wishes to illustrate. Then an example can be shortened. An alternative is to refer to an example from the short selection of texts at the end of the grammar. The advantage of this is that the reader will have access to the context of the example.

Some linguistic phenomena in a language are more frequent than others. Information about frequency of a form, or construction, is useful to include if available. In his summary article on serial verb constructions, Dixon (2006b: 338) mentions the differences in textual frequency of serial verb constructions between the languages discussed in the volume which Dixon's article summarizes. In Tariana, more than 70 per cent of textual clauses include a serial verb. In Ewe, Eastern Kayah Li, and Dumo, between 20 and 50 per cent do so. Serial verb constructions in Mwotlap, Toqabaqita, and Lakota occur only in 5–20 per cent of clauses, while in Khwe they occur in less than 1 per cent of clauses. These facts are relevant for establishing the functional load of a construction, and how important it is in the language.

15.1.5 On linguistic terminology

In order to make yourself, and your grammar, understood, you need to be clear and explicit in using linguistic terminology (see §1.7.3). Whichever term you use, be consistent, clear, and explain its meaning well.

Some terms in linguistics are well-established. A grammar writer does not have to explain basic terms, such as phonemes, allophones, morphemes, affixes, negation, tense, aspect, and gender. A grammar that provides a definition of every single grammatical term (as if it were an elementary textbook in general linguistics) is bound to be pedantic, drawn out, and boring. However, some terms which have come on to the linguistic scene relatively recently could well have to be explained. For example, a brief definition of 'mirativity' (grammaticalized expression of surprise) or 'serial verb constructions' may be handy if the grammar writer wants to make sure their readers follow. These definitions will be accompanied by references to the relevant sources. An alternative could be a brief glossary of terms at the end of the grammar.

Ideally, a grammar writer should consider framing their discussion within a typological perspective. Linguistic typologists are among the primary readership of any grammar. Linguistic typology involves a comprehensive investigation of parameters for cross-linguistic variation in languages, with the aim of uncovering and understanding the range of structures and means available in human languages. It also involves establishing cross-linguistic generalizations that hold for all, or most, human languages. A grammar writer needs to show how a structure found in the language under consideration accords with established parameters of cross-linguistic variation, and perhaps expands them. For example, in analysing noun incorporation, a grammar writer ought to consult the typological parameters formulated in Mithun (1984), to see if they apply, and how.

If a language displays a phenomenon which the grammar writer considers unusual, a typological perspective is highly welcome. Tamambo, an Oceanic language from Vanuatu, displays a correlation between irrealis and habitual aspect. In her incisive grammar of Tamambo, Jauncey (2011: 302–4) offers brief justification for this uncommon connection, providing a number of references and typological analogies to justify the connection between irrealis and habituality in the language she is analysing.

A brief cross-linguistic characterization of a linguistic phenomenon at the beginning of a chapter may offer additional help to a reader.

To know what is unusual and what is not, a grammarian needs to be well-read. It is essential to have read, in some detail, several good grammars, some in one's area of expertise, and some in other areas. This is a way of acquiring a good feel for cross-linguistic variation, and learning how to write a grammar.

Analysing a language is a journey of discovery. Putting an analysis out as a coherent piece of work, and sharing it with others, is yet another journey, perhaps equally exciting. Reading a grammar, and taking it all in, is an integral part of this act of sharing.

15.2 To read a grammar

Ideally, a grammar—just like any book, be it a scholarly monograph, or a novel—should be read as a coherent whole. Reading the grammar from beginning to end rather than choosing topics selectively is the key to getting into the spirit of the language, and understanding the author's line of thought and argumentation. All this is trivial and common sense; yet, many self-proclaimed typologists—many of whom have never done fieldwork (let alone written a grammar themselves)—scour grammars for one particular category or meaning, without taking in the whole thing. As a result, their account is typically deficient.

A grammar is written as an integrated whole. To understand what follows, one needs to have digested what precedes. The reader is urged to study a grammar from beginning to end, as one would read most books, and not as a random selection of essays on whatever grammatical topic takes their fancy.

As was mentioned in Chapter 2, a summary linguistic profile of the language at the very start of the grammar will highlight its most distinctive and noteworthy features. This is a way of letting your readership know what to expect.

To facilitate the readers' task, a grammar may contain some indications as to how it can be read. Paraphrasing Dixon's words (2005: xiii), a grammar 'is, of course, designed to be read from first to last page. But other strategies are possible'. Chapter 3 of Dixon's grammar of Jarawara provides an overview of the main points of the grammar. Later chapters deal with particular grammatical topics, and 'assume familiarity with the information given in Chapter 3'. Chapter 2 offers a detailed discussion of highly complex phonological rules in this language; Dixon (2004a: xviii) suggests that 'it is not necessary to read the whole of Chapter 2 before consulting the grammatical chapters'. The reader is advised to look at the general statement of vowels and consonants, and an overview of phonological rules—without these they may have difficulties taking in the rest of the grammar.

It is highly advisable to include notes on the structure of the grammar and the most appropriate way of reading it either in the introductory chapter or in a special section on conventions—like creating a road-map of what is to come. Some chapters within a grammar may be less integral than the rest. Some could be read independently, just for the sake of the phenomena described there. For example, Chapter 18 of my grammar of Tariana (Aikhenvald 2003), dealing with serial verb constructions and verb compounding, is a fairly self-contained analysis of these structures and can be read in isolation (after some acquaintance with the language's profile and its general features, outlined in Chapter 1). But Chapter 19, on complex predicates and multi-verb constructions (other than serial verbs) has to be read after Chapter 18—otherwise it would be hard to understand.

Chapter 3, 'Grammatical relations', of my grammar of Manambu (Aikhenvald 2008) is essential for understanding the rest of the grammar: without reading it, even the glossing of examples may not make sense. But the detailed discussion of phonological rules in Chapter 2 can be skimmed, if the reader is more keen to learn about morphology, syntax, and semantics. Chapter 22, dealing with genetic and areal relationships of the language, can be read on its own, in conjunction with the relevant parts of the introductory chapter, detailing the socio-cultural background of the Manambu, and the linguistic family Manambu belongs to. An anthropologist or a lexicographer interested in semantic notions in a Papuan language from the East Sepik might just read parts of Chapter 21, 'Issues in semantics and features of lexicon'.

It is not necessary for a scholar interested in some particular aspect of language to read every word of the grammar. However, it is important for them to look at all sections that may be relevant to the topic in hand. Someone interested in reciprocals should look at the appropriate chapter of the grammar, but should also follow through cross-references to other parts, including perhaps grammatical relations, noun phrase structure, and clause types.

The texts at the end of the grammar should be carefully chosen to provide maximum exemplification of as many significant grammatical patterns as possible. However, thirty or so pages of texts can never cover every facet of the language. It will always be the case that a number of significant properties of a language will be scarcely exemplified in a small selection of texts.

Examples within a grammar should be read and thought through, based on the glosses, which reveal what they mean and how they are structured in the language under study. The way examples are translated often does not reflect the actual structure of the language. Sadly, some arm-chair typologists and self-proclaimed proponents of time-line theories read just the translations of examples and draw ill-informed conclusions on the basis of the structure of the language in which the grammar is written. This is a lamentable malpractice to be avoided.

In summary: to make the most of a grammar one reads, it is important to follow the author's argumentation, and gradually come to understand the structure of the language as it is being uncovered. In turn, the grammar writer must endeavour to maintain standards of clarity, cohesion, and precision of argumentation throughout their work (mentioned in §1.7.2).

15.3 Envoi: the makings of a reference grammar

In Antoine Meillet's words (1926: 16), 'a language makes up . . . a system in which everything holds together' (see §1.4.1). And so does a reference grammar, which will form the major part of documenting the language for the present-day readership and for posterity.

A model reference grammar makes the language come alive and live on. No language is boring, simple, or 'primitive'. Sadly, some grammars are. It is important that your grammar does not fall into this category.

Glossary of terms

This short glossary explains the ways in which some core linguistic terms are used throughout this book. Where appropriate, I give the number of a section where a particular point is discussed in detail, or for which it is relevant. Complementary terms are marked as Compl. Synonyms are marked as Syn.

A: subject of a transitive verb, a core syntactic function.

ABESSIVE: a marker indicating that something or someone is absent, meaning 'without' something or someone (see §6.4). Syn: PRIVATIVE.

ABLATIVE: a marker indicating movement away from an object or a person. See §6.4.

ABSOLUTIVE: case inflection marking intransitive subject (S) and transitive object (O). Compl: ERGATIVE (see §6.4, §§10.4–10.5).

ABSOLUTIVE-ERGATIVE SYSTEM: a system of grammatical marking whereby A is marked with ergative case, and S and O are marked in the same way with absolutive case (see §6.4, §§10.4–10.5).

ACCENT: a prosody realized through auditory prominence within a PHONOLOGICAL WORD, characterized by some or all of loudness, pitch, vowel quality, and length. Syn: STRESS (see §4.2).

ACCUSATIVE: case inflection marking transitive object (O) (see §6.4, §10.3). Compl: NOMINATIVE.

ACTIVE VERB: a verb whose subject is agentive and may control the action. Compl: STATIVE VERB (see §5.5, §10.5.2).

ACTIVE-STATIVE: a label covering SPLIT-S and FLUID-S systems (see §10.5).

ADDRESSEE: core or peripheral argument referring to someone to whom someone else speaks.

ADESSIVE: a marker indicating the position of an object next to another object, or on the surface of another object (see §6.4).

ADJECTIVE: word class whose members typically refer to properties and have two main functions: (a) stating that something has a certain property by occurring in intransitive predicate slot or as copula complement; and (b) specifying the referent of the head noun in a noun phrase by functioning as a modifier to this noun (see §5.6, §§8.1–8.3).

ADJUNCT: same as ARGUMENT, PERIPHERAL.

ADPOSITION: a marker of a grammatical relation realized as a separate phonological word, but not as an affix. See also PREPOSITION, POSTPOSITION.

ADVANCED TONGUE ROOT VOWEL HARMONY: In the production of vowels considered +ATR, the tongue is drawn forward, and the space between the tongue root and the back of the throat is widened. In vowels which are –ATR, the tongue is retracted and the space is narrowed (see §4.1.2).

ADVERB: a word class whose major role is modifying a verb (see §5.7, §8.5).

AFFINAL: kinship relation which involves link by marriage rather than by blood. Opposite: CONSANGUINEAL (see §2.5).

AFFIX: a bound form which is added to a root or to a stem. See also PREFIX, SUFFIX (see §3.3).

AGGLUTINATING: a type of language where words are easily segmentable into a sequence of morphemes, each of which typically conveys one meaning (see §2.1). Syn: AGGLUTINATIVE.

AGREEMENT: when two words in a syntactic construction (for example, a noun and modifying adjective within a noun phrase) are marked for the same grammatical category. For instance gender (an inherent category for the noun, and an agreement category for the adjective).

AIRSTREAM MECHANISM: a mechanism for initiating the flow of air facilitating speech; see also PULMONIC, GLOTTALIC (see §4.1.1).

ALIENABLE POSSESSION: a construction in which the possessed noun does not have a close or inherent connection with the possessor (see §6.3). Compl: INALIENABLE POSSESSION.

ALLATIVE: a marker indicating movement to or towards something.

ALLOMORPH: one of several alternative forms of a morpheme.

ALLOPHONE: a possible pronunciation variant of a phoneme.

AMBITRANSITIVE: a verb which can function in both a transitive and an intransitive clause, of type S=A or S=O. Syn: LABILE (see §5.5.1).

ANALYTIC: a type of language whose words each have a small number of grammatical components. Compl: SYNTHETIC (see §2.1).

ANAPHORA: a personal pronoun or a demonstrative referring to something which was stated earlier in the discourse; see TEXTUAL ANAPHORA, SUBSTITUTION ANAPHORA (see §9.2.2).

ANDATIVE: a spatial marker (typically, on verbs) indicating the direction 'away' from the speaker. Compl: VENTIVE.

ANTIPASSIVE: valency-reducing derivation which puts the underlying A (transitive subject) argument into derived S (intransitive subject) function, and places the underlying O argument into a peripheral function (see §7.3.1 and Box 7.2).

APPLICATIVE: valency-increasing derivation which can operate on an intransitive clause, putting the underlying S argument into A function and introducing a new O argument (which may have been in peripheral function—instrumental, comitative, beneficiary, etc.—in the underlying clause), or on a transitive verb, whereby a new O argument is co-opted from a peripheral argument, and the underlying O either assumes a peripheral function, or the verb becomes ditransitive (see §7.3.2 and Box 7.4).

APPREHENSIVE: clause or a verbal form whose meaning is 'for fear that, lest (such and such thing should happen)'.

AREAL FEATURE: a linguistic feature characteristic of a LINGUISTIC AREA and indicative of language contact within the area (see §2.3.3, §14.2).

ARGUMENT, CORE: an obligatory argument for a specific verb which must be either explicitly stated or be recoverable from the context.

ARGUMENT, PERIPHERAL: non-core argument, which is optional; typical non-core arguments include instrument, accompaniment, recipient, beneficiary, time, place, manner. Syn: ADJUNCT, OBLIQUE.

ARTICLE: a determiner whose prototypical role is to mark an NP head as definite or indefinite (see §6.5).

ARTICULATOR: an active articulator (for instance, tongue tip) is brought in contact with, or into approximation with, a passive articulator (for example, the teeth) (see §4.1.1).

ASPECT: verbal category which covers composition of an event (perfective versus imperfective); sometimes also covers boundedness and completion (see §7.2.3).

ASSIMILATION: a process by which one sound changes to become more similar to a neighbouring sound, for example, -*nb*- becoming -*mb*-. Opposite: DISSIMILATION.

ASSUMED EVIDENTIAL: information source supplied on the basis of logical conclusion and also sometimes general knowledge and experience (see §7.2.5).

ATELIC: an event which is unbounded and has no end-point (see §7.2.3). Compl: TELIC.

ATR VOWEL HARMONY: see ADVANCED TONGUE ROOT VOWEL HARMONY.

AUGMENTED: pronoun paradigm in which one or more further participants are added to each term in a minimal paradigm. Compl: MINIMAL (see §9.1.1).

AUXILIARY: verb from a small closed class which accompanies another (lexical) verb from an open class carrying grammatical specifications. An auxiliary (also called auxiliary verb) typically inflects for tense or aspect, instead of the lexical verb inflecting for these categories (see §7.6.2).

BENEFACTIVE: an applicative derivation which adds a beneficiary participant to the verb (see §7.3.2 and Box 7.4).

BENEFICIARY: peripheral argument referring to someone who will benefit from the activity, e.g. *John wrote a letter for Mary*[BENEFICIARY].

BORROWING: transfer of linguistic features of any kind from one language to another as the result of contact.

BOUND FORM: form which cannot occur on its own but must occur attached to another form, e.g. prefix *in*- or suffix -*ing* in English. Compl: FREE FORM.

BOUND PRONOUN: pronominal agreement marking on the verb or on noun (see §9.1.6). Syn: CROSS-REFERENCING. Compl: FREE PRONOUN.

BOUNDEDNESS: grammatical category indicating whether or not an activity has an endpoint. See TELIC, ATELIC (see §7.2.3).

CASE: a system of nominal inflection marking the syntactic function of a noun phrase in a clause (see §6.4).

CATAPHORA: a personal pronoun or a demonstrative referring to something which is stated further on in the discourse, see TEXTUAL CATAPHORA, SUBSTITUTION CATAPHORA (see §9.2.2).

CAUSATIVE: valency-increasing derivation introducing a causer as an A-argument (see §7.3.2 and Box 7.3).

CLASSIFIERS: a set of free or bound forms categorizing the referents of the noun in terms of their sex, shape, composition, arrangement, and so on (see §6.1).

CLITIC: a morpheme which cannot form a phonological word, but may be able to form a grammatical word, with special phonological properties different from those of both an affix and an independent word (see §3.2 and §4.4). See also ENCLITIC, PROCLITIC.

CODA, OR SYLLABLE CODA: part of the syllable that comes after its vowel, or nucleus.

CODE-SWITCHING: alternative use of two languages either within a sentence or across sentence boundaries.

COGNATES: linguistic forms which are related historically, that is, go back to a single original form.

COMITATIVE: (a) an affix, added to a noun, with a meaning 'together with NOUN' or 'having a NOUN'; (b) an applicative derivation which adds a comitative participant to the verb (that is, someone together with whom the action was performed) (see §7.3.2 and Box 7.4).

COMMON ARGUMENT: an argument shared by main clause and relative clause in a relative clause construction (see §12.2.1).

COMPARATIVE CONSTRUCTION: a construction which typically involves comparing two participants (the comparee and the standard) in terms of a property (the parameter); this being marked by an index of comparison (see §11.1.4).

COMPLEMENT CLAUSE: a special clause type whose exclusive function is to occupy an argument slot of a main verb (see §12.2.2).

COMPLEMENT-TAKING VERB: a verb which may have a complement clause as one of its argument slots (see §12.2.2).

COMPLEMENTARY DISTRIBUTION: a situation whereby two or more items (sounds or forms) occur in mutually exclusive environments (see §4.1).

COMPLEMENTATION STRATEGY: a syntactic construction used in lieu of a COMPLEMENT CLAUSE construction (see §12.2.2).

COMPLEMENTIZER: grammatical form which marks a complement clause (see §12.2.2).

COMPLETION: grammatical category covering perfect and imperfect (see §7.2.3).

COMPOSITION: grammatical category covering perfective and imperfective (see §7.2.3).

COMPOUND: a word formed from two or more words or forms of words (see §6.6, §7.5).

CONDITIONAL: a grammatical form marking a clause expressing condition, or a clause containing a condition.

CONSANGUINEAL: kinship relation which involves link by blood rather than by marriage. Opposite: AFFINAL (see §2.5).

CONSTITUENT: a word, a construction, or a phrase that fills a slot in syntactic structure.

CONSTITUENT ORDER: the order in which phrasal constituents occur in a clause. This is often confused with WORD ORDER (see §3.10, Chapters 11 and 12).

CONSTRUCTION: type of clause or phrase with specified properties.

CONTENT INTERROGATIVE: question which enquires concerning a core or a peripheral argument, or predicate, or an action or state or property (see §11.3.2). Syn: CONTENT QUESTION.

CONTENT QUESTION: same as content interrogative.

CONTINUOUS: an event or a process viewed as continuing over an appreciable period of time. Syn: DURATIVE, PROGRESSIVE.

CONTOUR TONE: a tone characterised by a movement or potential movement in pitch, e.g. down-gliding, and up-gliding, rather than a specific pitch level (in contrast to REGISTER TONE) (see §4.2).

CONVERB: a non-finite verb form marking adverbial subordination (see §7.6.3, §12.2.3).

CONVERGENCE: a process whereby languages in contact gradually become more like each other in terms of grammatical categories and constructions (see §2.3.3, §14.2).

COPULA: a form (often a verb) which indicates a relationship between the copula subject and the copula complement, as the verb *be* in English *The Amazon is a long river.*

COPULA CLAUSE: a clause with a relational meaning between the copula subject and the copula complement (see §3.9, §11.1.1).

COPULA COMPLEMENT (CC): the argument in a copula clause which is shown to be in a specified relation to the copula subject.

COPULA SUBJECT (CS): the argument in a copula clause which has subject properties and is the topic for the discourse in which it occurs.

CORE ARGUMENT: an obligatory argument for a specific verb which must be either explicitly stated or be recoverable from the context.

CORE MEANING: main (and default) meaning of a category or a lexical item. Syn: MAIN MEAN-ING. Compl: EXTENSION OF MEANING.

CREOLE: a language historically developed from a PIDGIN. A pidgin develops from trade or other contact; it has no native speakers, its range of use and vocabulary are limited and its structure is simplified. It later becomes the only form of speech common to a community, is learned by new speakers, acquires native speakers, and is used for all purposes; its structure and vocabulary become more complex. At this stage, it becomes a Creole.

CREOLIZATION: the historical process involved in the development of CREOLES.

CROSS-REFERENCING: pronominal agreement marking on the verb or on the noun (see §9.1.6). Syn: BOUND PRONOUN.

DATIVE: (a) a case which typically marks the beneficiary of 'give', the addressee of 'tell', and the person to whom something is 'shown' for 'show'; (b) an applicative which adds an addressee or a beneficiary participant to the verb as its O argument (see §7.3.2 and Box 7.4).

DEBITIVE: modality indicating obligation. Syn: DEONTIC.

DECLARATIVE: a mood used in statements (see §7.2.1).

DEICTIC: category related to DEIXIS.

DEIXIS: the ways in which the reference of an element is determined with respect to speaker, addressee, or temporal or spatial setting, typically involving pointing.

DELAYED IMPERATIVE: a command 'do later'. Also see DISTANCE IN TIME (see §11.3.1).

DEMONSTRATIVE: grammatical element whose primary function is to point to an object in the situation of discourse; may also have anaphoric and/or cataphoric functions (see §9.2).

DEONTIC: form or category expressing obligation or recommendation. Syn: DEBITIVE.

DEPENDENT CLAUSE: a clause constituting a syntactic element within another clause. Syn: SUB-ORDINATE CLAUSE.

DERIVATION: optional morphological process which applies to a root or to a stem, and may derive a stem; may or may not change word class.

DESUBORDINATION: a process whereby a subordinate clause acquires the status of a main clause.

DETERMINER: grammatical modifier within a noun phrase, typically covering demonstratives and articles.

DIACHRONIC DESCRIPTION: description of a language system taking account of historical changes. Compl: SYNCHRONIC DESCRIPTION.

DIFFERENTIAL OBJECT MARKING: Marking Os differently depending on their definiteness, spec-ificity and topicality is also known as 'differential object marking' (see §10.7).

DIFFUSION: the spread of a linguistic feature within a geographical area or between languages. Diffusion can be unilateral (where A affects B) or multilateral (where A affects B in some ways and B affects A in others) (see §2.3.3, §14.2).

DIPHTHONG: a vowel phoneme which has two or more phonetic components (see §3.1 and §4.1.3).

DIRECT EVIDENTIAL: an evidential which covers speakers' or participants' own sensory experi-ence of any kind. Often the same as EXPERIENTIAL EVIDENTIAL and VISUAL EVIDENTIAL (see §7.2.5).

DIRECT SPEECH: verbatim or close to verbatim quotation of what was said (see §12.5).

DIRECT SPEECH COMPLEMENT: verbatim quotation of what someone else has said which appears in a complement clause slot of a verb of speech (see §12.5).

DIRECTIONAL: a form indicating movement to a location.

DIRECTIVE: speech act by which a speaker directs and orders action(s) by others.

DISSIMILATION: a process by which one sound changes to become different from a neighbouring sound. Opposite: ASSIMILATION.

DISTANCE IN SPACE: an imperative-specific category with the meaning of 'do (something) here (or near the speaker/addressee)' or 'do (something) there (or far from speaker/addressee)' (see §11.3.1).

DISTANCE IN TIME: an imperative-specific category with the meaning of 'do (something) now' or 'do (something) later'. Similar to DELAYED IMPERATIVE, IMMEDIATE IMPERATIVE (see §11.3.1).

DITRANSITIVE: clause type with three core arguments, in A (transitive subject), O (transitive object), and E (extension to core) functions; verb which occurs in such a clause. Syn: EXTENDED TRANSITIVE.

DUAL: a term in the category of 'number' which distinguishes two objects or individuals (see §6.2).

DURATIVE: an event or a process viewed as continuing over an appreciable period of time (see §7.2.3). Syn: CONTINUOUS, PROGRESSIVE.

E: a syntactic function which constitutes an extension to the core in an extended intransitive or an extended transitive clause (see §3.9).

ELATIVE: marker indicating direction of movement of an object out of the inside of another object (see §6.4).

ELISION: process by which a vowel is lost.

ENCLITIC: clitic attached at the end of a phonological word. See also CLITIC, PROCLITIC (see §3.2, §4.4).

EPISTEMIC MEANINGS: meanings of (a) possibility or probability of an event or (b) of the reliability of information (see §7.2.4).

EPISTEMIC MODALITY: modality associated with epistemic meanings.

ERGATIVE: case inflection marking transitive subject (A) (see §6.4, §§10.4–10.5). Compl: ABSOLUTIVE.

EVIDENTIAL, EVIDENTIALITY: grammatical marking of information source (see §7.2.5).

EVIDENTIAL EXTENSION: an extension for a non-evidential category (such as tense, aspect or modality) to refer to an information source. Syn: EVIDENTIAL STRATEGY (see §7.2.5).

EVIDENTIAL STRATEGY: use of a non-evidential category (such as tense, aspect, or modality) to refer to an information source. Syn: EVIDENTIAL EXTENSION.

EXCLUSIVE: non-singular first person pronoun referring to the speaker and one or more other people who do not include the addressee (see §9.1.1). Compl: INCLUSIVE.

EXTENDED INTRANSITIVE: clause type with two core arguments, in S (intransitive subject) and E (extension to core) functions; a verb which occurs in such a clause (see §3.9).

EXTENDED TRANSITIVE: clause type with three core arguments, in A (transitive subject), O (transitive object) and E (extension to core) functions; verb which occurs in such a clause (see §3.9). Syn: DITRANSITIVE.

EXTENSION OF MEANING: additional meaning of a category or a lexical item realized under particular circumstances. Compl: CORE MEANING.

EXTENT: grammatical category covering punctual and durative (see §7.2.3).

EYEWITNESS EVIDENTIAL: an evidential—typically in a small system with two choices—referring to something the speaker has seen or witnessed. Syn: FIRSTHAND EVIDENTIAL (see §7.2.5).

FIRSTHAND EVIDENTIAL: an evidential—typically in a small system with two choices—referring to something the speaker has seen, heard, or otherwise experienced. Opposite of NON-FIRSTHAND EVIDENTIAL. Syn: EYEWITNESS EVIDENTIAL (see §7.2.5).

FLUID-S: a system whereby some verbs may have their S argument (intransitive subject) marked either like the transitive subject A (S_a) or like the object O (S_o) with a predictable difference in meaning (see §10.5).

FOCAL CLAUSE: the clause in a combination of linked clauses which carries the mood of the sentence (see §12.6).

FOCUS: a grammatical mechanism for marking a part of a clause for prominence, or contrast, or as new information (see §13.1.2).

FORMAL MARKEDNESS: a term in a grammatical system which has zero realization—or a zero allomorph—is said to be formally unmarked.

FREE FORM: a form which can occur on its own and then constitutes a grammatical word. Compl: BOUND FORM.

FRUSTRATIVE: verbal form (often classified as a type of modality) indicating that the action was done in vain (see §7.2.4).

FUNCTIONAL LOAD OF A CONTRAST OR A FORM: the extent to which a contrast or a form are utilized in a language.

FUNCTIONAL MARKEDNESS: a term in a grammatical system which is used as a generic cover term—or in underspecified context—is said to be functionally unmarked.

FUSIONAL: a type of language whose words consist of morphemes which are 'fused' together and are not segmentable (see §2.1).

GENDER: small closed system of agreement classes whose semantics involves some of sex (masculine, feminine, sometimes also neuter), animacy, humanness, and rationality. Membership must be marked outside the noun itself (within the noun phrase or on the verb) (see §6.1). Syn: NOUN CLASS.

GENITIVE: marker of a possessive relationship within a noun phrase. Compl: PERTENSIVE.

GERUND: a nominalized form of a verb, similar to CONVERB (see §7.6.3).

GLOTTALIC AIRSTREAM MECHANISM: air movement initiated in the glottis (see §4.1.1).

GRAMMATICAL MEANING: a meaning which must be expressed in a given language (Boas 1938: 132).

GRAMMATICAL WORD: a unit within the hierarchy of grammatical units defined on grammatical criteria (see §4.4).

GRAMMATICALIZATION: process whereby an item with lexical status changes into an item with grammatical status (Heine and Kuteva 2002). A typical example of grammaticalization is the verb 'finish' becoming a marker for 'completed' aspect.

HEAD: obligatory nucleus of a phrase which determines the grammatical profile and form of the whole phrase (for example, gender in a noun phrase).

HEARSAY EVIDENTIAL: information known through verbal report (see §7.2.5). Syn: REPORTED EVIDENTIAL, SECONDHAND EVIDENTIAL.

HEAVY SYLLABLE: a syllable that counts as two units (rather than one) rhythmically, and for the purposes of stress assignment. Typically contains a long vowel, or a diphthong, or ends in a consonant (see §4.1.3). Compl: LIGHT SYLLABLE.

HETERORGANIC: sequence of sounds which have different place of articulation, e.g. *nb*.

HOMORGANIC: sequence of sounds which have the same place of articulation, e.g. *mb*.

HORTATIVE: command addressed to first person (see §11.3.1).

IDEOPHONE: forms whose phonetic form is perceived as imitating a sound or an activity someone or something makes, or a sound associated with something that objects denote. Ideophones often have unusual phonetic and phonological properties (see §4.1.5, §5.8).

ILLATIVE: a marker indicating direction of an object towards another object, or towards its surface (see §6.4).

IMMEDIATE IMPERATIVE: a command 'do immediately'. Also see DISTANCE IN TIME (see §11.3.1).

IMPERATIVE: a mood used in commands (see §11.3.1).

IMPERFECT: an event which began in the past and is still continuing (see §7.2.3). Compl: PERFECT.

IMPERFECTIVE ASPECT: a verbal form used to refer to actions extending over a period of time, or continuously (see §7.2.3). Compl: PERFECTIVE ASPECT.

IMPERSONAL, OR IMPERSONAL PERSON MARKER: a pronoun or a pronominal marker on a verb or noun with the meaning 'one in general, everyone' (see §9.1).

IMPERSONAL PASSIVE: a valency-reducing derivation which puts the underlying O argument into derived S (intransitive subject) function and removes the underlying A (transitive subject) (see §7.3.1 and Box 7.1).

INALIENABLE POSSESSION: a construction in which the possessed noun has a close or inherent connection with the possessor (see §6.3). Compl: ALIENABLE POSSESSION.

INCEPTIVE: same as INCHOATIVE.

INCHOATIVE: indicating the initiation of an action or a process (see §7.2.3).

INCLUSIVE: non-singular first person pronoun referring to the speaker and one or more other people including the addressee (see §9.1.1). Compl: EXCLUSIVE.

INDIRECT SPEECH: reporting what someone else has said by adapting deictic categories (e.g. person) to the viewpoint of the reporter (see §12.5). Compl: DIRECT SPEECH.

INESSIVE: a marker indicating position of an object inside another object (see §6.4).

INFERENTIAL (a) synonym for INFERRED EVIDENTIAL; (b) inference as part of the meaning of a non-firsthand evidential (see §7.2.5).

INFERRED EVIDENTIAL: information source based on conclusions drawn on the basis of what one can see, or the result of something happening (see §7.2.5).

INFLECTION: morphological process which obligatorily applies to a root or derived stem of a particular word class, producing a grammatical word.

INFORMATION SOURCE: grammatical marking of how one knows something (see §7.2.5).

INSTRUMENTAL: (a) an affix, added to a noun, indicating weapon, tool or material with which the action is performed; (b) an applicative derivation which adds an instrumental participant to the verb as its O argument (see §7.3.2 and Box 7.4).

INTERJECTION: conventionalized sound, typically expressing the speaker's emotional response or reaction to something (see §4.1.5, §5.8).

INTERNAL CHANGE: morphological process which involves changing a vowel or a consonant in the middle of a word.

INTERROGATIVE: a mood used in questions (see §7.2.1, §11.3.2).

INTERROGATIVE WORD: word occurring in a content question which establishes its status as a question (see §7.2.1, §11.3.2).

INTONATION: type of prosody realized by pitch, which generally applies to a clause or a sentence.

INTRANSITIVE: clause type with one core argument (in S, intransitive subject) function; verbs which occur in such clauses. Compl: TRANSITIVE.

IRREALIS: verbal form referring to hypothetical events and/or something that has not happened (see §7.2.6). Compl: REALIS.

ISOLATING: a type of language in which most grammatical words consist of one morpheme (see §2.1).

JUSSIVE: command addressed to third person (see §11.3.1).

LABILE: older name for AMBITRANSITIVE.

LANGUAGE OBSOLESCENCE: a process whereby a language gradually falls into disuse.

LENITION: the replacement of a sound by another sound that has weaker articulation (involving less muscular tension), e.g. *p > w, k > h, s > h.*

LIGHT SYLLABLE: a syllable that counts as one unit, rhythmically, and for the purposes of stress assignment. Typically contains a short vowel and no consonant coda (see §4.1.3). Compl: HEAVY SYLLABLE.

LINGUA FRANCA: a language used for communication between groups who have no other language in common (see §2.4).

LINGUISTIC AREA: a geographically delimited region including languages from two or more language families, or different subgroups of the same family, sharing significant traits, or combinations of traits most of which are not found in languages from these families or subgroups spoken outside the area (see §2.3.3, §14.2). Syn: SPRACHBUND.

LOCATIVE: (a) a case which typically marks location at, on, in, or near the referent of the noun phrase to which it is attached; (b) an applicative which adds a locative participant to the verb as its O argument (see §7.3.2 and Box 7.4).

METATHESIS: phonological change or process which involves a change in the order of sounds.

MINIMAL: pronoun paradigm in which 'me and you' is a term on a par with first person singular and second person singular (see §9.1.1). Compl: AUGMENTED.

MIRATIVE: grammatical marking of 'unprepared mind', including unexpected and also surprising information (see §7.2.4).

MODAL VERB: a verb with a modal meaning, which includes possibility, probability (epistemic meanings), necessity, obligation (deontic meanings), desire, and intention.

MODALITY: grammatical category covering the degree of certainty of a statement (EPISTEMIC), obligation (DEONTIC), and permission (see §7.2.4). This should not be confused with MOOD.

MOOD: grammatical category expressing a speech act (e.g. statement: indicative mood; question: interrogative mood; command: imperative mood) (see §7.2.1, §11.3).

MORA: unit of syllable weight applicable to languages where long (or HEAVY) syllables are distinguished from short (or LIGHT) syllables (see §4.2).

MORPHEME: the minimum meaningful unit of speech (see Chapter 3).

MORPHOLOGICAL PROCESS: process which applies to a root.

MORPHOLOGY: part of grammar which studies the structure of words. Compl: SYNTAX.

MORPHOPHONOLOGICAL PROCESS: a phonological process conditioned by morphological environment (e.g. occurring on a boundary between a prefix and a root).

MORPHOPHONOLOGY: part of grammar which is concerned with morphologically conditioned alternations.

MULTILATERAL DIFFUSION: the spread of a linguistic feature within a geographical area or between languages where A affects B in some ways and B affects A in others. Compl: UNILATERAL DIFFUSION (see §2.3.3, §14.2).

NEUTRALIZATION: when a certain grammatical or phonological contrast does not apply in a certain environment, it is said to be neutralized in this environment.

NOMINAL HIERARCHY: hierarchy of items which can be head of a noun phrase, according to how likely they are to occur in A (transitive subject) or O function (see §10.5.1 and Figure 10.1).

NOMINALIZATION: morphological derivation which forms a noun from a verb, an adjective, or a word of another word class.

NOMINATIVE: case inflection marking intransitive subject (S) and transitive subject (A). Compl: ACCUSATIVE (see §6.4, §§10.4–10.5).

NOMINATIVE-ACCUSATIVE SYSTEM: a system of grammatical marking whereby A and S are marked in the same way with nominative case, and O is marked with accusative case (see §6.4, §§10.4–10.5).

NON-CANONICAL MARKING OF CORE ARGUMENTS: situation when most of the instances receive a certain marking, and a minority of instances display different marking, is referred to as non-canonical (see §10.6).

NON-EYEWITNESS EVIDENTIAL: an evidential—typically in a small system with two choices—referring to something the speaker has not seen or witnessed (see §7.2.5). Opposite of EYEWITNESS EVIDENTIAL. Syn: NON-FIRSTHAND EVIDENTIAL.

NON-FIRSTHAND EVIDENTIAL: an evidential, typically in a small system with two choices, referring to something the speaker has not seen, heard or otherwise experienced, and to something the speaker may have inferred, assumed, or (in some systems) learnt from someone else's verbal report (see §7.2.5). Opposite of FIRSTHAND EVIDENTIAL. Syn: NON-EYEWITNESS EVIDENTIAL.

NON-SPATIAL SETTING: covers the range of parameters which describe the setting for activities or states other than those referring to spatial location or direction (see §7.2).

NON-VISUAL EVIDENTIAL: information source involving hearing, smelling, feeling, and sometimes also touching something (see §7.2.5). Syn: NON-EYEWITNESS EVIDENTIAL.

NOUN: word class whose primary function is as head of a noun phrase (see Chapter 6).

NOUN INCORPORATION: the incorporation of a noun—generally in underlying S (intransitive subject) or O (object) function—into a verb to create a complex stem.

NOUN PHRASE (NP): a constituent which can fill an argument slot in a clause. It may have a noun, a pronoun, or a demonstrative as its HEAD (see §6.7).

NUMBER: grammatical system referring to the quantity of referents, one of whose terms is singular.

O: the object of a transitive verb, a core syntactic function.

OBLIQUE: same as ARGUMENT, PERIPHERAL.

ONOMATOPOEIA: forms whose phonetic form is perceived as imitating a sound someone or something makes, or sound associated with something that they denote.

ONSET, OR SYLLABLE ONSET: the part of the syllable that comes before its vowel, or nucleus.

OPTATIVE: a grammatical form whose main meaning is to express wishes.

PARENTHETICAL: 'a word, phrase, or sentence which interrupts a sentence and which bears no syntactic relation to that sentence at the point of interruption' (Trask 1993: 199) (see §13.1.4).

PASSIVE: valency-reducing derivation which puts underlying O (direct object) argument in derived S (intransitive subject) function and places underlying A (transitive subject) argument in a peripheral function (see §7.3.1 and Box 7.1).

PAUCAL NUMBER: number referring to a relatively small number greater than two (see §6.2).

PERFECT: a verbal form focusing on the results of an action or process, thus relating a past event to the present. An event or a process is then viewed as completed in the past but still relevant for the present (see §7.2.3). Compl: IMPERFECT.

PERFECTIVE ASPECT: a verbal form which specifies that the event is regarded as a whole, without respect for its temporal constituency (even though it may be extended in time) (see §7.2.3). Compl: IMPERFECTIVE ASPECT.

PERIPHERAL ARGUMENT: non-core argument, which is optional; typical non-core arguments include instrument, accompaniment, recipient, beneficiary, time, place, manner (see §3.9). Syn: ADJUNCT, OBLIQUE.

PERLATIVE: a marker of movement through an object (see §6.4).

PERSON: speech act participants, always including 1st person (speaker), 2nd person (addressee), and sometimes also 3rd person (neither speaker nor addressee) (see §9.1.1).

PERTENSIVE: marker of a possessive relationship within a noun phrase which is added to the possessed item (see §6.3). Compl: GENITIVE.

PHASAL VERB: verb referring to beginning, continuing, or ending of an activity (see §7.2.3).

PHASE OF ACTIVITY: characterization of an activity as beginning, continuing, or ending (see §7.2.3).

PHONEME: the minimum segmentable unit in phonology which helps differentiate meanings (see Chapters 3 and 4).

PHONETICS: articulatory and/or acoustic study of the sounds of speech (see Chapter 3).

PHONOLOGICAL WORD: a unit in the hierarchy of phonological units defined on the basis of phonological criteria, typically including stress and tone (see §4.3).

PHONOLOGY: description of the phonetic contrasts which are used to distinguish between different words in a given language (see Chapter 3).

PHONOTACTICS: statement of which consonants and vowels occur in which position in a syllable or within a phonological word (see §4.1.4).

PHRASE: a constituent which can fill a slot in clause structure (noun phrase in an argument slot, and verb phrase in predicate slot).

PIDGIN: a simplified form of speech developed from trade or other contact; it has no native speakers, its range of use and vocabulary are limited and its structure is simplified. It later becomes the only form of speech common to a community, is learned by new speakers, acquires native speakers, and is used for all purposes; its structure and vocabulary become more complex. At this stage, it becomes a CREOLE.

PITCH: the property of sounds which corresponds to the physical parameter of frequency (see §4.2).

PITCH ACCENT: an accent realized primarily by differences in pitch between accented and unaccented syllables (see §4.2).

PIVOT: a topic recognizable as such through its grammatical properties (see §12.4).

PLURACTIONAL: verbal forms which may refer to a multiplicity of objects, subjects, and repetition and even intensity of activity (see §7.2.3).

PLURAL: a term in the category of 'number' which distinguishes more than one objects or individuals in a singular-plural system, and more than two in a singular-dual-plural system (see §6.2).

POLAR INTERROGATIVE: question which enquires whether or not the statement is correct (also known as 'yes/no' question) (see §11.3.2). Syn: POLAR QUESTION.

POLAR QUESTION: same as POLAR INTERROGATIVE.

POLARITY: grammatical system whose terms are negative and positive.

POLYSYNTHETIC: a highly SYNTHETIC language (see §2.1).

POSTPOSITION: an adposition which follows the constituent for which it provides grammatical marking.

POTENTIAL: a grammatical form whose main meaning is to express possibility.

PRAGMATICS: meanings created by the context of use.

PREDICATE: the central and obligatory structural component of a clause, generally realized by a verb phrase, with verb as head. The predicate determines the number and type of core arguments required in a clause (see §3.9, Chapter 10).

PREFIX: an AFFIX which precedes a root or to a stem. See also AFFIX, SUFFIX (see §3.3).

PREPOSITION: an ADPOSITION which precedes the constituent for which it provides grammatical marking. See also ADPOSITION, POSTPOSITION.

PRIVATIVE: a marker meaning 'without' something, similar to ABESSIVE.

PROCLITIC: a CLITIC attached at the beginning of a phonological word (see §3.2, §4.4). See also CLITIC, ENCLITIC.

PROGRESSIVE: an event or a process viewed as continuing over an appreciable period of time. Syn: CONTINUOUS, DURATIVE.

PROLATIVE: a marker indicating movement along something (see §6.4).

PRONOUN: small closed class of grammatical items which relate to person, and can be free or bound forms (see §9.1).

PROSODY: rhythm and intonation in speech; non-segmental features of sounds; also used to refer to a system of phonological contrasts which has scope over a sequence of segments (see §§4.2–4.3).

PROTO-LANGUAGE: putative ancestor language for a group of modern languages proven to be genetically related, with each having developed by regular changes from the proto-language.

PULMONIC AIRSTREAM MECHANISM: air movement initiated in the lungs (see §4.1.1).

PUNCTUAL: an action which happens instantaneously (see §7.2.3).

QUOTATIVE: (a) verbal form or a particle introducing a verbatim quotation of what someone else has said; (b) in some grammars of North and South American Indian languages, same as REPORTED EVIDENTIAL (see §7.2.5).

REALIS: a category which encompasses real events or states, which have happened or are happening (see §7.2.6). Compl: IRREALIS.

REALITY STATUS: a grammatical category covering REALIS and IRREALIS (see §7.2.6).

REANALYSIS: a historical process by which a morphosyntactic device comes to be assigned a different structure from that which it had, without necessarily changing its surface form and with little change to its semantics.

RECIPROCAL: clause describing several instances of an activity such that what is A (transitive subject) argument in one instance is O argument in another (see §7.3, §9.1.5).

REDUPLICATION: morphological process which involves repeating all or part of the root or stem of a word before, after, or in the middle of it.

REFLEXIVE: a category or a clause where underlying A and O arguments have the same reference (see §7.3, §9.1.5).

REGISTER TONE: a tone characterized by a different level of pitch (in contrast to CONTOUR TONE) (see §4.2).

RELATIVE CLAUSE: clause which modifies the head of a noun phrase. Relative clause and main clause share a common argument (see §12.2.1).

REPORTED EVIDENTIAL: a marker of information source; that is, an evidential whose main meaning is marking what has been learnt from someone else's verbal report (see §7.2.5). Syn: HEARSAY EVIDENTIAL, SECONDHAND EVIDENTIAL.

RESULTATIVE: a verbal form referring to the results of an action or a process (see §7.2.3).

S: subject of an intransitive verb, a core syntactic function.

S=A AMBITRANSITIVE: a verb used transitively and intransitively, such that its S (intransitive subject) argument corresponds to the A (transitive subject) when it is used transitively.

S=O AMBITRANSITIVE: a verb can be used transitively and intransitively such that its S (intransitive subject) argument corresponds to the O (transitive object) when it is used transitively.

S_a: an intransitive verb whose subject (S) is marked in the same way as the subject (A) of a transitive verb (see §10.5).

SCOPE: the part of a sentence, of a clause or of a word which a modifier, an affix, or a negator has effect over.

SECONDARY CONCEPTS: provide modification for primary verbs, either as independent verbs or as affixes (see §5.5).

SECONDHAND EVIDENTIAL: (a) based on verbal report from someone who said it (as opposed to THIRDHAND); (b) same as REPORTED EVIDENTIAL, HEARSAY EVIDENTIAL (see §7.2.5).

SEMANTIC ROLE: the types of participant used with verbs of a certain semantic type.

SEMANTIC TYPE: a set of words with a similar set of meanings and grammatical properties.

SENSORY: referring to perception by physical senses.

SERIAL VERB CONSTRUCTION: a single predicate consisting of two or more verbs each of which could be used as a predicate on its own. A serial verb construction refers to one event and has single mood, modality, polarity, and tense/aspect value (see §7.6.1).

SHIFTER: grammatical item whose reference changes depending on who is speaking (pronouns) or what the place or time is (see §§9.1–9.2).

SINGULAR: a term in the category of 'number' which distinguishes just one object or individual (see §6.2).

S_o: an intransitive verb whose subject (S) is marked in the same way as the object (O) of a transitive verb (see §10.5).

SPEECH ACT: an utterance 'conceived as an act by which the speaker does something' (Matthews 2007: 349). If one says *Go away!*, one performs an act of command. If one says *Who is it?*, the act is of asking a question (see §11.3).

SPEECH ACT PARTICIPANTS (SAP): first person (speaker) and second person (addressee).

SPLIT-S: a system whereby some verbs may have their S argument (intransitive subject) marked like the transitive subject A (S_a) and others have it marked like the object O (S_o); also called active/stative (see §10.5).

STATIVE VERB: a verb referring to a state and whose subject is not agentive and does not control the state (see §5.5, §10.5.2). Compl: ACTIVE VERB.

STEM: the nucleus of a word to which a morphological process may apply, forming a grammatical word (see §3.3).

STRESS: a prosody realized through auditory prominence within a PHONOLOGICAL WORD, characterized by some or all of loudness, pitch, vowel quality, and length (see §4.2). Syn: ACCENT.

SUBGROUP: set of languages within a language family which descend from a single ancestor language, this being itself a descendant of the proto-language for the whole language family.

SUBORDINATE CLAUSE: a clause constituting a syntactic element within another clause (see §12.2). Syn: DEPENDENT CLAUSE.

SUBORDINATOR: overt marker of a subordinate clause.

SUBSTITUTION ANAPHORA: a personal pronoun or a demonstrative referring to a participant mentioned earlier in the discourse. Compl: TEXTUAL ANAPHORA (see §9.2.2).

SUBSTITUTION CATAPHORA: a personal pronoun or a demonstrative referring to a participant mentioned further on in the discourse. Compl: TEXTUAL CATAPHORA (see §9.2.2).

SUBTRACTION: morphological process which involves deleting some material from the root (see §3.3).

SUFFIX: an affix which follows a root or a stem. See also AFFIX, PREFIX (see §3.3).

SUPPLETION: a morphological process in which one form replaces another in a given context; for example English *better* is a suppletive form of *good* (see §3.3).

SUPPORTING CLAUSE: the clause in a combination of linked clauses which does not carry the mood of the sentence (see §12.6).

SWITCH REFERENCE: a grammatical system whereby a marker indicates whether the subject of a dependent (medial) clause is identical or not with that of the main (final) clause (see §12.3).

SYLLABLE: a phonological unit centred on a nucleus (typically, a vowel) which may be preceded or followed by one or more consonants (see §4.1.3).

SYNCHRONIC DESCRIPTION: description of a language system at one point in time, without taking account of historical changes. Compl: DIACHRONIC DESCRIPTION.

SYNTAX: study of the organization and interrelation of units of grammar above the level of 'word'.

SYNTHETIC: a language whose words consist of a large number of grammatical components. Compl: ANALYTIC (see §2.1).

TELIC: an event which is bounded and has an end-point (see §7.2.3). Compl: ATELIC.

TENSE: grammatical category which refers to time (see §7.2.2).

TEXTUAL ANAPHORA: a demonstrative referring to a stretch of text earlier in the discourse; Compl: SUBSTITUTION ANAPHORA (see §9.2.2).

TEXTUAL CATAPHORA: a personal pronoun or a demonstrative referring to a participant mentioned further on in the discourse. Compl: SUBSTITUTION CATAPHORA (see §9.2.2).

THIRDHAND: based on a verbal report from someone else who in their turn acquired the information through another verbal report (see §7.2.5).

TOPIC: an argument which occurs in a succession of clauses in discourse and binds them together thematically (see §13.1).

TRANSITIVE: clause type with two core arguments, in A (transitive subject) and O (transitive object) functions; verbs which occur in such clauses. Compl: INTRANSITIVE.

TRANSLATIVE: a marker that indicates a change in state of a noun (see §6.4).

TRIAL: term in a grammatical number system referring to three entities (see §6.2).

TRIPARTITE MARKING: when each of the transitive subject (A), intransitive subject (S), and transitive object (O) receive a distinct case marking (see §10.2).

UNILATERAL DIFFUSION: the spread of a linguistic feature within a geographical area or between languages where A affects B. Compl: MULTILATERAL DIFFUSION (see §2.3).

VALENCY: the number of core arguments required by a verb.

VALENCY-CHANGING: derivations which may increase valency (causative, applicative) or decrease it (passive, antipassive, some varieties of reciprocal and reflexive).

VENTIVE: a spatial marker (typically, on verbs) indicating the direction 'towards' the speaker. Compl: ANDATIVE.

VERB: word class whose primary function is as head of predicate (see §5.5, Chapter 7).

VERB PHRASE: a constituent which can fill the predicate slot within a clause (see §7.7).

VERBALIZATION: word-class changing derivation which forms a verb stem from a noun or an adjective (see §7.5).

VERBLESS CLAUSE: similar to a copula clause but with the predicate slot left empty. It indicates a relational meaning between the verbless clause subject and the verbless clause complement.

VERBLESS CLAUSE COMPLEMENT (VCC): the argument in a verbless clause shown to be in a specified relation to the verbless clause subject (see §3.9, §11.1.2).

VERBLESS CLAUSE SUBJECT (VCS): the argument in a verbless clause which is topic for the discourse in which it occurs and which may share properties with A of a transitive clause and S of an intransitive clause (see §3.9, §11.1.2).

VISUAL EVIDENTIAL: information source involving knowledge obtained through seeing something (see §7.2.5).

VOWEL HARMONY: prosody applying over a phonological stretch (typically, a phonological word) whereby all the vowels within the stretch agree in some feature, e.g. front/back (see §4.3).

WORD ORDER: the order in which words occur in a phrase, or a clause, or a sentence. Distinct from (but often confused with) CONSTITUENT ORDER (see §3.10).

ZERO: a term in a system which has no overt marking is said to have zero realization.

ZERO DERIVATION: a word-class-changing derivation with zero marking.

References

Abbott, M. 1991. 'Macushi', pp. 23–160 of *Handbook of Amazonian Languages*, vol. 3, edited by D. C. Derbyshire and G. K. Pullum. Berlin: Mouton de Gruyter.

Abdul-Fetouh, H. M. 1969. *A Morphological Study of Egyptian Colloquial Arabic*. The Hague: Mouton.

Abercrombie, David. 1967. *Elements of General Phonetics*. Edinburgh: Edinburgh University Press.

Abondolo, Daniel. 1998. *Uralic*. London: Routledge.

Adams, K. L. 1989. *Systems of Numeral Classification in the Mon-Khmer, Nicobarese and Aslian Subfamilies of Austroasiatic*. Canberra: Pacific Linguistics.

Adams, Valerie. 1973. *An Introduction to Modern English Word Formation*. London: Longman.

Adelaar, W. F. H. 1990. 'The role of quotations in Andean discourse', pp. 1–12 of *Unity in Diversity. Papers presented to Simon C. Dik on his 50th birthday*, edited by Harm Pinkster and Inge Genee. Dordrecht: Foris publications.

Aikhenvald, Alexandra Y. 1995a. *Bare*. Munich: Lincom Europa.

Aikhenvald, Alexandra Y. 1995b. 'Person-marking and discourse in North-Arawak languages', *Studia Linguistica* 49: 152–95.

Aikhenvald, Alexandra Y. 1996. 'Words, phrases, pauses and boundaries: evidence from South American Indian languages', *Studies in Language* 20: 487–517.

Aikhenvald, Alexandra Y. 1998. 'Warekena', pp. 215–439 of *Handbook of Amazonian Languages*, edited by D. C. Derbyshire and G. K. Pullum, vol. 4. Berlin: Mouton de Gruyter.

Aikhenvald, Alexandra Y. 2000. *Classifiers: A Typology of Noun Categorization Devices*. Oxford: Oxford University Press.

Aikhenvald, Alexandra Y. 2002a. 'Typological parameters for the study of clitics, with special reference to Tariana', pp. 42–78 of Dixon and Aikhenvald (eds).

Aikhenvald, Alexandra Y. 2002b. *Language Contact in Amazonia*. Oxford: Oxford University Press.

Aikhenvald, Alexandra Y. 2003. *A Grammar of Tariana, from North-west Amazonia*. Cambridge: Cambridge University Press.

Aikhenvald, Alexandra Y. 2004a. 'The adjective class in Tariana', pp. 97–124 of *Adjective Classes: A Cross-linguistic Typology*. edited by R. M. W. Dixon and Alexandra Y. Aikhenvald. Oxford: Oxford University Press.

Aikhenvald, Alexandra Y. 2004b. *Evidentiality*. Oxford: Oxford University Press.

Aikhenvald, Alexandra Y. 2004c. 'Gender', Article 98, pp. 1031–45 of *Morfologie/Morphology. Ein Handbuch zur Flexion und Wortbildung/A Handbook on Inflection and Word Formation*, 2 Halbband, edited by Geert E. Boij, Christian Lehmann, Joachim Mugdan, and Stavros Skopetas. Mouton de Gruyter.

Aikhenvald, Alexandra Y. 2006a. 'Grammars in contact: a cross-linguistic perspective', pp. 1–66 of *Grammars in Contact: A Cross-linguistic Typology*, edited by Alexandra Y. Aikhenvald and R. M. W. Dixon. Oxford: Oxford University Press.

Aikhenvald, Alexandra Y. 2006b. 'Classifiers and noun classes, semantics', pp. 463–70 of vol. 1 (article 1111) of *Encyclopedia of Language and Linguistics*, 2nd edition, edited by Keith Brown. Elsevier: Oxford.

Aikhenvald, Alexandra Y. 2006c. 'Evidentiality in grammar', pp. 320–5, vol. 4 (article 0252), of *Encyclopedia of Language and Linguistics*, 2nd edition, edited by Keith Brown. Elsevier: Oxford.

Aikhenvald, Alexandra Y. 2006d. 'Serial verb constructions in typological perspective', pp. 1–68 of *Serial Verb Constructions: A Cross-linguistic Typology*, edited by A. Y. Aikhenvald and R. M. W. Dixon. Oxford: Oxford University Press.

Aikhenvald, Alexandra Y. 2007a. 'Linguistic fieldwork: setting the scene', *Language Typology and Universals* 60 (1): 3–10.

Aikhenvald, Alexandra Y. 2007b. 'Typological dimensions in word formation', pp. 1–65 of *Language Typology and Syntactic Description*, vol. 3, edited by T. Shopen. Cambridge: Cambridge University Press.

Aikhenvald, Alexandra Y. 2008. *The Manambu Language of East Sepik, Papua New Guinea*. Oxford: Oxford University Press.

Aikhenvald, Alexandra Y. 2009. 'Syntactic ergativity in Paumarí', pp. 111–27 of *Topics in Descriptive and African Linguistics. Essays in Honor of Distinguished Professor Paul Newman*, edited by Samuel Dyasi Obeng. Munich: Lincom Europa.

Aikhenvald, Alexandra Y. 2010. *Imperatives and Commands*. Oxford: Oxford University Press.

Aikhenvald, Alexandra Y. 2011a. 'Word-class changing derivations in typological perspective', pp. 221–89 of *Language at Large. Essays on Syntax and Semantics*, by Alexandra Y. Aikhenvald and R. M. W. Dixon. Leiden: Brill.

Aikhenvald, Alexandra Y. 2011b. 'Speech reports: a cross-linguistic perspective', pp. 290–326 of *Language at Large. Essays on Syntax and Semantics*, by Alexandra Y. Aikhenvald and R. M. W. Dixon. Leiden: Brill.

Aikhenvald, Alexandra Y. 2011c. 'Versatile cases', pp. 3–43 of *Language at Large. Essays on Syntax and Semantics*, by Alexandra Y. Aikhenvald and R. M. W. Dixon. Leiden: Brill.

Aikhenvald, Alexandra Y. 2012a. *Languages of the Amazon*. Oxford: Oxford University Press.

Aikhenvald, Alexandra Y. 2012b. 'Round women and long men: shape and size in gender choice in Papua New Guinea and beyond', *Anthropological Linguistics* 54 (1): 33–86.

Aikhenvald, Alexandra Y. 2012c. 'The essence of mirativity', *Linguistic Typology* 16 (3): 435–85.

Aikhenvald, Alexandra Y. 2013a. 'Possession and ownership: a cross-linguistic perspective', pp. 1–64 of *Possession and Ownership: A Cross-linguistic Typology*, edited by Alexandra Y. Aikhenvald and R. M. W. Dixon. Oxford: Oxford University Press.

Aikhenvald, Alexandra Y. 2013b. 'Perception and cognition in Manambu, a Papuan language from New Guinea', pp. 137–60 of *Perception and Cognition in Language and Culture*, edited by Alexandra Y. Aikhenvald and Anne Storch. Leiden: Brill.

Aikhenvald, Alexandra Y. 2013c. 'Possession and ownership in Manambu, a Papuan language from New Guinea', pp. 107–25 of *Possession and Ownership: A Cross-linguistic Typology*, edited by Alexandra Y. Aikhenvald and R. M. W. Dixon. Oxford: Oxford University Press.

Aikhenvald, Alexandra Y. 2013d. 'A story of love and debt: the give and the take of linguistic fieldwork', *The Asia-Pacific Journal of Anthropology* 14: 172–82.

Aikhenvald, Alexandra Y. 2014. 'Language contact', pp. 295–317 of *How Languages Work*, edited by Carol Genetti. Cambridge: Cambridge University Press.

Aikhenvald, Alexandra Y. Forthcoming-a. 'Sentence types', to appear in *Handbook of Mood and Modality*, edited by Ian Nuyts and Johan van der Auwera. Oxford: Oxford University Press.

Aikhenvald, Alexandra Y. Forthcoming-b. Proto-Arawak.

Aikhenvald, Alexandra Y. and R. M. W. Dixon (eds). 2001. *Areal Diffusion and Genetic Relationships: Case Studies in Comparative Linguistics*. Oxford: Oxford University Press.

Aikhenvald, Alexandra Y. and R. M. W. Dixon (eds.) 2006. *Serial Verb Constructions: A Cross-linguistic Typology*. Oxford: Oxford University Press.

Aikhenvald, Alexandra Y. and R. M. W. Dixon. 2011a. *Language at Large. Essays on Syntax and Semantics*. Leiden: Brill.

Aikhenvald, Alexandra Y. and R. M. W. Dixon. 2011b. 'Dependencies between grammatical systems', pp. 170–204 of Aikhenvald and Dixon 2011a.

Aikhenvald, Alexandra Y. and R. M. W. Dixon. 2011c. 'Non-ergative associations between S and O', pp. 143–69 of *Language at Large. Essays on Syntax and Semantics*, edited by Alexandra Y. Aikhenvald and R. M. W. Dixon. Leiden: Brill.

Aikhenvald, Alexandra Y. and R. M. W. Dixon. (eds.) 2013. *Possession and Ownership: A Cross-linguistic Typology*, edited by Alexandra Y. Aikhenvald and R. M. W. Dixon. Oxford: Oxford University Press.

Aikhenvald, Alexandra Y. and R. M. W. Dixon. (eds). 2014. *The Grammar of Knowledge: A Cross-linguistic Typology*, edited by Alexandra Y. Aikhenvald and R. M. W. Dixon. Oxford: Oxford University Press.

Aikhenvald, Alexandra Y. and Diana Green. 2011. 'Palikur and the typology of classifiers', pp. 394–450 of Aikhenvald and Dixon 2011a.

Aikhenvald, Alexandra Y. and Pieter Muysken. (ed.). 2011. *Multi-verb Constructions: A View from the Americas*. Leiden: Brill.

Aikhenvald, Alexandra Y. and Anne Storch. (eds). 2013. *Perception and Cognition in Language and Culture*. Leiden: Brill.

Aikhenvald, Alexandra Y. and Anne Storch. 2013. 'Linguistic expression of perception and cognition: a typological glimpse', pp. 1–46 of *Perception and Cognition in Language and Culture*, edited by Alexandra Y. Aikhenvald and Anne Storch. Leiden: Brill.

Aikhenvald, Alexandra Y., R. M. W. Dixon, and Masayuki Onishi. (eds). 2001. *Non-canonical Marking of Subjects and Objects*. Amsterdam: John Benjamins.

Alpher, Barry. 1991. *Yir-Yoront Lexicon: Sketch and Dictionary of an Australian Language*. Berlin: Mouton De Gruyter.

Altmann, Hans. 1993. 'Satzmodus', pp. 1006–29 of *Syntax. Ein internationales Handbuch zeitgenössiger Forschung. An International Handbook of Contemporary Research*, edited by Joachim Jacobs, Arnim von Stechow, Wolfgang Sternefeld, and Theo Vennemann, vol. 1. Berlin: Walter de Gruyter.

Ameka, Felix K. 1991. *Ewe: Its grammatical constructions and illocutionary devices*, PhD thesis. Canberra: Australian National University.

Ameka, Felix K. 1992. 'Interjections: the universal yet neglected part of speech', *Journal of Pragmatics* 18: 101–18.

Ameka, Felix K. 2013. 'Possessive constructions in Likpe (Sɛkpɛlé)', pp. 224–42 of *Possession and Ownership: A Cross-linguistic Typology*, edited by Alexandra Y. Aikhenvald and R. M. W. Dixon. Oxford: Oxford University Press.

Ameka, Felix K., Alan Dench, and Nicholas Evans. 2006. *Catching Language: The Standing Challenge of Grammar Writing*. Berlin: Mouton De Gruyter.

Amha, Azeb. 2001. *The Maale Language*. Leiden: CNWS.

Amha, Azeb. 2007. 'Non-verbal predication in Wolaitta', pp. 99–117 of *Deictics, Copula and Focus in the Ethiopian Convergence Area*, edited by Joachim Crass and Ronny Meyer. Köln: Rüdiger Köppe Verlag.

Amha, Azeb. 2012. 'Omotic', pp. 423–504 of *Afroasiatic Languages*, edited by Zygmunt Frajzyngier. Cambridge: Cambridge University Press.

Amha, Azeb and Gerrit J. Dimmendaal. 2006. 'Verbal compounding in Wolaitta', pp. 319–37 of *Serial Verb Constructions: A Cross-linguistic Typology*, edited by Alexandra Y. Aikhenvald and R. M. W. Dixon. Oxford: Oxford University Press.

Amith, Jonathan D. and Thomas C. Smith-Stark. 1994. 'Transitive nouns and split possessive paradigms in Central Guerrero', *International Journal of American Linguistics* 60: 342–68.

Andersen, Torben. 1988. 'Ergativity in Päri, a Nilotic OVS language', *Lingua* 75: 289–324.

Anderson, S. R. 1992. *A-Morphous Morphology*. Cambridge: Cambridge University Press.

Andrews, Avery D. 2007. 'Relative clauses', pp. 206–36 of *Language Typology and Syntactic Description*, edited by T. Shopen. Cambridge: Cambridge University Press.

Andvik, Eric. 2003. 'Tshangla', pp. 439–55 of *The Sino-Tibetan Languages*, edited by Graham Thurgood and Randy J. LaPolla. London: Routledge.

Anttila, Raimo. 1989. *Historical and Comparative Linguistics*. Amsterdam: John Benjamins.

Appel, René and Pieter Muysken. 2005. *Language Contact and Bilingualism*. Amsterdam: Academic Archive.

Ashton, E. O. 1947. *Swahili Grammar (including Intonation)*. London: Longmans.

Aspinion, Robert. 1953. *Aprenons le berbère: Initiation aux dialectes chleuhs*. Paris: Félix Moncho.

Austin, Peter. 1998. 'Crow is sitting chasing them: grammaticalization and the verb "to sit" in the Mantharta languages, Western Australia', pp. 19–35 of *Case, Typology and Grammar*, edited by Anna Siewerska and Jae Jung Song. Amsterdam: John Benjamins.

Auwera, Johan van der. 2011. 'Phasal adverbials in the languages of Europe', pp. 25–146 of *Adverbial Constructions in the Languages of Europe*. Berlin: De Gruyter.

Barnes, Janet. 1999. 'Tucano', pp. 207–26 of *The Amazonian Languages*, edited by R. M. W. Dixon and Alexandra Y. Aikhenvald. Cambridge: Cambridge University Press.

Barnhart, Robert K. 2008. *Chambers Dictionary of Etymology*. Edinburgh: Chambers.

Baron, Dennis. 1986. *Grammar and Gender*. New Haven and London: Yale University Press.

Basso, Ellen B. 2007. 'The Kalapalo affinal civility register', *Journal of Linguistic Anthropology* 17: 161–83.

Basso, Keith H. 1970. '"To give up on words": silence in Western Apache culture', *Southwestern Journal of Anthropology* 26: 213–30.

Bauer, Laurie, and Rodney Huddleston. 2002. 'Lexical word-formation', pp. 1621–777 of *The Cambridge Grammar of the English Language*, by Rodney Huddleston and Geoffrey K. Pullum (chief authors). Cambridge: Cambridge University Press.

Baugh, Albert C. 1957. *A History of the English Language*. 2nd edn, New York: Appleton-Century-Crofts.

Baxter, A. N. 1988. *A Grammar of Kristang (Malacca Creole Portuguese)*. Canberra: Pacific Linguistics.

Beck, David. 2002. *The Typology of Part-of-speech Systems: The Markedness of Adjectives*. New York: Routledge.

Becker, A. J. 1975. 'A linguistic image of nature: the Burmese numerative classifier system', *Linguistics* 165: 109–21.

Beckwith, C. I. 1998. 'Noun specification and classification in Uzbek', *Anthropological Linguistics* 40: 124–40.

Benveniste, Émile. 1971. 'Delocutive verbs', pp. 239–46 of his *Problems of General Linguistics*, translated by Mary E. Mack. Coral Gables: University of Miami Press. [Original: *Problèmes de linguistique générale*. 1966. Paris: Editions Gallimard.]

Berlin, B. 1968. *Tzeltal Numeral Classifiers: A Study in Ethnographic Semantics*. The Hague: Mouton.

Bhat, D. N. S. 2004. *Pronouns*. Oxford: Oxford University Press.

Blake, Barry J. 2001. *Case*. Cambridge: Cambridge University Press.

Bloomfield, Leonard. 1933. *Language*. New York: Holt.

Boas, Frans. 1938. 'Language', pp. 124–45 of *General Anthropology*, edited by Franz Boas. Boston, New York: D. C. Heath and Company.

Boas, Frans and Ella Deloria. 1941. *Dakota Grammar*. Washington: US Govt. Print. Office.

Bonvillain, N. 1978. 'Linguistic change in Akwesasne Mohawk: French and English influences', *International Journal of American Linguistics* 44: 31–9.

Borgman, D. M. 1990. 'Sanuma', pp. 17–248 of *Handbook of Amazonian Languages*. vol. 2, edited by D. C. Derbyshire and G. K. Pullum. Berlin: Mouton de Gruyter.

Bossong, Georg. 1991. 'Differential object marking in Romance and beyond', pp. 143–70 of *New Analyses in Romance Linguistics*, edited by D. Wanner and D. Kibbee (eds). Amsterdam: John Benjamins.

Bowden, John. 2001. *Taba: Description of a South Halmahera Language*. Canberra: Pacific Linguistics.

Breedveld, J. O. 1995. 'The semantic basis of noun class systems: the case of the KE and NGE classes in Fulfulde', *Journal of West African Languages* XXV: 63–74.

Brenzinger, Matthias and Anne-Marie Fehn. 2013. 'From body to knowledge: perception and cognition in Khwe-||Ani and Tsi'ixa', pp. 161–92 of Aikhenvald and Storch (eds).

Bril, Isabelle. 2004. 'Coordinating strategies and inclusory constructions in New Caledonian and other Oceanic languages', pp. 499–534 of *Coordinating Constructions*, edited by Martin Haspelmath. Amsterdam: John Benjamins.

Bril, Isabelle. 2013. 'Ownership, part–whole, and other possessive-associative relations in Nêlêmwa (New Caledonia)', pp. 65–89 of *Possession and Ownership: A Cross-linguistic Typology*, edited by Alexandra Y. Aikhenvald and R. M. W. Dixon. Oxford: Oxford University Press.

Brinton, Laurel J. 1988. *The Development of English Aspectual System*. Cambridge: Cambridge University Press.

Brinton, Laurel J. 2000. *The Structure of Modern English: A Linguistic Introduction*. Amsterdam: John Benjamins.

Brody, Jill. 1995. 'Lending the "unborrowable": Spanish discourse markers in Indigenous American languages', pp. 132–47 of *Spanish in Four Continents. Studies in Language Contact and Bilingualism*, edited by Carmen Silva-Corvalán. Washington: Georgetown University Press.

Brosnahan, P. 1961. *The Sounds of Language*. Cambridge: W. Heffer and Sons Ltd.

Brown, P. and S. C. Levinson. 1987. *Politeness: Some Universals in Language Usage.* Cambridge: Cambridge University Press.

Brown, R. 1981. 'Semantic aspects of some Waris predications', pp. 93–123 of *Syntax and Semantics in Papua New Guinea Languages*, edited by K. J. Franklin. Ukarumpa: Summer Institute of Linguistics.

Brownie, John and Marjo Brownie. 2007. *Mussau Grammar Essentials.* Data Papers on Papua New Guinea Languages, vol. 52. Ukarumpa: SIL-PNG Academic Publications.

Bruce, Les. 1985. *The Alamblak Language of Papua New Guinea (East Sepik).* Canberra: Pacific Linguistics.

Bruce, Les. 1988. 'Serialisation: from syntax to lexicon', *Studies in Language* 12: 19–49.

Burquest, Donald A. and David L. Payne. 1993. *Phonological Analysis: A Functional Approach.* Dallas, TX: Summer Institute of Linguistics.

Burridge, Kate. 2004. 'Changes within Pennsylvania German grammar as enactments of Anabaptist world view', pp. 207–30 of *Ethnosyntax. Explorations in Grammar and Culture*, edited by Nicholas J. Enfield. Oxford: Oxford University Press.

Burridge, Kate. 2006a. 'Complement clause types in Pennsylvania German', pp. 49–71 of *Complementation: A Cross-linguistic Typology*, edited by R. M. W. Dixon and Alexandra Y. Aikhenvald. Oxford: Oxford University Press.

Burridge, Kate. 2006b. 'Language contact and convergence in Pennsylvania German', pp. 179–200 of *Serial Verb Constructions: A Cross-linguistic Typology*, edited by Alexandra Y. Aikhenvald and R. M. W. Dixon. Oxford: Oxford University Press.

Burridge, Kate. 2007. 'A separate and peculiar people—fieldwork and the Pennsylvania Germans', *Language Typology and Universals* 60 (1): 32–41.

Butt, John and Carmin Benjamin. 2004. *A New Reference Grammar of Modern Spanish.* 4th edn, London: Hodder Arnold.

Bybee, Joan. 1985. 'Diagrammatic iconicity in stem-inflection relations', pp. 11–48 of *Iconicity in Syntax*, edited by John Haiman. Amsterdam: John Benjamins.

Camp, E. and M. Liccardi, 1965. 'Itonama', pp. 223–383 of *Gramáticas estructurales de lenguas bolivianas*, vol. III, edited by E. Matteson. Riberalta: Instituto Lingüístico de Verano.

Campbell, Lyle. 1997. 'Amerindian personal pronouns: A second opinion', *Language* 73: 339–51.

Carlin, Eithne B. 2004. *A Grammar of Trio, a Cariban Language from Suriname.* Frankfurt am Main: Peter Lang.

Carlson, Robert. 1994. *A Grammar of Supyire.* Berlin: Mouton de Gruyter.

Carpenter, K. 1986. 'Productivity and pragmatics of Thai classifiers', *Berkeley Linguistics Society: Proceedings of the annual meeting* 12: 14–25.

Chafe, Wallace L. 1967. *Seneca Morphology and Dictionary.* Washington, DC: Smithsonian Press.

Chafe, Wallace L. 1970. *A Semantically Based Sketch of Onondaga.* Supplement to the International Journal of American Linguistics 36 (2).

Chafe, Wallace L. 1976. 'Givenness, contrastiveness, definiteness, subjects, topics, and point of view', pp. 25–55 of *Subject and Topic*, edited by Charles N. Li. New York: Academic Press.

Chafe, Wallace L. 1987. 'Cognitive constraints on information flow', pp. 21–51 of *Coherence and Grounding in Discourse*, edited by Russell S. Tomlin. Amsterdam: John Benjamins.

Chafe, Wallace L. 1990. 'Uses of the defocusing pronominal prefixes in Caddo', *Anthropological Linguistics* 31: 57–68.

Chafe, Wallace L. 1994. *Discourse, Consciousness and Time: The Flow and Displacement of Consciousness Experience in Speaking and Writing.* Chicago: University of Chicago Press.

Chafe, Wallace L. 2004. 'Masculine and feminine in the Northern Iroquioan languages', pp. 99–109 of *Ethnosyntax. Explorations in Grammar and Culture*, edited by N. J. Enfield. Oxford: Oxford University Press.

Chaker, Salem. 1983. *Un parler berbère d'Algérie (Kabylie). Syntaxe.* Aix-en-Provence: Publications Université de Provence.

Chao, Y. 1968. *A Grammar of Spoken Chinese.* Berkeley and Los Angeles: University of California Press.

Chapman, S. and D. C. Derbyshire. 1991. 'Paumari', pp. 161–354 of *Handbook of Amazonian Languages*, edited by D. C. Derbyshire and G. K. Pullum, vol. 3. Berlin: Mouton de Gruyter.

Chaumeuil, Jean-Pierre. 1993. 'Des esprits aux ancêtres: Procédés linguistiques, conceptions du langage et de la société chez les Yagua de l'Amazonie péruvienne', *L'Homme. 33e Année.* No 126/128. *La remontée de l'Amazonie*: 409–27.

Chelliah, Shobhana and Willem de Reuse. 2010. *Handbook of Descriptive Linguistic Fieldwork.* London: Springer.

Chirikba, Viacheslav. 2008. 'The problem of the Caucasian Sprachbund', pp. 25–93 of *From Linguistic Areas to Areal Linguistics*, edited by Pieter Muysken. Amsterdam: John Benjamins.

Christaller, J. 1875. *A Grammar of the Asante and Fante Languages Called Twi.* Basel: Basel Evangelical Missionary Society.

Chung, S. and A. Timberlake. 1985. 'Tense, aspect and mood', pp. 202–58 of *Language Typology and Syntactic Description*, vol. III, edited by T. Shopen. Cambridge: Cambridge University Press.

Clark, Eve V. 1978. 'Locationals: existential, locative, and possessive constructions', pp. 85–126 of *Universals of Human Language*, vol. 4. *Syntax*, edited by Joseph H. Greenberg. Stanford, CA: Stanford University Press.

Clark, Eve V. and Herbert H. Clark. 1979. 'When nouns surface as verbs', *Language* 55: 767–811.

Clyne, Michael, Catrin Norrby, and Jane Warren. 2009. *Language and Human Relations. Styles of Address in Contemporary Languages.* Cambridge: Cambridge University Press.

Coates, Jennifer. 2003. 'Address', pp. 33–4 of *International Encyclopedia of Linguistics*, 2nd edn, edited by William J. Frawley. Oxford: Oxford University Press.

Cole, Peter. 1982. *Imbabura Quechua.* Amsterdam: North-Holland.

Collinder, Björn. 1965. *An Introduction to the Uralic Languages.* Berkeley: University of California Press.

Comrie, Bernard. 1976a. *Aspect.* Cambridge: Cambridge University Press.

Comrie, Bernard. 1976b. 'The syntax of causative constructions', pp. 261–312 of *Syntax and Semantics*, vol. 6, *The Grammar of Causative Constructions*, edited by Masayoshi Shibatani. New York: Academic Press.

Comrie, Bernard. 1984. [Plenary session discussion], pp. 255–87 of *Interrogativity. A Colloquium on the Grammar, Typology and Pragmatics of Questions in Seven Diverse Languages*, edited by William S. Jr. Chisholm. Amsterdam: John Benjamins.

Comrie, Bernard. 1985. *Tense.* Cambridge: Cambridge University Press.

Comrie, Bernard. 2003. 'Recipient person suppletion in the verb "give"', pp. 265–81 of *Language and Life. Essays in Memory of Kenneth L. Pike*, edited by Mary Ruth Wise, Thomas

N. Headland, and Ruth M. Brend. Summer Institute of Linguistics International and the University of Texas at Arlington.

Comrie, Bernard and Sandra A. Thompson. 1985. 'Lexical nominalization', pp. 349–98 of *Language Typology and Syntactic Description*, vol. III, *Grammatical Categories and the Lexicon*, edited by T. Shopen. Cambridge: Cambridge University Press.

Cook, Eung-Do. 2004. *A Grammar of Dëne Sųłiné (Chipewyan)*. Algonquian and Iroquoian Linguistics special Athabaskan number. Memoir 17.

Corbett, Greville. 1991. *Gender*. Cambridge: Cambridge University Press.

Corbett, Greville. 2000. *Number*. Cambridge: Cambridge University Press.

Corominas, J. 1954. *Diccionario Crítico Etimológico de la Lengua Castellana*, vol. III. Berna: Editorial Francke.

Cowell, Andrew. 2007. 'Arapaho imperatives: indirectness, politeness and communal "face"', *Journal of Linguistic Anthropology* 17: 44–60.

Cowell, M. W. 1964. *A Reference Grammar of Syrian Arabic*. Washington DC: Georgetown University Press.

Cruse, Alan. 2006. *A Glossary of Semantics and Pragmatics*. Edinburgh: University of Edinburgh Press.

Curnow, Timothy J. 1997. *A grammar of Awa Pit*. PhD thesis. Canberra: Australian National University.

Daguman, Josephine. 2004. *A grammar of Northern Subanen*. PhD dissertation, RCLT, La Trobe University.

Davies, E. 1986. *The English Imperative*. London: Croom Helm.

Davies, J. 1981. *Kobon*. Amsterdam: North-Holland.

Dean, Bartholomew. 2009. *Urarina Society, Cosmology, and History in Peruvian Amazonia*. Gainesville: University Press of Florida.

Dehé, N. and Y. Kavalova. 2007. *Parentheticals*. Amsterdam: John Benjamins.

DeLancey, S. 1997. 'Mirativity: the grammatical marking of unexpected information', *Linguistic Typology* 1: 33–52.

Dench, A. 2001. 'Descent and diffusion: the complexity of the Pilbara situation', pp. 105–33 of *Areal Diffusion and Genetic Relationships: Case Studies in Comparative Linguistics*, edited by Alexandra Y. Aikhenvald and R. M. W. Dixon. Oxford: Oxford University Press.

Derbyshire, Desmond C. 1985. *Hixkaryana and Linguistic Typology*. Dallas: SIL and the University of Texas at Arlington.

Deutscher, Guy. 2006. 'Complement clause types and complementation strategies in Akkadian', pp. 159–77 of *Complementation: A Cross-linguistic Typology*, edited by R. M. W. Dixon and Alexandra Y. Aikhenvald. Oxford: Oxford University Press.

Deutscher, Guy. 2009. 'The semantics of clause linking in Akkadian', pp. 56–73 of *The Semantics of Clause Linking: A Cross-linguistic Typology*, edited by R. M. W. Dixon and Alexandra Y. Aikhenvald. Oxford: Oxford University Press.

Diessel, Holger. 1999. *Demonstratives: Form, Functions and Grammaticalization*. Amsterdam: John Benjamins.

Dimmendaal, Gerrit J. 1983. *The Turkana Language*. Dordrecht: Foris Publications.

Dimmendaal, Gerrit J. 1998. 'A syntactic typology of the Surmic family from an areal and historical-comparative point of view', pp. 35–81 of *Surmic Languages and Cultures*, edited by Gerrit J. Dimmendaal and Marco Last. Köln: Rüdiger Köppe Verlag.

Dimmendaal, Gerrit J. 2000. 'Number marking and noun categorization in Nilo-Saharan languages', *Anthropological Linguistics* 42: 215–61.

Dixon, R. M. W. 1972. *The Dyirbal Language of North Queensland*. Cambridge: Cambridge University Press.

Dixon, R. M. W. 1977. *A Grammar of Yidiñ*. Cambridge: Cambridge University Press.

Dixon, R. M. W. 1979. 'Delocutive verbs in Dyirbal', pp. 21–38 of *Studies in Descriptive and General Linguistics: Festschrift for Winfred P. Lehmann*, edited by Paul. J. Hopper. Amsterdam: John Benjamins.

Dixon, R. M. W. 1980. *The Languages of Australia*. Cambridge: Cambridge University Press.

Dixon, R. M. W. 1982. *Where Have all the Adjectives Gone? and Other Essays in Semantics and Syntax*. Berlin: Mouton.

Dixon, R. M. W. 1988. *A Grammar of Boumaa Fijian*. Chicago: University of Chicago Press.

Dixon, R. M. W. 1989. 'The Dyirbal kinship system', *Oceania* 50: 245–68.

Dixon, R. M. W. 1991. *A New Approach to English Grammar, on Semantic Principles*. Oxford: Clarendon Press.

Dixon, R. M. W. 1994. *Ergativity*. Cambridge: Cambridge University Press.

Dixon, R. M. W. 2000. 'A typology of causatives: form, syntax and meaning', pp. 30–83 of *Changing Valency: Case Studies in Transitivity*, edited by R. M. W. Dixon and Alexandra Y. Aikhenvald. Cambridge: Cambridge University Press.

Dixon, R. M. W. 2002. *Australian Languages: Their Nature and Development*. Cambridge: Cambridge University Press.

Dixon, R. M. W. 2004a. *The Jarawara Language of Southern Amazonia*. Oxford: Oxford University Press.

Dixon, R. M. W. 2004b. 'Adjective classes in typological perspective', pp. 1–49 of *Adjective Classes: A Cross-linguistic Typology*, edited by R. M. W. Dixon and Alexandra Y. Aikhenvald. Oxford: Oxford University Press.

Dixon, R. M. W. 2005. *A Semantic Approach to English Grammar*. 2nd edn, Oxford: Oxford University Press.

Dixon, R. M. W. 2006a. 'Complement clause types and complementation strategies in typological perspective', pp. 1–48 of *Complementation: A Cross-linguistic Typology*, edited by R. M. W. Dixon and Alexandra Y. Aikhenvald. Oxford: Oxford University Press.

Dixon, R. M. W. 2006b. 'Serial verb constructions: Conspectus and coda', pp. 338–50 of *Serial Verb Constructions: A Cross-linguistic Typology*, edited by A. Y. Aikhenvald and R. M. W. Dixon. Oxford: Oxford University Press.

Dixon, R. M. W. 2007a. 'Field linguistics: a minor manual', *Language Typology and Universals* 60 (1): 12–31.

Dixon, R. M. W. 2007b. 'Clitics in English', *English Studies* 88: 574–600.

Dixon, R. M. W. 2008. 'Deriving verbs in English', *Language Sciences* 30: 31–52.

Dixon, R. M. W. 2009. 'The semantics of clause linking in typological perspective', pp. 1–55 of *The Semantics of Clause Linking: A Cross-linguistic Typology*, edited by R. M. W. Dixon and Alexandra Y. Aikhenvald. Oxford: Oxford University Press.

Dixon, R. M. W. 2010a. *Basic Linguistic Theory*, vol. 1. *Methodology*. Oxford: Oxford University Press.

Dixon, R. M. W. 2010b. *Basic Linguistic Theory*, vol. 2. *Grammatical topics*. Oxford: Oxford University Press.

Dixon, R. M. W. 2011. 'Features of the noun phrase in English', pp. 494–518 of *Language at Large. Essays on Syntax and Semantics*, edited by Alexandra Y. Aikhenvald and R. M. W. Dixon. Leiden: Brill.

Dixon, R. M. W. 2012. *Basic Linguistic Theory*, vol. 3. *Further Grammatical Topics*. Oxford: Oxford University Press.

Dixon, R. M. W. 2014. *Making New Words: Morphological Derivations in English*. Oxford: Oxford University Press.

Dixon, R. M. W. Forthcoming. *Edible Gender, Mother-in-law Style and other Grammatical Wonders*. Oxford: Oxford University Press.

Dixon, R. M. W. and Alexandra Y. Aikhenvald (eds) 2000. *The Amazonian Languages*. Cambridge: Cambridge University Press.

Dixon, R. M. W. and Alexandra Y. Aikhenvald. 2002. 'Word: a typological framework', pp. 1–41 of *Word: A Typological Framework*, edited by R. M. W. Dixon and Alexandra Y. Aikhenvald. Cambridge: Cambridge University Press.

Dixon, R. M. W. and Alexandra Y. Aikhenvald (eds) 2002. *Word: A Typological Framework*. Cambridge: Cambridge University Press.

Dixon, R. M. W. and Alexandra Y. Aikhenvald (eds) 2004. *Adjective Classes: A Cross-linguistic Typology*. Oxford: Oxford University Press.

Dixon, R. M. W. and Alexandra Y. Aikhenvald. 2006. *Complementation: A Cross-linguistic Typology*, edited by R. M. W. Dixon and A. Y. Aikhenvald. Oxford: Oxford University Press.

Dixon, R. M. W. and Alexandra Y. Aikhenvald (eds) 2009. *The Semantics of Clause Linking: A Cross-linguistic Typology*. Oxford: Oxford University Press.

Dixon, R. M. W. and Grace Koch. 1996. *Dyirbal Song Poetry*. Santa Lucia: University of Queensland Press.

Doke, C. M. 1935. *Bantu Linguistic Terminology*. London: Longmas, Green.

Donohue, Mark. 1997. 'Tone systems in New Guinea', *Linguistic Typology* 1: 347–86.

Dorian, Nancy C. 2010. *Investigating Variation: The Effects of Social Organization and Social Setting*. New York: Oxford University Press.

Downing, Pamela. 1996. *Numeral Classifier Systems: The Case of Japanese*. Amsterdam: John Benjamins.

Du Bois, John. 1987. 'The discourse basis of ergativity', *Language* 63: 805–55.

Dunn, Michael. 1999. *A grammar of Chukchi*. PhD thesis. Australian National University, Canberra.

Durie, M. 1988. 'Verb serialisation and "verbal prepositions" in Oceanic languages', *Oceanic Linguistics* 27: 1–23.

Durie, M. 1997. 'Grammatical structures in verb serialisation', pp. 289–354 of *Complex Predicates*, edited by A. Alsina, J. Bresnan, and P. Sells. Stanford, CA: CSLI.

Ebeling, C. L. 1966. 'Review of Chikobava and Cercvadze's *The Grammar of Literary Avar*'. *Studia Caucasica* 2: 58–100.

Eberhard, David. 2009. *Mamaindê Grammar: A Northern Nambiquara Language in its Cultural Context*. Utrecht: LOT.

Ekdahl, Elizabeth M. and Joseph E. Grimes. 1964. 'Terena verb inflection', *IJAL*, 30: 261–8.

Elliott, D. E. 1974. 'Toward a grammar of exclamations', *Foundations of Language* 11: 231–46.

Elliott, J. 2000. 'Realis and irrealis: Forms and concepts of the grammaticalisation of reality', *Linguistic Typology* 4: 55–90.

Emeneau, M. B. 1956. 'India as a linguistic area', *Language* 32: 3–16.

Enfield, Nicholas J. (ed.) 2004. *Ethnosyntax: Explorations in Grammar and Culture*. Oxford: Oxford University Press.

Enfield, Nicholas J. 2004a. 'Introduction', pp. 3–30 of Enfield (ed.).

Enfield, Nicholas J. 2004b. 'Adjectives in Lao', pp. 323–47 of *Adjective Classes: A Cross-linguistic Typology*, edited by R. M. W. Dixon and Alexandra Y. Aikhenvald. Oxford: Oxford University Press.

Enfield, Nicholas J. 2007. *A Grammar of Lao*. Berlin: Mouton de Gruyter.

England, Nora C. 1983. *A Grammar of Mam, a Mayan Language*. Austin: University of Texas Press.

England, Nora C. 1992. 'Doing Mayan linguistics in Guatemala', *Language* 68: 29–35.

Epps, Patience. 2008. *A Grammar of Hup*. Berlin: Mouton de Gruyter.

Erelt, Mati. 2007. 'Structure of the Estonian language. Syntax', pp. 93–129 of *Estonian Language*, edited by Mati Erelt. Tallinn: Estonian Academy Publishers.

Evans, Barrie. 1994. *Draft Grammar of Pular*. Conakry: Mission Protestante Réformée.

Evans, Nicholas. 2000. 'Kinship verbs', pp. 103–72 of *Approaches to the Typology of Word Classes*, edited by P. M. Vogel and B. Comrie. Berlin: Mouton de Gruyter.

Evans, Nicholas and Toshiki Osada. 2005. 'Mundari: the myth of a language without word classes', *Linguistic Typology* 9: 351–90.

Fabricius, Anne H. 1998. *A Comparative Survey of Reduplication in Australian Languages*. Munich: Lincom Europa.

Farr, Cynthia J. M. 1999. *The Interface between Syntax and Discourse in Korafe, a Papuan Language of Papua New Guinea*. Canberra: Pacific Linguistics.

Feldpausch, Tom and Becky Feldpausch. 1992. *Namia Grammar Esssentials*. Ukarumpa: SIL.

Fleck, David W. 2006. 'Antipassive in Matses', *Studies in Language* 30: 541–73.

Fleck, David. Forthcoming. *A Grammar of Matses*.

Fleck, David and Robert S. Voss. 2006. 'On the origin and cultural significance of unusually large synonym sets in some Panoan languages of Western Amazonia', *Anthropological Linguistics* 48: 335–68.

Fodor, I. 1984. 'Language reforms of the past and in the developing countries', pp. 441–54 of vol. III of *Language Reform: History and Future*, edited by I. Fodor and C. Hagège. Hamburg: Buske Verlag.

Foley, William A. 1986. *The Papuan Languages of New Guinea*. Cambridge: Cambridge University Press.

Foley, William A. 1991. *The Yimas Language of New Guinea*. Stanford, CA: Stanford University Press.

Foley, William A. and M. Olson. 1985. 'Clausehood and verb serialisation', pp. 17–60 of *Grammar Inside and Outside the Clause*, edited by J. Nichols and A. C. Woodbury. Cambridge: Cambridge University Press.

Fortescue, M. 1984. *West Greenlandic*. London: Routledge.

Fortescue, M. 2003. 'Evidentiality in West Greenlandic: a case of scattered coding', pp. 291–306 of *Studies in Evidentiality*, edited by Alexandra Y. Aikhenvald and R. M. W. Dixon. Amsterdam: John Benjamins.

Frajzyngier, Zygmunt. 1993. *A Grammar of Mupun*. Berlin: Dietrich Riemer Verlag.

Frajzyngier, Zygmunt. 2002. *A Grammar of Hdi*. Berlin: Mouton De Gruyter.

Friedman, Victor. 2006. 'Balkanizing the Balkan Sprachbund: a closer look at grammatical permeability and feature distribution', pp. 201–19 of *Grammars in Contact: A Cross-linguistic Typology*, edited by Alexandra Y. Aikhenvald and R. M. W. Dixon. Oxford: Oxford University Press.

Fries, Charles C. and Kenneth L. Pike. 1949. 'Coexistent phonemic systems', *Language* 25: 29–50.

Gary Olmsted, Judith and Saad Gamal-Edin. 1982. *Cairene Egyptian Colloquial Arabic*. Amsterdam: North Holland.

Gaztambide Arrillaga, Carlos. 1990. *El idioma indígena taíno en las Antillas*. Serie Gaztambide Arrillaga de historia y lingüística. Estudio de Investigación Filológica. Tomo XXII. Puerto Rico, Ramallo Bros.

Genetti, Carol. 2005. 'The participial construction of Dolakhā Newar: syntactic implications of an Asian converb', *Studies in Language* 29: 35–87.

Genetti, Carol. 2006. 'Complement clause types and complementation strategy in Dolakha Newar', pp. 137–58 of *Complementation: A Cross-linguistic Typology*, edited by R. M. W. Dixon and Alexandra Y. Aikhenvald. Oxford: Oxford University Press.

Genetti, Carol and Laura D. Crain. 2003. 'Beyond preferred argument structure: sentences, pronouns and given referents in Nepali', pp. 197–224 of *Preferred Argument Structure: Grammar as Architecture for Function*, edited by John W. Du Bois, Lorraine E. Kumpf, and William J. Ashby. Amsterdam: John Benjamins.

Genetti, Carol and Kristine Hildebrandt. 2004. 'The two adjective classes in Manange', pp. 74–96 of *Adjective Classes: A Cross-linguistic Typology*, edited by R. M. W. Dixon and Alexandra Y. Aikhenvald. Oxford: Oxford University Press.

Geraghty, Paul. 2000. 'Possession in the Fijian languages', *Sprachtypologie und Universalienforschung* 53 (3/4): 243–50.

Gildea, Spike. 2000. 'On the genesis of the verb phrase in Cariban languages: diversity through reanalysis', pp. 65–105 of *Reconstructing Grammar: Comparative Linguistics and Grammaticalization*, edited by Spike Gildea. Amsterdam: John Benjamins.

Givón, Talmy. 1970. 'Notes on the semantic structure of English adjectives', *Language* 46: 816–37.

Givón, Talmy. 1991. 'Some substantive issues concerning verb serialisation: grammatical vs cognitive packaging', pp. 137–184 of *Serial Verbs: Grammatical, Comparative and Cognitive Approaches*, edited by C. Lefebvre. Amsterdam: John Benjamins.

Givón, Talmy. 2011. *Ute Reference Grammar*. Amsterdam: John Benjamins.

Goddard, Cliff. 1983. *A semantically-oriented grammar of the Yankunytjatjara dialect of the Western Desert language*. PhD dissertation, Australian National University.

Goddard, Cliff. 2005. *The Languages of East and Southeast Asia: An Introduction*. Oxford: Oxford University Press.

Gomez, Gale G. 1990. *The Shiriana dialect of Yanam (Northern Brazil)*. PhD dissertation, Columbia University.

Grandi, Nicola. 2002. *Morfologie in contatto. Le costruzioni valutative nelle lingue del Mediterraneo*. Pavia: Francongeli.

Gray, L. H. 1971. *Introduction to Semitic Comparative Linguistics*. Amsterdam: Philo Press.

Greenberg, Joseph H. 1963. 'Some universals of grammar with particular reference to the order of meaningful elements, pp. 58–90 of *Universals of Language*, edited by Joseph H. Greenberg. Cambridge, MA: MIT Press.

Grevisse, Maurice. 1986 *Le bon usage. Grammaire française*. Douzième édition refondue par André Goosse. Paris-Gembloux: Duculot.

Guérin, Valérie. 2007. 'Definiteness and specificity in Maˇvea', *Oceanic Linguistics* 46: 538–53.

Guillaume, Antoine. 2004. *A grammar of Cavineña, an Amazonian language of northern Bolivia*. PhD thesis, La Trobe University.

Guillaume, Antoine. 2008. *A Grammar of Cavineña*. Berlin: Mouton de Gruyter.

Gumperz, J. J. and R. Wilson. 1971. 'Convergence and creolization: a case from the Indo-Aryan/ Dravidian Border in India', pp. 151–68 of *Pidginization and Creolization of Languages*, edited by D. Hymes. Cambridge: Cambridge University Press.

Haig, Geoffrey. 2001. 'Linguistic diffusion in present-day East Anatolia: from top to bottom', pp. 195–224 of *Areal Diffusion and Genetic Relationships: Case Studies in Comparative Linguistics*, edited by Alexandra Y. Aikhenvald and R. M. W. Dixon. Oxford: Oxford University Press.

Haiman, John. 1980. *Hua: A Papuan Language of the Eastern Highlands of New Guinea*. Amsterdam: John Benjamins.

Haiman, John. 1983. 'Iconic and economic motivation', *Language* 59: 781–819.

Haiman, John and Pamela Munro (eds). 1983. *Switch-reference and Universal Grammar*. Amsterdam: John Benjamins.

Hale, Kenneth L. 1966. 'Kinship reflections in syntax: some Australian languages', *Word* 22: 318–24.

Hale, Kenneth L. 1973. 'Deep-surface canonical disparities in relation to analysis and change: an Australian example', pp. 401–58 of *Current Trends in Linguistics*, vol. 11—*Diachronic, Areal and Typological Linguistics*, edited by T. A. Sebeok. The Hague: Mouton.

Hale, Kenneth L. 1975. 'Gaps in grammar and culture', pp. 295–315 of *Linguistics and Anthropology: In Honor of C. F. Voegelin*, edited by M. D. Kinkade et al. Lisse: Peter de Ridder Press.

Hale, Kenneth L. 1976. 'The adjoined relative clause in Australia', pp. 78–105 of *Grammatical Categories in Australian Languages*, edited by R. M. W. Dixon. Canberra: AIAS.

Halpern, A. 1998. 'Clitics', pp. 101–22 of *The Handbook of Morphology*, edited by A. Spencer and A. M. Zwicky. Oxford: Blackwell.

Halpern, A. M. 1942. 'Yuma kinship terms', *American Anthropologist* 44: 425–41.

Hardman, M. J. 1986. 'Data-source marking in the Jaqi languages', pp. 113–36 of *Evidentiality: The Linguistic Coding of Epistemology*, edited by W. L. Chafe and J. Nichols. Norwood, NJ: Ablex.

Harms, Philip Lee. 1994. *Epena Pedee Syntax*. Dallas: SIL and University of Texas at Arlington.

Harris, Alice C. 2000. 'Where in the word is the Udi clitic?' *Language* 76: 593–616.

Haspelmath, Martin. 1993. *A Grammar of Lezgian*. Berlin: Mouton de Gruyter.

Haspelmath, Martin. 1997. *Indefinite Pronouns*. Oxford: Oxford University Press.

Haspelmath, Martin (ed.). 2004. *Coordinating Constructions*. Amsterdam: John Benjamins.

Haspelmath, Martin. 2004. 'Coordinating constructions: an overview', pp. 3–39 of *Coordinating Constructions*, edited by Martin Haspelmath. Amsterdam: John Benjamins.

Haspelmath, Martin, Matthew S. Dryer, David Gil, and Bernard Comrie. 2005. *The World Atlas of Language Structures*. Oxford: Oxford University Press.

Haviland, John. 1979. 'Guugu Yimidhirr', pp. 1–180 of *Handbook of Australian Languages*, edited by R. M. W. Dixon and Barry J. Blake. Canberra: The Australian National University Press and Amsterdam: John Benjamins.

Heine, Bernd. 1993. *Auxiliaries: Cognitive Forces and Grammaticalization*. New York: Oxford University Press.

Heine, Bernd. 1997a. *Possession: Cognitive Sources, Forces and Grammaticalization*. Cambridge: Cambridge University Press.

Heine, Bernd. 1997b. *Cognitive Foundations of Grammar*. New York: Oxford University Press.

Heine, Bernd. 2000. 'Polysemy involving reflexive and reciprocal markers in African languages', pp. 1–29 of *Reciprocals: Forms and Functions*, edited by Zygmunt Frajzynguer and Tracy S. Curl. Amsterdam: John Benjamins.

Heine, Bernd and Tania Kuteva. 2001. 'Convergence and divergence in the development of African languages', pp. 393–411 of *Areal Diffusion and Genetic Relationships: Case Studies in Comparative Linguistics*, edited by Alexandra Y. Aikhenvald and R. M. W. Dixon. Oxford: Oxford University Press.

Heine, Bernd and Tania Kuteva. 2002. *World Lexicon of Grammaticalization*. Cambridge: Cambridge University Press.

Henderson, Eugénie J. A. 1951. 'The phonology of loanwords in some South-east Asian languages.' *Transactions of the Philological Society*: 131–58.

Henderson, John. 2002. 'The word in Eastern/Central Arrernte', pp. 100–24 of *Word: A Typological Framework*, edited by R. M. W. Dixon and Alexandra Y. Aikhenvald. Cambridge: Cambridge University Press.

Herbert, R. K. 1990. 'Hlonipha and the ambiguous woman', *Anthropos* 85: 455–73.

Hercus, Luise A. 1994. *A Grammar of the Arabana-Wangkangirru Language, Lake Eyre Basin, South Australia*. Canberra: Pacific Linguistics.

Hewitt, George. 1979. *Abkhaz*. London: Routledge.

Hewitt, George. 1996. *Georgian: A Learner's Guide*. London: Routledge.

Hill, D. 1992. *Longgu grammar*. PhD thesis, Australian National University.

Hill, Jane H. 2005. *A Grammar of Cupeño*. Berkeley: University of California Press.

Hill, Jane H. and Ofelia Zepeda. 1999. 'Language, gender, and biology: pulmonic ingressive airstream in women's speech in Tohono O'odham', *Southwest Journal of Linguistics* 18: 15–40.

Hinds, John. 1986. *Japanese*. London: Croom Helm.

Hock, Hans Henrich. 1991. *Principles of Historical Linguistics*. Berlin: Mouton de Gruyter.

Hockett, Charles F. 1954. 'Two models of grammatical description', *Word* 10: 210–31.

Holes, Clive. 1990. *Gulf Arabic*. London: Routledge.

Holes, Clive. 1995. *Modern Arabic: Structures, Functions and Varieties*. London and New York: Longman.

Holisky, Dee Ann. 1987. 'The case of the intransitive subject in Tsova-Tush (Batsbi)', *Lingua* 71: 103–32.

Holisky, Dee Ann and Rusudan Gagua. 1994. 'Tsova-Tush (Batsbi)', pp. 147–212 of *The Indigenous Languages of the Caucasus*, vol. 4. *North East Caucasian languages*. Part 2, edited by Rieks Smeets. New York: Caravan Books.

Holzknecht, Suzanne. 1987. 'Word taboo and its implication for language change', *Language and Linguistics in Melanesia* 18: 43–69.

Hopper, Paul J. and Sandra Thompson. 1980. 'Transitivity in grammar and discourse', *Language* 56: 251–99.

Hosokawa, K. 1991. *The Yawuru language of West Kimberley: a meaning-based description*, PhD thesis, Australian National University.

Hualde, José Ignacio and Jon Ortiz de Urbina. 2003. *A Grammar of Basque*. Berlin: Mouton de Gruyter.

Huddleston, R. D. 2002. 'Clause type and illocutionary force', pp. 851–945 of *The Cambridge Grammar of the English Language*, edited by Rodney Huddleston and Geoffrey K. Pullum. Cambridge: Cambridge University Press.

Hyman, Larry M. 1975. *Phonology: Theory and Analysis*. New York: Holt, Rinehard and Winston.

Hyman, Larry M. 1988. 'The phonology of final glottal stops', *Proceedings of W.E.C.O.L.* 111–30.

Hyman, Larry M. 1990. 'Boundary tonology and the prosodic hierarchy', pp. 109–26 of *The Phonology–Syntax Connection*, edited by Sharon Inkelas and Draga Zec. Chicago: University of Chicago Press.

Hyslop, Catriona. 2001. *The Lolovoli Dialect of the North-east Ambae Language, Vanuatu*. Canberra: Pacific Linguistics.

Hyslop, Catriona. 2004. 'Adjectives in North-East Ambae', pp. 262–82 of *Adjective Classes: A Cross-linguistic Typology*, edited by R. M. W. Dixon and Alexandra Y. Aikhenvald. Oxford: Oxford University Press.

Ikoro, Suanu. 1996. 'Igbo.' Project 'The categories of human languages.' Canberra: ANU.

Ingram, Andrew. 2006. 'Serial verb constructions in Dumo', pp. 202–22 of *Serial Verb Constructions: A Cross-linguistic Typology*, edited by Alexandra Y. Aikhenvald and R. M. W. Dixon. Oxford: Oxford University Press.

Iwasaki, Shoichi and Preeya Ingkaphirom. 2005. *A Reference Grammar of Thai*. Cambridge: Cambridge University Press.

Jacobsen, William, Jr. 1979. 'Noun and verb in Nootkan', pp. 83–155 of *The Victorian Conference on Northwestern Languages*, edited by Barbara S. Efrat. British Columbia Provincial Museum, Heritage Record No. 4.

Jakobson, R. O. 1957. *Shifters, Verbal Categories, and the Russian Verb*. Cambridge, MA: Harvard University.

Jarkey, Nerida. 2006. 'Complement clause types and complementation strategy in White Hmong', pp. 115–36 of *Complementation: A Cross-linguistic Typology*, edited by R. M. W. Dixon and Alexandra Y. Aikhenvald. Oxford: Oxford University Press.

Jauncey, Dorothy G. 1997. *A grammar of Tamambo*, PhD thesis, Australian National University.

Jauncey, Dorothy G. 2011. *Tamambo, the Language of West Malo, Vanuatu*. Canberra: Pacific Linguistics.

Johnstone, Barbara. 2000. 'The individual voice in language', *Annual Review of Anthropology* 29: 405–24.

Jones, W. and P. Jones. 1991. *Barasano Syntax*. University of Texas at Arlington.

Judy, R. and J. E. Judy. 1965. 'Movima', pp. 131–222 of *Gramáticas estructurales de lenguas bolivianas*, vol. III, edited by E. Matteson. Riberalta: Instituto Lingüístico de Verano.

Juntanamalaga, P. 1988. 'Social issues in Thai Classifier Usage', *Language Sciences* 10: 313–30.

Kabuta, N. S. 2001. 'Ideophones in Cilubà', pp. 139–55 of Voeltz and Kilian-Hatz (eds.)

Kaltenböck, Gunther, Heine, Bernd, and Kuteva, Tania. 2011. 'On thetical grammar', *Studies in Language* 35: 852–97.

Keating, E. 1997. 'Honorific possession: power and language in Pohnpei, Micronesia', *Language and Society* 26: 247–68.

Keenan, Edward L. and Bernard Comrie. 1977. 'Noun phrase accessibility and universal grammar', *Linguistic Inquiry* 8: 63–99.

Keenan, Edward L. and Bernard Comrie. 1979. 'Data on the noun phrase accessibility hierarchy', *Language* 55: 333–51.

Kenesei, I., R. M. Vago, and A. Fenyvesi. 1998. *Hungarian*. London: Routledge.

Kerr, Isabel J. 1995. *Gramática pedagógica del cuiba-wáimonae*. Bogotá: Asociación Instituto Lingüístico de Verano.

Kibrik, A. E. 1994. 'Khinalug', pp. 367–406 of *The Indigenous Languages of the Caucasus*, vol. 4. *North East Caucasian Languages*. Part 2, edited by Rieks Smeets. New York: Caravan Books.

Kilian-Hatz, Christa. 1999. 'Ideophone: Eine typologische Untersuchung unter besonderer Berücksichtigung afrikanischer Sprachen'. *Habilitationschrift*. Cologne: University of Cologne.

Kimball, G.D. 1991. *Koasati Grammari*. Lincoln: University of Nebraska Press.

King, Gareth. 1993. *Modern Welsh*. London: Routledge.

König, Christa. 2008. *Case in Africa*. Oxford: Oxford University Press.

König, Ekkehard and P. Siemund. 2007. 'Speech act distinctions in grammar', pp. 276–324 of *Language Typology and Syntactic Description*, vol. 1. *Clause Structure*, edited by T. Shopen. Cambridge: Cambridge University Press.

Kossmann, Maarten. 1997. *Grammaire du parler berbère de figuig*. Paris, Louvain: Éditions Peeters.

Kossmann, Maarten. 2012. 'Berber languages', pp. 18–101 of *Afroasiatic Languages*, edited by Zygmunt Frajzyngier. Cambridge: Cambridge University Press.

Krauss, Michael E. 1992. 'The world's languages in crisis', *Language* 68: 4–10.

Krishnamurti, Bhadriraju. 2007. 'Fieldwork on Konda, a Dravidian language', *Language Typology and Universals* 60 (1): 56–66.

Kruspe, Nicole. 2004. *A Grammar of Semelai*. Cambridge: Cambridge University Press.

Kundama, J. and P. Wilson, with A. Sapai. 2006. *Ambulas Dictionary*. Ukarumpa: Summer Institute of Linguistics.

Künnap, Ago. 1992. 'Elanud kord . . .' ('Once upon a time . . .'), *Keel ja kirjandus* 4: 209–15.

Kuteva, Tania. 2001. *Auxiliation: An Enquiry into the Nature of Grammaticalization*. New York: Oxford University Press.

Ladefoged, Peter. 1975. *A Course in Phonetics*. New York: Harcourt Brace Jovanovich.

Ladefoged, Peter and Maddieson, Ian. 1996. *The Sounds of the World's Languages*. Oxford: Blackwell.

Lambrecht, Knud. 1994. *Information Structure and Sentence Form: Topic, Focus and Mental Representations of Discourse Referents*. Cambridge: Cambridge University Press.

Lang, Adrienne. 1973. *Enga Dictionary with English Index*. Canberra: Pacific Linguistics.

Laoust, E. 1928. *Cours de berbère marocain. Dialectes du Maroc Central*. Paris: Librarie orientaliste Paul Geuthner.

Lehmann, Thomas. 1993. *A Grammar of Modern Tamil*. Pondicherry: Pondicherry Institute of Linguistics and Culture.

Lehmann, Winfred P. 2004. 'Some proposals for historical linguistic grammars', *Southwest Journal of Linguistics* 23: 145–56.

Lewis, Geoffrey L. 1953. *Teach Yourself Turkish*. London: The English Universities Press Ltd.

Lewis, Geoffrey L. 1967. *Turkish Grammar*. Oxford: Clarendon Press.

Lewis, Geoffrey L. 2000. *Turkish Grammar*. 2nd edn, Oxford: Oxford University Press.

Lewis, M. P. (ed.). 2009. *Ethnologue: Languages of the World*. 16th edn, Dallas: SIL International, <http//www.ethnologue.com>.

Li, Charles N. and Sandra A. Thompson. 1976. 'Subject and topic: a new typology of language', pp. 457–89 of *Subject and Topic*, edited by Charles N. Li. New York: Academic Press.

Li, Charles N. and Sandra A. Thompson. 1981. *Mandarin Chinese: A Functional Reference Grammar*. Berkeley: University of California Press.

Liberman, Anatoly (ed.) 1991. *The Legacy of Genghis Khan and Other Essays on Russia's Identity*, by Nikolai Sergeevich Trubetzkoy. Ann Arbor: Michigan Slavic Publications.

Lichtenberk, F. 1983a. 'Relational Classifiers', *Lingua* 60: 147–76.

Lichtenberk, F. 1983b. *A Grammar of Manam*. Honolulu: University of Hawaii Press.

Lichtenberk, F. 2000. 'Inclusory pronominals', *Oceanic Linguistics* 2000: 1–32.

Lichtenberk, F. 2008. *A Grammar of Toqabaqita*. Berlin: Mouton de Gruyter.

Lindau, Mona. 1985. 'The story of r', pp. 157–68 of *Phonetic Linguistics*, edited by Victoria A. Fromkin. Orlando, FL: Academic Press.

Löftstedt, Leena. 1966. *Les expressions du commandement et de la défense en latin et leur survie dans les langues romanes*. Helsinki: Société Néophilologique.

Lord, C. 1975. 'Igbo verb compounds and the lexicon.' *Studies in African Linguistics* 6: 23–48.

Lowe, Ivan. 1999. 'Nambiquara languages', pp. 269–92 of *The Amazonian Languages*, edited by R. M. W. Dixon and A. Y. Aikhenvald. Cambridge: Cambridge University Press.

Luo, Yongxian. 2013. 'Possessive constructions in Mandarin Chinese', pp. 186–207 of *Possession and Ownership: A Cross-linguistic Typology*, edited by Alexandra Y. Aikhenvald and R. M. W. Dixon. Oxford: Oxford University Press.

Macaulay, Monica. 1996. *A Grammar of Chalcatongo Mixtec*. Berkeley: University of California Press.

McCawley, N. 1973. 'Boy! Is syntax easy!.' *Papers from the Ninth Regional Meeting of the Chicago Linguistic Society* edited by C. Corum, T. Smith-Stark and A. Weiser: 369–77.

MacDonald, Lorna. 1990. *A Grammar of Tauya*. Berlin: Mouton de Gruyter.

McDonald, M. and S. A. Wurm. 1979. *Basic Materials in Waŋkumara (Gaḷali): Grammar, sentences and vocabulary*. Canberra: Pacific Linguistics.

McFarland, Teresa Ann. 2009. *The phonology and morphology of Filomeno Mata Totonac*. PhD dissertation, University of California, Berkeley.

McLendon, S. 2003. 'Evidentials in Eastern Pomo with a comparative survey of the category in other Pomoan languages', pp. 101–30 of *Studies in Evidentiality*, edited by Alexandra Y. Aikhenvald and R. M. W. Dixon. Amsterdam: John Benjamins.

Maiden, Martin and Cecilia Robustelli. 2007. *A Reference Grammar of Modern Italian*. 2nd edn, New York: MacGraw Hill.

Marchand, Hans. 1969. *The Categories and Types of Present-day English Word-formation: A Synchronic-Diachronic Approach*. München: C. H. Beck'sche Verlagsbuchhandlung.

Marnita, Rina A. S. 1996. *Classifiers in Minangkabau*. MA thesis, Australian National University.

Martin, Samuel E. 1975. *A Reference Grammar of Japanese: A Complete Guide to the Grammar and Syntax of the Japanese Language*. Ruttland: Charles E. Tuttle Company.

Masica, Colin. 1991. *The Indo-Aryan Languages*. Cambridge: Cambridge University Press.

Maslova, Elena. 2003. *A Grammar of Kolyma Yukaghir*. Berlin: Mouton de Gruyter.

Mathiot, M. (ed.) 1979. *Ethnology: Boas, Sapir and Whorf revisited*. The Hague: Mouton.

Mathiot, M. and M. Roberts. 1979. 'Sex roles as revealed through referential gender in American English', pp. 1–47 of *Ethnology: Boas, Sapir and Whorf revisited.*, edited by M. Mathiot. The Hague: Mouton.

Matisoff, James A. 1973. 'Rhinoglottophilia: the mysterious connection between nasality and glottality', pp. 265–87 of *Nasalfest: Papers from a symposium on nasals and nasalization*, edited by Charles A. Ferguson, Larry M. Hyman and John J. Ohala. Stanford University: Language Universals Project.

Matthews, P. H. 2007. *Oxford Concise Dictionary of Linguistics*. Oxford: Oxford University Press.

Maybury-Lewis, David. 1968. *Akwẽ-Shavante Society*. Oxford: Clarendon Press.

Meillet, Antoine. 1926. *Linguistique historique et linguistique générale*. Paris: Champion.

Merlan, Francesca. 1976. 'Noun incorporation and discourse reference in Modern Nahuatl', *International Journal of American Linguistics* 42: 177–91.

Merlan, Francesca. 1983. *Ngalakan Grammar, Texts and Vocabulary*. Canberra: Pacific Linguistics.

Michael, Lev D. 2013. 'Possession in Nanti', pp. 149–66 of *Possession and Ownership: A Cross-linguistic Typology*, edited by Alexandra Y. Aikhenvald and R. M. W. Dixon. Oxford: Oxford University Press.

Migliazza, Ernest C. 1972. *Yanomama grammar and intelligibility*. PhD thesis, Indiana University.

Mihas, Elena. 2010. *Essentials of Ashéninca Perené grammar*. PhD dissertation. The University of Wisconsin-Milwaukee.

Miller, Amy. 2001. *A Grammar of Jamul Tiipay*. Berlin: Mouton de Gruyter.

Milner, G. B. 1956. *Fijian Grammar*. Suva: Fiji Government Press.

Miracle, A. W. Jr. and J. de Dioz Yapita Moya. 1981. 'Time and space in Aymara', pp. 33–56 of *The Aymara Language in its Social and Cultural Context: A Collection of Essays on Aspects of Aymara Language and Culture*, edited by Martha Hardman. Gainesville: University Presses of Florida.

Mithun, Marianne. 1984. 'The evolution of noun incorporation', *Language* 60: 847–94.

Mithun, Marianne. 1987. 'Is basic word order universal?', pp. 281–328 of *Coherence in Grammar and in Discourse*, edited by R. S. Tomlin. Amsterdam: John Benjamins.

Mithun, Marianne. 1991. 'Active/agentive Case Marking and Its Motivations', *Language* 67: 510–46.

Mithun, Marianne. 1995. 'On the relativity of irreality', pp. 367–88 of *Modality in Grammar and Discourse*, edited by Barbara Fox and P. J. Hopper. Amsterdam: John Benjamins.

Mithun, Marianne. 1996. 'Multiple reflections of inalienability in Mohawk', pp. 633–49 of *The Grammar of Inalienability: A Typological Perspective on Body Part Terms and the Whole-Part Relation*, edited by Hilary Chappell and William McGregor. Berlin: Mouton de Gruyter.

Mithun, Marianne. 1999. *The Languages of Native North America*. Cambridge: Cambridge University Press.

Mithun, Marianne. 2000. 'The reordering of morphemes', pp. 231–58 of *Reconstructing Grammar: Comparative Linguistics and Grammaticalization*, edited by Spike Gildea. Amsterdam: John Benjamins.

Mithun, Marianne. 2001. 'Understanding and explaining applicatives', *CLS 37: Proceedings of the Thirty-seventh Meeting of the Chicago Linguistic Society: Functionalism and formalism in linguistic theory*, vol. 37(1): 73–97. Chicago Linguistic Society.

Mithun, Marianne. 2007. 'What is a language? Documentation for diverse and evolving audiences', *Language Typology and Universals* 60 (1): 42–55.

Molochieva, Zarina. 2010. *Tense, aspect, and mood in Chechen*. PhD disseration, University of Leipzig.

Monier-Williams, Sir Monier. 1899. *A Sanskrit-English Dictionary, Etymologically and Philologically Arranged, with Special Reference to Cognate Indo-European Languages*. Oxford: Clarendon Press.

Moravcsik, Edith. 2003. 'A semantic analysis of associative plurals', *Studies in Language* 27: 469–503.

Mous, Maarten. 1993. *A Grammar of Iraqw*. Hamburg: Helmut Buske.

Munro, Pamela. 1976. *Mojave Syntax*. New York: Garland.

Munro, Pamela. 1982. 'On the transitivity of "say" verbs', pp. 301–19 of *Syntax and Semantics*, vol. 15. *Studies in Transitivity*, edited by Paul J. Hopper and Sandra A. Thompson. New York: Academic Press.

Murkelinskij, G. B. 1967. 'The Lak language' ('Lakskij jazyk'), pp. 488–507 of *Jazyki narodov SSSR*, vol. IV, edited by E. A. Bokarev et al. Moscow: Nauka.

Nadkarni, M. V. 1975. Bilingualism and syntactic change in Konkani', *Language* 51: 672–83.

Nedjalkov, Igor. 1997. *Evenki*. London: Routledge.

Nelson Francis, W. 2003. 'Dialectology', pp. 430–5 of *International Encyclopedia of Linguistics*, vol. 1, edited by William J. Frawley. Oxford: Oxford University Press.

Newman, Paul. 1990. *Nominal and Verbal Plurality in Chadic*. Dordrecht: Foris.

Newman, Paul. 2000. *The Hausa Language: An Encyclopedic Reference Grammar*. New Haven: Yale University Press.

Newman, Roxana Ma and Vincent J. van Heuven. 1981. 'An acoustic and phonological study of pre-pausal vowel length in Hausa', *Journal of African Languages and Linguistics* 3: 1–18.

Nikolaeva, Irina and Maria Tolskaya. 2001. *A Grammar of Udihe*. Berlin: Mouton de Gruyter.

Noonan, Michael. 1992. *A Grammar of Lango*. Berlin: Mouton de Gruyter.

Nordlinger, R. and Sadler, L. 2004. 'Nominal tense in cross-linguistic perspective', *Language* 80: 776–806.

Ochs Keenan, Elinor and Bambi B. Schieffelin. 1976. 'Topic as a discourse notion: a study of topic in the conversations of children and adults', pp. 336–84 *Subject and Topic*, edited by Charles N. Li. New York: Academic Press.

Okamoto, Shigeko. 1995. '"Tasteless" Japanese: less "feminine" speech among young Japanese woman', pp. 297–325 of *Gender Articulated: Language and the Socially Constructed Self*, edited by Kira Hall and Mary Buchholtz. London: Routledge.

Olawsky, Knut. 2006. *A Grammar of Urarina*. Berlin: Mouton de Gruyter.

Onishi, Masayuki. 1994. *A grammar of Motuna*. PhD thesis, Australian National University.

Onishi, Masayuki. 2001. 'Non-canonically marked subjects and objects: parameters and properties', pp. 1–52 of *Non-canonical Marking of Subjects and Objects*, edited by Alexandra Y. Aikhenvald, R. M. W. Dixon, and Masayuki Onishi. Amsterdam: John Benjamins.

Overall, Simon. 2008. *A grammar of Aguaruna*. PhD thesis, La Trobe University.

Overall, Simon. 2009. 'The semantics of clause linking in Aguaruna', pp. 167–92 of *The Semantics of Clause Linking: A Cross-linguistic Typology*, edited by R. M. W. Dixon and Alexandra Y. Aikhenvald. Oxford: Oxford University Press.

Owens, Jonathan. 1985. *A Grammar of Harar Oromo (Northeastern Ethiopia)*. Hamburg: Helmut Buske Verlag.

Owens, Jonathan. 1996. 'Grammatisierung, Semantisierung und Sprachkontakt: Arabisch im Tschad-See-Gebiet', pp. 79–85 of *Sprachkontakt und Grammatikalisierung*, edited by M. Haase and N. Nau. Special issue of *Sprachtypologie und Universalienforschung* 49(1).

Owens, Jonathan. 2006. *A Linguistic History of Arabic*. Oxford: Oxford University Press.

Padgett, Jaye. 2007. 'Glides, Vowels, and Features', *Lingua* 118 (12): 1937–55.

Pan, Chia-jung. 2012. *A grammar of Lha'alhua, an Austronesian language of Taiwan*. PhD thesis, James Cook University.

Pandharipande, Rajeshwari V. 1997. *Marathi*. London: Routledge.

Parker, Steve. 1996. 'Toward a Universal Form for "Yes": or, Rhinoglottophilia and the Affirmation Grunt', *Journal of Linguistic Anthropology* 6: 85–95.

Patz, Elisabeth. 1991. 'Djabugay', pp. 245–347 of *The Handbook of Australian languages*, vol. 4, edited by R. M. W. Dixon and Barry J. Blake. Melbourne: Oxford University Press.

Pawley, Andrew K. 1987. 'Encoding events in Kalam and English: different logics for reporting experience', pp. 329–60 of *Coherence and Grounding in Discourse*, edited by Ross Tomlin. Amsterdam: John Benjamins.

Pawley, Andrew K. 1993. 'A language which defies description by ordinary means', pp. 87–129 of *The Role of Theory in Language Description*, edited by William A. Foley. Berlin: Mouton de Gruyter.

Payne, Doris L. 1990. *The Pragmatics of Word Order: Typological Dimensions of Verb Initial Languages*. Berlin: Mouton de Gruyter.

Payne, Doris L. and Thomas E. Payne. 1990. 'Yagua', pp. 249–474 of *Handbook of Amazonian Languages*, vol. 2, edited by D. C. Derbyshire and G. K. Pullum. Berlin: Mouton de Gruyter.

Payne, John R. 1985. 'Negation', pp. 197–242 of *Language Typology and Syntactic Description*, Vol. 1. *Clause structure*, edited by T. Shopen. Cambridge: Cambridge University Press.

Payne, John R. and Rodney Huddleston. 2002. 'Nouns and noun phrases', pp. 323–523 of *The Cambridge Grammar of the English Language*, edited by Rodney Huddleston and Geoffrey K. Pullum. Cambridge: Cambridge University Press.

Pedersen, Holger and Henry Lewis. 1937. *A Concise Comparative Celtic Grammar*. Göttingen: Vandenhoeck and Ruprecht.

Peterson, David A. 2003. 'Hakha Lai', pp. 409–26 of *The Sino-Tibetan Languages*, edited by Graham Thurgood and Randy J. LaPolla. London: Routledge.

Peterson, David A. 2007. *Applicative Constructions*. Oxford: Oxford University Press.

Picanço, Gessiane. 2005. *Mundurukú: phonetics, phonology, synchrony, diachrony*. PhD dissertation, University of British Columbia.

Pike, Kenneth L. 1947a. 'Grammatical prerequisites to phonemic analysis', *Word* 3: 155–72.

Pike, Kenneth L. 1947b. *Phonemics: A Technique for Reducing Languages to Writing*. Ann Arbor: University of Michigan Press.

Pike, Kenneth L. 1948. *Tone Languages: A Technique for Determining the Number and Types of Pitch Contrasts in a Language, with Studies in Tonemic Substitution and Fusion*. Ann Arbor: University of Michigan Press.

Pike, Kenneth L. 1952. 'More on grammatical prerequisites', *Word* 8: 108–21.

Poplack, Shana. 1993. 'Variation theory and language contact', pp. 251–86 of *American Dialect Research: An Anthology Celebrating the 100th Anniversary of the American Dialect Society*, edited by D. Preston. Amsterdam: Benjamins.

Post, Mark W. 2007. *A grammar of Galo*. PhD thesis, La Trobe University.

Post, Mark W. 2008. 'Adjectives in Thai: implications for a functionalist typology of word classes', *Linguistic Typology* 12: 339–81.

Post, Mark W. 2009. 'The semantics of clause linking in Galo', pp. 74–95 of *The Semantics of Clause Linking: A Cross-Linguistic Typology*, edited by R. M. W. Dixon and Alexandra Y. Aikhenvald. Oxford: Oxford University Press.

Price, Glanville. 2008. *A Comprehensive French Grammar*. London: Blackwell.

Quirk, R., S. Greenbaum, G. Leech, and J. Svartvik. 1985. *A Comprehensive Grammar of the English Language*. London: Longman.

Radetzky, Paula K. 2003. *The functions and evolution of topic and focus markers*. PhD dissertation, University of California, Berkeley.

Ramirez, Henri. 1994. *Le Parler Yanomami des Xamatauteri*. Paris.

Ramirez, Henri. 1997. *A fala Tukano dos Yepâ-masa. Tomo 1. Gramática*. Manaus: Inspetoria Salesiana Missionária da Amazônia CEDEM.

Rankin, Robert L. 2004. 'The history and development of Siouan positionals with special attention to polygrammaticalization in Dhegiha', *Language Typology and Universals* 57 (2/3): 202–27.

Reid, N. 1990. *Ngan'gityemerri. A language of the Daly river region, Northern Territory of Australia*. PhD thesis, Australian National University.

Ribeiro, Eduardo Rivail. 2006. 'Subordinate clauses in Karajá', *Boletim do Musu Paraense Emílio Goeldi. Ciências humanas*, 1 (1): 17–46.

Rice, Keren. 1990. 'Predicting rule domains in the phrasal phonology', pp. 289–312 of *The Phonology–Syntax Connection*, edited by Sharon Inkelas and Draga Zec. Chicago: University of Chicago Press.

Richards, Cara B. 1974. 'Among the liberated', pp. 401–19 of *Many Sisters: Women in Cross-cultural Perspective*, edited by Carolyn J. Matthiasson. New York: Free Press.

Roberts, John R. 1987. *Amele*. London: Croom Helm.

Roberts, John R. 1997. 'Switch-reference in Papua New Guinea: a preliminary survey', pp. 101–241 of *Papers in Papuan Linguistics* 3. Canberra: Pacific Linguistics.

Rodrigues, Aryon D. 1983. 'Silêncio, pausa e nasalisação', *YIII Encontro Nacional de Linguística*, Rio de Janeiro.

Rodrigues, Aryon D. 1999. 'Macro-Jê', pp. 165–206 of Dixon and Aikhenvald (eds).

Rood, David S. 1976. *Wichita Grammar*. New York: Garland.

Routamaa, Judy. 1994. *Kamula Grammar Essentials*. Ukarumpa: Summer Institute of Linguistics.

Rubino, Carl Alvez. 1997. *Reference grammar of Ilocano*. PhD disseration, UCSb.

Rushforth, S. 1991. 'Uses of Bearlake and Mescalero (Athapaskan) Classificatory Verbs', *International Journal of American Linguistics* 57: 251–66.

Sadock, J. and A. Zwicky. 1985. 'Speech act distinctions in syntax', pp. 155–96 of *Language Typology and Syntactic Description*, edited by T. Shopen. Cambridge: Cambridge University Press.

Saltarelli, Mario. 1988. *Basque*. London: Routledge.

Sands, A. Kristina. 2012. *Complement Clauses and Grammatical Relations in Finnish*. Munich: Lincom Europa.

Sapir, Edward. 1921. *Language*. New York: Harcourt, Brace and World.

Sapir, Edward. 1922. 'The Takelma language of southwestern Oregon', pp. 1–296 of *Handbook of American Indian Languages*, Part 2, edited by Franz Boas. Washington: Smithsonian Institution.

Sapir, Edward. 1929. 'Male and female forms of speech in Yana', pp. 79–83 of *Donum Natalicium Schrijnen*, edited by St. W. J. Teeuwen. Nijmegen-Utrecht.

Sapir, Edward. 1930. 'Southern Paiute, a Shoshonean language', *Proceedings of the American Academy of Arts and Science*, 65: 1–3.

Sapir, Edward. 1936. 'Internal linguistic evidence suggestive of the northern origin of Navaho', *American Anthropologist*, n.s., 38: 224–35, reprinted as pp. 213–24 of *Selected Writings of Edward Sapir in Language, Culture and Personality*, edited by David G. Mandelbaum. Berkeley and Los Angeles: University of California Press.

Sarvasy, Hannah. Forthcoming. *A grammar of Nungon, from Morobe Province, Papua New Guinea*. PhD thesis, JCU, Cairns.

Saxena, Anju. 1988. 'On syntactic convergence: the case of the verb "say" in Tibeto-Burman', *Berkeley Linguistics Society Proceedings* 14: 375–88.

Schachter, Paul. 1985. 'Parts-of-speech systems', pp. 1–61 of *Language Typology and Syntactic Description*, vol. I, *Clause structure*, edited by T. Shopen. Cambridge: Cambridge University Press.

Schachter, Paul and Fe T. Otanes. 1972. *Tagalog Reference Grammar*. Berkeley and Los Angeles: University of California Press.

Schaub, Willi. 1985. *Babungo*. London: Croom Helm.

Schieffelin, Bambi. 1985. 'The acquisition of Kaluli', pp. 525–93 of *The Cross-linguistic Study of Language Acquisition*, vol. 1. *The Data*, edited by D. Slobin. Hillsdale, NJ: Lawrence Erlbaum Asociates.

Schultze, Wolfgang. 2004. 'Review article, Alice C. Harris. Endoclitics and the origins of Udi morphosyntax. Oxford: Oxford University Press', *Studies in Language* 28: 419–44.

Seiler, H. 1977. *Cahuilla Grammar*. California: Malki Museum Press.

Seki, Lucy. 2000. *Gramática da língua Kamaiurá*. Campinas: Editora da Unicamp.

Senft, Gunter and Ellen B. Basso. 2009. *Ritual Communication*. Oxford: Berg.

Sherzer, Joel. 1990. *Verbal Art in San Blas: Kuna Culture through its Discourse*. Albuquerque: University of New Mexico Press.

Shibamoto, Janet S. 1987. 'The womanly woman: manipulation of stereotypical and nonstereotypical features of Japanese female speech', pp. 26–49 of *Language, Gender and Sex in Comparative Perspective*, edited by Susan U. Philips, Susan Steele, and Christine Tanz. Cambridge: Cambridge University Press.

Shibatani, Masayoshi. 1990. *The Languages of Japan*. Cambridge: Cambridge University Press.

Shibatani, Masayoshi. 2006. 'Honorifics', pp. 381–90 of *Encyclopedia of Language and Linguistics*, edited by Keith Brown. Oxford: Elsevier.

Shvedova, N. Ju. 1970. *The Grammar of Modern Russian Literary Language* (Grammatika sovremennogo russkogo literaturnogo jazyka). Moscow: Nauka.

Silva, Cácio and Elisângela Silva. 2012. *A língua dos Yuhupdeh: introdução etnolíngüística, dicionário Yuhup-Português e glossário semântico-gramatical.* São Gabriel da Cachoeira: Pró-Amazonia.

Silver, S. and W. Miller. 1997. *American Indian Languages: Cultural and Social Contexts.* Tucson: The University of Arizona Press.

Silverstein, Michael. 1976. 'Hierarchy of features and ergativity', pp. 112–71 of *Grammatical Categories in Australian Languages*, edited by R. M. W. Dixon. Canberra: Australian Institute of Aboriginal Studies.

Simons, Gary. 1982. 'Word taboo and comparative Austronesian linguistics', pp. 157–226 of *Papers from the Third International Conference on Austronesian Linguistics, vol. 3: Accent on Variety*, edited by Amran Halim, Lois Carrington and Stephen A. Wurm. Canberra: Pacific Linguistics.

Slater, K. W. 2002. *A Grammar of Mangghuer: A Mongolic Language of China's Qinghai-Gansu Sprachbund.* London and New York: Routledge Curzon.

Smeets, Ineke. 1989. *A Mapuche grammar.* PhD thesis, University of Leiden.

Smeets, Ineke. 2008. *A Grammar of Mapuche.* Berlin: Mouton de Gruyter.

Smith-Stark, S. 1974. 'The plurality split.' *Papers from the Annual Regional Meeting of the Chicago Linguistic Society* 10: 657–71.

Sneddon, James N. 1996. *Indonesian Reference Grammar.* Sydney: Allen and Unwin.

Sohn, Ho-min. 1994. *Korean.* London: Routledge.

Sohn, Ho-min. 2004. 'The adjective class in Korean', pp. 223–41 of *Adjective Classes: A Cross-linguistic Typology*, edited by R. M. W. Dixon and Alexandra Y. Aikhenvald. Oxford: Oxford University Press.

Sparing-Chávez, M. 2003. 'I want to but I can't: the frustrative in Amahuaca', *Summer Institute of Linguistics Electronic Working Papers* SILEWP 2003-002.

Spencer, Katharine. 2008. 'Kwomtari grammar esentials', pp. 53–77 of *Kwomtari Phonology and Grammar Essentials*, edited by Murray Hornsberger, Carol Hornsberger and Ian Tupper. Data Papers on Papua New Guinea languages, vol. 5. Ukarumpa: SIL-PNG Academic Publications.

Steuernagel, Karl. 1961. *Hebräische Grammatik.* Leipzig: Brockhaus.

Stirling, Lesley. 1998. 'Isolated *if*-clauses in Australian English', in pp. 273–94 in *The Clause in English: In Honour of Rodney Huddleston*, edited by P. Collins and D. Lee. Amsterdam: John Benjamins.

Storch, Anne. 2011. *Secret Manipulations: Language and Context in Africa.* New York: Oxford University Press.

Storch, Anne. 2013. 'Knowing, smelling and telling tales in Luwo', pp. 47–68 of *Perception and Cognition in Language and Culture*, edited by Alexandra Y. Aikhenvald and Anne Storch (eds). Leiden: Brill.

Sulkala, H. and M. Karjalainen. 1992. *Finnish.* London: Routledge.

Sun, Hongkai and Guangkun Liu. 2009. *A Grammar of Anong: Language Death under Intense Contact*, translated, annotated, and supplemented by Fengxiang Li, Ela Thurgood, Graham Thurgood. Leiden: Brill.

Tamura, Suzuko. 2000. *The Ainu Language.* Tokyo: Sanseido.

Tauli, V. 1984. 'The Estonian language reform', pp. 309–30 of Vol. III of *Language Reform. History and Future*, edited by I. Fodor and C. Hagège. Hamburg: Buske Verlag.

Taylor, D. M. 1977. *Languages of the West Indies.* Baltimore: John Hopkins University Press.

Thiesen, Wesley and David Weber. 2012. *A Grammar of Bora with Special Attention to Tone.* Dallas, TX: SIL International.

Thomas, D. D. 1971. *Chrau Grammar.* Honolulu: University of Hawaii Press.

Thompson, Chad. 1996. 'On the grammar of body parts in Koyokon Athabaskan', pp. 651–76 of *The Grammar of Inalienability: A Typological Perspective on Body Part Terms and the Part–Whole Relation*, edited by Hilary Chappell and William McGregor. Berlin: Mouton de Gruyter.

Thompson, Sandra and R. E. Longacre. 1985. 'Adverbial clauses', pp. 171–234 of *Language Typology and Syntactic Description*, vol. II, edited by T. Shopen. Cambridge: Cambridge University Press.

Timberlake, A. 2007. 'Aspect, tense, mood', pp. 280–333 of *Language Typology and Syntactic Description*, vol. III, edited by T. Shopen. 2nd edn, Cambridge: Cambridge University Press.

Topping, Donald M. 1973. *Chamorro Reference Grammar.* Honolulu: University of Hawaii Press.

Trask, R. L. 1993. *A Dictionary of Grammatical Terms in Linguistics.* London: Routledge.

Treis, Yvonne. 2005. 'Avoiding their names, avoiding their eyes: how Kambaata women respect their in-laws', *Anthropological Linguistics* 47: 292–320.

Trubetzkoy, Nicolai S. 1939. *Grundzüge der Phonologie* (Travaux du Cercle Linguistique de Prague, No. 7).

Trudgill, Peter. 2011. *Sociolinguistic Typology: Social Determinants of Linguistic Complexity.* Oxford: Oxford University Press.

Underhill, Robert. 1976. *Turkish Grammar.* Cambridge, MA: MIT Press.

Urmson, J. O. 1952. 'Parenthetical verbs', *Mind* 61: 480–96.

Vallauri, E. L. 2004. 'Grammaticalization of syntactic incompleteness: free conditionals in Italian and other languages.' *SKY Journal of Linguistics* 17: 189–215.

van der Voort, Hein. 2004. *A Grammar of Kwaza.* Berlin: Mouton de Gruyter.

van Driem, George. 2007. 'A holistic approach to the fine art of grammar writing: The Dallas Manifesto', pp. 93–184 of *Recent Studies in Nepalese Linguistics*, edited by Novel Kishore Rai, Yogendra Prasad Yadav, Bhim N. Regmi, and Balaram Prasain. Kathmandu: Linguistic Society of Nepal.

van Eijk, Jan and Hess, Thom. 1986. 'Noun and verb in Salish', *Lingua* 69: 319–31.

Vance, Timothy J. 1987. *An Introduction to Japanese Phonology.* Albany, NY: S.U.N.Y. Press.

Velázquez-Castillo, Maura. 1996. *The Grammar of Possession: Inalienability, Incorporation and Possessor Ascension in Guaraní.* Amsterdam: John Benjamins.

Verhaar, John W. M. 1995. *Towards a Reference Grammar of Tok Pisin: An Experiment in Corpus Linguistics.* Honolulu: University of Hawai'i Press.

Viitso, Tiit-Rein. 2007. 'Structure of the Estonian language. Phonology, morphology and word formation', pp. 9–92 of *Estonian Language*, edited by Mati Erelt. Tallinn: Estonian Academy Publishers.

Vogel, Petra M. and Bernard Comrie (eds) 2000. *Approaches to the Typology of Word Classes.* Berlin: Mouton de Gruyter.

de Vries, Lourens. 2005. 'Towards a typology of head-tail linkage in Papuan languages', *Studies in Language* 29: 363–84.

de Vries, Lourens. 2013. 'Seeing, hearing and thinking in Korowai, a language of West Papua', pp. 111–36 of *Perception and Cognition in Language and Culture*, edited by Alexandra Y. Aikhenvald and Anne Storch (eds). Leiden: Brill.

Voeltz, F. K. Erhard and Christa Kilian-Hatz (eds) 2001. *Ideophones*. Amsterdam: John Benjamins.

Wali, Kashi and Omkar N. Koul. 1997. *Kashmiri*. Oxford: Routledge.

Waltereit, Richard. 2002. 'Imperatives, interruption in conversation, and the rise of discourse markers: a study of Italian *guarda*', *Linguistics* 40: 987–1010.

Watters, David E. 2002. *A Grammar of Kham*. Cambridge: Cambridge University Press.

Watters, David E. 2009. 'The semantics of clause linking in Kham', pp. 96–117 of *The Semantics of Clause Linking: A Cross-linguistic Typology*, edited by R. M. W. Dixon and Alexandra Y. Aikhenvald. Oxford: Oxford University Press.

Weber, David J. 1986. 'Information Perspective, Profile, and Patterns in Quechua', pp. 137–55 of *Evidentiality: The Linguistic Coding of Epistemology*, edited by W. L. Chafe and J. Nichols. Norwood, NJ: Ablex.

Weber, David J. 1989. *A Grammar of Huallaga (Huánuco) Quechua*. Berkeley: University of California Press.

Weinreich, Max. 1945. 'Der Yivo un di problemen fun undzer tsayt' (The YIVO and the problems of our time). *YIVO Bleter* 25, 1. In Yiddish.

Weinreich, U. 1953. *Languages in Contact*. New York: Linguistic Circle of New York.

Whorf, Benjamin Lee. 1956. *Language, Thought and Reality. Selected writings of Benjamin Lee Whorf*. Edited by John B. Carroll. Cambridge, MA: The MIT Press.

Wilson, P. 1980. *Ambulas Grammar*. Ukarumpa: Summer Institute of Linguistics.

Winford, Donald. 2003. *An Introduction to Contact Linguistics*. London: Wiley.

Zandvoort, R. W. 1975. *A Handbook of English Grammar*. London: Longmans.

Zanuttini, Raffaella and Paul Portner. 2003. 'Exclamatory clauses: at the syntax–semantics interface', *Language* 79: 39–81.

Index of languages, language families, and linguistic areas

This index contains a list of languages, established subgroups, language families, and linguistic areas mentioned in this book. Each language and subgroup is accompanied by an indication of its genetic affiliation, e.g. French (Romance, Indo-European). Subgroups and families are accompanied with the word 'languages', e.g. Romance languages. No affiliation is given for Creole languages.

The languages of Australia can be divided into about thirty-eight small genetic groups and there are numerous isolates (see Dixon 2002: xxx–xlii). They cannot all be shown to be genetically related. They do, however, constitute a large diffusion area and are referred to as 'Australian area'.

Papuan languages (or non-Austronesian languages of New Guinea) are highly diverse; in many cases their genetic classification is a matter of dispute. Languages and language families spoken in the Papuan region are referred to as 'Papuan region', e.g. Namia (Papuan region). If a family is well established, it is included, e.g. Alamblak (Sepik Hill, Papuan region). We eschew dubious and unjustified groupings (including Pama-Nyungan, Trans-New Guinea phylum and others: see p. 35).

Index of authors

Index of subjects

Entries in bold refer to the entry in the Glossary.